RE-VISIONING FAMILY THERAPY

RE-VISIONING FAMILY THERAPY

Race, Culture, and Gender in Clinical Practice

Edited by

MONICA McGOLDRICK

THE GUILFORD PRESS

New York   London

© 1998 Monica McGoldrick
Published by The Guilford Press
A Division of Guilford Publications, Inc.
72 Spring Street, New York, NY 10012
www.guilford.com

Printed in the United States of America

This book is printed on acid-free paper.

Last digit is print number: 9 8 7 6

Library of Congress Cataloging-in-Publication Data

Re-visioning family therapy : race, culture, and gender in clinical
   practice / edited by Monica McGoldrick
      p.   cm.
   Includes bibliographical references and index.
   ISBN 1-57230-027-2 (hc.)   ISBN 1-57230-824-9 (pbk.)
   1. Minorities—Mental health services—United States. 2. Family
psychotherapy—United States. 3. Minorities—United States—
Family relationships.   I. McGoldrick, Monica.
RC451.5.A2R4 1998
616.89′156′08900973—dc21   98-6174
                                                                CIP

*To Margaret Bush and Aunt Mamie Cahalane
and all those like them,
whose invisibility was a hidden shame, and
who bravely transformed the constraints of their lives
into a love that inspires and carries us through.*

Contributors

Rhea Almeida, LCSW, PhD, DVS, Executive Director, Institute for Family Services, Somerset, NJ; Family Institute of New Jersey, Metuchen, NJ

N. Norma Akamatsu, MSW, Northampton Institute for Family Therapy, Northampton, MA

Nancy Boyd-Franklin, PhD, Graduate School of Applied and Professional Psychology, Rutgers University, New Brunswick, NJ

Nollaig O'Reilly Byrne, MB, FRCP(C), Family Therapy Training Programmes, Department of Child and Family Psychiatry, Mater Misericordiae Hospital, Dublin Ireland

Fernando Colón, PhD, Ann Arbor Center for the Family, Ann Arbor, MI

Joel Crohn, PhD, Private Practice, San Rafael, Berkeley, CA

Ken Dolan-Del Vecchio, LCSW, DVS, Institute for Family Services, Somerset, NJ

Celia Jaes Falicov, PhD, Department of Psychiatry, University of California in San Diego, San Diego, CA; Private Practice, San Diego, CA

John Folwarski, MA, LCSW, Raritan Bay Mental Health Center, Perth Amboy, NJ

Roberto Font, LCSW, DVS, Institute for Family Services, Somerset, NJ

Anderson J. Franklin, PhD, Clinical Psychology Program, City College of New York, NY; Private Practice, Brooklyn, NY

Nydia Garcia-Preto, LCSW, Clinical Director, Family Institute of New Jersey, Metuchen, NJ; Private Practice, Metuchen, NJ

Robert-Jay Green, PhD, Coordinator, Family/Child Psychology Training, California School of Professional Psychology in Berkeley/Alameda, CA

Kenneth V. Hardy, PhD, Professor, Marriage and Family Therapy Program, Department of Child and Family Studies, College for Human Development, Syracuse University, Syracuse, NY

Paulette Moore Hines, PhD, Director, Office of Prevention Services, UMDNJ University Behavioral Health Care, Piscataway, NJ; The Family Institute of New Jersey, Metuchen, NJ

Thomas W. Johnson, LCSW, EdD, Private Practice, Metuchen, NJ

Michael S. Keren, PsyD, Department of Psychiatry, Robert Wood Johnson University of Medicine and Dentistry, Piscataway, NJ; Graduate School of Applied and Professional Psychology, Rutgers University, New Brunswick, NJ; Private Practice, Metuchen and Lawrenceville, NJ

Bok-Lim C. Kim, LCSW, Private Practice, Chula Vista, CA

Jodie Kliman, PhD, The Center for Multicultural Training in Psychology, Boston Medical Center, Boston, MA; The Family Institute of Cambridge, Watertown, MA; Private Practice, Brookline, MA

Joan Laird, MSW, LCSW, Smith College School for Social Work, Northampton, MA

Tracey A. Laszloffy, PhD, Marriage and Family Therapy Program, Department of Child and Family Studies, College for Human Development, Syracuse University, Syracuse, NY

Jayne Everette Mahboubi, ACSW, LCSW, Spelman College Counseling Services, Atlanta, GA; Private Practice, Smyrna, GA

Vanessa M. Mahmoud, LCSW, Midtown Psychotherapy Association, Spelman College, Atlanta, GA

Imelda Colgan McCarthy, PhD, Department of Social Policy and Social Work, University College Dublin, Ireland

Monica McGoldrick, LCSW, PhD (h.c.), Director, Family Institute of New Jersey, Metuchen, NJ; Private Practice, Metuchen, NJ; Associate Professor of Clinical Psychiatry, UMDNJ—Robert Wood Johnson Medical School; Visiting Professor, Fordham University, School for Social Service, New York, NY

Peggy McIntosh, PhD, Associate Director, Wellesley College Center for Research on Women, Wellesley, MA

Theresa Messineo, LCSW, DVS, Co-Director, Institute for Family Services, Somerset, NJ

Horace Miner (deceased), PhD, University of Michigan

Marsha Pravder Mirkin, PhD, Jean Baker Miller Institute, Stone Center, Wellesley College, Wellesley, MA; Private Practice, Newton, MA

Matthew R. Mock, PhD, Director, Family, Youth, and Children's and Multicultural Services, City of Berkeley Mental Health Division, Berkeley, CA; Director, Cross Cultural Counseling, Graduate School of Professional Psychology, John F. Kennedy University, Orinda, CA

Elaine Pinderhughes, PhD, Graduate School of Social Work, Boston College, Chestnut Hill, MA

Ashburn Pidcock Searcy, MD, Anesthesiologist, Private Group Practice, Marietta, GA

Carlos E. Sluzki, MD, Director, Psychiatric Services, Santa Barbara Cottage Hospital, Santa Barbara, CA; Department of Psychiatry, University of California at Los Angeles School of Medicine, Los Angeles, CA

Charles Waldegrave, MA (hons.) (Waik), MA (hons.) (Camb.), The Family Centre, Wellington, New Zealand

Froma Walsh, MSW, PhD, Center for Family Health, School of Social Service Administration, University of Chicago, Chicago, IL

Marlene F. Watson, PhD, Director, Graduate Programs in Couple and Family Therapy, Department of Mental Health Sciences, Allegheny University of the Health Sciences, Philadelphia, PA

Susan Weltman, LCSW, Center for Family Studies, Springfield, NJ; Private Practice, Metuchen, NJ

Rosemary Woods, LCSW, DVS, Co-Director, Institute for Family Services, Somerset, NJ

Acknowledgments

This book is the product of many conversations, painful moments of realization, and excitement about the possibilities of our field and our world. I am very grateful to Seymour Weingarten, Editor in Chief of The Guilford Press, for his support throughout this third book we have done together, which has meant a great deal to me. My deepest gratitude also goes to our thoughtful, caring, and wise editor, Rochelle Serwator, for her good counsel and for the generous efforts she has taken to make the book as clear and succinct as possible, and to Marie Sprayberry for her careful and thoughtful copyediting, which tightened the text even further.

I am extremely grateful as well to Rene Campbell, whose daily good humor and support make my work and life possible. Marijean Battistella provided good-natured and patient efforts with the many different people, ideas, titles, and fax and phone numbers that she had to master in a short time. Marty Jessun and Donna Maser's loyalty, generosity, and support to me and to the Family Institute of New Jersey also make my work and life possible. My colleagues and friends at the Institute and in our broader network are my mainstay. Robert-Jay Green helped me formulate the idea for the book, gave me courage, and was, as always, lovingly available for long-distance consultations that carried me through; he was also a brilliant contributor on his own to the final product. Rhea Almeida shared many hours of conversation about the ideas and reviewed many chapters, giving invaluable feedback.

My friends and family are my lifeline, and I thank them all—some long-time soulmates; some friends from my earliest childhood; some new but cherished brothers and sisters; some lost, and some refound over the years. All of them have been teaching me about these issues, long before I realized what I was learning. They include Nydia Garcia-Preto, Rhea Almeida, Paulette Moore Hines, Charlee Sutton, Froma Walsh, Carol Anderson, Betty Carter, Tom Johnson, Ken Hardy, Vanessa Mahmoud, Jayne Mahboubi, Elaine Pinderhughes, A. J. and Nancy Boyd Franklin, Eliana Gil, Sandy Leiblum, Nollaig O'Reilly Byrne and Imelda Colgan

McCarthy, Peggy Papp, Marianne Walters, Olga Silverstein, Celia Jaes Falicov, JoAnn Krestan, Jackie Hudak, Amy Bibb, Michael Rohrbaugh and Varda Shohom, John Folwarski, Rich and Jette Simon, Meyer Rothberg, Jane Sufian, Janey Hart, Jim Hawkins, Jimmy Michener, Joyce Richardson, Charlotte Fremon Danielson, Gerald Grow, Ariane Baer, Neale McGoldrick and Morna, Hugh, and Guy Livingston, Elliott and Marie Mottram, Mildred Cook, and Jack Mayer.

I thank my parents for giving me the courage to face truths about our family and about myself, which their strength helped me to acknowledge. And I thank my students and my clients, who have kept me from being self-satisfied and who inspire me every day. I am also grateful to the authors of the chapters, many of whom worked within very tight page constraints to conform to the space limitations of the book, and at the same time to infuse their creativity and knowledge into their cultural descriptions. Finally, I thank my husband, Sophocles, for his quiet smile and for being there for me and for our son in so many ways that make us flourish. I am indebted to both Sophocles, and my wonderful and amazing son, John, for putting up with my late nights of work on the computer, my hours on the phone, and my distraction as I struggled over these ideas and how we could articulate them to convey the messages that are so important for us all.

Preface

The failure of societies to tolerate diversity is the greatest single threat to the survival of civilization. This book grew out of our increasing need as family therapists to break out of the constraints of our traditional monocular vision of families as white, heterosexual, and middle-class, and to redefine the boundaries of our field. Our new cultural lens must take into account the diversity of U.S. society and the ways that societal oppression has silenced the voices and constrained the lives of family members, whole families, and whole communities since this nation was founded.

Larger forces of racial, sexist, cultural, classist, and heterosexist power hierarchies define the boundaries of our clients' lives. Specifically, they determine what get defined as "problems" and what services society will set up to respond to these problems. This book's aim is to broaden the focus of our work beyond the interior of the family, so that we can begin to see how our clients' lives are constrained by these larger societal structures and can develop new ways of working—ways based on a revised understanding of our society, ourselves, our histories, and our clients' lives.

Over the past few years, we have been struggling to envision theory and practice that will begin to transform our field so that we can see ourselves and our clients more clearly, and can provide services that will be more healing and will offer a sense of hope and belonging for all who seek our help. A companion volume to *Ethnicity and Family Therapy* (now in its second edition), which explores culture through the lens of ethnicity, *Re-Visioning Family Therapy: Race, Culture, and Gender in Clinical Practice* has evolved from our endeavor to expand our view of families and of family therapy from more inclusive cultural perspectives. The book includes many personal stories—known over the years to some of us, but now available for a wider audience—which help us pay attention to those who have been hidden from history.

Family therapy, like every institution, set of ideas and practices of our society, is always evolving. It originally developed primarily in reaction to Freudian psychology, which had focused on intrapsychic processes.

It provided a kind of corrective perspective, focusing attention on interpersonal processes between family members as central to understanding psychological functioning. Although some family therapists eschewed any other level of analysis than the interpersonal/family level, most came to think in terms of multiple systemic levels, from the biological to the familial to the cultural. However, it has been very hard to shift our thinking about therapy beyond the family to consider the therapeutic implications of the context in which families are embedded.

The idea of this book was to provide a broad range of brief chapters by many of those who have been working to re-vision the family therapy field through a cultural lens. In each chapter, the author or authors were given frustratingly little space and asked to present a few key ideas of clinical relevance in a reader-friendly format. All of the authors have attempted to contextualize the oppressions that are the focus of this book, to take into account the many complex factors that impinge on our vision, and to suggest re-visions for our clinical work. I applaud the authors for their courage to contend with these hard issues, and I rejoice in them as my cohort in going along through life. We know that we are not yet clear about how these power dimensions operate on us, but we are striving with each other's help to see the road more clearly.

The book is intended to be exciting and suggestive rather than comprehensive in its articulation of where we need to go in our work. Most of the material is intentionally personal. We want to make clear how unarticulated aspects of our history have influenced our need to change the future. Our ideas have evolved from our frustrations with the traditional boundaries of the field and our wish to expand our vision to see more clearly where we might go. This book has been an opportunity to push our own and each other's boundaries, in hopes that it will help transform our field to more inclusive practice. We hope the reader will give us the benefit of the doubt—realizing, as we realize ourselves, that many of these ideas are still in progress, awaiting the leavening of future conversations to help us see the issues more clearly. Ideally, a book like this will soon be out of date as the ideas expressed here become commonplace, accepted practice, and we will be forced to reformulate these ideas to accommodate changing times.

In the seven parts of this book, we have attempted to address not only our cultural diversity, but also the diverse ways in which we practice as family therapists. Sometimes discussions of diversity become so inclusive that racism is trivialized or ignored in the multiplicity of other "-isms." Other times discussion gets polarized as if we could focus on only one dimension at a time. As Beverly Tatum (1997) has noted in another context, those who have focused on racial identity development have done little to address gender, and feminist theorists have often done little to address race. Sometimes in discussions of diversity the "Black–White" issues predominate, leaving others feeling that their issues have no place. Sexism, anti-Semitism, ageism, homophobia and other oppressions are pushed into the background, as people argue over which oppression is the worst or most important. We hope this book will contribute to multilayered conversations about oppression and diversity.

The book includes chapters that focus specifically on racism and Whiteness. These are vital topics to consider if we are to embark on accountable and ethical practice. However, we still find it hard to raise some issues in the context of others. The question of how one can address sexism with a couple in which both partners are also victims of racism is a hot topic. The question of how to address the negativity about homosexuality within the African American community is equally challenging. Hall and Greene (1994) have addressed the ethical imperative for attending to the complexities centering around issues of feminism, racism, and homophobia in relation to African American families:

> The African American woman may perceive that feminists and the feminist movement underestimate the integral role of cultural traditions and racism in her life. In a parallel experience, many African American males equate feminism with lesbianism, anti-male and white perspectives. It is imperative that feminist family therapists examine how much of the negative perception of therapy and feminist family therapy within the African American community is based on realistic experiences as opposed to sexist attitudes and misconceptions. . . . The ethical inclusion of cultural pluralism, a cultural context for therapy, as well as the examination of the influence of white privilege in feminist family therapy is essential in the provision of appropriate and meaningful treatment. (pp. 6–7)

I believe we need to keep a multidimensional perspective, which can at the same time highlight the overwhelming horror of institutionalized racism, while not making light of other forms of oppression. We have to hold African American men accountable to women, and at the same time to understand the particular oppression they have been subjected to for generations. While moving against sexism, we have to hold those of us who are White feminist family therapists accountable for the ways in which privilege and unintentional racism perpetuate the very oppression they (we) should be well aware of. We must carefully and respectfully hold White men accountable for their privilege, entitlement, and lack of awareness of their role in perpetuating the current system. Their lack of consciousness is part of the structure of our society, which functions in such a way that the oppressed always know much more about the dominant groups than the dominant groups know about them, for the very reason that their survival depends on this understanding (Miller, 1976). This means that just as we must ask White men to take responsibility for learning to be uncomfortable with organizational structures that are dominated by White men, we who are White must learn to become uncomfortable when in segregated situations, when reading books (including books about feminism or homosexuality) that pertain only to White people, and so forth. We must become so uncomfortable that we are moved to do something about it.

I am hoping that this book will be another step toward finding ways to contain opposites, contradictions, and ambiguities. While not oversimplifying the issues, we must not obfuscate the prejudices and oppression that are defining and destroying us.

REFERENCES

Hall, R. L., & Green, B. (1994). Cultural competence in feminist therapy: An ethical mandate. *Journal of Feminist Family Therapy, 6*(3), 5–28.

Miller, J. B. (1976). *Toward a new psychology of women.* Boston: Beacon Press.

Tatum, B. D. (1997). Racial identity development and relational theory: The case of Black women in white communities. In J. V. Jordan (Ed.), *Women's growth in diversity: More writings from the Stone Center.* New York: Guilford Press.

Contents

PART V
THERAPY WITH DIFFERENT POPULATIONS

PART VI   MIGRATION

PART VII
NEW APPROACHES TO THERAPY PRACTICE   385

PART I

A FRAMEWORK FOR RE-VISIONING FAMILY THERAPY

Like other societal institutions, family therapy has been structured in ways that support the dominant value system and keep invisible certain hidden organizing principles of our lives, including culture, class, race, gender, and sexual orientation. The chapters in this section—indeed, in the book as a whole—evolved out of the work many in our field are doing to incorporate those hidden dimensions and to transform our definitions of "home" and "family" so that all Americans may feel safe and included. The first section of this book offers a framework for the possibilities of re-visioning family therapy from a contextual point of view.

In the opening chapter, I locate this re-visioning in the history of the family therapy field in general. Following the path laid out by Peggy McIntosh in the field of education, I try to contextualize the history and possible future of our field.

The next two chapters address the complexity of culture and cultural identity, and the need not to accept unquestioningly what is defined as "adaptive," "healthy," or "normal." Joan Laird describes ways we must transform our thinking to become aware of our multiple cultural selves, as well as ways we can move marginalized cultural experiences and ideas to the center of our awareness. Celia Falicov focuses on cultural relativity and describes a way we can rethink our concept of family triangles from this point of view.

Next, Jodie Kliman lays out the dimension of class—one of the essential and, until now, least visible elements of re-visioning family therapy from a cultural perspective. It goes unacknowledged that many groups in society are not represented in our institutions and do not have the same entitlements to participate even in our world of family therapy. It goes unsaid that where you come from does matter—that you cannot shed your past, become whatever you want, or move up in class just through hard work and desire. This chapter directly addresses the therapeutic, implications of class relations.

In the final chapters in this section, Froma Walsh and Paulette Hines discuss, from two different perspectives, issues of transcendence, spirituality, hope, and resilience—issues that have long been eschewed in our theory and practice. Such ideas have been people's primary resources in times of emotional distress for thousands of years. It is high time we reintegrated this dimension into our conceptual formulations. The belief in something beyond our individuality and our personal self-interest is our only hope for a positive future. We trust that in the next few years this area will begin to receive the attention it deserves, as more and more therapy incorporates transcendent ideas in our clinical assessment of families under stress and in our approaches to healing.

CHAPTER 1

Introduction

RE-VISIONING FAMILY THERAPY
THROUGH A CULTURAL LENS

Monica McGoldrick

> Please call me by my true names,
> so I can wake up
> and so the door of my heart can be left open.
> —THICH NHAT HANH, "Please Call Me by My
> True Names" (1991, pp. 123–124).

This chapter takes a brief look at the dominant discourses within family therapy, examining the ways in which we as family therapists have organized our theory and practice, and illustrating how this replicates the dominant value systems of U.S. society. Family therapy is evolving to become more relevant to the needs of our society and more inclusive of the individuals who make it up. This is, however, a slow and difficult evolution, and not without a backlash within the movement. In the latter portion of the chapter, I map out a series of phases that describe both the past and the possible future of family therapy. Our movement into the last of these phases, I hope will result in a transformation of theory and practice.

One problem we face in family therapy and in U.S. society as a whole is the definition of "family." Our entire business world and our entire educational system are organized to accommodate a type of family structure that represents only 3% of U.S. households—nuclear family units with employed fathers and homemaker mothers who devote themselves to the care of their husbands and children (Barnett & Rivers, 1996; Stacey, 1996). Most family therapy, like our dominant social ideology in general, has tended to be oriented toward this view of families as self-sufficient and usually nuclear units. However, our definition of a two-parent family as critical for child development has always been a euphemism for a family with a mother who is perpetually on call for everyone both emotionally and physically, and a distant, money-providing father. Families with such a structure cannot help being problematic.

The underlying issue here is our insistence in the United States on defining ourselves and others as (positively) "autonomous" or (negatively) "dependent." Poor families are seen as deficient, because they are obviously and critically dependent on systems beyond themselves for their survival; yet all families are dependent for their survival on systems beyond themselves. But those of us who are of the dominant groups fail to realize this, because of the ways the government and others support us. Our needs are met, taken for granted, and so rendered invisible to us (Coontz, 1992). Schools, courts, the police, and all other societal institutions operate for the protection and benefit of the dominant groups. Thus, those of us who make the rules and definitions are kept blind to our privilege (see McIntosh, Chapter 11, this volume) and to our dependence on those who take care of us. So the real problem is not the dependence of certain people on the society, but the delusion of autonomy. The dominant groups are using up the world's resources with no awareness or accountability (Ehrlich & Ehrlich, 1991; Ehrenreich, 1989). The economic system, the prison system, the drug rehabilitation industry, the gun industry, and the legal and governmental systems make money for the dominant groups of our society on the backs of the poor and the disenfranchised, who serve us in our homes, hotels, hospitals, and factories, making our clothing and supplies. We remain blind to our connection to them, not seeing our exploitation or the racism, sexism, and classism in our behavior. Furthermore, every American baby will have the same negative impact on the global environment in its lifetime as about 25 Indian babies (Ehrlich, Ehrlich, & Daily, 1995).

Paradoxically, the ideals stated, but not meant, by the U.S. Constitution could be the foundation of a truly egalitarian human partnership society (perhaps the first in human history)—but only if we acknowledge and deal with the pernicious, unspoken exclusions. To do this, we must acknowledge the issues. Our history books still brag about the foundation of our nation, minimizing the slaughter, slavery, and forced invisibility of more than half the population. This is hard to see, because what we overtly espouse mystifies the underlying facts of exclusion. Everything we say falls at the intersection between the spoken and the unspoken. But our society makes it very difficult to notice the unspoken or to hear the unsung voices.

Along with the members of all other institutions, we in family therapy need to revise our books to make room for the mystified underside of what has been spoken—the unspoken secrets that have structured the culture-, race-, class-, and gender-biased hierarchies that are the underpinnings of our society. It goes unacknowledged that non-Whites, the poor, women, and homosexuals are severely underrepresented in our institutions and do not have the same entitlements to participate even in our world of family therapy.

Family therapists must begin to think of families in terms of the communities they live in. We have ignored community, focusing in our field on the interior of the nuclear family in the present time—ignoring all that came before and all that provides the context for family experience. Children need more than one or even two adults to raise them, and adults need more than one or two close relationships to get them through life. As family therapists, we need to encourage our clients to go beyond the dominant culture's definitions of "family"—to pay attention to relationships with siblings, nieces, nephews, grandchildren, aunts, and uncles. And beyond this, we need to attend to friendships, and to the health, safety, and community contexts in which families find themselves. We need to consider the role of housekeepers, maids, and nannies, as well as that of godparents, teachers, and other mentors, in the rearing of children. We need to attend to the whole fabric of the family and community in order to raise our children.

THE PROBLEMS OF NAMING

We in family therapy get paid by the names we give to the problems our clients present to us. This naming is a powerful issue. An early 19th-century physician in the United States, Samuel Cartwright, described two mental disorders prevalent among slaves (Tarvis, 1992; Thomas & Sillen, 1974):

1. "Drapetomania," which was characterized by a single symptom: the uncontrollable urge to escape slavery. This was literally a "flight-from-home mania."
2. "Dysathesia aethiopia," for which many symptoms were described: destroying property on the plantation, being disobedient, talking back, fighting with masters, and refusing to work.

These diagnoses turned the desire for liberty into a sickness that was the problem of the slave, not the slave owner. The slave owner—the oppressor—became completely invisible in this nomenclature. Using labels to control others continues pretty much unabated even in family therapy.

We are much readier to diagnose the victims of abuse than the abusers. We have our favorite acronyms: MPD (multiple personality disorder), PTSD (posttraumatic stress disorder), SCSA (survivors of child sexual abuse), and so on—defining the whole life course of those who have experienced trauma, but leaving out of our descriptions those who traumatize others, just as we did with slavery. Racism is not only not a diagnosis; it is not even listed in the index for the over-800-page DSM-IV! We also obscure who does what to whom in our nomenclature by our naming: "alcoholic family," "violent family," "schizophrenic family," and so on (terms I myself used for years).

The DSM-IV claims that its naming is based on "scientific evidence," although a significant part of this research has been funded by drug companies (Kupers, 1995). This diagnostic manual includes a specific diagnosis (301.6, dependent personality disorder) for the person who has trouble disagreeing with others because of the fear of losing their approval or support. The description adds a note that this diagnosis is not to include realistic fears or worries about reprisals, but gives no guidelines as to how one would assess whether a person's fears are realistic, perhaps because of race or gender. The DSM-IV has no comparable diagnosis for those who are pathologically fearful of intimacy or dependence, those who are unable to develop friendships, those who have a need for sexual conquests, or those who react to their fear of aging by leaving their similar-age partners and establishing sexual relationships with persons the age of their children (Kupers, 1995). Similarly, the manual has failed to come up with a diagnosis not only for those who are racist, but also for those who are misogynistic or homophobic.

Indeed, it is not sufficient, according to the DSM-IV, to have been physically or sexually violent to receive a diagnosis of conduct disorder or antisocial personality disorder. The most one can give in a case of violence without the other required symptoms is one of four "V-codes": sexual abuse of child, physical abuse of child, physical abuse of adult, or sexual abuse of adult. Not one sentence of description or explanation is provided for any of these. And this situation exists in a society where a woman is beaten on the average every 18 seconds, and physical abuse is the most common cause of injury for women (more widespread than breast cancer or car accidents) (U.S. Department of Justice, 1994).

At the same time, families of color, families of the poor, and immigrant families, whose norms and values are different from those within our naming scheme, remain peripheralized, invalidated, and pathologized as deficient or dysfunctional—or, worse, invisible within our society. Many family therapists are still trained without reference to the insidious role that hierarchies related to culture, class, race, and gender play in the United States. We are taught concepts of human development, psychopathology, and family functioning within the totally skewed patriarchal, racist, classist framework of the dominant White groups in our society. We are taught that you can learn about "men's issues" and not mean issues of African American men, because their experiences are never referred to. In general, when we have talked about "couple therapy" or "child sexual abuse" or "the family life cycle" or "dual-career families" or "genograms," we have referred only to White families.

BEYOND THE TYRANNY OF LABELS: MAKING ROOM FOR BOTH GROUP CONNECTIONS AND UNIQUENESS

Labels can be reassuring or dangerous because they define boundaries— who is in and who is out. Our labels for ourselves may be reassuring because they define groups to which we belong, thus overcoming our sense of isolation. But they also define the limits of that belonging. If we label ourselves "woman," "African American," "lesbian," "son," and so on, we are by those definitions "not-man," "not-Bosnian Muslim," "not-heterosexual," "not-daughter," and so forth.

Coming to define myself as "Irish American," for example, has been an affirmation at the deepest level of my belonging (see my discussion of this in Chapter 16). It gave me a profound sense that neither I nor the other members of my family were alone in our ways of seeing the world— that much of what I thought was strange or eccentric had a meaning because of our cultural history. At a certain point, however, when I define myself as "Irish American" (or by any other fixed group identity), the boundary becomes exclusionary and distances me from others who are not Irish, to whom I may need to emphasize my connections more explicitly.

As a society, we need to transform the way we think about definitions of sameness and difference. I believe our survival as human beings depends on whether we can remove the blinders of denial that prevent our seeing our human connectedness to each other. At the same time, we must make more room to tolerate our differences. We must develop a perspective on our identity that allows for at least three levels:

1. Our uniqueness as individuals.
2. Our various group identities that give us a sense of "home"— that define who we are in relation to others.
3. Our common partnership with every other human being, without which we will surely perish.

Dealing with the subject of cultural diversity is therefore a matter of balance between validating the differences among us and appreciating the forces of our common humanity. Group boundaries may prevent people from defining themselves in all their complexity. They may emphasize distinction from outsiders rather than affiliation with group members; this reflects a negative rather than affirmative way of defining ourselves. Group boundaries may also define covert power hierarchies, which remain invisible and therefore have a pernicious effect, as when ethnic differences are described in such a way that the status differences between groups are marginalized. We as family therapists need to help our clients develop multiple affiliative group identities, to increase the flexibility of their lives in accordance with their ever-evolving circumstances. To do this we must expand our psychological theories of development to describe our identities with all their multiplicity and complexity (McGoldrick & Carter, 1998).

If we look carefully enough, all of us are a hodge-podge. Developing "cultural competence" requires us to go beyond the dominant values and explore the complexity of culture and cultural identity—not without values and judgments about what is adaptive, healthy, or "normal," but without accepting unquestioningly our society's definitions of these culturally determined categories. Our clients should not have to suppress parts of themselves in order to "pass for normal" according to someone else's standards. Nor can we simply accept our clients' definitions of their problems. Their very descriptions reflect the prejudices that we all absorb from the dominant culture. No one lives outside the issues of sexism or racism or classism or other labeling, which results in the invisibility and oppression of so many in our society.

The goal is to create a world we can each call home—a place where we will each have a voice, where our flowing sense of group identities gives us more a sense of boundaries that include than of divisions that exclude. The notion of culture is almost a mystical sense of connection with all the threads of which our human community is woven.

Clinically, we must find ways of working that hold each person accountable for his or her behavior, including intentional or unintentional sexism, racism, or other unjust behavior, at the same time that we must convey a message of love and belonging. This requires that we move beyond our denial of our connectedness to each other.

BACKLASH WITHIN FAMILY THERAPY

In family therapy, as in every other structure of our society, we see repeated efforts to silence the voices of the previously unheard who are beginning to speak up. The field has for some years been reeling from the backlash of the feminist critique. Many men have withdrawn from professional meetings. Now, as the issues of culture and race are beginning to be asserted, people say, "We better go slow, or Whites will retreat from our organizations." But we will not have a future if we have only a White future. We cannot go on the way we were going. It was our path that was a dead end, not our moves to change the path.

One aspect of the backlash is the accusation that those who advocate attention to oppression, culture, and diversity are trying to put us into a straightjacket of "political correctness" (Tataki, 1997). The first *Networker* on cultural diversity was entitled "Multiculturalism: Has It Got Us All Walking on Eggshells (*Family Therapy Networker*, 1994)." This draws our attention to the discomfort of the privileged rather than to the pain of the oppressed. Such discussion implicitly blames those who attempt to discuss their oppression for making the privileged uncomfortable—thus blocking discussion of privilege. The truth is that those who draw our attention to such social phenomena as the absence of people of color in our professional organizations, or inequities in the status of women or minorities in terms of salary, power, and visibility, make us uncomfortable. We no longer feel "safe" in an atmosphere that values "political correctness." Reverting the discussion from the issues of inequity to the discomfort of the privileged blocks a necessary part of change, since those who experience social oppression never had the privilege of feeling "safe" in the first place.

Tamasese and Waldegrave (1993) have described how claims of injustice are often overtly acknowledged in "liberal therapeutic environments," but then subtly avoided. They describe three techniques by which accountability for injustice is undermined. "Paralysis," a response of overwhelming guilt, can end up entrenching the status quo. People become so overwhelmed by their own pain that, fearing the possibility that they might offend again in the future, they do nothing and feel impotent. Others respond in a "patronizing" way, taking on the issue of the oppressed to the extent that they inappropriately become self-appointed spokespeople for them. A third response is "individualizing," whereby people separate themselves from their cultural or gender histories and claim that they can only be responsible for their personal behavior:

> [This] cleverly sidesteps the institutional and collective reality of discrimination. It is the collective of men and the history of patriarchy, which has created the environment that privileges the decisions and actions of men over women. No matter how committed to women a man may be, he may still continue to benefit at every level in a patriarchal society, at their expense. (Tamasese & Waldegrave, 1993, p. 32)

Individualizing, through which a person denies the relevance of discussion at a group level, makes it impossible to discuss issues of power, privilege, and accountability. Individualizing also includes attempts to deny belonging to the category of privilege. A person may deny being "White," for example, maintaining that other categories, such as class, culture, or personal history, are more relevant. A person may do this by referring to a great grandfather who was Cherokee, or to centuries of oppression as Irish, Jewish, or gay, or to class oppression for being "poor White trash" or having a mentally ill or abusive parent. Some people challenge the very existence of categories at all, saying that we are all just human beings and that reference to such social groupings foments trouble. Such people prefer to hold up cherished myths about being color-blind or preferring to judge people as individuals. This response, too, makes discussion of the problems of racism, sexism, and other discrimination impossible.

There are many signs of backlash within our organizations. For example, people of color are often blamed for not wanting to join our associations. Faculty members may say, "We would love to hire a minority faculty person, but we can't find any," or "We invited so-and-so, but she is a prima donna and didn't respond." Most don't question their standards for defining a "senior family therapist." Requirements such as having the "right "credentials, being in the field for a long time, or training with the field's leaders set up a conundrum, since the very problem to be solved is that family therapy, like society at large, has excluded and marginalized people of color. Most clinicians of color have not defined themselves as family therapists because they have not felt at home in our context. We have not realized that we have to change both our context and our requirements in order to welcome them in. Therapists who say that they are willing to mentor someone from a disadvantaged group, but their offers have not been accepted, fail to consider the reasons why a person from such a group might not want to join with us. Our institutions themselves have to change. Would I feel comfortable in a situation if I were the only person of my group included, and if I were expected to represent all others of my group? I doubt it.

Some members of the dominant group make subtly disqualifying comments: "These issues just aren't relevant to my work. This topic doesn't interest me. I think we need to talk about managed care instead." Or "We did cultural diversity last year; we need something new this year." This attitude assumes that we can continue our old routines without changing our institutional structures—that we can allow those who experience oppression to speak out every so often, and then we can go back to business as usual.

Others in power try to promote conflicts among those without power in our society. The top 1 million people in the United States make as much money as the next 100 million put together. As African American law professor Derrick Bell (1993) has pointed out, if people realized their commonalities and shared interests across racial lines, it would create a revolution. So it is much safer for the dominant group to promulgate myths that it is "angry" Black men, "controlling" women, or "perverse" homosexuals we really have to fear, rather than the power structure that holds the dominant group in place. An example of this within family therapy would be Jim Coyne's (1992) blaming of working mothers for keeping invisible minority child care workers in their families, while leaving out of his description the men in these families who leave home and child responsibilities to their wives, while they define the laws of the society and control employment and family structures.

THE EVOLUTION OF FAMILY THERAPY

Peggy McIntosh (1983, 1990) has described five phases of educational and personal "re-vision" with regard to both gender and race. Using these different lenses, we might broaden our perspective as family therapists to include the categories of culture, class, race, and gender in our thinking.

Starting with Phase 1, in which women and minorities were absent from academic discussion, McIntosh describes several evolutionary stages of re-visioning curricula to include a shifting consciousness of these dimensions. For example, she takes the discipline of history and explores how it can differ at each phase of re-visioning. In the first phase, history is about the ordering of events of achievement, accomplishment, and success; wars and rulers; and so forth. A course may be organized around "Man's Quest for Knowledge."

As notions of history first expand (Phase 2), the lens may be widened to include some women and/or members of ethnic minorities in the discussion of history. For example, Elizabeth Cady Stanton, Frederick Douglass, Clara Barton, and Sacagawea, may be included, but the topics of interest remain the same—an ordering of events and accomplishments, and a focus on certain individuals. The principle difference is that by broadening our lens to include some "second-stringers" who have also had an impact on history, science, or the arts, we do begin to include some women and some minorities in our discussion.

As consciousness evolves (Phase 3), there begins to be a rethinking of the place of women and ethnic minorities in society. History courses may begin to focus on them as "a problem," discussing how women struggled to get the vote, the history of the antislavery movement, and so forth. In this phase there is a consciousness that prior curricula have ignored them. The question is asked, for example, "Did women have a 'Renaissance'?" and the answer given is, of course, "No, and neither did people of color, at least not during the 'Renaissance.' " Efforts to change this exclusion focus on the social forces that have kept women and minority groups invisible.

In Phase 4, conceptions of history undergo a more radical transformation. The historian is now included in the notion of history. Instead of being an "objective" ordering of the "facts" of the past, history becomes an interactive process, where the historian influences the stories and there is a fluidity in perspectives about history.

In Phase 5—a phase that McIntosh says she herself cannot clearly envision—history will itself be reconceived to include us all.

Following McIntosh, I would like to suggest several phases through which we can imagine the field of family therapy as evolving.

Traditional Universalist Perspective

The traditional, universalist perspective was the primary lens in family therapy in the 1960s and 1970s, and continues in some quarters as we approach the 21st century. The primary definers of families and family therapy in this era were people like Bowen, Minuchin, Ackerman, Whitaker, Jackson, Watzlawick, Weakland, Fisch, Bateson, Framo, Boszormenyi-Nagy, the Milan group, Lidz, Fleck, Erickson, and Haley. One of the very few prominent women in the field in this early era was Virginia Satir; she played a major role until a quadrennial meeting of the *Family Process* advisory editors in 1974, which set up a confrontational plenary session entitled "Is Virginia Satir Dangerous for Family Therapy?" In this session Satir and Kitty LaPerriere were pitted against Sal Minuchin and Frank Pittman. It is hard to conceive that the field would have tolerated a plenary session entitled "Is Murray Bowen Dangerous for Family Therapy?" or "Is Sal Minuchin Dangerous for Family Therapy?" Satir never attended another major family therapy meeting after that, and devoted more and more time to working abroad.

Within this traditional framework, family therapy was (and often still is) white male family therapy—invented by White men, whose theories implicitly defined "family" to mean an intact, middle-class, heterosexual, White family, organized with the man as head of the household and the woman as primary caretaker of all family relationships. The theoretical focus was on family members interacting as systemic units, with no acknowledgment of their unequal power to influence interactions.

Common concepts taught about the understanding of family relationships included complementarity, homeostasis, triangles, pursuer–distancer, recursive feedback loops, cognitive-behavioral exchanges, enmeshment–disengagement, and overfunctioning–underfunctioning. One prime theoretician, Bowen, emphasized a scale of "differentiation" as the measure of human maturity; according to his theory, people defining themselves primarily by the standards of others would score lower on this scale. The fact that such self-definitions have been required of women and minorities was not mentioned. Similarly, the structural approach, another leading approach to family therapy in this era, tended to hold women responsible for family problems, without reference to their unequal power position within the family. Men were expected to control their families, and women were expected to take care of the needs of all family members.

Within this traditionalist lens, neither racism (except in the cases of Minuchin, Auerswald, and a few others) nor sexism was considered as relevant in understanding systems. Problems were formulated and assessed according to unquestioned White male definitions (the DSM categories). No reference was made to race as a category requiring attention in the family therapy field. No one pointed out that there were no people of color in the field as either leaders or followers. (The structural group did train many people of color and focused a lot of its work on families of color; its training was, however, one of the most conservative in its advocating of patriarchal gender arrangements.)

Gender Perspective

In the late 1970s and early 1980s, a new gender lens was being developed. Its emergence was heralded by articles by Rachel Hare-Mustin (1978) in the United States and by Kerrie James and Deborah McIntyre (1983) in Australia, as well as by the establishment in 1977 of the Women's Project (whose founders were Marianne Walters, Betty Carter, Peggy Papp, and Olga Silverstein). Women began to notice that the field was defined primarily or exclusively by men. A few women had risen to prominence before the feminist critique of the field: Virginia Satir and Mara Selvini Palazzoli, as well as Peggy Papp, Kitty LaPerriere, and others. However, the majority of presenters at conferences were White men; the leading texts were authored by White men; the primary research in the field was led by White men; and it was still assumed that a "family" was White, middle-class, heterosexual, and intact, unless otherwise noted. Women's lack of power in "families" was still a nontopic.

At the beginning of the 1980s, the journals and professional organizations had a predominance of White heterosexual men at the helm. *Family Process* had about 10% women on its editorial board, while its primary board had only one woman. Almost all presenters at every quadrennial meeting were men. By the 1982 *Family Process* meeting, "Epistemology, Efficacy, and Ethics," a few "junior" women had become advisory editors, but the program was still very much in the hands of the men who ran the organization. One woman, Olga Silverstein, was invited by these men to critique Mara Selvini Palazzoli's ideas, and Selvini Palazzoli responded hotly. This division between the only two women presenters seemed to be constructed into the program. (The men who commented on each others' work were known friends and supporters of each other.) Bell (1993) has written of how those without a voice in our society are pitted against each other in order to keep invisible the role of the dominant group in maintaining the status quo.

At the *Family Process* meeting in 1986, one person of color was invited to give a presentation—an African American specialist on AIDS, who was not a family therapist. Although the ratio of male to female presenters was still about 14:1, a panel of all women was arranged on gender issues (scheduled on the last morning of the conference, a Sunday). It was clear that "women's issues" were still seen as a domain exclusive to women and separate from "regular family theory and practice." There was almost no notice taken of the fact that nearly all the participants were White, so the infusion of the feminist critique was really a White feminist critique.

Two pivotal networking meetings of women family therapists in 1984 and 1986, called "Stonehenge," solidified a collaboration among women therapists that had been missing until then. A third meeting of women family therapists—an international meeting held in 1990 in Denmark— expanded the networking with other countries. The consciousness raising of women's networking was initially related more to gender than to race and culture, which took almost 10 more years to get on the table. A critique of the organization of the field began to evolve. But the primary ideas and readings in most family training programs were still those of white heterosexual men. In 1990 *Family Process,* under pressure from below, strove to have at least one-third women and 10% minorities on its advisory editorial board.

As the members of the Women's Project and others began to write about and give presentations on feminist family therapy, the absence of women and ethnic minorities in many discussions was increasingly recognized as a problem. New areas of research emerged, bringing into focus the inequality of gender roles in families, the oppression of women, violence against women in families, and mother blaming in family therapy. Still, the first-ever plenary presentation on male violence, which laid out the most basic dimensions of the problem in society and called for the development of therapeutic models to address them, was criticized as an appallingly unjust, unbalanced attack on men, in particular because the issue of women's violence was not addressed. And this issue has still not become a topic of mention by mainstream men in our field.

When the American Family Therapy Academy (AFTA), which for the first time in the late 1980s had a predominance of White women in leadership positions, planned an annual conference with mostly women presenters, there was an outraged reaction by White male leaders. They had not noticed that during the first decades of family therapy, most presentations and virtually all the key awards had gone to White men. In the mid-1980s, four women (the founders of the Women's Project) had to share one award, and the awards committee proposed that two others (Goldner and Hare-Mustin) share another, because neither had "quite done enough" to deserve a full award for her contribution to gender awareness. By the 1990s AFTA had a president and a vice president who were both women. The organization's programs dealt with cultural diversity 3 years in a row, but worried that the emphasis on these "nondominant" concerns (women and culture) was causing men to leave the organization. It wasn't until the mid-1990s that there was any public acknowledgment of the heterosexist bias of the field, and several books and articles began to appear about gay, lesbian, and bisexual families. Also in the mid-1990s, some of the major texts began to include a section on feminist family therapy, although its issues were still not acknowledged by most of the prominent men in the field.

Cultural Perspectives

During the late 1980s, an expanded cultural perspective emerged, although one strong thread had been developed from the 1960s through the work of a small minority of theoreticians and clinicians whose work focused on the poor. This group included the authors of *Families of the Slums* (Minuchin, Montalvo, Guerney, Rosman, & Schumer, 1967) and a few others, including Auerswald, and Sluzki, who spoke and wrote about multiproblem, poor, minority families. Others, such as Nancy Boyd Franklin and Elaine Pinderhughes, wrote about African American families, racism, and the poor; however, these were generally seen as special topics, not pertaining to family therapy itself. Similarly, writing on couple therapy, child abuse, the family life cycle, and other issues pertinent to family therapy continued to use White, nuclear, heterosexual, middle-class families as the norm and neglected to consider cultural differences and social inequalities. Even a family's third generation was often referred to as an "extended family," as if "family" included only those living together in the present. Family therapy conferences included one or two presenters from minority groups, who were asked to present on issues of "minority families," as opposed to "families." By 1985 the AFTA had given about 75 awards, but not one to a man or woman of color. The two best-known men of color of the early family therapy movement, Harry Aponte and Braulio Montalvo, did not receive awards until the 1990s.

The emerging cultural perspective expanded the ways families and family therapy were thought about to include the dimensions of ethnicity and culture, although (again) these dimensions were for a long time viewed as "add-ons" or "special features" of certain families, rather than as basic dimensions for understanding all families. Gradually perspectives began to expand beyond just asking that more minorities be included in leadership positions. Beginning in the 1990s, cultural diversity workshops became more common at major family therapy meetings. African Americans appeared on panels; more books and articles began to appear on Black families and other cultural minority families; there was some acknowledgment of how researchers had ignored the experience of families of color. Accepted definitions in the field of family therapy were also now open to question: It was being recognized that these definitions had labeled both people of color and women as deficient—"undifferentiated," "enmeshed," or being highly emotional.

"Minority" scholarships were awarded by a few institutions to encourage a changing in the preponderance of White therapists, but the amount of these scholarships was relatively small, and the reluctance of people of color to sign on for family therapy training was seen as their problem. Despite acknowledging the paucity of Black clients, practicing family therapists (who were still almost all White) frequently worked in private practice, which, for all intents and purposes, was alien and inaccessible to people of color or the poor. As discussed earlier, institutes expressed interest in having at least one Black faculty member, but were not prepared to make more fundamental changes in their structure and organization.

In the early 1990s, the American Association for Marriage and Family Therapy, with much fanfare, gave out a mere $5,000 in minority scholarships. The annual AFTA meeting had a plenary session on culture, where it was intended that people of privilege would begin to take some responsibility for their own part in cultural problems. Three White therapists presented three White cases and had a panel of discussants including one African American, who said that he imagined that if he had been the therapist in these cases, race would have been an issue, because he rarely had the luxury of a case in which race was not an issue. This point was not taken up by the other discussants, who moved on to other issues.

Transforming Our Vision

A fourth lens, requiring second-order change, began developing later in the 1990s. From this perspective, all families, not just "minorities," are seen as embedded in and bounded by class, culture, gender, and race. Moreover, how a society defines gender, race, culture, and class relationships is viewed as critical to understanding how *all* family processes are structured.

Family therapy from this perspective aims to meet the needs of people of many cultural backgrounds. Courses on couple therapy include Black couples, Chinese and other Asian couples, interracial couples, and gay couples. The faculty and students of training programs are more culturally diverse. Again, this requires second-order change on the part of the leaders of the field, to make room for the inclusion of knowledge and teaching other than that of the dominant groups. Faculties of training programs are in the process of being reconstituted so that they can reflect diversity, and subject matter is likewise being rethought from a more inclusive perspective. Emphasis is shifting from the teachings of a few highly valued leaders to experiential and reciprocal learning. The wisdom and strengths of American Indian, African American, and other "minority" cultures are becoming integral components of family therapy theories.

Student training includes home visits and studies of the cultural values and healing customs of Muslim families, Asian Indian families, and Latino families. Students are encouraged to collaborate with indigenous community cultural leaders to help families. Questions about how families are located in their communities are becoming routine in assessment. Assumptions of the student and faculty are examined, as are those in the family therapy literature. The field is expanding to include study of healing in cultures around the world. Spiritual, physical, psychological, and biological solutions to problems are increasingly employed in an integrated way.

FAMILY THERAPY REDEFINED AND RECONSTRUCTED TO INCLUDE US ALL

Although we need to continue working in the directions outlined above, this final phase is hard to envision, just as it has been for Peggy McIntosh in the field of education. Its description must await our learning to see around the next corner. Surely in this latest phase, family intervention will occur in more flexible contexts with a more diverse array of helpers and a more flexibly defined "family." Intervention strategies will draw from cultural healing the world over. Family therapy training may focus on how we can understand those who are different from ourselves. It is so difficult even to picture a world not divided by our current hierarchical structures that it is hard to imagine what healthy families or therapy may come to look like. One thing seems sure: As we expand the boundaries of our field, we open up enormous possibilities for helping families in multiple contexts and with a great variety of healing tools—from music, meditation, prayer, and poetry to community meetings and empowerment. I hope that this book provides a small window into this new world of possibilities.

REFERENCES

Bell, D. (1993). *Faces at the bottom of the well: The permanence of racism.* New York: Basic Books.

Coontz, S. (1992). *The way we never were: American families and the nostalgia trap.* New York: Basic Books.

Coyne, J. (1992, May–June). *Family Therapy Networker,* [Letter to the editor on "Stonewalling feminism"], p. 3.

Ehrenreich, B. (1989). *Fear of falling: The inner life of the middle class.* New York: Harper.

Ehrlich, P., & Ehrlich, A. (1991). *Healing the planet.* New York: Addison-Wesley.

Ehrlich, P., Ehrlich, A., & Daily, G. C. (1995). *The stork and the plow: The equity answer to the human dilemma.* New Haven: Yale University Press.

Family Therapy Networker. (1994, July/August). Multiculturalism: Has it got us all walking on eggshells?

Hanh, T. N. (1991). *Peace is every step.* New York: Bantam.

Hare-Mustin, R. (1978). A feminist approach to family therapy. *Family Process, 17,* 181–194.

James, K., & McIntyre, D. (1983). The reproduction of families: The social role of family therapy? *Journal of Marital and Family Therapy, 9,* 119–129.

Kupers, T. A. (1995). The politics of psychiatry: Gender and sexual preference in DSM-IV. *Masculinities, 3*(2), 67–78.

McGoldrick, M., & Carter, B. (1998). Self in context: The individual life cycle in systemic perspective. In B. Carter & M. McGoldrick (Eds.), *The expanded life cycle: Individual, family, community.* Needham Height, MA: Allyn & Bacon.

McIntosh, P. (1983). *Interactive phases of curricular re-vision: A feminist perspective* (Working Paper No. 124). Wellesley, MA: Wellesley College Center for Research on Women.

McIntosh, P. (1990). *Interactive phases of curricular and personal re-vision with regard to race* (Working Paper No. 219). Wellesley, MA: Wellesley College Center for Research on Women.

Minuchin, S., Montalvo, B., Guerney, B. G., Jr., Rosman, B. L., & Schumer, F.

(1967). *Families of the slums: An exploration of their structure and treatment*. New York: Basic Books.

Stacey, J. (1996). *In the name of the family: Rethinking family values*. Boston: Beacon.

Tavris, C. (1992). *The mismeasure of women*. New York: Simon & Schuster.

Tamasese, K., & Waldegrave, C. (1993). Culture and gender accountability in the 'just therapy' approach. *Journal of Feminist Family Therapy, 5*(2), 29–45.

Tataki, R. (1997). At the end of the century: The "Culture Wars" in the U.S. In R. Tataki (Ed.), *From different shores*. New York: Oxford University Press.

Thomas, A., & Sillen, S. (1974). *Racism and psychiatry*. Secaucus, NJ: Citadel.

U.S. Department of Justice. (1994, January). *Violence against women: A national crime victimization survey report*.

CHAPTER 2

Theorizing Culture
NARRATIVE IDEAS
AND PRACTICE PRINCIPLES

Joan Laird

"Cultural diversity," "multiculturalism," "culturally sensitive practice," "cultural competence"—these have become the buzz phrases of the 1990s in the mental health professions. But the term "culture" covers a territory that contains vast possibilities for understanding and interpretation. We use words like "culture," "gender," "race," "ethnicity," "social class," and "sexual orientation" as if they had consistent definitions and as if we had some agreement on their meanings.

As mental health practitioners, we are repeatedly exhorted to become culturally competent and to practice ethnic-sensitive practice. This usually means educating ourselves about the characteristics of the "other," and discovering what the study of a group of people—with origins different from our own, from another nation, with another skin color, with different genitalia, with same-sex life partners—can tell us about ourselves. To learn about the other, said anthropologists, was to learn about us. As Bateson (1979) put it, "it takes two somethings to create a difference" (p. 68). Thus, you may know you are French because someone else is Swedish; I know I am short (in this context) because you are tall. In Western culture, at least, we've organized ourselves around "difference" and particularly around binary oppositions—male–female, Black–White, gay–straight, rich–poor. To be culturally competent has meant, then, to know about and to appreciate "difference." But "different from" often means "less than." Are there any other ways to think about thinking about culture?

"Culture" is a vast interdisciplinary topic that has generated floods of literature and research in the social sciences in the last decade, as well as central discussions in academia, in organizations, within the popular culture, and, of course, at professional conferences. How do we move beyond the cliché-ridden, often rather meaningless or undefined ways these notions are tacked on to diagnostic and other clinical languages, receiving little more than honorable mention? How do we surface our own cultural stories, our cultural identities? And, when it is important— as it almost always is—how do we locate the cultural stories and meanings of the people with whom we work?

My purpose in this chapter is to offer a number of ideas or metaphors that may be useful for thinking about how to think about "culture," and, using those ideas, to generate some principles for practice. These ideas are inspired by work from many directions, among them the postmodern movement, the interdisciplinary movement, the feminist critique, voices from various margins, and new work on gender and sexuality. I intend for these ideas to apply to any of the cultural categorizations we make in identifying and characterizing each other and in labeling various social groupings—categorizations such as gender, race, ethnicity, social class, or sexuality. These categorizations, these self-representations, are overlapping and simultaneous; we can "theorize" them using common points of reference.

THE NEED TO MOVE
BEYOND STATIC NOTIONS OF CULTURE

Many clinicians believe that these dimensions of human experience are vitally important, but have very different ideas about the meanings of these cultural categorizations and how they should be thought about in practice. In the ethnicity area, for example, some clinicians have argued that culture is "camouflage" (Friedman, 1980); that is, it is used in families in manipulative or controlling ways as a red herring, in order to preserve the status quo, bind children to their parents, keep family boundaries closed, and so on. Others, like Montalvo and Gutierrez (1983), have seen culture or ethnicity as a potential "mask" that can obscure people's problem-solving modes:

> By using cultural constraints selectively . . . the family can pull the therapist away from reality. The therapist is made to deal instead with a cultural image of the ethnic group. In the process the family—as simply people having difficulties in solving problems—is lost. (p. 16)

These authors have believed that if one is simply a good listener, or, as in the case of various family therapies, able to surface the family structure, rules, and other patterns, what is important about culture will emerge. One needs no special knowledge.

McGoldrick (1993), perhaps the most articulate and dedicated spokesperson in the clinical arena for the importance of the cultural dimension in family life, has taken a very different position. She points out that "ethnicity patterns our thinking, feeling and behavior in both obvious and subtle ways, playing a major role in determining what we eat, how we work, how we relate, how we celebrate holidays and ritual, and how we feel about life, death, and illness" (p. 335). In McGoldrick's view, although to learn about ethnic group practices and beliefs is to risk stereotyping, to pretend that there are no patterns is to mystify and disqualify human experience and to "perpetuate negative stereotyping" (p. 335).

Falicov (1995), in one kind of effort to avoid the risks of stereotyping, advocates what she calls a "multidimensional, comparative" training framework. "Culture is viewed as occurring in multiple contexts that create common 'cultural borderlands' as well as diversity; unpredictability and possibility, as well as regularity and constraint" (p. 373). She uses what she terms "basic parameters" common to all families—parameters such as ecological niche, migration patterns, degrees of acculturation, or life cycle events—to think comparatively. I see this effort, in part, as one of learning about how diverse people approach common human experiences rather than about ethnic groups or entities. It is one way of shifting the center and avoiding the "different from/less than" trap that comes from always beginning with the dominant experience.

My own view both combines and is somewhat different from any of these positions. I agree with McGoldrick about the power of culture and ethnicity (and gender, sexuality, social class, etc.) in shaping the self and the human story, and about how important it is for clinicians to learn how to access these stories. If we are to unpack cultural stories, we need to know enough to ask good questions, to "notice" culture in its many guises. I also believe, unlike Montalvo or Friedman, that whatever our therapeutic models, listening and questioning in and of themselves are not quite good enough, and that special "knowledges" are helpful as long as we hold them tentatively. For if we do not learn about our own cultural selves and the culture of the other, it will be difficult to move beyond our own cultural lenses and biases when we encounter practices that we do not understand or find distasteful; we will not be able to ask the questions that help surface subtle ethnic, gender, or sexuality meanings; and we may not see or hear such meanings when they are right there in front of us. Our own cultural narratives help us to organize our thinking and anchor our lives, but they can also blind us to the unfamiliar and unrecognizable and they can foster injustice. One needs only to think about the gender blindness that dominated the mental health professions for nearly a century to understand how invisible crucial influences on people's lives can be. Moreover, such blindness largely continues today in relation to lesbian, gay, bisexual, and transsexual people. Learning about culture(s) can teach us how to ask good questions in a way that not only helps to surface for our inspection our clients' cultural meanings, but makes it possible for them to hear their own cultural stories in a newly reflective way. It is this cultural questioning process, not cultural characteristics, that has transferability across cultural categories.

On the other hand, we also need to move beyond the curiously static and decontextualized ways in which ethnicity is often theorized, taught, and applied in clinical practice. We have leaned on theories and definitions of ethnicity that stress clusters of attributes and experiences—what might be called "first-order learning"—rather than learning how to learn about culture. We are urged to help people preserve their culture, as if culture were a set of essential and unchanging characteristics, an "it" that is identifiable and preservable in unaltered form. Making the argument in relation to gender, Goldner (1991) argues that an internally consistent idea of gender identity is not possible or even desirable. In her view, gender coherence, consistency, conformity, and identity are culturally mandated normative ideas that become absorbed uncritically and sometimes problematically. I suggest that the same may be said of ethnicity, race, social class, sexuality, and other cultural identities. These normative ideas, in which we are all embedded, encourage stereotyping, narrow our field of possibilities, and prevent us from recognizing the dynamic complexity and continuously changing nature of ethnic, racial, gender, social class, or sexual identity and experience. We are constrained by our nouns, as words like "nature," "identity," and "culture" itself imply that these are "things" we can hold for a moment in time. We also find it enormously difficult either to pivot or to shift the center, to divest ourselves of our canons or at least hold them more tentatively, to move our positions, and both to begin with and to enter the experiences and meanings of our informants. The challenge, as bell hooks (1984) frames it, is to move the subjugated experience from margin to center.

My own stance might be described as one of "informed not-knowing" (Shapiro, 1995). "Not-knowing" is used here in the sense that Anderson and Goolishian (1992) use it, to mean that we are never "expert," "right," or in full possession of "the truth." On the other hand, I believe that only if we become as informed as possible—about ourselves and those whom we perceive as different—will we be able to listen in a way that has the potential for surfacing our own cultural biases and recognizing the cultural narratives of the other. Learning about culture from one friend, one book, one client, one trip, gives us the possibility of hearing and seeing even more at the next opportunity; it enriches our repertoire of good and important questions. Furthermore, as investigators, ethnographers, therapists, we are "positioned subjects who are prepared to know certain things and not others" (Rosaldo, 1989, p. 8).

MORE DYNAMIC NOTIONS OF CULTURE: SOME SUGGESTIONS

In this section, I suggest a number of ideas or concepts that have the potential for helping us move away from more essentialist and fixed notions of culture. The terms I use all argue for the "moveable feast" metaphor—that is, the idea that gender, race, and other cultural notions are constantly in motion, changing in meanings and definitions on the parts of both the beholder and the beheld.

Culture Is Performative and Improvisational

Culture is performed; its forms and meanings are situated and communicated in various "contexts for action, interpretation, and evaluation" (Bauman, 1986). We "perform" our cultural stories of gender, ethnicity, race, and so on, as we move through the days in time and space. Furthermore, each performance, each enacted storying, is both unique and at the same time located in and related to the larger social discourses of meaning from which we gather narrative threads, symbols, and ritual possibilities—a combination of tradition and imagination (Laird, 1989). This process can be thought of as "improvisational," a term that I first heard used in reference to culture by Myerhoff (1978). She suggested that we make culture up and we make ourselves up as we go along, forcing our experiences to fit into particular sets of meanings. Myerhoff discovered that a group of aging Jews in Venice, California, who thought they were preserving Yiddishkeit, were largely making it and themselves up through highly improvisational story and ritual; these 80- and 90-year-olds were not so much recreating the old as creating the new. Drawing on the work of Kenneth Burke, she suggested that they were "dancing an attitude." This is what we do: We dance attitudes.

Culture Is Fluid/Emergent

Culture is contextual. Thus, because no two contexts are ever quite the same, it is always more or less changing and it is always emerging. Who we are changes from moment to moment in shifting settings. We are all multiple cultural selves. I am culturally different when I am in a classroom on the campus of Smith College; vacationing in my Maine cabin in the woods; marching in the Gay, Lesbian, Bisexual March in Washington; driving in heavy traffic by myself; driving in heavy traffic with a casual friend or acquaintance; eating dinner at the college president's house; or visiting my mother in central Florida. What I am aware of is that I change various cultural markers and symbols, as well as my relationships with various stereotyped notions of culture; I alter my language and my topics of conversation, my costuming, my positioning, how much and what I eat or drink. I become more or less feminine or masculine, more or less gay or straight, more or less middle-class, more or less my mother (Protestant, English, and German in heritage) or my father (Catholic, Irish, and French-Canadian). I never wear jeans to the college president's house; I never call anyone an "ass———" when I am performing professionally in public; and I try not to swear in front of my tiny granddaughter. I don't talk about my career in the same way when I am with my family as when I am with my friends or colleagues. I never wear a pink triangle in Maine—one neighbor is a very conservative, rigid, militaristic sort of person (and so I make up ideas about *his* culture!) The point is that I, like all of us, can dance an attitude.

This is not to trivialize, for example, the importance and centrality to our lives of race, gender, or other aspects of cultural identity. African American family therapist Ken Hardy (1996) has pointed out that race is always salient for him as a person and as a therapist, whether he is working with a White family or another Black man, in a way that it may not (but would, if we could shift the center) feel salient for a White therapist working with a White family. For Hardy, it is always part of the "discourse in the mirrored room" (Hare-Mustin, 1994). Goldner (1988) argued that gender is a fundamental organizing force in family life, even more universal than other mediating variables, such as race, class, or ethnicity. Any cultural categorization or identity—gender, race, class, sexuality—seems more salient at the margins, where there is heightened awareness of how one may be defined as "other" and deprivileged. Furthermore, if one lives on the margins rather than in the center, it is more important to maintain what some have called a "dual perspective"—one informed eye on the dominant culture and the other on one's own. Nevertheless, other than skin color (which itself has different meanings in differing contexts) and one's anatomically distinct characteristics (which can be altered), very little about gender, race, or any other cultural category can be construed as unchanging.

Chicano anthropologist Renato Rosaldo (1989) calls these shifts in context "cultural borderlands," and suggests that they should be regarded as "sites of creative cultural production" (p. 208). Culture is creative and unpredictable, and because it is creative, it has its distinctive tempo, and it permits people to develop timing, coordination, and a knack for responding to contingencies. These qualities constitute social grace, which in turn enables an attentive person to be effective in the interpersonal politics of everyday life. (p. 112)

As one of Weston's (1996) informants told her in a comment sure to confuse those who think that "lesbian" implies "masculine," or who think that "butch" and "femme" are constant categories that imply imitating heterosexual norms for masculinity and femininity,

I think I was much more butch before I ever came out. Coming out has been a process of getting in touch with the feminine in me. It gave me the courage to do it and it gave me support to do it by giving me a community that allegedly respects women. When I'm femme, I'm really femme, and when I'm butch, I'm pretty butch. I'd say I'm more butch and femme than most. (p. 111)

Culture Is Intersection

One is never simply a Chicano or a man or gay or working-class or an American. The same person may be, in any one moment, all of these things and much more. None of these categorizations is stable or fixed, and no one is ever one of these stories without at the same time all of the others, although one story, one self, may be more salient in one context and time than in another. For a lesbian with children, being a woman/ mother may be far more important at particular times in her life than her sexual orientation, shaping her activities, her friends, and her presentation of self (Lewin, 1993). As in the turning of a kaleidoscope, variously colored and shaped pieces fall into patterned arrangements where one or the other color or pattern seems to stand out. Recent scholars (e.g., Anderson & Collins, 1992; Spelman, 1988) have reminded us that neither race, class, nor gender (and, I would add, any cultural categorization) ever stands alone. Carrying the cultural narrative of a middle-aged, heterosexual, Irish American, working-class woman from Boston implies different meanings and different experiences than being a middle-aged, heterosexual, Irish American, middle-class woman from Boston; being an Irish American working-class woman may have very different meanings than being an American Indian working-class woman; and so on. A New York City Puerto Rican man with a doctorate in engineering may speak a constellation of languages: the English of the engineer, of the consultant, of the educated man in his office in the city; another type of English when he is at home with his equally well-educated, White, British American wife; and Puerto Rican Spanish when he returns to rural Puerto Rico for a family reunion. An African American college teacher may use one type of language in her classroom, another in her church, and a third when she returns to her old neighborhood. She is differently African American in each context, drawing on various parts of her ethnic self-story. All are emergently ethnic, differentially performing their ethnicities, drawing on traditional ideas as well as assimilating and acculturating according to the situation. Gender is raced and classed, and shifts in meaning with age, sexual orientation, and other "selves." Similarly, ethnicity is gendered, raced, classed, and so on.

Furthermore, there is tremendous within-group diversity. One can never assume common sets of meanings within any one grouping—not even all middle-class, middle-aged, White, English-descent, heterosexual, feminist, East Coast men share common meanings about gender (or, for that matter, anything else). But the commonalities we've learned about in their life narratives can help us to ask good questions: How is *this* person performing culture?

Culture Is Definitional and Constitutive

Culture is not measurable or generalizable; it cannot be defined, except perhaps in a way that is satisfying to sociologists who are comforted by statistical portraits (which do indeed stimulate certain kinds of important questions)—by the numbers of in-group members who are bar mitzvahed, who intermarry, who attend Sunday school, who march on St. Patrick's Day, or who can speak the native language. Ethnicity, for example, or race cannot be decontextualized and held up for examination and definition, because it is not a thing, an object; it is a narrativized cluster of meanings drawn from past, present, and future that is itself definitional and constitutive. Part of one's cultural identity may be strengthened in situations of contrast or difference—as Bateson implied, these situations provide information. A man may feel more "manly" when performing a task that requires physical strength. A woman may develop a heightened consciousness of her usually dormant Jewish heritage when she is with her British-American in-laws for a holiday. These moments, these points of intersection, lead us (at least in this context) to strengthen certain parts of our cultural selves. Ethnicity, gender, social class, and other narratives not only mirror or recreate existing meanings, but create new ones as they are being performed and improvised. The larger culture, the ethnic group, the family, offer us symbols, stereotypes, narratives from which to choose as we, in *bricolage* fashion, constitute and reconstitute ourselves. The adult lesbian or gay "coming-out" experience offers a clear example of how this process can work.

In a fascinating description of the relationships between race, ethnicity, class, and particularly gender on the one hand and sexual orientation on the other, Weston (1996), through extended narrative interviews, pivots around and deconstructs the "tomboy" story as new lesbians draw upon this larger cultural story in a retrospective effort to make sense of current action and to construct a lesbian identity. She says:

> You might think that lesbians would want to dismiss the tomboy-grows-into-a-dyke narrative for the stereotype it is. But drawing upon the inversion model, a woman can use gender to argue for the "realness" of her gay identity. How? She slips continuity into her descriptions of the ways she has gendered herself over the years. She reminds you that her first words were, "Play ball," but forgets to tell you about the time she tried out for cheerleading or homecoming queen. (p. 44)

"Is gendering," Weston asks, "usually consistent over a lifetime, or is consistency an impression produced by the stories people tell about those formative years?" (p. 45). The tomboy narrative, she argues, is raced and classed—a story told far more by white working-class women to make sense of their emerging lesbian identities.

Culture Is Political

We know that all stories, whether they are about race, gender, or physical ability, are not equal; that is, people do not have equal voice in shaping their personal narratives, nor do all people have equal opportunities to have their particular stories prevail. Feminist family therapists have demonstrated, for example, how powerfully gendered social discourses and personal gender premises influence how we construct our narratives (Goldner, Penn, Sheinberg, & Walker, 1990; Hare-Mustin, 1994; Laird, 1989). Our personal and family narratives are shaped and constrained by larger cultural narratives that provide the possibilities from which we can choose to make meaning. When these narratives are "problem-saturated" (White & Epston, 1990), invisible, and/or unjust, or simply narrow and constraining, they can, most benignly, inhibit the ways individuals can make sense of themselves and their experiences. More lethally, they can influence the development of shameful, defeating, and even deadly self-narratives.

In sum, I suggest that culture (whether we are talking about gender, age, race, or other cultural categories) is an individual and social construction, a constantly evolving and changing set of meanings that can be understood only in the context of a narrativized past, a cointerpreted present, and a wished-for future. It is always contextual, emergent, improvisational, transformational, and political; above all, it is a matter of linguistics or of languaging, of discourse. It is meaning-defined and itself definitional and constitutive.

IMPLICATIONS FOR PRACTICE

Growing out of these thoughts on culture, and drawing on narrative, constructionist, and other postmodern ideas as they are emerging in the family therapy field, the following suggestions seem relevant to a stance for therapy that is culturally sensitive.

Making "Culture" the Central Metaphor for Therapy

The concept of "culture"—with a small "c" and meant to include any of the sociocultural categorizations we, in interaction with others, make up about ourselves or others make up about us—should be the central metaphor for practice, not a peripheral one. Culture and all of its ingredients are more experience-near, closer to the ground of everyday life and everyday experience, than the more abstract and objectifying metaphors usually invented to label consumers of mental health services.

Culture is constituted through language, through narrative, story, and social discourse. These narratives are performed in private, when one of our multiple selves is talking to another, or in public, when we are talking to the "other." Culture is put into action by people themselves to constitute and define themselves. The cultural metaphor avoids the machine-like, corporate, experience-distant metaphors of structural and family systems theories, as well as the pathologizing metaphors of psychoanalytic and psychodynamic theories. There is no enmeshed or disengaged dysfunctional family here; nor is there some imagined, tripartite homunculus constructing the rules of the road, directing traffic, and punishing road offenses. Neither is the cultural metaphor as reductionistic as some of the behavioral therapy metaphors, for there is room here for behavior, internal narrative, thought, emotion, language, fantasy, myth, speech, action, and intersubjectivity. It is indeed a metaphor that allows for movement between inner experience and the outer world.

This does not mean that it is a metaphor without risk. Cultural categorizations may be abused in the service of stereotyping, power politics, and such severe forms of oppression as the appalling practice of "ethnic cleansing" (otherwise known as genocide), violence against women, or gay-bashing. Although "culture" may be misused by some to justify oppression within families or in the larger world—to heighten and exploit "difference," rather than to foster the appreciation of diversity—when used intelligently and empathically, it is a way of entering the lives of people by listening to their own voices, their own everyday experiences.

Taking an Ethnographic Stance

Borrowing from the anthropologists and congruent with the notion of culture as metaphor, several writers in the family field, myself included, have argued for assuming the ethnographic metaphor in practice (Anderson & Goolishian, 1992; Falicov, 1995; Laird, 1989, 1994, 1995, 1996). What this stance most fundamentally is about is figuring out how, when entering the experience of another individual or group of individuals, to be as unfettered as possible with one's own cultural luggage—how to leave at home one's powerful cultural assumptions and to create the conversational spaces wherein the voices of the "other" can emerge. Anderson and Goolishian (1992), in their effort to deconstruct the ethnographic stance, have argued that it is the client who is the expert; as therapists, we do (or should) enter the experience of the other as "not-knowing." Dyche and Zayas (1995) suggest that "cultural naiveté," and "respectful curiosity" are as important as knowledge and skill. Knowledge, or what they call "cultural literacy," they believe, can obscure our views and privilege our own representations over those of our clients.

It is important to point out that we can never completely leave our own cultural assumptions behind. Even the choices we make about to whom to talk or where to position the video camera reflect our own cultural visions and thus direct our gaze. We cannot escape culture; we can only try to meet it on its own terms. This is why it is so vital, as so many scholars have cautioned, to keep working on understanding our own "local knowledges," our own cultural narratives, and to make them as accessible as possible to ourselves and transparent to others.

Furthermore, as I have said earlier, we must be highly informed "not-knowers" if we are to ask good questions. What we learn about the culture of one society is not replicable and transferable to another society, just as what we learn about the experiences of one individual or family is not replicable and transferable to another. What *are* replicable and transferable, however, are ideas. Ideas that emerge from one ethnographic or practice experience generate questions to ask of another group, another person. We do not know, in any prior way, the experiences of our informants; leaning on prior understandings or our own professional "knowledges" may well close us off from understanding the meanings of the person or family in view, and create what it is we expected to see. But as "informed not-knowers," we may bring a wealth of expertise in asking good questions—questions that help to make more visible (both to us and to the "other") their meanings, as well as the sources of those meanings.

Assuming a Narrative Stance

In the last several years, a number of therapists have pioneered and articulated a narrative stance for therapy (e.g., Andersen, 1991; Anderson & Goolishian, 1992; Hoffman, 1992; White & Epston, 1990). The literature on narrative therapy is rapidly expanding, as therapists draw on the work of the pioneers, add to and deepen the ideas, and make applications to various kinds of problems and populations. There is not sufficient space here to review this work. I simply state that I believe the therapeutic stance implied—a stance that is highly respectful, collaborative, and nonhierarchical—is one that encourages the expression of multiple ideas and possibilities; avoids blame or pathologizing; searches for strengths rather than defects; is grounded in a value stance; and fosters transparency on the part of the therapist (i.e., a situating of the therapist's ideas in her or his own experience). It is a stance uniquely suited to culturally sensitive practice.

Deconstructing Cultural Self-Narratives

Although the idea of deconstructing cultural self-narratives is a simple one, it gets lost in translation in many therapies. Many therapists who hope and plan to practice in a culturally sensitive way fail to see or hear the cultural, because their own prior texts are so powerful. Most therapists emphasize "listening." But listening usually means listening for something in particular—for example, for therapist–client relational or transferential material; for evidence to make a diagnosis; for material to confirm our impressions of dysfunction or pathology. Deconstructing the cultural self-narrative also means listening and questioning, but not based on prior assumptions. It means exploring how client cultural meanings and cultural premises (whether linked to race, ethnicity, social class, gender, sexuality, work, religion or mourning, etc.) are being performed, and how they are influencing both the self-story and the problem (Akamatsu, 1995). Furthermore, it means listening "radically," in a way that Weingarten (1995) defines as "authenticating"—a way that is respectful, accepting, and welcoming; a way that searches for the unsaid as well as the said, the invisible as well as the visible.

It is important to recognize that there will be many differing cultural narratives in the same family (those stories also gendered, raced, classed, aged, etc.), responsive to differences in degrees of acculturation, access to new cultural narratives, generational differences, and many other influences. East Indian parents now raising their children in the United States may be hurt and bewildered when their daughter chooses to live in a coed dorm at her university or dates a European American man, while a Chinese American husband may be in despair at the freedoms his wife is claiming in this country. Can we listen in ways that are authenticating and socially just and responsible for all concerned?

Locating Cultural Narratives
in the Larger Social Discourse

"Local knowledges" (Geertz, 1983) do not spring simply from the local experience, no matter how intersubjective they may be. For example, in mainstream U.S. society, a teenage girl's profound contempt for her mother is very likely to be connected to a much more pervasive profound contempt of women. For the young girl to accept, value, and identify with her mother may mean envisioning for herself a future filled with both subtle and overt forms of oppression—a future she sees as intolerable. By repudiating her mother, perhaps she can venture down another path in her own adult life. An African American man's depression or his fury toward his wife may have its roots in larger devaluing and invalidating narratives of the Black man's experience. Our self-narratives are embedded in larger social discourses, negotiated over time within relations of knowledge and power (Foucault, 1980), which gain acceptance as "truth." These narratives can be subjugating; they can cut us off from a fuller range of possibilities for ourselves and our lives. Thus, as Hare-Mustin (1994) phrases it, it is crucial to bring these larger social discourses into the mirrored room and to challenge them. Whose stories have prevailed in the shaping of our clients' cultural narratives? Do these stories fit their lived experiences? Are they nurturing, strengthening, and potentiating stories, or are they self-defeating ones? Do they trivialize or even render invisible some of the clients' experiences? Do their self-stories demean their own worth and ideas, and privilege the ideas and interpretations of others? Do their stories contain contradictions or double binds that are invalidating? For example, is a woman of color receiving competing messages about who she is and what she should be choosing from the dominant society and from her own ethnic group? Is a poor woman on Aid to Families with Dependent Children being told on the one hand that she lacks a work ethic, and on the other hand, when she locates work, being blamed for neglecting her children because there is no affordable day care? Is a father told on the one hand that it is his job to shoulder the breadwinning responsibilities by working harder or accepting a second job, and on the other faulted for not being available for or nurturing to his children? Is he taught to bury his emotions, to be a warrior, and to solve problems and handle challenges aggressively, but punished when he uses these same self-narratives to "discipline" his wife and children? Can transsexuals find any stories that affirm their identity narrative, in which to locate their own isolating and invisible experiences? Are our stories liberating or subjugating?

Resisting Culture or Interrogating the Subjugating Narrative

Most of us have been taught to respect rather than to question differing cultural practices—sometimes even when they seem brutal, such as bride burning in India, supercision of young males in New Guinea puberty rites, or the clitoridectomy of young females in some African tribes. Taken to its isolationist extreme, a hands-off stance in the face of genocide (e.g., the slaughter of Jews, Cambodians, and Bosnian Muslims) has been tolerated worldwide.

Less dramatically, in our training programs, in our classrooms, and in our therapy offices, we have learned and have taught others to respect differences in what are called ethnic or cultural or class or gender or sexuality values, both within families and in and between ethnic groups. Dilemmas arise, however, when those differences privilege the position of one group or subgroup of a family and deprivilege or subjugate the experiences of another. For example, the Latino gay man (Morales, 1996) and the African American lesbian (Greene, 1994) may be unacceptable in their larger ethnic groups or families, while the voices of the Chinese girl child or even the middle-class European American woman may be deprivileged in relation to the family males.

Weingarten (1995) describes, for example, how mothers in this society are constrained by cultural messages about what constitutes "good" and "bad" mothering, so that their effort is to story their lives in ways that will be acceptable within these definitions, not in ways that more accurately reflect their lived experiences. Women's narratives, we have learned, are often silenced, and even their speech genres are ridiculed (Laird, 1989).

Such differences present a dilemma for some narrative therapists, who see bringing culture into the therapy room in a way that challenges dominant discourses as an imposition of personal politics (e.g., Hoffman, 1992). Others, more concerned about subjugation and injustice, take a very different stance. White (1994), for example, argues that every therapeutic act is a political one, and that clients need to be helped to deconstruct not only their self-narratives but also the dominant cultural narratives and discursive practices that constitute their lives. "Deconstruction" means to explore how these dominating discourses are shaped, to examine whose interests they serve and whose they may subjugate, and to expose the marginalized possibilities. How have these dominant and subjugated narratives influenced the "local" story or the story at hand in the clinical situation? This does not mean that therapists deliver their political views as truths, but that they remain sensitive to the spoken stories as well as to the underlying ones that have not been voiced due to lack of power or knowledge. Alertness to the privileging of some narratives in unjust and colonizing dominant discourses allows us to open up conversational spaces in which new and more potentiating narratives may emerge.

Moving beyond the Mirrored Room toward a Culturally Just Practice

Finally, and most neglected, is the role of the family therapist in moving beyond the therapeutic conversation to a position between client and community. Minuchin (1991) wonders whether postmodern theory is rescuing us from having to face the evils and hopelessness in the world around us, reducing our concerns to the individual story, when the plots of these stories are often dictated by powerful forces outside the interviewing room.

Justice is raced, gendered, and classed—a lesson cast in bold relief in the last several years with the Rodney King beating, the Anita Hill and Clarence Thomas case (Morrison, 1992), the U.S. Navy Tailhook incident, and the ongoing O. J. Simpson saga. It is our responsibility not only to surface cultural stories of oppression and marginalization in people's lives in our offices, but to go beyond the case to help our clients tell their stories in new and larger contexts, and to bear witness to those suppressed stories ourselves in the schools, courts, legislatures, and mass media. In other words, we need to add our own voices when those larger cultural discourses do not fairly represent the experiences of our clients and do not allow their stories to be heard.

REFERENCES

Akamatsu, N. N. (1995). The defiant daughter and compliant mother: Multicultural dialogues on woman's role. *In Session: Psychotherapy in Practice, 1*(4), 43–55.

Andersen, T. (1991). *The reflecting team: Dialogues and dialogues about the dialogues.* New York: Norton.

Anderson, H., & Goolishian, H. (1992). The client is the expert: A not-knowing approach to therapy. In S. McNamee & K. Gergen (Eds.), *Therapy as social construction* (pp. 25–39). Newbury Park, CA: Sage Publications.

Anderson, M. L., & Collins, P. H. (Eds.). (1992). *Race, class, and gender: An anthology.* Belmont, CA: Wadsworth.

Bateson, G. (1979). *Mind and nature: A necessary unity.* New York: Dutton.

Bauman, R. (1986). *Story, performance, and event: Contextual studies of oral narrative.* Cambridge, England: Cambridge University Press.

Dyche, L., & Zayas, L. H. (1995). The value of curiosity and naivete for the cross-cultural therapist. *Family Process, 34*(4), 389–399.

Falicov, C. J. (1995). Training to think culturally: A multidimensional comparative framework. *Family Process, 34,* 373–388.

Foucault, M. (1980). *Power/knowledge: Selected interviews and other writings.* New York: Pantheon.

Friedman, E. (1980). Systems and ceremonies. In E. A. Carter & M. McGoldrick (Eds.), *The family life cycle: A framework for family therapy* (pp. 429–460). New York: Gardner Press.

Geertz, C. (1983). *Local knowledge: Further essays in interpretive anthropology.* New York: Basic Books.

Goldner, V. (1988). Genderation and gender: Normative and covert hierarchies. *Family Process, 27,* 17–31.

Goldner, V. (1991). Toward a critical relational theory of gender. *Psychoanalytic Dialogues, 1*(3), 249–272.

Goldner, V., Penn, P., Sheinberg, M., & Walker, G. (1990). Gender paradoxes in volatile attachments. *Family Process, 29*(4), 343–364.

Greene, B. (1994). Lesbian women of color: Triple jeopardy. In L. Comas-Díaz & B. Greene (Eds.), *Women of color: Integrating ethnic and gender identities in psychotherapy* (pp. 389–427). New York: Guilford Press.

Hardy, K. (1996, June). *The ethics of participation: Bringing culture into the room. A narrative therapy approach (Reflections).* Paper presented at the annual meeting of the American Family Therapy Academy,

Hare-Mustin, R. (1994). Discourses in the mirrored room: A postmodern analysis of therapy. *Family Process, 33*(1), 19–35.

Hoffman, L. (1992). A reflexive stance for family therapy. In S. McNamee & K. J. Gergen (Eds.), *Therapy as social construction* (pp. 2–24). Newbury Park, CA: Sage.

hooks, b. (1984). *Feminist theory: From margin to center.* Boston: South End Press.

Laird, J. (1989). Women and stories: Restorying women's self-constructions. In M. McGoldrick, C. Anderson, & F. Walsh (Eds.), *Women in families: A framework for therapy* (pp. 427–450). New York: Norton.

Laird, J. (1994). "Thick description" revisited: Family therapist as anthropologist–constructivist. In E. Sherman & W. J. Reid (Eds.), *Qualitative research in social work* (pp. 175–189). New York: Columbia University Press.

Laird, J. (1995). Family-centered practice in the postmodern era. *Families in Society: The Journal of Contemporary Human Services, 76*(3), 150–162.

Laird, J. (1996). Family-centered practice with lesbian and gay families. *Families in Society: The Journal of Contemporary Human Services, 77*(9), 559–572.

Lewin, E. (1993). *Lesbian mothers: Accounts of gender in American culture.* Ithaca, NY: Cornell University Press.

McGoldrick, M. (1993). Ethnicity, cultural diversity, and normality. In F. Walsh (Ed.), *Normal family processes* (2nd ed., pp. 331–360). New York: Guilford Press.

Minuchin, S. (1991). The seductions of constructivism. *Family Therapy Networker, 15*(5), 47–50.

Montalvo, B., & Gutierrez, M. (1983). A perspective for the use of the cultural dimension in family therapy. In C. Falicov (Ed.), *Cultural perspectives in family therapy* (pp. 15–32). Rockville, MD: Aspen Systems.

Morales, E. (1996). Gender roles among Latino gay and bisexual men: Implications for family and couple relationships. In J. Laird & R.-J. Green (Eds.), *Lesbians and gays in couples and families: A handbook for therapists* (pp. 272–297). San Francisco: Jossey-Bass.

Morrison, T. (1992). *Race-ing justice, en-gendering power: Essays on Anita Hill, Clarence Thomas, and the construction of social reality.* New York: Pantheon.

Myerhoff, B. (1978). *Number our days.* New York: Simon & Schuster.

Rosaldo, R. (1989). *Culture and truth: The remaking of social analysis.* Boston: Beacon Press.

Shapiro, V. (1995). Subjugated knowledge and the working alliance: The narratives of Russian Jewish immigrants. *In Session: Psychotherapy in Practice, 1*(4), 9–22.

Spelman, E. (1988). *Inessential woman: Problems of exclusion in feminist thought.* Boston: Beacon Press.

Weingarten, K. (1995). Radical listening: Challenging cultural beliefs for and about mothers. *Journal of Feminist Family Therapy, 7*(1–2), 7–22.

Weston, K. (1996). *Render me, gender me: Lesbians talk sex, class, color, nation, studmuffins. . . .* New York: Columbia University Press.

White, M. (1994). *The politics of therapy: Putting to rest the illusion of neutrality* [Mimeograph]. Adelaide, South Australia: Dulwich Centre.

White, M., & Epston, D. (1990). *Narrative means to therapeutic ends.* New York: Norton.

CHAPTER 3

The Cultural Meaning of Family Triangles

Celia Jaes Falicov

"Triangles" are pivotal constructs in family therapy. Symptoms of family distress have been regularly linked to the presence of family triangles (Ackerman, 1966; Bowen, 1972; Haley, 1967, 1976; Minuchin, 1974; Satir, 1967; Fogarty, 1979; Lerner, 1989; Feldman, 1994). Several hypotheses have been used to explain the link between triangles and family dysfunction. One is the idea that any persistent tension, conflict, or anxiety between two people can be diffused by involving a third party. A similar idea is that triangular processes detour a couple from underlying marital conflict; in such a case, the conflict is often manifested as disagreements over a third party, such as a child or an older parent. This latter form—the alliance between two members of different generations (usually a parent and child against the other parent), called the "cross-generational coalition"—has been focused on as being especially malevolent or "perverse."

Many therapists not only believe that unresolved marital conflicts "cause" the intrusion or the recruitment of a third party; they also believe that a triangle has the "effect" of weakening necessary boundaries around the couple, and thus further precludes the resolution of the underlying marital discord. Consequently, a therapist who detects a cross-generational coalition tends automatically to strengthen the boundary around the couple, and to extrude, block, or free up the person caught in the middle, while simultaneously addressing the underlying marital conflict.

In this chapter, I argue that the uncritical pathologizing of triangles (particularly cross-generational coalitions) and the automatic goal of restoring the boundary around the marital couple are based on *local* cultural[1] constructions that reflect and support the ideology of a particular

37

kind of family: the American middle-class nuclear family. In families from other ethnicities, races, and social classes, and from rural rather than urban settings, placing strong boundaries around a conflicted couple and blocking the participation of other family members may cause strain by undermining other central family ties (Hoffman, 1981) or other potential avenues for conflict resolution.

To demonstrate how triangles take on their meanings and implications from the social context and the cultural constructions in which they are embedded, I compare cross-generational coalitions in families with different cultural visions and different prioritizing of the marital and the intergenerational relationships. First, I focus on the principles of organization that affect the meaning of triangles in collectivistic and individualistic settings. These contexts vary in their ideological narratives regarding (1) connectedness and separateness, and (2) generation and gender hierarchies. Second, I show that these differences have implications for communication styles and for conflict resolution, and therefore that they influence how (and how much) a triangular pattern reveals or contributes to family distress.

INDIVIDUALISTIC AND COLLECTIVISTIC CONTEXTS

Connectedness and Separateness

The relatively isolated nuclear family is at the center of individualistic societies, and at the center of the nuclear family is the marital bond. Relative discontinuity with the families of origin of husband and wife is culturally supported. In fact, boundaries around the couple must be closely guarded, because the very existence of the family depends on the quality of the marital tie. Thus, intimate disclosure between parents and children is thought to interfere with this necessary separation. Healthy development is therefore equated with leaving home and individuation from one's own parents, so that attachment to a spouse becomes primary. This is also the view of contemporary psychological theory,[2] which clearly favors the values of the middle-class American family.

The nuclear family embedded in an extended, collectivistic network exists within a wholly dissimilar field of social interactions. In this type of family, the marital tie is not elevated above all others, and lifelong parent–child bonds insure continuity with the family of origin (Hsu, 1971; Bohannon, 1971). From a multiculturalist perspective, it is imperative not to pathologize this lifelong connectedness and interdependence, which are characteristic of many ethnic groups (Tamura & Lau, 1992;

McGoldrick, Giordano, & Pearce, 1996) and of many social minorities, whose life conditions often make of the parent–child dyad a more enduring or stable relationship than the marital bond. A most evocative description of familistic preferences in Asian collectivistic settings is given by Alan Roland (1988). He described a "familial self" for Japanese and Indians that contrasts with the "individual self" of mainstream Americans. The "familial self" involves connectedness, emotional involvement, empathy with and receptivity to one's family of origin, and strong identification with the honor and reputation of the extended family over attachments to outsiders.

Nevertheless, family therapists of disparate orientations, from strategic to intergenerational, subscribe to the cultural narrative that optimal development requires a stance of differentiation from one's family of origin. Some go to great lengths to create a boundary between the couple and the families of origin. Milton Erickson (reported in Haley, 1973), for example, instructed a woman to throw up on the floor (albeit apologetically) when her parents-in-law visited unannounced, so that they would become more "respectful of her needs." Poor taste aside, it is hard to picture this strategy working within a richly connected network of relatives. But it is also possible that a person raised in a collectivistic environment would be less likely to advance "her needs" for privacy as being so crucial.

Hierarchies: Generation and Gender

In individualistic cultures, the family's leadership structure depends upon reaching marital agreement and a satisfactory quid pro quo through many implicit and explicit conversations and negotiations (Lederer & Jackson, 1968; Walsh, 1989). Horizontal, egalitarian, and symmetrical interactions are stressed, even when actual practices deviate from these ideals. All siblings are supposed to be equal in duties and privileges. Husband and wife expect joint domestic authority and strive for the proverbial "united parental front" because parental consensus is thought to be crucial. Spouses expect equal affective involvement with, and equal rights over, the children. A child is expected to love and be loyal to both parents equally and not to take sides. Parental authority is precarious and withers away as children advance in age and become colleagues and "friends" of their parents (Bohannon, 1971; Williamson, 1982).

On the other hand, in collectivistic extended families, vertical relationships and age hierarchies are stressed, with leadership and authority firmly vested in the older generation throughout life (Hsu, 1971; Tamura & Lau, 1992). To take one example, Mexican Americans respect the parents' hierarchical position throughout life, and move very slowly from a position of inequality toward greater equality near the end of the parents' lives (Clark & Mendelson, 1975). Compare this parent–child attachment and lifelong respect with the prescriptions of mainstream psychological theory, which equate emotional maturity with the adult development of "personal authority" (Williamson, 1982).

Many collectivistic cultures are based on patriarchal privilege. Ideally, men have public authority over women. The husband has authority over his wife, and the brother over his sister. The father's leadership and executive role distance him from his wife and from the children. In fact, greater affective closeness between the mother and children is culturally expected (Slater, 1992; Del Castillo, 1996).

Asymmetries among the children or siblings are also common. A son or daughter may gain ascendancy, obligations, privilege, and access to adult information by being the oldest, parentified, or favorite son or daughter. This child may be in an apprenticeship role to take future care of the land, the inheritance, the aging parents, or the surviving parent. Or this child may be the culture and language "broker" or "go-between" for the immigrant parents.

Implications for Communication Styles and Conflict Resolution

The ideologies described above regarding connectedness and hierarchies have implications for communicating and for managing conflicts. True to their wish to preserve family connectedness and avoid interpersonal conflict, collectivistic cultures favor indirect, implicit, and covert communications. People publicly agree with others in order not to make them uncomfortable. This superficial harmony may be accompanied by talking behind a person's back to a third party for two reasons: first, simply to decompress and reduce tension about some difficult aspect of the relationship; or, second, actually to engage the listener as a helper in changing the other person, with whom the speaker does not wish or dare to negotiate directly.

Furthermore, in extended networks, the permeable nuclear boundaries allow inclusion of parents, siblings, and even friends. They fulfill many instrumental functions and reduce tensions by providing emotional outlets in the form of "gossip" and "secrets" about the spouse, in-laws, or other relatives. Many rapport-based alliances are acceptable, particularly when they follow gender lines. These "light" triangles, rather than being detrimental, may actually enhance the stability of the marriage (Komarovsky, 1967). Tannen (1990) aptly describes women's socialization to "trouble talk," and to sharing details of theirs and other people's lives as a basic ingredient of intimacy—a view not espoused by most men. Mexican working-class women may consider it permissible to be disrespectful about their husbands when talking to other women (Benería & Roldán, 1987).

"Gossip" serves an important function in many cultures. For example, among Filipinos, gossip is an intricate way to criticize another's values or actions, without causing open conflict (Cimmarusti, 1996). The person criticized inevitably becomes aware of the criticism when another family member reports what is being said. This information can become an impetus for the recipient to change his or her behavior. According to Cimmarusti, the widespread practice of gossip leads to considerable (often functional) triangulation among first-generation Filipino Americans:

> The process of triangulation, so often seen as dysfunctional by Western-culture clinicians, can be successfully employed by first-generation Filipino-American families and their second-generation offspring, especially in dealing with their parents. That is, concerns or complaints about a person can be relayed to that person without straining relationships or exacerbating conflict. For example, one family member tells another about concerns or complaints she/he has about a third member. When the person told has an appropriate family role, she/he can relay these concerns to the third party in a functional fashion. (1996, p. 211)

The opposite of gossip is communication characterized by assertiveness, direct expressions of opinions, demands for clarification, and a reluctance to participate in other people's problems. These forms of communication are more congruent with the ideals of differentiation prevalent in individualistic cultures and in conventional psychological theory. For example, during a consultation interview, a well-known White family therapist (implying "codependent" behavior) instructed a White middle-class daughter to interrupt her mother when the mother talked to her about her father's excessive drinking, and to tell her: "Don't involve me in your life. You have to live with your mistakes, or do something about it. Let me go on with my life. He is your guy, not mine."

There are many reasons why such an intervention may backfire with members of collectivistic cultures. First, a differentiated stance with clear and assertive communication is antithetical to the values of receptivity, concern, and obligation that are part of being socialized into an interconnected family network. A "hands-off" attitude may be perceived as selfish or disrespectful, and may puzzle a mother who may not have a cultural code about the autonomy and separation of the daughter. Indeed, the daughter may be the most valuable and powerful ally in engaging the father in a process of change. The daughter also may feel guilty for being disloyal to her mother's plight.

The value of *familismo* among Latinos stresses the duties of family members to help one another always, but particularly in the face of serious problems. Inclán and Hernandez (1993) offer a fitting cross-cultural critique of the therapy construct of "codependence" as being based on an individualistic cultural narrative.

CROSS-GENERATIONAL AND SAME-GENERATION COALITIONS IN CULTURAL CONTEXT

In the larger field of the collectivistic narrative, the constellation of ties that is likely to upset the family balance is different from that which may upset a small nuclear unit.

Cross-Generational Coalitions

In the nuclear family, unresolved marital disagreements pose a major threat to the continuity and the authority structure of the family. Ideally, children should be equally attached to the mother and to the father. Therefore, if one parent enlists the cooperation of a child in a marital struggle, or if the child becomes more sympathetic toward one parent, this imbalance may be construed as a covert attack on the excluded parent. A cross-generational coalition strikes at the nuclear family foundation of ideals of individuation, marital unity, parental consensus and equidistance from children, direct communication, and egalitarian hierarchies.

Cross-generational coalitions are common in nuclear families living in collectivistic settings, but there are several reasons why they do not have the same unbalancing effect. Lines of authority are clearly defined *a priori*, and the exclusion of the father may not be read as a threat, because marital disclosure and parental consensus are not essential for the continuity of the family. In patriarchal extended settings, the mother's asymmetrical position in the family's hierarchy may prompt her to form a coalition with one son, either to challenge the father through the son, or simply because a strong relationship with the son may increase her influence (Lamphere, 1974; Romanucci-Ross, 1973; Del Castillo, 1996) or even her closeness with the husband.

It may even be that the family members regard this "traditional" triangular arrangement as unsatisfactory, but they may argue that it provides a necessary balance. Such is the case with the *hausfrau* of the German patriarchal household (Slater, 1977), who publicly endorses the father's authority, while privately siding with the children. The children may indeed feel more distant from the father than from the mother, but they still respect his authority. In fact, children in rigid, patriarchal families often feel that actively enlisting the mother's secret cooperation is the only way to obtain privileges and handle the father's strictness.

Observing this cross-generational coalition, many American-trained therapists may interpret the problem as stemming from a gender-based marital imbalance, and may attempt to disentangle the son or daughter from the middle so as to work on the marital power asymmetry and the wife's oppression. However, cautious inquiry and curiosity about how belief systems and ideologies are tied to the triangles observed should precede any jumping to conclusions about their meaning and functionality. Therapists should consider that cross-generational coalitions may be common "cultural solutions" that have a negative or positive impact, depending on the family's personal and cultural ideology. Cross-generational coalitions may indeed in some cases perpetuate a painful marital status quo that needs to be uncovered and counteracted with cultural resistance. But in other cases these coalitions may actually help redress imbalances of power that are not easy to change for an individual alone. Or they may help initiate a process of change, because the alliance between the mother and offspring dislodges the father from his patriarchal entrenchment.

Each client's generation needs to be taken into account, as it is so intricately tied to cultural ideology. An older Latina woman, for example, may resist a therapist's suggestion of weakening the tie with a son or daughter and developing a more egalitarian relationship with her husband. She may favor holding on to a value system that, in her view, affords her respect and protection in spite of considerable self-sacrifice (Vasquez & Gil, 1996). This resistance is sometimes accompanied by a well-founded fear that a direct demand for her rights could lead to divorce—a much greater evil than an unhappy marriage for a member of the older generation, especially for a woman.

Same-Generation Coalitions

In the collectivistic setting, threats to the continuity and hegemony of the intergenerational tie need to be severely countered. Therefore, a different type of triangle from the cross-generational coalition is threatening—a triangle in which the strong dyad is not between two members of different generations in the same family, but between two people of the same generation. One is a family member, the other an outsider to the family.

A same-generation coalition may indeed have dangerous implications for a family bent on preserving the primacy of the intergenerational dyad. A parent, especially a mother, may react negatively to a son's new-found intense closeness with an "outsider," such as a girlfriend or a new wife—particularly if the latter conceives of her love relationship as exclusive rather than inclusive of the husband's family. A same-generation coalition arises also from a marriage in which the husband supports the wife in disengaging from her "overbearing" mother, or, conversely, the wife wins the husband over from his "excessive" attachment to his mother.

These are adaptive processes from the vantage point of the marital bond, but may be very disturbing to an intergenerational tie in which the expectation is for lifelong, intense parent–child involvement. For example, whereas a White American man may "separate" from his parents by expecting his new wife to succeed him in continuing the closeness, or to handle conflicts with his mother (Silverstein & Rashbaum, 1994; Walters, Carter, Papp, & Silverstein, 1988; Friedman, 1985; Meyerstein, 1996), a "typical" Mexican man may not be stirred by the same cultural strivings for autonomy. It is likely that he will maintain an emotionally devoted and loyal relationship with his mother, without resorting to his wife's help at all. Both types of family situations may create considerable stress for the young wife, but the developmental meaning attached to the cross-generational triangle is different in each case.

Triangles, then, take on their meaning and implication in part from the underlying cultural code that defines their degree of acceptability and interpersonal usefulness in the culture. The potential for problems in a triangle depends on its congruence with the total social field.

FAMILY TRIANGLES IN TRANSITION

In reality, invidualistic and collectivistic families are not as separate and distinct as the descriptions to this point may have suggested. Even the most traditional families are constantly exposed, through globalization, urbanization, and migration, to contemporary nuclear ideologies; and even the most individualistic families have contacts with the extended families they come from. In spite of these complex realities of family life, American psychotherapy is biased toward the nuclear husband–wife bond, and regards continued attachment to parents as secondary.

A therapist must accept family variation in the meanings attached to the intergenerational and the marital bond, and the complex interconnection between the various family dyads. Thus, a therapist needs to develop a curious, open-minded attitude, and should closely examine the ramifications of a particular triangle in each particular family.

Consider this example: In an Italian American family where the husband is a fisherman at sea for several months a year, the benefits of his wife's ties to her own mother outweigh the adjustment costs that arise when he returns. The mother and daughter function as allies to keep the daughter's family together; for instance, the mother helps the daughter with the children (one of whom is physically challenged), and thus relieves pressure on the daughter's husband. Among other things, the mother–daughter interactions include frequent venting of complaints about the absent spouse. The Italian collectivistic background of the family, the husband's seasonal occupation, and the child's handicap may all contribute to the continuation of the mother–daughter attachment. These circumstances do not necessarily require the strengthening of the marital (or parental) relationship by blocking the wife's mother from "interfering" in the nuclear family. Rather than helping this family acculturate to the dominant American, couple-oriented model, the issue may be how to help this family alternate the two family models at different times in ecologically useful ways, perhaps by better orchestrating the entrances and exits of the family members involved.

When it appears that there is a clash of traditional and modern values, it is more productive to label families as being in "cultural transition"—that is, in a state and process of coexistence of different cultural ideologies and codes (for further discussion, see Falicov, 1995). Immigrant families often move from settings where there is a larger emphasis on tradition, generational continuity, and authority to rapidly changing settings that emphasize the centrality of the marital bond and generational discontinuity.

When a triangle is detected in a family, these questions must be asked: Is this family's cultural ideology in transition toward the individualistic code of husband–wife centrality? Or does the nuclear unit need to be simultaneously congruent with the collectivistic values of the intergenerational bond? To help resolve these dilemmas, it is important to understand the trajectory of migration and acculturation, because this information provides valuable guidelines about past and future family shapes.

In the following example, it seemed appropriate to help resolve two cross-generational coalitions by strengthening the marital bond, given the family's new ecological setting. A migrant Mexican man sided with his mother in a triangle involving his mother and his wife. He had insisted on leaving their baby daughter in Mexico with his mother, while he and his wife moved to the United States. He reasoned, "There is no love like a mother's love." At the time, he was unaware of the implications of his thinking for the mother of his child, because his definition of "mother" was limited only to his own mother. This pattern of leaving a child in the native land with a grandmother when moving to the United States to find better opportunity is not uncommon among Latinos. Consequently, a therapist must not pathologize such a decision, but rather must recognize it (and even "normalize" it) as a legitimate attempt to resolve the practical and emotional problems of separation and still maintain some continuity with the family of origin. The biological mother, who was culturally accustomed to relying on the paternal grandmother, accepted the decision to leave her baby daughter, but only temporarily. Over time, she appealed to her husband to reincorporate the child into the nuclear family she had formed with her husband in the United States. The reunification of the family was stressful for all involved, and the child became triangulated between the mother and father and between the grandmother and mother, as a symbolic emotional link between the extended and the nuclear families.

Although adaptive to the immediate circumstances of migration, the decision to leave a child behind with a relative can eventually erode the husband–wife tie, preventing the formation of the strong marital bond that becomes so essential in the new setting. This particular family had made a commitment to remain in the United States (after two "trial" returns to Mexico). The parents agreed that developing a strong parental alliance would probably serve their family goals better than maintaining the permeable boundaries with the grandmother—a situation that implied a "ping-pong," precarious position for the young child. Note that the decision to promote marital unity in this family was not based on the usual inference that underlying marital problems were the cause of the triangular process. Instead, prioritizing the marital over the intergenerational bond was considered to be the most effective way of empowering this particular family, given its new setting. It was important to amplify the biological mother's voice and the need to reunite with her child; it was also important to strengthen the marital bond. Yet, to be culturally attuned, these issues were broached without pathologizing the father's attachment to his own mother, whom he could continue to honor and send money to.

Keeping a curious and open mind, a therapist needs to explore the meaning and function of a particular triangle within a family's cultural and ecological context, and determine which pathways to transition make more sense for each family.

CONCLUSION

Triangles cannot be isolated from their cultural context, reified, and assumed to have the same universally problematic implications in all cases. Family therapists' views about triangles mirror several core American cultural assumptions about how family ties are balanced. A richer theoretical and technical vocabulary about triangles in different ethnic backgrounds and social classes is required to explore the potentially benign or malevolent meaning of triangles.

ACKNOWLEDGMENT

Some ideas in this chapter appeared previously in Falicov and Brudner-White (1983).

NOTES

1. It is important to remember that almost all "universal" psychological theories are in fact based on less than a third of the world population—the portion that lives in the United States and in Western Europe (Triandis, 1996).

2. Clients may not agree with this view of development. Some studies have found a very large discrepancy between therapists' equation of normality with individual separation from families of origin on the one hand, and with many clients' continued wish for closeness and togetherness with their families on the other (Rogers & Leichter, 1964; Kazak et al., 1989).

REFERENCES

Ackerman, N. W. (1966). *Treating the troubled family.* New York: Basic Books.

Benería, L., & Roldán, M. (1987). *The crossroads of class and gender: Industrial homework, subcontracting and household dynamics in Mexico City.* Chicago: University of Chicago Press.

Bohannon, P. J. (1971). Dyad dominance and household maintenance. In F. K. Hsu (Ed.), *Kinship and culture.* Chicago: Aldine.

Bowen, M. (1972). Family psychotherapy. *American Journal of Orthopsychiatry, 31,* 40–60.

Cimmarusti, R. A. (1996). Exploring aspects of Filipino-American families. *Journal of Marital and Family Therapy, 22*(2), 205–217.

Clark, M., & Mendelson, M. (1975). Mexican-American aged in San Francisco. In W. C. Sze (Ed.), *Human life cycle.* New York: Jason Aronson.

Del Castillo, A. R. (1996). Gender and its discontinuities in male/female domestic relations: Mexicans in cross-cultural context. In D. Marciel & I. D. Ortiz (Eds.), *Chicanas/Chicanos at the crossroads: Social, economic and political change.* Tucson: University of Arizona Press.

Falicov, C. J. (1995). Cross-cultural marriages. In N. S. Jacobson & A. S. Gurman (Eds.), *Clinical handbook of couple therapy.* New York: Guilford Press.

Falicov, C. J., & Brudner-White, L. (1983). The shifting family triangle: Cultural and contextual relativity. In C. J. Falicov (Ed.), *Cultural perspectives in family therapy.* Rockville, MD: Aspen Systems.

Feldman, P. (1994). The use of therapeutic questions to restructure dysfunctional triangles in marital therapy: A psychodynamic family therapy approach. *Journal of Family Psychotherapy, 5*(3), 55–67.

Fogarty, T. (1979). Triangles. In *The best of the family*. Washington, DC: The Center for Family Learning.

Friedman, E. H. (1985). *Generation to generation: Family process in church and synagogue*. New York: Guilford Press.

Haley, J. (1967). Toward a theory of pathological systems. In G. Zuk & I. Boszormenyi-Nagy (Eds.), *Family therapy and disturbed families*. Palo Alto, CA: Science and Behavior Books.

Haley, J. (1973). *Uncommon therapy: The psychiatric techniques of Milton E. Erickson*. New York: Norton.

Haley, J. (1976). *Problem-solving therapy*. San Francisco: Jossey-Bass.

Hoffman, L. (1981). *Foundations of family therapy*. New York: Basic Books.

Hsu, F. K. (Ed.). (1971). *Kinship and culture*. Chicago: Aldine.

Inclán, J., & Hernandez, M. (1993). Cross-cultural perspectives and codependence: The case of poor Hispanics. *American Journal of Orthopsychiatry, 62*(2), 145–255.

Kazak, A. E., McCannell, K., Adkins, E., Himmelberg, P., & Grace, J. (1989). Perception of normality in families. *Journal of Family Psychology, 2*(3), 277–291.

Komarovsky, M. (1967). *Blue collar marriage*. New York: Random House.

Lamphere, L. (1974). Strategies, cooperation and conflict among women in domestic groups. In M. Z. Rosaldo & L. Lamphere (Eds.), *Women, culture and society*. Stanford, CA: Stanford University.

Lederer, W. J., & Jackson, D. D. (1968). *The mirages of marriage*. New York: Norton.

Lerner, H. G. (1989). *The dance of intimacy: A woman's guide to courageous acts of change in key relationships*. New York: Harper & Row.

McGoldrick, M., Giordano, J., & Pearce, J. K. (Eds.). (1996). *Ethnicity and family therapy* (2nd ed.). New York: Guilford Press.

Meyerstein, I. (1996). A systemic approach to in-law dilemmas. *Journal of Marital and Family Therapy, 22*(4), 469–480.

Minuchin, S. (1974). *Families and family therapy*. Cambridge, MA: Harvard University Press.

Rogers, C., & Leichter, H. (1964). Laterality and conflict in kinship ties. In W. Goode (Ed.), *Readings on the family and society*. Englewood Cliffs, NJ: Prentice-Hall.

Roland, A. (1988). *In search of self in India and Japan: Toward a cross-cultural psychology*. Princeton, NJ: Princeton University Press.

Romanucci-Ross, L. (1973). *Conflict, violence and morality in a Mexican village*. Chicago: University of Chicago Press.

Satir, V. (1967). *Conjoint family therapy*. Palo Alto, CA: Science and Behavior Books.

Silverstein, O., & Rashbaum, B. (1994). *The courage to raise good men*. New York: Viking.

Slater, P. E. (1977). *Footholds*. New York: Dutton.

Slater, P. E. (1992). *The glory of Hera: Greek mythology and the Greek family.* Princeton, NJ: Princeton University Press.

Tamura, T., & Lau, A. (1992). Connectedness versus separateness: Applicability of family therapy to Japanese families. *Family Process, 31*(4), 319–340.

Tannen, D. (1990). *You just don't understand: Women and men in conversation.* New York: Ballantine Books.

Triandis, H. C. (1996). The psychological measurement of cultural syndromes. *American Psychologist, 51*(4), 407–415.

Vasquez, C. I., & Gil, R. M. (1996). *The María paradox: How Latinas can merge Old World traditions with New World self-esteem.* New York: Putnam.

Walsh, F. (1989). Reconsidering gender in the marital quid pro quo. In M. McGoldrick, C. Anderson, & F. Walsh (Eds.), *Women in families: A framework for family therapy.* New York: Norton.

Walters, M., Carter, B., Papp, P., & Silverstein, O. (1988). *The invisible web: Gender patterns in family relationships.* New York: Guilford Press.

Williamson, D. S. (1982). Personal authority in family experience via termination of the intergenerational hierarchical boundary: Part III. Personal authority defined, and the power of play in the change process. *Journal of Marital and Family Therapy, 8*(3), 309–323.

CHAPTER 4

Social Class as a Relationship
IMPLICATIONS FOR FAMILY THERAPY

Jodie Kliman

Social class shapes all family experience in a class-stratified society, yet our ideas about class and its influence on family life are often vague and contradictory. Implicit rules against discussing class and prevailing, contradictory beliefs about upward mobility and classlessness strengthen its fundamental influence. Dominant discourse acknowledges class only for the very rich or poor. In this chapter, I explore the operations of class on the lives of *all* families and their implications for family therapy.

Generations of implicit and explicit communication construct each family's narratives about class. They affect how family members define themselves and are defined, what they value, and how they organize daily life and meet its challenges. Class narratives delineate what is acceptable and even conceivable for family, network, and community (Kliman & Madsen, 1998). Class disparities can divide the daily lives of different families—and their members—into separate worlds.

UNDERSTANDING SOCIAL CLASS

My understandings of class evolve with the class and cultural narratives of my own family and work life, both of which change with the economy. They change as I learn about the class experiences of clients and colleagues. As part of a society that mystifies class, I cannot claim to know what social class *is*; rather, I offer an exploration of social class. Defining social class is a complex venture. Class involves multiple relationships to economic and other social structures: race, ethnicity, religion, gender, sexuality, physical and mental well-being, and geography. It also involves relationships between classes. One's economic and social circumstances exist in relation to those of others.

Definitions of class shift with context. Sometimes class means money, which is equated with power. Sometimes other, vaguer, criteria of social status prevail. A professor is seen as being in a higher class than a contractor with equal income and an associate's degree, but not if she is Latina and the male contractor is from "an old family" of British stock. A Black executive has less effective class standing than his White subordinate when he tries to hail a cab, get service at an upscale store, or buy an elegant home. Women's and children's class status plummets after divorce. Saying that someone who acts tactlessly, talks with a full mouth, or ornately decorates home and body "has no class" suggests entirely different meanings for "class."

Economic and other social definitions are best integrated, as economic and other forms of domination operate together. Atop the class pyramid are the "ruling class" (Marx, 1932) and the "(nonruling) capitalist class." Next is the "professional/managerial class," or "professional middle class" (Ehrenreich, 1989)—salaried and self-employed professionals and managers who as a class support the class and cultural status quo. The "working class" includes salaried workers of lower social status, but not necessarily lower income, than the lower ranks of the professional managerial class. The lower ranks of the working class live in the grinding poverty of low wages and no benefits or security. Finally, the "underclass" consists of (mostly poor) people living outside the legitimate economy (Inclán & Ferran, 1990)—through public assistance, through the underground economy, or at the margins of society. These categories reflect exploitative class relationships, contradicting popular ideas about upper, upper-middle, middle, lower-middle, and lower socioeconomic status, which miss the economic relationship between one family's wealth and privilege and another's poverty and oppression.

Class weaves itself into personal, family, cultural, and community ties to local, national, and global economies. The extent to which the work done in one's network is alienated or self-determining builds narratives of self, family, and community, which shape psychological experience. One's place in the economy is defined by occupation and earned income, but also by *un*earned income, assets, and inheritances; credit lines; consumption of goods and services; employment security; debt load; and the number of paychecks one is from homelessness. These factors are shaped by race, ethnicity, gender, and physical and mental well-being, all of which govern economic access. These phenomena change as the economy generates fewer goods and more services, information, money management, and so on. Class is partly determined by how autonomous, supervised, respected, or demeaned one's work is. Telemarketers must request bathroom breaks; therapists must justify treatment plans to insurance gatekeepers; and chief executive officers (CEOs) give themselves huge bonuses while laying off workers. Each relationship to work affects what workers and their children expect of life.

Class position governs access to resources: health care, political influence, housing, interest rates, and information. Does one use emergency rooms or top specialists? Do kin, day care centers, or nannies help with babies? Do teens pay into or draw on family coffers? Do parents remove lead paint from a new home or pray that toddlers won't eat lead paint chips? A professor gets a life-saving second opinion. The professor's nanny, an "illegal," uninsured alien, is turned away at the emergency room. A professional faxes 50 resumés in the time it takes an unskilled worker to apply in person for three advertised jobs.

Economic resources buffer families against misfortune; being without such resources multiplies misfortune's impact, as does discrimination based on race, gender, sexual orientation, or health. An elderly widow is secure in a paid-off house. A family sharing a grandmother's subsidized housing becomes homeless on her death. A ruling-class "cut-up" expelled from prep school enters another. Similar behavior in a barrio yields a criminal record. Divorce forces a realtor and her children to cut back painfully, but leaves their day-care provider's family without heat. The White children of a surgeon and a depressed homemaker addicted to alcohol and pills get by with help from family, friends, and paid caretakers. The Black children of a single mother who lost her job to alcohol and crack abuse wind up in foster care, separated from mother, each other, friends, school, and kin. Poverty and oppression increase vulnerability to the chronic stressors implicated in asthma, hypertension, and substance abuse (Hines, 1988). Poor mothers with inadequate prenatal care and diet are exposed to environmental hazards implicated in infants' prematurity, low birth weight, birth defects, retardation, lead- or drug-related impulsivity and learning disabilities, and drug addiction or HIV at birth. Addressing children's medical needs creates additional stress when doctors, pharmacies, and groceries are three bus rides away.

Class involves a multilevel relationship between families and community, regional, national, and global economies. Boyd-Franklin (1993) reported that poor Black communities may define working-poor families as middle-class by virtue of their being employed and "their values, aspirations, and expectations for their children" (pp. 363–364). A janitor and a hotel worker, in her parents' two-family house on a gentrifying city block, are "poor neighbors." In a ghetto or poor farm community with dying schools, they are among its few two-income households. The children of suburban teachers lead protected lives. The children of teachers at the edge of a ghetto wracked by violence, arson, and drugs, and those of nearby drug dealers, are both (if not equally) at risk of undereducation, seduction by drugs or gangs, assault, and murder. Class position and its meanings extend beyond one's household or family, encompassing one's neighborhood, network, and local, national, and global economies.

In a racist and classist society, neither class nor race can be understood by itself (Kliman, 1994). Together, they shape family dilemmas and possibilities. Dominant U.S. discourse equates "White" with "middle-class" and "Black" with "poor." Immigrants and people of color, assumed to be poor and uneducated, are patronized by bureaucrats and health care workers, suspected by police and store clerks, and lied to by realtors and employers. Racism intensifies class oppression, disproportionately undereducating and impoverishing people of color. Whereas 12% of whites live under the poverty line, 15% of Asians and Pacific Islanders, 31% of Latinos and Native Americans, and 33% of African Americans do so (Sklar, 1995, pp. 11–12). Over 15% of adult and 46.8% of teenaged Black men are *officially* unemployed; still more are underemployed. Those with jobs earn nearly a third less than Whites (Rubin, 1994). Black males ages 15–19 are shot to death at ten times the rate of their white agemates; black males ages 20–24 are fatally shot eleven times more often than white males of the same age (U.S. Bureau of the Census, 1994, p. 101). In 1989, 25% of all Black men in their 20s were incarcerated, on probation, or parole, as were 10% of Latino and 6.25% of White men (Sklar, 1995, pp. 120–121). These figures reflect the synergy of racism and class.

Patriarchy and class structure combine to shape family life profoundly. Although most women outside the ruling class and underclass now do paid work, the "glass ceiling" is intact. Of course, poor women have always done productive labor (as peasants, slaves, or factory workers); only in recent decades have they been expected to join privileged women in focusing on domestic life. Women, to whom child care, elder care, or health emergencies fall, earn less than men and account for most involuntarily part-time and temporary workers. Working-class women are at greatest risk of harassment on entering "male" work domains. (The military, long a path to upward mobility, is a bastion of sexual harassment.) Educational expectations are lower for women, although they are equalizing somewhat in the professional middle class. Racism adds a twist: Women of color are more often accepted by schools and employers than men of color, perhaps because they are less threatening to whites (Boyd-Franklin, 1993; Hines, 1988). Women who are single, divorced, widowed, or in lesbian partnerships have lower income and status than do wives. Single-mother households' poverty (U.S. Bureau of the Census,

1994, p. 470) and stress levels are blamed on mothers—not on capitalism, patriarchy, or fathers who don't support their children.

When dominant U.S. discourse admits to class, it explains it most often in two contradictory and decontextualized ways. One explains class standing by individual attributes. Thus, laziness, ignorance, dependence, and moral turpitude (e.g., drugs or unwed motherhood) cause poverty, whereas initiative, talent, competitiveness, and greed generate wealth. The second suggests a natural order of things in which "we will always have the poor among us," or "we can't all be rich." Both explanations obscure one class's power over others. Class stratification is a predictable structural outcome of a free-market, capitalist society. Those with privilege and power live well at the expense of those without either (Sklar, 1995). It is also a predictable outcome of the institutionalized racism, patriarchy, and colonialism on which U.S. society was founded. Institutionalized inequity at many levels determines who has privilege and power. Exploring the role of class in family life is an exercise in social justice.

TWO FAMILIES

In order to explore how class circumstances and narratives shape family life and therapy, let us consider two families separated by class. Both are Anglo American, Protestant, Northeastern families with troubled adolescents; one is professional managerial class, the other working-class.

Jim and Abby Sinclair—a certified public accountant and a grade school teacher, respectively, living in a wealthy suburb—and their children are in turmoil over 17-year-old Eddie's learning problems, truancy, and poor college prospects (see Figure 4.1 for the Sinclair family's genogram). Eddie is smoking marijuana daily, experimenting with stronger drugs, and drinking on weekends. Jim and Abby are pouring their college and retirement savings into tutors and therapy. Eddie mostly acts angrily alienated, but occasionally seems very sad and lonely for family contact. Family conflict is escalating; Jim has started working more nights and weekends; Abby is snapping more, and is evading relatives' and friends' questions about Eddie's college plans. Jeannie, 24, an assistant broker with an MBA degree, is angry at Eddie for his expensive problems and at her parents for paying for them. Family therapy has begun at Eddie's guidance counselor's urging.

The Sinclairs' jobs and address (the only class-related data most therapists ask for) do not reveal their complex class background. Abby's forebears were lawyers, but Jim's were hardscrabble farmers. Although Jim and Abby share distress over Eddie's substance abuse, his failing grades

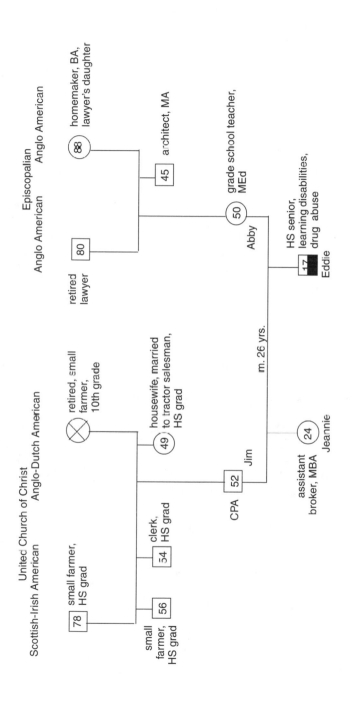

FIGURE 4.1. The Sinclair family. The half-shaded square represents substance abuse.

evoke different responses that reflect their disparate class histories. They argue and blame each other about how to help or discipline him. Their therapist can productively ask what family members know and think about each other's expectations for work, school, and family responsibilities, and how these expectations relate to class. She can explore how different family stories about education and work color their responses to the current crisis. Implicit, class-based expectations of life influence Jim's shame over his son's failures, Abby's worry about being a bad mother, Eddie's angry protests that he might just do his schoolwork if everyone left him alone, and Jeannie's resentment toward Eddie.

Class is least visible in therapy when everyone is, or is assumed to be, professional managerial class. Most therapists may assume that Eddie can count on family for shelter, low-level job contacts, and therapy instead of jail, and that his teachers expect him to graduate. A therapist who is attuned to class, however, can productively note how valuable such class buffers are, and can help deconstruct class-based constraints (e.g., opinions about not going to college). Through her own class lens, the Sinclairs' therapist may read Jim's shame over Eddie's academic future as a "middle-class success hangup," or may recognize it as a painful reliving of how he felt about his own parents' "lack of class" compared to his in-laws. She may view Abby's apparent capitulation to Eddie's behavior as a vicarious rebellion against her father's severe standards, or may note that Abby has no class context for understanding her son's behaviors. She may see Eddie as a spoiled and entitled brat or as a self-destructing victim of rigid class expectations. She may see Jeannie as entitled or responsible.

Dick and Suzanne Scott, high school graduates in a depressed former mill town, are parents to Alice, 23, Thomas, 21, and Matthew, 17 (see Figure 4.2 for the Scotts' genogram). Alice lives with her husband; both sons live at home. Like Eddie Sinclair, Matt has learning disabilities, does poorly in school, drinks heavily, and is often truant. An arrest for drunk driving led to court-ordered therapy. An expectant father, he has lost peers to drugs and prison. He sees little future for himself, and no point to finishing school or finding work. With help from their older son's paycheck, the Scotts support Matt and their aging parents on insecure, underpaid jobs with no benefits. They worry over Matt's ending up unemployed or in prison. Angry at Matt's girlfriend for getting pregnant, they fret over their unborn grandchild's care, as neither family has savings, health insurance, or extra room.

Dick and Suzanne both grew up working-class in a factory town that assured semiskilled workers employment, benefits, and upward mobility. Their older son, Tom, has a trade and steady work. Alice went to community college, got an office job, and married a middle-class co-

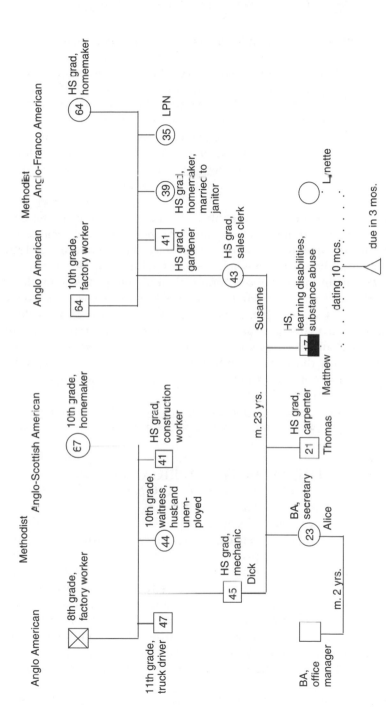

FIGURE 4.2. The Scott family. The half-shaded square represents substance abuse.

worker. Matt, however, knows only economic decline: unemployment, falling real wages, drugs, violence, and urban decay. Without the buffering resources Eddie Sinclair's class enjoys, Matt's prospects are grim.

Their therapist can ask how coming of age in such different economic times affects the parents' and Matt's expectations for themselves and each other. He can inquire how the family used family and community resources to help Tom and Alice graduate, and to keep Matt in school as long as they have in a crowded school without adequate special education resources. Detailed questioning helps identify family competencies and resources. It also explicitly introduces class into therapy. An originally working-class therapist can describe discovering resources (e.g., summer camp jobs) rarely accessible to the poor. A therapist who once thought everyone got math tutors, summer jobs in relatives' offices, and college tuition can note how much class privilege helped him succeed and can wonder aloud where he would be today without it. Deconstructing class relations in therapy both counters their shaming effects and helps therapists guard against falling back on privilege themselves (e.g., as experts or success stories). It facilitates *collaborative* cross-class explorations into resources that poor and working-class families rarely hear about. The therapist can share his expertise about resources as the family shares theirs about how those resources would work in their class context. He must be open about his own class experiences and avoid imposing his own meanings on school difficulties, drinking problems, and teen parenthood. He must find out what they mean to all family members, and must neither pathologize nor romanticize the unfamiliar.

THERAPEUTIC IMPLICATIONS
OF CLASS RELATIONS

Talking about class counters the obscuring and perpetuation of class privilege in therapy. Collaboratively exploring class relationships, in and out of therapy, challenges the psychic constraints of class. The myth that almost everyone has "enough," or could if they tried, skews families' self-perceptions in all classes. So does discreetly restricting social welfare to the privileged (tax loopholes, corporate subsidies, and universities' affirmative action for big donors' heirs). Economic shifts affect families of all classes—the newly rich, as well as those who can no longer reach goals formed in easier times. Externalizing the impact of economic forces counters self-blame and mutual recriminations about "not being good enough."

As the economy "trickles up," disparities in income grow. In 1992,

CEOs made a staggering 157 times as much as their employees (Sklar, 1995, p. 8). Less privileged families' shame often abates on learning about how wealth (net worth)—that is, the sum of all one's assets (including bank accounts, real estate, insurance, inheritances, investments, etc.) minus all one's debts (Sklar, 1995)—is distributed. In 1989, the richest 1% held 39% of the nation's wealth; the richest fifth owned 85%; and the poorest fifth, whose debts exceeded their assets, held 1.4% of the nation's wealth (Sklar, 1995, p. 6).

Poverty for many is the price of riches for a few. In 1993, 15% of all U.S. residents, 23% of all children, 12% of the elderly, and 24% of the severely disabled lived below the $14,654 official poverty line for a family of four (Sklar, 1995, pp. 11–12). The officials who set the 1960s poverty line viewed it as realistic on an emergency basis only and suggested 150% of that figure, or $21,981, as more livable (Sklar, 1995, p. 12). Yet 25% of all U.S. residents, 34% of children, 27% of the elderly, and 42% of the severely disabled live below that line, which does not reflect soaring housing or medical costs (Sklar, 1995), or the fact that 25% of all U.S. families have no health insurance (Knox, 1996).

Such figures help families reconsider their circumstances without economics lectures. Being asked why their lives contrast so sharply with TV families' can be eye-opening and energizing for them. Families denied mortgages or college loans can locate their difficulties in the economic system, not in their own failings. Detailed questions about the ingenuity and work needed to keep a poor household going can focus on strengths and survival skills, not self-blame or helplessness. Professional managerial class and working-class families benefit from detailed questions about their generation's downward mobility. Overlooking class promotes selective attention to individual failures and selective inattention to constraining social factors. Understanding their class situation helps families to develop self-respecting family narratives and to draw on family and community resources in new ways. This counters the experiences of isolation, shame, and immobilization that blame-the-victim ideologies engender.

As workers are forced from steady jobs with benefits into underpaid and insecure work, their families should note that corporate profit and control *require* unemployment (Sklar, 1995). Families losing welfare benefits should know that the upper classes still get their tax breaks and corporate welfare is thriving. Many dual-career couples feel like failures for not owning houses their fathers' sole income could once buy. Their thinking may shift on learning that from 1946 to 1956, the GI Bill made a whole generation upwardly mobile by giving veterans no down payment, low-interest home loans, college tuition and stipends, and free family medical care (Brady, 1996).

CLASS INFLUENCES ON THERAPY

Therapists need navigational tools to discern the complex ways class enters the therapeutic enterprise. Unless wealth, poverty, or class mobility (or therapists' high fees and fancy offices) make it salient, families and therapists rarely think about class. Making class an open subject can alleviate shame, guilt, resentment, and stigma. It can also open therapists' own class-bound moral judgments to question. The beliefs, practices, and incomes to which therapists are trained support existing class structure. Less fortunate clients understandably see even therapists who object to that structure accordingly. Most therapists do lead professional managerial class lives, even though they have begun to lose autonomy and income to budget cuts and managed care. Therapists are becoming "proletarianized" but hold onto middle-class beliefs. Therapy is an encounter between several sets of values, assumptions, and behaviors—those that evolve in the therapist's and family members' class contexts. As therapists, our views of family members' class positions and histories often differ from theirs. Our own struggles, shame, confusion, domination, silence, guilt, entitlement, or loss in our family class histories affect our responses to clients. Our values and struggles may resonate, clash with, illuminate, or obscure our clients' struggles.

Family therapy often involves cross-class relationships that do not acknowledge class disparities. Relying on a "don't ask, don't tell" policy allows therapy to glide over questions of class and to overlook fundamental differences. When multiclass families neglect their own complex class histories, contradictory class expectations continue to evoke painful and confusing responses. When a bus driver's daughter and a doctor's son describe, unquestioned, growing up "middle-class" (despite endless conflicts over table manners and money) or see the therapist, a longshoreman's son, as "middle-class," these complexities are lost. Clients may wrongly assume that their therapists hold values "appropriate" to their class. Therapists may be perplexed to feel eager to please or defensive about their training, office decor, or fees with wealthy families. What's more, not all therapists identify themselves as "middle-class." Those who grew up working-class can feel uncomfortable dissonance when their privilege is assumed. It can be freeing to acknowledge their actual experience. Wealthy therapists can feel uncomfortable in a different way when seen as middle-class. Privileged therapists must carefully avoid using class privilege, for instance, to define clients' class experience or judge their class-influenced behaviors. Respectful, collaborative conversations about therapists' own class dilemmas in therapy can limit such harm.

I invite the reader to pursue further inquiry into the importance of social class in the lives of all families and in family therapy practice—inquiry based on understanding social class as a *relationship* that permeates all social and psychological experience. It is a relationship that requires special care, with constant attention to social justice and self-awareness.

ACKNOWLEDGMENTS

I thank Bill Madsen, my coauthor on a related chapter, and Laura Chasin, Jeffrey Kerr, and Michele Bograd for sharing ideas about class in our own lives. I also thank David Trimble and Kathy Weingarten for their invaluable conceptual and stylistic help.

REFERENCES

Boyd-Franklin, N. (1993). Class, race, and poverty. In F. Walsh (Ed.), *Normal family processes* (2nd ed.). New York: Guilford Press.

Brady, J. (1996, August 4). In appreciation, the GI Bill. *Parade Magazine,* pp. 4–5.

Ehrenreich, B. (1989). *Fear of falling: The inner life of the middle class.* New York: HarperCollins.

Hines, P. (1988). The family life cycle of poor black families. In B. Carter & M. McGoldrick (Eds.), *The changing family life cycle: A framework for family therapy* (2nd ed.). New York: Gardner Press.

Inclán, J., & Ferran, E. (1990). Poverty, politics, and family therapy: A role for systems theory. In M. Mirkin (Ed.), *The social and political contexts of family therapy.* Boston: Allyn & Bacon.

Kliman, J. (1994). The interweaving of gender, class, and race in family therapy. In M. Mirkin (Ed.), *Women in context: Toward a feminist reconstruction of psychotherapy.* New York: Guilford Press.

Kliman, J., & Madsen, W. (1998). Social class and family life cycles. In B. Carter & M. McGoldrick (Eds.), *The expanded life cycle: Individual, family, community.* Needham Heights, MA: Allyn & Bacon.

Knox, R. (1996, October 23). 1 in 4 find health care unavailable. *The New York Times,* pp. A1, A20.

Marx, K. (1932). *Capital, the Communist manifesto, and other writings.* New York: Modern Library.

Rubin, L. (1994). *Families on the fault line: America's working class speaks about the family, the economy, race, and ethnicity.* New York: HarperPerennial.

Sklar, H. (1995). *Chaos or community: Seeking solutions, not scapegoats for bad economics.* Boston: South End Press.

U.S. Bureau of the Census. (1994). *Statistical abstract of the United States.* Washington, DC: U.S. Government Printing Office.

CHAPTER 5

Beliefs, Spirituality, and Transcendence
KEYS TO FAMILY RESILIENCE

Froma Walsh

Family life and the world around us have changed so dramatically in recent years that while we yearn for strong and enduring relationships, we are unsure how to shape and sustain them to weather the storms of life. With widespread concern about family breakdown, we need more than ever to understand and encourage the processes that foster relational hardiness. A resilience-based approach aims to identify and fortify key interactional processes that enable families to withstand and rebound from crisis and challenge (Walsh, 1996, 1998). This chapter examines the importance of family beliefs and spirituality, in particular, as vital sources of resilience in rising above adversity.

THE NEED FOR A RESILIENCE-BASED APPROACH TO FAMILY THERAPY

Throughout the field of mental health, medical and psychoanalytic treatment paradigms influenced an early emphasis on therapist strategies to alter family pathology. The skewed focus on family deficits led clinicians to be blind to family strengths and pessimistic about change. Extending more recent strength-based, collaborative approaches to family therapy, a resilience-based approach shifts the perspective from viewing families as damaged to seeing them as challenged (Walsh, 1993).

All families face life crises, such as an untimely death, traumatic separation, or job loss; some suffer persistent stresses, such as poverty, serious illness, or abuse. Yet, while some families are shattered, others rise to the challenge and emerge strengthened through the process. When families seek help in distress, a resilience-oriented approach encourages their own healing resources and, by empowering families, reduces vulnerability to future stress. In strengthening resilience, we inspire people to believe in their own possibilities for regeneration. Therapy best fosters hardiness by activating the relationship network as a healing environment for the relief of suffering and renewal of life passage. Our faith in all families' desire to be healthy and their potential for healing and growth can encourage their best efforts.

The notion of healing is important in resilience. Distinct from curing, recovery, or problem resolution, healing is a natural process in response to injury or trauma. Sometimes people heal physically but don't heal emotionally, mentally, or spiritually; or badly strained relationships remain unhealed. Some may recover from an illness but may not regain the spirit to live and love fully. Yet people are able to heal psychosocially even when we do not heal physically, or when a traumatic event can't be reversed. Similarly, resilience can be forged even when problems can't be solved and when they recur. The literal meaning of "healing" is becoming whole. When necessary, it also involves compensating for losses.

Treatment and healing are quite different concepts. Treatment is externally administered; healing comes from within the person, the family, and the community. In the West, scientific medicine has been focused on identifying external agents of disease and developing technological weapons against them. Metaphors of war are prominent—fighting, combating, destroying disease. An unbalanced view focused on pathology rather than health contributes to pessimism (Weil, 1994). In contrast, Eastern medicine is based on a set of beliefs about healing processes and the importance of mind–body interactions. The healing system is a functional system, not an assemblage of structures. Chinese medicine, for instance, explores ways of increasing internal resilience as resistance to disease, so that whatever harmful influences we are exposed to, we can remain healthy. In the psychosocial realm, this belief in strengthening protective processes assumes that individuals and their families—like the body—have a natural ability to heal and grow stronger. Mechanisms of diagnosis, self-repair, and regeneration exist in all of us, that can be activated as the need arises. Knowledge about the healing system enables clinicians to enhance these processes as the best hope for recovery when crises occur. Resilience-based therapy mobilizes individual, family, and community resources to promote healing and growth.

THE POWER OF BELIEFS:
KEYS TO RESILIENCE

In the empirically based Western world, it is often said that seeing is believing. A Kiowa Indian would say, "It may have to be believed to be seen." Beliefs are at the very heart of who we are and how we make sense of our experience. They are the lenses through which we view the world, influencing what we see and do not see as we move through life, as well as what we make of our perceptions (Wright, Watson, & Bell, 1996). Families develop shared beliefs, influenced by their position and experiences in the world over time (Falicov, 1995; McGoldrick, Giordano, & Pearce, 1996). They are reaffirmed and altered over the family life cycle and across the generations. Belief systems provide a meaningful orientation for understanding one another and approaching new challenges. They are expressed in the narratives we construct together, guiding our expectations and actions. Belief systems enable us to organize our experience in the social world so as to make sense of crisis experiences (Reiss, 1981).

We can help individuals and their families alter constraining beliefs, which perpetuate problems and limit options, and encourage facilitative beliefs, which increase options for problem resolution, healing, and growth (Wright et al., 1996). In the rest of this chapter, we will consider how core beliefs and spiritual connections act as vital sources of resilience which can enable us, and our clients, to transcend adversity.

Strength in Connection and Collaboration

"We shall overcome!" The clarion cry of the 1960s civil rights movement has inspired hope and creative action in many parts of the world, based on the belief that strength is best forged through collaboration. This simple yet profound phrase expresses the core conviction in relational resilience: In joining together, we strengthen our ability to overcome adversity (Walsh, 1998). Highly resilient people reach out for help when needed, turning to kin, social, and religious support systems, as well as helping professionals. Mutual support promotes relational resilience, strengthening families and their communities.

Resilience has generally been viewed in terms of individual traits (Garmezy, 1991; Rutter, 1987; Wolin & Wolin, 1993), reflecting the American ethos of the rugged individual, as if resilient persons grew themselves up. Either they had the "right stuff" all along (a biological hardiness) or acquired it on their own. This individualistic philosophy has left us out of touch with the communal and the interpersonal, contributing to the fragmentation and alienation so many individuals and families experience today (Bellah et al., 1985).

Cross-cultural research finds that resilience is relationally based (Walsh, 1996). Family and community connections are lifelines in times of distress (Walsh & McGoldrick, 1991). For children and adults overcoming a range of adverse conditions, the most significant positive influence is a supportive relationship with others who believe in them, with whom they can identify, who advocate on their behalf, and from whom they can gather strength to overcome crisis and hardship (Werner & Smith, 1992).

Yet our culture's dim view of families as hopelessly dysfunctional has led many to dismiss family potential as a source of resilience, and to encourage family blame and disconnection (Rubin, 1997), not seeing possibilities for repair. Moreover, cultural myths of "the normal family," based in socially constructed views of normality, have constrained our vision of relational possibilities and stigmatized those not conforming to the standard (Walsh, 1993). Contrary to the belief that one family model is essential, research reveals that healthy functioning can be found in a wide diversity of family arrangements. What matter more than a family's form are its relational resources. A resilience-based approach is founded on the conviction that there are many pathways in relational resilience and that all families have the potential for repair.

Making Meaning of Adversity

The meaning of adversity, like all experience, is socially constructed and filtered through family transactions. In the pain and uncertainty wrought by a life crisis, core beliefs come to the fore. We attempt to make sense of how things have happened through causal and explanatory attributions (Kluckhohn, 1960). Western culture emphasizes personal responsibility in the belief that we are masters of our own fate. In American culture, we hold a curious split image of individual and family responsibility, crediting individuals for their success but blaming their families—especially mothers—for their problems (McGoldrick, Anderson, & Walsh, 1989).

In many traditional cultures, people turn to highly respected folk healers for explanations and solutions to their problems. Blame is often externalized, as in beliefs that others who are envious, spiteful, or wish harm may have brought about their plight. In many cultures and religions, adversity is ascribed to one's fate. Hindus may believe that misfortune is the result of bad karma, perhaps owing to circumstances in a previous life. For Muslims, what happens in life is determined by Allah's will. A Moroccan friend once told me of his father's drinking and abandonment and his mother's retreat into her own sorrows. When, from an American perspective, I was puzzled that he harbored no anger or blame toward them for his life difficulties, he replied: "But you don't understand. I'll always be grateful to my parents; they gave me life."

How a problem is viewed and how distress is handled vary with different family and cultural norms. Poverty, for instance, does not carry the same stigma in many places as it does in the United States. In Morocco, even the poorest families may not hesitate to disclose their economic situation. Poverty indicates only a lack of material goods at the present time; it is a regrettable hardship, but does not reflect negatively on personal character or family failing. It simply means that Allah has not smiled on this family, for reasons beyond normal comprehension. There is even wide variation among people within cultures. For example, epidemiologists find in the United States that at any given time, 75% of all people are "symptomatic," experiencing physical or psychological distress. Yet most define it as part of normal life and don't seek treatment (Kleinman, 1988). Therapists need to be mindful of such different outlooks in working with families. An integral part of the therapy process involves understanding the meanings each family makes of its challenges, particularly in the light of its own cultural belief system.

Sense of Coherence

How families make sense of a crisis situation and how they endow it with meaning are most crucial for resilience. A "sense of coherence" is a global orientation to life expressing the extent to which the world is seen as comprehensible, manageable, and meaningful (Antonovsky, 1979). It involves confidence in the ability to clarify the nature of problems so that they seem ordered, predictable, and explicable. A sense of coherence includes existential feelings of social integration and purpose in life, as opposed to a sense of alienation, drifting, or stuckness. To meet diverse challenges, this orientation emphasizes flexibility in selecting varied coping strategies to fit the situation and the culture. In today's rapidly changing world, we must search for meaning and pattern in the midst of uncertainty and in relation to shifting social contexts (Gergen, 1989). We can help families seek coherence in the diversity and discontinuities of their experience for healthy adaptations to unexpected events in their lives.

Adversity: Learning and Integration

Resilience is promoted when hardship or tragedy can be viewed as instructive and can serve as an impetus for growth. Research on high-functioning middle-class families found that they viewed causes and effects as multiple, recursive influences and avoided blaming or typecasting others as villains or victims (Beavers & Hampson, 1990). In contrast, more dysfunctional families tend to believe one explanation almost fanatically, are locked into an idea of single causation, and are prone to blaming and scapegoating. Believing it's a waste of time to be bound up in regret, blaming, or nursing old wounds, resilient people attempt to draw lessons from their experience that can be valuable in guiding their future course. They are accountable for their own part when something has gone wrong and learn not to repeat mistakes. In accepting what has happened, they try to incorporate what was learned into attempts to live better lives and to help that others can gain from their experience.

Being able to give meaning to a precarious situation makes it easier to bear. It can also be transforming, bringing clarity and new vision to life. Perceptions of a current crisis intersect with legacies of previous experience in the multigenerational system to forge its meaning and our response (Carter & McGoldrick, 1989). A faulty notion of resilience sees it as invulnerability, simply breezing through a crisis and bouncing back unscathed, at the cost of cutting off from painful experience. Rather, true resilience is forged by coming to terms with experience and integrating that understanding with new challenges.

Several other key beliefs are particularly important in facilitating resilience and thus enabling individuals and families to surmount crisis and hardship. These include hope; initiative and invention; perseverance; encouragement and confidence; and humor.

Hope: A Positive Outlook

Considerable research evidence documents the strong effects of an optimistic orientation in coping with stress and crisis. Epidemiologists find that "positive illusions" sustain hope in the face of crisis, such as a life-threatening illness, and enable people to make their best efforts to overcome the odds (Taylor, 1989). "What oxygen is to the lungs, such is hope to the meaning of life" (Brunner). Many families in chronically impoverished minority ghettos have lost hope, suffering a deprivation of both "bread" and "spirit" in the persistent racism, lack of opportunity, and failure of our social safety net (Aponte, 1994). This poverty of despair robs them of meaning and purpose. When the present is bleak, we must sustain hope in order to envision and strive for a better future (West, 1996). Hope for a better life for their children keeps many parents from being defeated by their immediate plight. In the words of Martin Luther King, "We must accept finite disappointment, but we must never lose infinite hope."

Initiative and Invention

Resilient persons are masters of the art of the possible (Higgins, 1994). They take stock of their situation—their challenges, constraints, values, and resources—and then focus their energies on making the most of their options. Families today must be inventive. They need to envision new models of human interaction to fit new life challenges, drawing on a wide variety of inspirations—from past experience, family myths, and creative fantasy to new and untried solutions. Bateson (1994) stresses the need for an attitude of improvisation: "Adaptation comes out of encounters with novelty that may seem chaotic. In trying to adapt, we may need to deviate from cherished values, behaving in ways we have barely glimpsed, seizing on fragmentary clues" (p. 8).

Immigration, for instance, poses challenges of loss and adaptation, with resilience forged through interweaving the old with the new for continuity and change. Immigrant women have often found food and cooking to be both a source of livelihood in the new land and a cherished link to the families and homelands they had to abandon. My grandmother Frimid came to Milwaukee with my grandfather from Budapest to escape pogroms against the Jews in the late 1880s. She started a catering business and raised geese in their backyard for *pâté de foie gras,* while her husband, who had been a Talmudic scholar, became a shopkeeper. Drawing on her memories of life in Hungary, she found that one year the strange weather reminded her of a certain season in Hungary when the onion crops had failed. She withdrew all their savings from the bank and invested them in onions. Sure enough, the crop failed; having cornered the market, she had a windfall. Her picture on the front page of the newspaper was captioned, "Frimid: The Onion Queen." Family stories of her bold resilience have been a source of inspiration for me, as her namesake.

Resilience also requires us to accept the limits of our power—appraising what we can and cannot change, and then putting their best efforts into what is possible. A philosophical acceptance is most common among older people (an important source of wisdom with aging) and for those from Eastern traditions, who are less focused on mastery and more attuned to living in harmony with nature. Control issues are more difficult for those with a Western mindset, who can be uncomfortable in situations beyond their control. High-functioning families understand that success in human endeavors depends in part on variables beyond their control, but that with goals and purpose they can make a difference in their own lives and those of others. When problems are overwhelming, family members can be encouraged to carve out a part they can influence. Although Western medicine provides an illusion of control over life and death, we live in an uncertain universe and cannot master death. Family members can actively choose ways to participate in caregiving and/or prepare for death, make the most of the time they have together, and find solace in loving one another well in the face of loss. We need to rethink our view of mastery to include *how* we rise to a challenge and seize opportunities before us.

Perseverance

Martin Seligman's (1990) concept of "learned optimism" has important implications for cultivating resilience. In his earlier work on "learned helplessness," he found that people can be conditioned to give up trying to solve problems. When people learn that their actions are futile, and nothing they do matters, they no longer initiate action and become passive, dependent, and hopeless. This despair can deplete the immune system, impair health, and hasten death. Interestingly, Seligman's own family experience contributed to his insights. When he was 13, his father was paralyzed by a series of strokes that left him, in Seligman's words, "physically and emotionally helpless." That foundation-shaking event first depressed the boy, but later lit a fire in him to do something to understand and overcome the problem. (Of note, Seligman shifted his research attention to learned optimism when he reached the same age as his father at his paralysis.) The question that intrigued him was this: Why did it spark that fire and not render him helpless, too? He became convinced that the difference had to do with initiative, dogged determination, and persistence: "I don't lie down and die." Seligman has contended that if helplessness can be learned, then it can be unlearned by successful experiences in which people come to believe that their efforts and actions can work. Yet a cheerful mindset is not sufficient: conditions must offer predictable and achievable rewards to reinforce efforts.

Encouragement and Confidence

The extraordinary courage shown by an ordinary person can also have profound meaning and inspiration for others, encouraging them to be bold. Rosa Parks is well remembered as the African American woman whose refusal to sit in the back of the bus became an inspiring moment at the start of the civil rights movement. Her courage shaped the spirit of the times. One's courage and the encouragement of family and community are intertwined. Supportive relationships build and sustain courage, especially in the face of overwhelming odds. In the gay community, the formation of strong social networks, "families of choice," have been vital in sustaining the lives of persons dealing with AIDS (Weston, 1994).

The courage shown in the everyday life of ordinary families often goes unnoticed. In the Cabrini Green projects in Chicago, parents and their children must pass gangs and drug-infested courtyards daily to go to work and school; returning at night is always hazardous (Kotlowitz, 1991). In a study of the family impact of neighborhood violence, interviews with mothers revealed enormous courage in steeling themselves each morning to get their families through another harrowing day, and trying, against all odds, to get ahead so that their children could have a better life. In families that coped the best, mothers had learned to carefully discriminate street sounds and activities for immediate risk of danger, and tried to keep a watchful eye on their children as best they could.

We need models and mentors for resilience. We often fail to see the many examples of heroism in our own families and communities. In her winning school essay on the theme "A Woman I Most Admire" (*New York Times*, OpEd page, March 25, 1995), Amelia Chamberlain wrote about watching her mother leave for work:

> I watch from the house in wonder. How does she do it? How does she always remember to give me $3.60 for lunch money? How does she always remember to tell me that she loves me? How does she work all night and do errands all day? How does she raise me and my sisters on her own? She never gives up or says, "I can't go today." She never, ever, doesn't get up, no matter how little sleep she's gotten.

Her story speaks to the courage in ordinary families, making the best of their difficult lives. Such stories of resilience inspire us to see unrecognized strengths and new possibilities for family healing in every family we work with.

Resilience is bolstered by unwavering confidence through an ordeal: "We always believed we would find a way." This conviction and relentless search for solutions fuels optimism and makes family members active participants in the problem-solving process. Confidence that each member will do his or her best builds relational resilience as it reinforces individual efforts. One woman credited her endurance in battling cancer to her partner's unfailing encouragement and their rock-solid relationship. This enabled her not to give up on life, but to engage in every means to recover as fully as possible.

Humor

Studies of resilience all find humor to be invaluable in coping with adversity. Norman Cousins (1989) posited that if negative emotions can produce harmful chemical changes in the body, then positive emotions should have a therapeutic value. He attributed much of his own recovery from a life-threatening disease to his self-generated program, which included "laughter therapy" (watching old Marx Brothers films). Recent medical studies show that humor can bolster both our spirits and our immune systems, encouraging healing and recovery from serious illness. For families as well, humor helps members cope with grim situations, reduce tensions, and accept limitations. Realization that we have the capacity to envision perfection yet are destined to flounder can encourage a sense of humility and an appreciation of paradox in our shared humanity (Beavers & Hampson, 1900).

TRANSCENDENT BELIEFS

"Transcendent beliefs" provide meaning and purpose beyond ourselves, our families, and immediate crisis situations. The need to find greater meaning in our lives is most commonly met through religious or spiritual faith and cultural heritage. It may also be found in ideological views, such as deep philosophical or political convictions. Transcendent beliefs offer clarity about our life and solace in distress; they render unexpected events less threatening and enable acceptance of situations that cannot be changed.

Values and Purpose

Understanding the connectedness of life as a whole and in relation to others involves a sense of higher values, purpose, and meaning. To accept the inevitable risks and losses in loving, families need a system of values and beliefs that transcends the limits of their experience and knowledge. This enables family members to view their particular reality, which may be painful, uncertain, and frightening, from a perspective that makes some sense of events and allows for hope. Without such perspectives, we are vulnerable to despair. Transcendent values, whether conventional or unique, enable us to define our lives in meaningful ways.

In today's cynical social and political climate, holding ideals may seem naive, and yet they are needed more than ever in facing unprecedented challenges. In times of tragedy—whether the ravages of war, a terrorist bombing, or the brutal assault of a child—it requires strong idealistic beliefs to hold fast to fundamental values and strive toward a better day. As family therapist Richard Chasin has observed: "Randomness takes the blue ribbon; evil takes the red; but from time to time justice shows." Martin Luther King has been a guiding spirit to so many oppressed people through his abiding faith that social justice will prevail. Not a passive faith to wait for God's deliverance, his was a rallying call for personal responsibility and collective action to bring about change.

Religion and Spirituality

Many of our most fundamental beliefs are founded in religion and spirituality. Religions are organized belief systems that include shared and institutionalized moral values, beliefs about God, and involvement in a religious community. Religions provide consistent patterns for living out these values and beliefs, as well as congregational support in times of crisis. Rituals and ceremonies offer participants a sense of collective self and, as Taggart (1994, p. 32) so aptly puts it, "a place in the chaos of reality." Congruence between religious beliefs and practices yields a general sense of well-being and wholeness, while incongruence commonly induces shame or guilt.

Spirituality, an overarching construct, involves personal beliefs, such as those about an ultimate human condition or set of values toward which we strive, a supreme being, or a unity with nature and the universe. It may also include numinous experiences, which are holy or mystical and difficult to define or explain in ordinary language and imagery (Griffith & Griffith, in press). Spirituality involves an active investment in an internal set of values—a sense of meaning, inner wholeness, and connection with others. It invites an expansion of awareness, with personal responsibility for and beyond oneself.

Spirituality can be experienced either within or outside formal religious structures. Some adhere to religious rituals without finding spiritual meaning in them. Others disavow formal religion, yet find spirituality in daily life. Universally, the spirit is seen as the vital essence, the source of life and power. In many languages the word for "spirit" and "breath" are the same: Greek, *pneuma*; Hebrew, *reach*; Latin, *spiritus*; Sanskrit, *spiritus* (Weil, 1994).

Faith can be even more important in sustaining resilience than frequent participation in religious services or activities. Medical studies suggest that faith, prayer, and spiritual rituals can actually strengthen health and healing by triggering emotions that influence the immune and cardiovascular systems (Dossey, 1993). One study of elderly patients who had undergone open-heart surgery found that those who were able to find some hope, solace, and comfort in their religious outlook had a survival rate three times higher than those who did not. What matters most is drawing on the power of faith to give meaning to a precarious situation.

Spiritual beliefs and practices vary greatly. Spiritual connectedness and renewal can be found in communion with nature, or in attractions to gurus or places with high spiritual energy—healing waters, pilgrimages, sacred shrines and temples. Beauty in many forms can have spiritual, healing effects. We can be inspired by great art, music, literature, and drama that express our common humanity. Music and dance are powerful ecstatic experiences in many cultures, from African American gospel singing to the purification and trance ceremonies of Gnawa nomadic tribes of the Sahara. The Choctaw Indians say, "To watch us dance is to hear our hearts speak."

For me, music has a deep spiritual resonance, as well as a bond with my mother and my daughter. When I was growing up, my mother was a concert pianist, a music teacher, and the organist at our Jewish temple. With an ecumenical command of great hymns and religious music, she was also in demand to play for holidays, weddings, and funerals for congregations of various Christian denominations in our town. Music, whether secular or religious, was a transcendent experience for her—as it became for me, accompanying her on those many occasions, and inheriting her love of all forms of music, from classical to jazz. Although I don't quite share my teenage daughter's taste in alternative rock, I love her deep passion for music.

Our imaginations, too, can transport us beyond a crisis situation, enable us to envision new possibilities, or illuminate pathways out of our dilemmas. Creativity is often born of adversity. In his essays, the writer Ralph Ellison described his own creative process as trying, to the best of his ability, to transform the brutalizing elements of the African American experience into art. His goal was not to escape but to work through the experience, to transcend it, just as through music, the blues transcend the painful conditions with which they deal.

The linchpins of resilience, faith, and intimacy are linked (Higgins, 1994). Faith is inherently relational, from early childhood when fundamental meanings about life are shaped within caregiving relationships. Caring about others both sustains us and infuses our lives with meaning. Viktor Frankl (1946/1984), in recounting life in Nazi prison camps, came to the realization that salvation is found through love. As he visualized the image of his wife, a thought crossed his mind: "I didn't even know if she were still alive. I knew only one thing—which I have learned well by now: Love goes very far beyond the physical person of the beloved. It finds its deepest meaning in his spiritual being, his inner self."

Spirituality and religion have long been neglected in the mental health field; they have been considered not the province of secular therapies, but matters best left to the clergy or faith healers to address. With growing awareness of their profound influence, we are only beginning to appreciate the spiritual dimension in the healing art of psychotherapy (Walsh, in press). Seligman (1990) believes that the soul—that which is deep within the personality—is the key to change, and that therapeutic efforts need to take the human spirit into account. Yet we must be cautious not to attribute failure to a lack of spiritual purity. New Age practitioners, emphasizing mental influences over physical states, have at times blamed patients' failure to recover on deficient mental attitudes or health practices.

We also need to understand the many aspects of spirituality in the lives of our clients, and the different kinds of impacts it can have. For example, spiritual distress can impede coping and an ability to invest life with meaning. Religious beliefs may become harmful, as when a mother's self-destructive drinking is based on her conviction that her child's death is God's punishment for not having baptized the child. A crisis may precipitate a questioning of long-held spiritual beliefs, or may launch a quest for a new form or dimension that can be sustaining.

Wright and her colleagues (1996) urge systems-oriented professionals to conceptualize persons as biopsychosocial–spiritual beings and to acknowledge that suffering, and often the injustice or senselessness of it, are spiritual issues. It is crucial to explore spiritual questions and beliefs that have profound implications for recovery, healing, and resilience. We also need to examine our own spiritual beliefs and the values embued in our professional ethos. The tradition of separating psychotherapy from religion has marginalized spiritual beliefs to such an extent that clients may only reveal the parts of their experience that fit normative expectations, editing out the spiritual dimension of their experience. Therefore, we therapists should not simply wait for our clients to bring up spiritual matters, presuming them to be unimportant if not voiced. Instead, we need to show comfort and respectful curiosity in exploring the spiritual domain experienced by each client. We can explore spiritual experiences that have been positive, such as moments of inner peace and communion, which can be drawn upon and expanded as sources of resilience.

TRANSFORMATION: GROWTH THROUGH CRISES AND TRANSITIONS

Though painful and disruptive, life crises and developmental transitions can serve as an impetus for reflection on assumptions, which can catalyze growth and transformation. Resilient individuals and families commonly emerge from shattering crises with a heightened moral compass and sense of purpose in their lives (Coles, 1997). A recent news story told of the life of James Coleman, Jr., the first African American appointed to the New Jersey Supreme Court. The son of a sharecropper, he transcended early life trauma: "I've learned to use the hardships that I endured from that time to become my source of strength. I converted the energy and, to some extent, the anger that the system caused within me, into motivation." In turn, he dedicated his life to a career in justice based on fairness and what he believed to be right.

The Chinese pictogram for "crisis" is composed of the symbols for danger and opportunity. As crises are assimilated, they may come to be seen as a gift that opens a new phase of life or new potentials. Most resilient families believe that their trials have made them more than what they would have been otherwise. One couple I know nearly lost a son in a freak accident that shook the very foundation of the family. For all the family members, this crisis became an epiphany, crystallizing a stronger sense of life purpose, dedication to practicing their values more fully, and a deeper appreciation of loved ones.

Much can be learned from studies of resilience to inform programs and interventions to strengthen families in crisis or persistent distress. First, we can encourage a family belief system and a community environment that increase both hope and possibilities. Small successes lead to larger ones in a ripple effect, building confidence to master more difficult challenges. Second, we can build collaboration and mutual support, so that shared efforts make a difference. Third, we can offer the perspective that adversity and failure are to be expected as normal parts of life and can be valuable ways of learning. Most importantly, we can convey our conviction in each family's worth and potential for resilience.

Resilience involves a process of coming to terms with all that has happened, reaching new emotional and relational equilibrium with changed circumstances, and becoming more resourceful in facing whatever lies ahead. Our beliefs are our most powerful options of all. When we can construct some valuable meaning out of our life struggles, they can become transforming experiences, enabling us to approach the best in our humanity.

REFERENCES

Antonovsky, A. (1979). *Health, stress, and coping: New perspectives on mental and physical well being.* San Francisco: Jossey-Bass.

Aponte, H. (1994). *Bread and spirit: Therapy with the poor.* New York: Norton.

Bateson, M. C. (1994). *Peripheral visions.* New York: HarperCollins.

Beavers, W. R., & Hapson, R. B. (1990). *Successful families.* New York: Norton.

Bellah, R., et al. (1985). *Habits of the heart: Individualism and commitment in American life.* Berkeley: University of California Press.

Carter, B., & McGoldrick, M. (Eds.). (1989). *The changing family life cycle: A framework for family therapy* (2nd ed.). Boston: Allyn & Bacon.

Coles, R. (1997). *Moral intelligence of children.* New York: Random House.

Cousins, N. (1989). *Head first: The biology of hope.* New York: Dutton.

Dossey, D. (1993). *Healing words: The power of prayer and the practice of medicine.* New York: Harper.

Falicov, C. J. (1995). Training to think culturally: A multidimensional comparative framework. *Family Process, 34,* 373–388.

Frankl, V. (1984). *Man's search for meaning.* New York: Simon & Schuster. (Original work published 1946)

Garmezy, N. (1991). Resiliency and vulnerability to adverse developmental outcomes associated with poverty. *American Behavioral Scientist, 34,* 416–430.

Gergen, K. (1989). Understanding, narration, and the cultural construction of the self. In J. Stigler, R. Shweder, & G. Herdt (Eds.), *Cultural psychology.* Cambridge, England: Cambridge University Press.

Griffith, J., & Griffith, M. (in press). *Conversations with God.* New York: Basic Books.

Higgins, G. O. (1994). *Resilient adults: Overcoming a cruel past.* San Francisco: Jossey-Bass.

Kleinman, A. (1988). *The illness narratives: Suffering, healing, and the human condition.* New York: Basic Books.

Kluckhohn, F. R. (1960). Variations in the basic values of family systems. In N. W. Bell & E. F. Vogel (Eds.), *The family.* Glencoe, IL: Free Press.

Kotlowitz, A. (1991). *There are no children here.* New York: Doubleday.

McGoldrick, M., Anderson, C., & Walsh, F. (Eds.). (1996). *Women in families: A framework for family therapy.* New York: Norton.

McGoldrick, M., Giordano, J., & Pearce, J. K. (Eds.). (1996). *Ethnicity and family therapy* (2nd ed.). New York: Guilford Press.

Reiss, D. (1981). *The family's construction of reality.* Cambridge, MA: Harvard University Press.

Rubin, L. (1996). *The transcendent child: Tales of triumph over the past.* New York: Basic Books.

Rutter, M. (1987). Psychosocial resilience and protective mechanisms. *American Journal of Orthopsychiatry, 57,* 316–331.

Seligman, M. (1990). *Learned optimism.* New York: Random House.

Taggart, S. R. (1994). *Living as if: Belief systems in mental health practice.* San Francisco: Jossey-Bass.

Taylor, S. E. (1989). *Positive illusions: Creative self-deception and the healthy mind.* New York: Basic Books.

Walsh, F. (1993). Conceptualization of normal family processes. In F. Walsh (Ed.), *Normal family processes* (2nd ed.). New York: Guilford Press.

Walsh, F. (1996). Strengthening family resilience: Crisis and challenge. *Family Process, 35,* 261–281.

Walsh, F. (1998). *Strengthening family resilience.* New York: Guilford Press.

Walsh, F. (Ed.). (in press). *Spiritual resources in family therapy.* New York: Guilford Press.

Walsh, F., & McGoldrick, M. (Eds.). (1991). *Living beyond loss: Death in the family.* New York: Norton.

Weil, A. (1994). *Spontaneous healing.* New York: Knopf.

Werner, E. E., & Smith, R. S. (1992). *Overcoming the odds: High risk children from birth to adulthood.* Ithaca, NY: Cornell University Press.

West, C. (1996, March). Plenary Address, *Family Therapy Networker* Symposium, Washington, DC.

Weston, K. (1991). *Families we choose: Lesbians, gays, and kinship.* New York: Columbia University Press.

Wolin, S., & Wolin, S. (1993). *The resilient self: How survivors of troubled families rise above adversity.* New York: Villard.

Wright, L., Bell, J. M., & Watson, W. L. (1996). *Beliefs: The heart of healing in families and illness.* New York: Basic Books.

CHAPTER 6

Climbing Up the Rough Side of the Mountain
HOPE, CULTURE, AND THERAPY

Paulette Moore Hines

Recently, a young therapist questioned what (if any) impact she could possibly have on a family that had been in and out of the mental health system for 16 years. The therapist's frustration was heightened by the fact that the mother seemed less disturbed than she, the therapist, about her family's situation. She wondered, "Is this mission impossible, or have I invested in a career that makes very little real difference in the lives of the people I am trying to help? Am I helping my clients to be hopeful, or are they teaching me to be hopeless?"

These same questions prompted me to review my own experiences, both personal and professional. How could I face an aunt and cousin who had lost four children in a house fire? How could I embrace my own pain without showing despair when meeting with a mother who was desperately trying to achieve some distance from the grief she had felt since the traumatic death of one of her twin sons? She and her husband had watched and participated in an unsuccessful rescue effort as their son cried for help. What could I possibly say to a young, homeless, penniless, formerly middle-class couple with three growing children whose prayers for employment had gone unanswered for 3 years?

Given the social, economic, and political times in which we all live, we are repeatedly confronted with the issues of hope and hopelessness. As therapists, we sometimes feel overwhelmed about the possibility that the problems our clients present can be resolved. Some clients, in contrast, appear undaunted, and we are either amazed at their survival skills or convinced they are in denial. In other instances, our clients convey a sense of hopelessness, a dis-ease of spirit, while we as therapists see possibilities and struggle to help them free themselves from self-imposed limitations. A third scenario is one in which both our clients and we ourselves have a sense of helplessness.

In spite of the pull to supply our clients with the answers to their problems, neither our personal life experiences nor our professional training prepare us to envision the answers to some dilemmas. We must also confront the reality that there are some problems for which there may be no concrete resolution, either immediately or in the long term.

In the face of such circumstances, the ability genuinely to convey and encourage hope is key to retaining clients in the helping process and to motivating them to make behavioral and cognitive shifts that can enhance their functioning and improve the quality of their lives. This chapter advances the premise that every culture has means of preserving the lessons that have been learned over generations about psychological survival. Using African American culture as an example, the chapter explores the therapeutic benefit of turning to the wisdom of those who have survived circumstances that confound us and our clients (Walsh, 1993), and it offers guidelines regarding how clients can make this connection. The chapter further highlights the importance of our being able to tap readily into our own reservoirs of hope, when it is lacking in our work.

BELIEFS AND WELL-BEING

There is a clear relationship between our beliefs and our emotional and behavioral functioning. Our belief systems help us to organize the barrage of stimuli, ideas, emotions, and memories that constitute our lives into systems of coherent meaning (Taggart, 1994), without which we would experience unbearable chaos. Beliefs, embraced intuitively and uttered spontaneously in crisis situations, may either function as anchors during a storm or promulgate a sense of hopelessness and helplessness. Fortunately, our beliefs are acquired through life experiences, worship, and cultural exposure, and they can be altered likewise (Cooper-Lewter & Mitchell, 1986).

Counseling and therapy are not modalities that African Americans turn to easily, even in the 1990s. When they do, few walk in and request treatment for their hopelessness. Nevertheless, there is no greater challenge to be faced by African Americans and those who work with them than maintaining and encouraging, in more culturally laden terms, the will to "keep on keeping on."

CONNECTING WITH THE PAST
IN ORDER TO MOVE FORWARD

Struggle characterizes our African American history, our present, and no doubt our future. We African Americans have historically recognized that maintaining the will to live life to its fullest and never to give up is vital to our physical, psychological, and spiritual survival, and we have proved to be masters at doing so under unimaginable circumstances. Without hope, for example, the slaves who traveled the Underground Railroad would have succumbed, and the outward symbols of racist segregation would not have been outlawed. As we approach the 21st century, the issue of "keeping our hope alive" remains central to the well-being and literal survival of African Americans, collectively and individually. For the majority of African Americans, freedom from the shackles of slavery has not given rise to freedom from pain and suffering.

Cornel West (1993) defines nihilism as the loss of hope and the absence of meaning. He suggests that since the civil rights movement, we African Americans have weakened our defenses against the pernicious external forces that have historically threatened our existence and well-being. African and African American tradition involves looking to our elders for the wisdom they have drawn from the research laboratories of life. Yet connecting with the oppression that our forebears experienced both during slavery and since the Civil War era brings forth conflicting wishes for many African Americans: the wish to forget the inhumanity our ancestors suffered, and the wish to remember their amazing capacity not only to survive but to transcend difficult circumstances and overwhelming odds.

Countless recognized and unsung heroes and "sheroes" were first physically enslaved and then segregated; the real victory was their audacity to believe in themselves, and to maintain a sense of dignity, self-respect, concern for one another, and hope for a better day. These were individuals who kept their spirits intact even though they were repeatedly treated as if they were dangerous or invisible. They had to struggle mightily to overcome the oppressive forces of poverty and racism. In short, the African American story is one of unrelenting struggle—people searching for a way to be happy, to function at their fullest potential, and to be free from the scars of the past and the restrictions of the present.

In recent years, African Americans have directed increasing attention to the link between escalating social, economic, health, educational, and political problems on the one hand, and the erosion of connections with cultural values and traditions on the other. Lerone Bennett (1991) wrote: "If we intend to redeem the pledges of the Black spirit, we must enter into an active dialogue with the voices of our tradition, which speak to us with recurring themes (p. 122). Bennett suggests that the voices of the past speak to us of hope, endurance, and daring. They tell us that life does not exist in the absence of connection with family and our culture. They tell us, among other things, that nothing can destroy us here if we keep the faith of our fathers and mothers and put our hands to the plow and hold on. They suggest that we can call upon the story of the collective and draw strength and direction.

African American culture is distinctive in the reliance placed upon oral communication to transmit beliefs, values, and traditions across generations. Proverbs and jokes; religious sermons and prayers; poetry; spirituals, the blues, and other forms of music; and stories and fables drawn from African and African American tradition are rich in wisdom about endurance and remaining spiritually healthy in spite of unrelenting oppression. Although the premises contained within these vehicles may be linked to either secular or religious sources, they are highly intertwined because of the strong spiritual orientation that permeates African American culture.

Folk Wisdom

Among African Americans, interest in preserving the wisdom of our elders is apparent in the recent popularity of what are known as "books of affirmation" (Copage, 1993; Riley, 1993; Vanzant, 1993). These old sayings, quotations, and proverbs drawn from African and African American experience are intended to pass on a message of empowerment. These messages have particular significance and familiarity for many African Americans. Some, such as "Stand tall, walk proud," and "Even an ant may harm an elephant," prompt us to let go of hopelessness and believe in ourselves. Others, such as "What storm is there which has no end?" and "Tough times don't last, tough people do," remind us that troubled times will come to an end. Yet others prompt us to take risks and to persevere: "If there is no struggle, there is no progress," "When life knocks you down, land on your back because if you can look up, you can get up," "You don't get there because, you get there in spite of."

Some messages connect us with our past and future, eliciting images of what has been and images of what can be. They draw attention to our interrelationship with one another through our commonalities in experience. These include the following: "Our successes have been earned while we stood on the shoulders of those who came before us," "Reach back, give back," "Look from whence you have come," "You are the son/daughter of kings and queens," "Black men, you were once great; you shall be great again. Lose not courage, lose not faith, go forward." The power of these messages to energize, mobilize, and promote transformation defies simple explanation, but it is readily apparent both inside and outside the therapeutic process.

Religious Beliefs

Two-thirds of the people of the United States consider religion to be important or very important in their lives, and may prefer approaches that are sympathetic to spiritual values (Bergin, 1991). Even when they are not involved with organized religion, African Americans tend to hold biblically based beliefs, although they may not identify them as such.

Cooper-Lewter and Mitchell (1986) have outlined a number of basic beliefs in African American culture that are tied to Judeo-Christian tradition and traditional African religion. These include reminders of the power of God (e.g., "God is in charge," "God knows everything and is an all-wise protector") and of the security that a just God offers (e.g., "God is just, fair, and impartial," "God is gracious, offering unqualified love," "God regards all persons as equal"). Common religious beliefs also pertain to the sanctity of life and basic human rights (e.g., "Each person is absolutely unique and worthy of respect," "We should not surrender to the pressures of life and give up in despair," "We are all related as a family"). The values that are encouraged by these beliefs parallel those espoused in the therapeutic community: forgiveness of self and others, self-discipline, respect for self and others, courage, honesty, ability to let go of negative emotional states, a sense of security, and so forth (Bergin, 1991).

When we African Americans call upon religion-based sources of inspiration, we call not only upon the wisdom of our ancestors, but upon the power of a higher spirit as well. Family stories, fables, poetic prayers, daily meditations, sermons, and such hymns and spirituals as "Let Me Tell You How to Move a Mountain" and "God Can Do Anything but Fail" contain messages that instruct us about the outlook that we "should" bring to situations in order to triumph over obstacles. They proclaim that no matter how bad things seem, everyone's life is worth living. They encourage perseverance, forgiveness, not wasting one's time on vengeance, celebrating one's uniqueness, self-understanding, and unconditional love. They encourage us never to feel alone. They remind us that God is mighty; when God is our partner, nothing can penetrate our armor. Although we may not know what the future holds, we need not be fearful, for we know that God holds the future. They remind us that no one can take our joy in life from us unless we give it away. We *can* move from obstacles to possibilities. We *can* run a race with one foot, if necessary.

This narrative has not only particular appeal, given the adversarial context in which African Americans have lived in this country, but far reaching implications. In a presentation focused on the power of religious beliefs, the Reverend Buster Soaries (1994) shared the following perspective:

> How do we account for the continued existence of African Americans in this country? For even when we were confronted by a political prison, when Blacks were in slavery and were not allowed to even meet together on a plantation, when we had to walk from Mississippi to Chicago—running from the Ku Klux Klan, when we were not even allowed to learn how to read, when we fought in armies and then were not allowed to be buried in [military] cemeteries, when we had to walk past beautiful schools to go to one room school houses, when we had to live in houses with outdoor bathrooms and people down the street had beautiful mansions, we could still say we have access to the God of heaven and earth. And that sense of resolution gives us on the one hand the capacity to accept our conditions without giving in to our conditions—to live in the world but not be of the world, to hear the cries of the world but not succumb to the pressures of the world.

An example of how individuals can be empowered by what many would regard as a relatively simple intervention lies in a story told by Evander Holyfield about his success, as a 25-1 underdog, in winning the world heavyweight boxing championship against Mike Tyson (Randolph, 1997). Evander's frustration and depression were building as each of his sparring partners beat him during his training. His wife suggested that his frustration and depression were the results of looking at God as though God was not big enough to handle the problem. This comment was based on the belief that there is danger in fighting life's battles alone, but that protection can be gained by putting on the armor of God, who is all-powerful, and allowing God to be our partner. She insisted that Evander get his songbook and sing with her the song "Be Magnified." After this, Evander constantly sang, "Heal my heart and show yourself strong. And in my eyes and with my song, oh Lord, be magnified." He noted that the music worked its magic; his speed, rhythm, and timing returned. Prior to going into the ring, he had his whole entourage sing the song. And, in one of the biggest upsets in boxing history, Evander won the fight.

During my childhood, my grandfather, a Baptist minister, often reiterated a concise translation of the scriptural text "I can do all things through Christ who strengtheneth me" (Philippians 4:13) in the form of "Never say you can't." This seemingly simple message embodied a number of powerful messages: It was not an invitation to be either grandiose or passive. It was a message that we should recognize and use the unique gifts that God bestows on each of us, to be mindful of the power of God, to pray before making major decisions and acting on them. When we lack any clue about how to proceed, or when we run out of steam and can't try or can't conceive what to do next, we should lean on God's strength and power. The implication of adopting such a perspective is clear: Solutions are more likely to be found when we continue to search for them.

CLINICAL IMPLICATIONS

The training of most therapists does not allow us to deal with spiritual beliefs and values easily. The anxiety associated with addressing religious beliefs is even greater, for a variety of reasons. First, unfamiliarity breeds discomfort. Second, many therapists interpret the mandate to be "neutral" in transactions with clients to mean that they should avoid discussions about religious beliefs and values. They fear they will abuse their power and influence clients toward adoption of their own viewpoints. Finally, some therapists perceive religion with suspicion because of the ways that it has been misused to support oppression.

Clearly, as therapists, we cannot possibly be familiar with the great variety of religious orientations that exist. However, to ignore the interrelationship among mind, body, and spirit is to draw an artificial distinction that distances us from our clients. Although we can abuse our influence, the truth is that we convey messages through our omissions as well as through what we say and do in therapy. We are probably less likely to influence changes in our clients' basic beliefs about religion than changes in other domains. We have also matured in our recognition that there can be healthy as well as unhealthy religiosity. A person's religious beliefs and values may heighten stress, provide a haven from stress, foster higher moral behavior, and/or promote personal growth and fulfillment (Spilka & Werme, 1971).

Regardless of whether their belief systems are grounded in secular and/or religious folkways, clients will vary in their abilities to readily articulate their basic beliefs. They will also vary in the extent to which they make a conscious, active effort to access cognitions (and associated images and positive "self-talk") that can empower them when they face obstacles. Therapists can help clients to pinpoint the basic beliefs that shape their world views, feelings, and behaviors by tracking their statements and asking direct questions. It is important to explore the personal meanings that underlie abstract belief statements (e.g., "I believe God will make a way") even when the language that clients use is familiar. Another key therapeutic task is to help clients understand that many of their beliefs are not based on absolutes, and that they may wish to evaluate whether it is worth holding on to a given belief that may have been helpful in the past but that may no longer serve them well. To the extent that it is relevant to clients' well-being and therapeutic goals, therapists should facilitate awareness of inconsistencies in beliefs, as well as inconsistencies between beliefs and behavior. The aim in these instances should be to help clients evaluate their positions, expand their perspectives, and draw their *own* conclusions about which beliefs they cling to and which they let go. In some instances, the challenge may be to help clients develop strategies to gain inspiration. In other instances, clients simply need to be encouraged to make more consistent use of the resources they have already identified and previously used, particularly in tough moments.

Working across Differences

Although many clients prefer therapists who share their beliefs and value systems, their bottom-line concern is having a place where they can talk openly without being judged. A therapist may have beliefs that are dissonant with a client's, or the therapist and client may share common beliefs that may originate from disparate sources. In either instance, it is possible for the therapist to be empathic and creative, and to generate hope in therapeutic transactions. When therapists greet clients with genuine respect and an openness to learning about them, there is a greater potential for discovering commonalities of experience that transcend differences. It may be difficult for therapists in the mainstream to experience the same emotion and empowerment as some clients do when listening to a spiritual; however, the same therapists can fully appreciate the notion that music, words, and images drawn from past experience can connect people, at a multisensory level, with memories of inner peace, hope, and memories of a point in time when they felt happy, protected, and/or safe. (For example, walking into the hallway of one's elementary grade school, or listening to "Twinkle, Twinkle, Little Star" or some other song cherished during childhood, may evoke memories and feelings of a point in time when one felt happy, protected, and safe.)

A Clinical Case Example

A brief but poignant illustration of the application of cultural narratives in the context of family therapy is provided by the case of a client, Jerry, who complained of anger and depression after he was demoted on his job. Jerry's preoccupation with what he viewed as an act of racial discrimination had resulted in considerable tension between him and his wife, as well as with his two adolescent children. He noted that he was never naive enough to assume that racism had disappeared, but his recent experience had left him feeling deflated and hopeless that a Black man could ever be treated justly in this society. The quality of his work had declined, and he had begun to have panic attacks when driving to work each day. He felt ashamed that his finances would not allow him to quit his position; he saw himself as the only one of four children that his aging parents could depend on for support, and he was also anxious about putting away funds for his own children's college education. Jerry had begun to withdraw from everyone and had lost interest in all of his former social and cultural activities. His wife complained that he would not share his thoughts and feelings with her; Jerry would either intellectualize or shut down completely. Jerry viewed himself as a hypocrite, in that he found himself unable to model positive functioning for his children.

During the review of Jerry's family history, he revealed that his grandfather was the person who had most significantly influenced him as a child. He recalled that one legacy passed on by his grandfather was the belief that "When one door closes, another opens." Within the context of a family session, we explored Jerry's thoughts about what his grandfather meant when he cited this adage, as well as what Jerry had wanted to convey to his children on the numerous occasions he had repeated these same words. Jerry had shared very little with his children or wife about his childhood. He assumed that they had little interest, but, even more, he feared he would be overwhelmed by feelings of loss. His two teenagers, who had done little to hide their reluctance to come to therapy, showed a high level of interest in the discussion about their ancestors. Jerry shared a story with his family about a time when his grandparents' farm was sold at auction following several years of bad crops, and the family was forced to give up most of their acquisitions. Although the bank had granted additional time to many of his grandfather's European American neighbors, his request for an extension had been denied. For the first time in many years, Jerry allowed himself to cry as he recalled the awe and pride he felt when his grandparents looked the auctioneer and bankers in the eye and walked proudly away from the home they had built themselves. His grandfather subsequently established a small trucking business, which sustained his family through the Great Depression.

When asked what advice his grandfather would give Jerry about coping with his current situation, Jerry imagined he would say, "Another person can't ride your back, unless it's bent." Discussion followed regarding how Jerry might better align his behavior with his grandfather's prescription. Among other things, Jerry reported that he had begun to read from a book of meditations daily. Aware that Jerry gave himself little or no room to lean on others for support even in the most difficult times, the therapist asked Jerry about the nature of his prayers. Not surprisingly, Jerry had operated from a firm conviction that it was OK for him to pray for others, but that it was selfish to ask for anything for himself. The therapist prescribed that Jerry begin a ritual of praying at least once a day, during which he was to ask God for help with his own problems.

During the next family session, Jerry reported that he was feeling considerably better. All of the family members were asked to discuss a challenging situation they had encountered, to which they could respond by putting the grandfather's prescription into practice. Jerry and his wife discussed with the therapist their varied notions about how they would recognize God's answer to Jerry's prayers. Jerry's unresolved guilt about being away at college during the last month of his grandfather's life surfaced. His inability to forgive himself had kept him distant from his grandmother during the remaining years of her life. Jerry was becoming very conscious of the double standards that he applied in his life, in that he was far more forgiving and less demanding of others than he was of himself.

The subsequent therapy continued to build on the value Jerry placed on his grandfather's wisdom and his heightened awareness that he had departed from it. He was asked (1) to project himself forward in time and to visualize himself having resolved his current dilemma by calling upon the cumulative wisdom of his ancestors; and (2) to define the minimal changes necessary to shift from his present (undesirable) situation to the scenario he had visualized in which his dilemma had been resolved. With the therapist's coaching, Jerry developed a plan to visualize his grandfather coaching him prior to each planned encounter with his boss. His boss seemed to be unbalanced by Jerry's calmness and self-confidence, and began to back down from the power and control games he had initiated shortly after Jerry's demotion. Jerry ultimately decided to take an early retirement package, and his wife agreed to support him in starting his own consulting firm.

Our Clients, Ourselves:
Avoiding the Hopelessness Trap

As therapists, we are generally attuned to the instances in which clients assume postures of hopelessness, imposing limitations on the possibilities that they can conceive because they are unable to see beyond their beliefs, imagination, and self-definition. We are less apt to recognize the negative influence that our own hopelessness has on our clients.

Most frequently, we have a sense of when our clients are likely to terminate therapy prematurely. This circumstance may result from our failure to communicate a sense of hope regarding the challenges the clients face. As one client put it, "Why invest my time and money in coming to see someone who only leaves me feeling worse?" African American clients, in particular, are very attuned to " negative vibes" (i.e., nonverbal messages), as well as to what is or is not communicated verbally. A message of hope that is insincere is unlikely to lead to positive results.

Within the context of a typical therapy hour, we have little time to process the barrage of information that is shared by clients. There is even less time available to ponder the roots and remedies to our own hopelessness, when it surfaces. We share with our clients a need to recognize when we are so afflicted; we also share a need to slow our pace occasionally, in order to embark on a process that can help us find a means of spiritual renewal.

Ongoing self-reflection and discussion with colleagues can provide insights that will assist us as therapists in mapping a path from hopelessness to hopefulness. Questions that may prove valuable in this process follow:

1. When you feel hopeless, what are the cues?
2. Is there a particular person, image, thought, or story that you are likely to access to help you cope?
3. What are the cultural messages and family stories that have been passed down to you about coping with adversity?
4. How are your personal beliefs and patterns of coping similar to or different from those held by most people in your family or culture?
5. Are there situations that are rightfully construed as hopeless?
6. Are there occasions when one may actually do harm by encouraging hope?
7. To what extent is your way of responding to adversity different from those of the clients who have proven most challenging to work with in therapy?
8. What strategies do you use to diminish burnout and revitalize yourself?
9. How do you distinguish between when it is reasonable to continue therapy with a client and when you feel you should transfer the case, because you feel hopeless about the potential for a positive outcome?

CONCLUDING STATEMENT

On occasion, our clients' well-being is tied to figuring out concrete solutions to their problems; more frequently, though, the key issue is a loss of the will that is necessary to pursue possibilities, however limited these may be. The basic premise of this chapter is that we therapists and our clients alike can find guidance regarding how to protect and heal our bruised spirits by turning to the wisdom of our ancestors, through whatever means this knowledge has been preserved. Within African American culture, proverbs, folk sayings, poetry, movies, literature, art, music, and stories drawn from African and African American tradition not only inspire but offer specific prescriptions about how to avoid and master obstacles in life. We will be wiser, happier, and more effective catalysts of change in our work as therapists if we attend to the *spiritual* as well as the physical and emotional dimensions of ourselves and our clients. We and our clients can be empowered by reaching into and beyond ourselves and tapping our cultural legacies.

REFERENCES

Bennett, L. (1991, February). Voices of the past. *Ebony*, pp. 120–122.

Bergin, A. (1991). Values and religious issues in psychotherapy and mental health. *American Psychologist, 46*(4), 394–403.

Cooper-Lewter, N., & Mitchell, H. (1986). *Soul theology*. Nashville, TN: Abingdon Press.

Copage, E. (1993). *Black pearls*. New York: Morrow.

Randolph, L. (1997, February). The lady and the champ Evander. *Ebony*, pp. 66–74.

Riley, D. (1993). *My soul looks back, 'less I forget*. New York: HarperCollins.

Soaries, B. (1994). *Religion and mental health*. Paper presented at the Culture, Class, and Race Conference, New Brunswick, NJ.

Taggart, S. (1994). *Living as if*. San Francisco: Jossey-Bass.

Spilka, B., & Werme, P. H. (1971). Religion and mental disorder: A research perspective. In M. Strommen (Ed.), *Research on religious development: A comprehensive handbook*. New York: Hawthorn.

Vanzant, I. (1993). *Acts of faith*. New York: Simon & Schuster.

Walsh, F. (Ed.). (1993). *Normal family processes* (2nd ed.). New York: Guilford Press.

West, C. (1993). *Race matters*. Boston: Beacon Press.

PART II

CHALLENGING RACISM IN IDEOLOGY AND TRAINING

The four chapters in this section guide us in the most important and as yet undeveloped area of re-visioning our field. Racism is perhaps the most pernicious element of our culture, and the hardest to deal with because of the extremely high level of segregation of our society. The forces for racial segregation are so powerful that, unless we make strong and deliberate efforts to nurture diversity, they will prevail. Whites have tended to keep themselves unaware of racism. It is not a category in our diagnostic manuals and has been invisible in our developmental theories and in our psychotherapy. Those of us who are White cannot assume that racism will disappear if we are all simply "good people," or if we leave it to people of color to deal with. It is time for us to come to grips with our role in perpetuating the problems of racism by refusing to let ourselves see them.

In these four chapters, Robert-Jay Green, Kenneth Hardy, Tracey Laszloffy, and Norma Akamatsu focus on changing our ideology and our training to incorporate cultural understandings and play our part in becoming accountable for racism. Unwittingly, our training programs have been part of the problem, reproducing the racist, sexist, classist, and heterosexist structures of the wider society. As these authors make clear, we cannot make revisions just by modifying our reading lists. We must radically change our programs so that our trainees can break through the dominant culture's blinders. These chapters provide concrete guidelines for transforming both our theory and our training to overcome these blinders. The authors of this section are in the forefront of these conversations, lighting the way for the rest of us in understanding what we have to do to stop being part of the problem of institutionalized racism, both intentional and unintentional, in our field.

CHAPTER 7

Race and the Field of Family Therapy

Robert-Jay Green

The practice of family therapy and its theoretical paradigm are undergoing momentous changes. As the field addresses intergroup race relations, delivery of culturally attuned mental health services, and training of multiculturally competent family therapists, the early promise of a multilevel theory of family functioning is about to be realized. In this chapter, I sketch the contours of a "multicultural family theory," highlighting central issues that need to be addressed in its development.

Throughout, I use examples pertaining primarily to African Americans families, drawn from my experiences over the last 8 years as a White researcher involved in a collaborative study of 95 inner-city African American families of children who attend Oakland's Chapter I schools.[1] A second major source of ideas has been an ongoing multicultural curricular reform effort at the California School of Professional Psychology, Berkeley/Alameda campus (see Green, Chapter 8, this volume). Much of what I write in this chapter applies to other disenfranchised groups (e.g., lesbians/gays and persons with physical disabilities), although there are very important differences among the various ethnic, racial, and other minority groups, resulting from each one's unique history and visibility vis-á-vis the larger culture (Atkinson & Hackett, 1995; Green, 1996; Laird & Green, 1996; Sue & Sue, 1990).

A PLURALISTIC SOCIETY

According to the 1990 U.S. Census, approximately 60 million people in this country (24% of the population) are African American, Latino American, Asian American/Pacific Islander, or Native American. The Bureau of the Census conservatively estimates that by the year 2050, this number will more than double to 122 million, or 40% of the total U.S. population (Olmedo, 1994). The 40% level is close to being reached already in California and in the Southwestern states, where current racial minority populations combined are expected to exceed 50% of the population by the year 2050. Given that such trends are predicted to continue beyond the year 2050, it is likely that at some point in the next century, Whites (European Americans) ultimately will constitute a minority group within the total U.S. population.

The rapidly changing racial composition of the United States carries profound implications for the future development of our field. In the personal realm, consciousness of one's own racial and ethnic identity (which always has been higher among people of color because of their visible differentness from the majority and their vulnerability to discrimination) is growing rapidly among Whites. Thus white family therapists now find themselves increasingly living and working in multiracial environments that stimulate curiosity about their own cultural differentness from others. The changing racial composition of our everyday contexts is creating a sea change in our consciousness, which in turn is affecting how we think about and do family therapy.

In contrast to the demographic trends in the U.S. population as a whole, current racial minority groups continue to be dramatically underrepresented among the ranks of family therapists. In a 1993 survey of graduate programs accredited by the American Association for Marriage and Family Therapy, fewer than 1% of master's degree graduates during the preceding 10-year period were African American, and only 1.8% of the doctoral degree graduates were African American (Wilson & Stith, 1993). In that same year, the American Family Therapy Academy—which is the organization of senior teachers and researchers in our field—had a membership that was only 1.4% African or African American, 1.1% Asian or Asian American, and 2.8% Latino or Latino American.

The discrepancy between the proportions of people of color in the general population and in the profession of family therapy means that racial minority families are usually treated by White majority family therapists and that the caseloads of white family therapists will increasingly be composed of families of color. For example, in 1995, the California Association of Marriage and Family Therapists conducted a survey of 12,900 marriage and family therapists in California and found that while 94% of marriage and family therapists in this state were European American, 66% (two-thirds) of their clients were from other racial groups (24% Latino, 19% African American, 15% Asian/Pacific Islander, 6% Native American, 2% other). As a harbinger of things to come nationally, most family therapy in California already involves families of color being treated by White therapists.

Because family therapy theories tend to reflect the kinds of client populations served, I think we can expect dramatic increases in treatment concepts pertaining to therapist–client racial diversity in the near future. Race will become a major nucleus around which new developments in the theory of family therapy will emerge. Moreover, I think that new ideas and techniques originating from this multicultural emphasis will prove valuable in all family therapy, including instances when White middle-class clients are being treated by White middle-class therapists. That is, the multicultural lens will bring into clearer focus the uniqueness of each race's normative family experience, including problems common to White middle-class families as a distinct cultural group. In addition, the study of therapist–client interracial differentness will help illuminate the more general process of negotiating differentness between therapist and client, regardless of race. For example, it is likely to stimulate studies of how other therapist–client differences affect treatment process and outcome (e.g., differences in social class background, age, gender, religion, national origin, sexual orientation, physical disability, and sociopolitical values).

In the coming years, family therapists who now feel that such questions are tangential to their everyday interests are likely to have a personal stake in the answers that unfold. They will be treating ever-growing numbers of clients who are not like themselves culturally, and they will find that the cutting-edge theories of family therapy will focus increasingly on specific interventions that are culturally attuned to specific groups' ways of being in the world. In this sense, the study of race and family functioning will not be simply another peripheral vein, but rather a chamber at the very heart of family therapy.

At present, we are facing a major theoretical task—to weave together multicultural theory (including factors of race, gender, ethnicity, social class, physical ability, sexual orientation, and age) and traditional family systems theory into a coherent whole (see Sue, Ivey, & Pederson, 1996, for an analogous effort in the field of counseling psychology). This new "Multicultural Family Systems Theory" must link the individual, family, and cultural perspectives in a manageable way; it must be flexible enough to encompass all manner of sociocultural diversity and practical enough to be applied in the new health care delivery and other treatment contexts.

As with earlier major innovations in our field (such as the shift from psychodynamic to structural/strategic approaches beginning in the mid-1970s, and the shift from systemic/strategic to feminist/constructionist/narrative approaches beginning in the mid-1980s), it is a good bet that it will take this reformation about 10 years to achieve solid footing and greater acceptance. In the remainder of this chapter, I expand on some of the themes introduced above, paying special attention to racism as a factor in the lives of families of color and its implications for multicultural family theory.

CULTURE, POWER, AND
THE FIELD OF FAMILY THERAPY

John Weakland, one of the pioneers of family therapy and a member of the group that formulated the "double-bind" concept, once described the differences between family therapy and all other mental health approaches in terms of its origins in anthropology:

> I think it was very important for our work that Gregory Bateson and I were both trained anthropologically. . . . Psychiatrists, and even psychologists, to a large extent, tend to view the world in terms of pathology. If something looks strange or different, their first thought is that it is some kind of pathology. Anthropology is different. If you go out into the field in a new society, then every damned thing they do seems strange. You can't get anywhere just by saying "It's all pathological. It's all crazy!" It's *your* job to make sense out of it, no matter how crazy it looks. This produces a very different slant on the observation of behavior. (Quoted in Bassi, 1991, pp. 69–70)

Although the field of family therapy rapidly moved away from this cultural anthropology stance to adopt cybernetic/systems metaphors, the enduring hallmark of family therapy has been its insistence on the intelligibility and adaptiveness of psychological symptoms when viewed in a social context.

Also, early in its development, the field of family therapy incorporated an explicit analysis of power relations in the society. For example, shortly after World War II, Nathan Ackerman (another of the founders of the field of family therapy) and Marie Jahoda coauthored a book titled *Antisemitism and Emotional Disorders: A Psychoanalytic Interpretation* (Ackerman & Jahoda, 1950). They were among the first to propose that prejudice (in this case, against Jews) was the result of unconscious defense mechanisms, particularly projection, by which individuals and social groups diverted inner frustrations, conflicts, hostility, feelings of inadequacy, and deprivations onto innocent out-groups such as racial/ethnic minorities. Later, Ackerman (1958) imported this same concept into his work with families, calling the process "prejudicial scapegoating" of the identified patient; this purportedly served the function of reducing other unresolved tensions within the family group, particularly in the parents' marriage.

Similar notions appeared in the work of other family theorists during the early to mid-1960s, including Ezra Vogel and Norman Bell's (1968) idea of the emotionally disturbed child as the "family scapegoat"; Murray Bowen's concept of the "family projection process" (1966) and, later, the "societal projection process" (1978); and R. D. Laing's (1965) concept of "mystification" (a term originally used by Karl Marx to describe the obfuscation of power relations that takes place in capitalist societies, which enables the continued exploitation of the proletariat by the aristocracy).

However, as historians of science have demonstrated, a field's theories and techniques tend to reflect sociopolitical developments in the society as a whole. Family therapy is no exception. Despite its auspicious anthropological beginnings and social consciousness immediately following World War II, our field's attention to social *power* issues waxed and waned, seemingly in response to national trends in political attitudes and leadership.

For example, in the late 1970s and early 1980s, the whole concept of power was dismissed as nonsystemic by some of the Batesonians, rendering the field of family therapy "neutral" (and silent) when it came to confronting even the most obvious of power inequities, such as racism, wife abuse, physical and sexual abuse of children, and discrimination against lesbians and gay men. There was a kind of collective silence among White family therapists about racial inequality in the United States during the period from 1970 to 1990. We knew it was there; many of us had lived through and participated in the civil rights and antiwar movements of the 1960s. However, like the nation's Republican presidents during the period from 1970 to 1990 (Richard Nixon, Gerald Ford, Ronald Reagan, and George Bush), White family therapists didn't talk much about race. The simple fact of the matter is that members of the dominant cultural group usually have the option of ignoring or denying that racism exists unless some extreme example in the news media temporarily and painfully intrudes into awareness. This is not an option for members of minority groups, whose consciousness is more or less always attuned to the possibility of becoming direct targets of discrimination (Grier & Cobbs, 1968).

What I wish to underscore here is that although our field started out with an anthropological stance and with a social analysis of power, subjugation, and prejudice in society, it soon became overly focused on intrafamilial relations. What remained of an analysis of power and scapegoating was confined mainly to within-family, parent–child relations, which were considered separately from the larger social milieu in which families were inextricably embedded.

Documenting parallel trends in the field of psychology, Sandra Graham (1992), in an article entitled "Most of the Subjects Were White and Middle Class," reported a steady and dramatic decline in research on African Americans published in American Psychological Association (APA) journals between 1970 and 1989. For example, during the 5-year period 1970–1974, 203 such articles appeared, whereas in 1985–1989, only 65 such articles (one-third as many) appeared. Over the entire 20-year period, only 3.6% of all published studies utilized an African American sample. Although I have not done a precise survey, I feel confident in saying that the percentage of articles on African Americans in the family therapy journals during this period was not much better than in the APA journals.

By the mid- to late 1980s, however, the pendulum began to swing back in the field of family therapy. Many who had initially been caught up in the pure systemic/cybernetic analogy became increasingly frustrated with the field's abstract intellectualism and inability to address the pressing social problems facing living and breathing people every day. Feminist family therapists led the way in the field's renewed interest in the analysis of power relations between the genders both in society and in the family. As Virginia Goldner (1988) pointed out, family therapists had dealt comprehensively with the issue of generational power arrangements in two- and three-generation families, but they did not address issues of gender-based power within the family and society, including men's violence toward women. However, in spite of their trenchant critiques, most of the White feminist authors did not extend their analysis of power relations to the domain of race relations and its implications for family life and family therapy.

Family therapists who did write about working with families of color tended to view the social context of racism as a set of fixed constraints (Haley, 1977; Minuchin, 1974; Minuchin, Montalvo, Guerney, Rosman, & Schumer, 1967). The therapeutic task became one of generating and selecting among behavioral options that did not involve challenging or even understanding those larger constraints. These theorists did not, for example, advocate discussion of racial issues or racism in therapy; nor did they advocate social activism on the part of family members as a constructive, self-affirming response to racism. It remained unclear, for example, how a therapist should respond if an African American client were spontaneously to make a straightforward comment about racism in the society at large or in her or his own personal experience. The implication, however, was that discussion of racial matters would be a distraction from the therapeutic task at hand, which was to solve a narrowly defined presenting problem by altering the intrafamilial interactions presumed to be maintaining it. Social forces beyond the family's control were to be accepted as givens; discussion of them would have been viewed as a relative waste of precious therapy time.

This model essentially required that all presenting problems be attributed to intrafamilial relations, with responsibility or blame apportioned among the family members as equitably as possible in order not to seem unfair. However, it may be extremely adaptive for members of a minority family to be able to attribute some amount of causal influence to oppressive forces outside the family, to take action in regard to such oppression when feasible, and simply to assess the limits of their own responsibility for creating and maintaining family problems.

Although there have been some outstanding contributions and increasing attention being paid to matters of ethnicity and culture in our field recently, one might say that these constitute only a first-order change. Much of the literature in this area has come from a small number of authors, most of whom are themselves members of cultural minority groups (e.g., the majority of contributors to McGoldrick, Giordano, & Pearce, 1996). A second-order change would seem to require that matters of race, ethnicity, social class, and prejudice become a fundamental, continuous, and visible focus in the work of a majority of family therapists and researchers, including White (European American) family therapists and researchers.

CULTURAL "DIFFERENTNESS" VERSUS INTERCULTURAL "OPPRESSION"

Among the barriers to this shifting of the gears, some of the issues before us require a different level of analysis than the intrafamilial one. When it comes to matters of social class, race, sexual orientation, or physical disability, for example, we are talking not only about power arrangements *within* couples or families, but also about *the unequal power of some families vis-á-vis other families in the society*. As I discuss later, in the section on service delivery systems, only some of the problems resulting from these intergroup inequities can be addressed with family therapy per se, whereas others may be more amenable to community-based family interventions that have a preventive/educational focus.

In this new era, we will need to distinguish clearly between matters of minority group *differentness* and matters of minority group *oppression*. I want to make very sure that we do not confuse ourselves about this distinction. We will need to broaden the conversation beyond our current emphasis (which mainly involves attempts to describe *intra*cultural patterns in the different ethnic groups) to include an explicit focus on *inter*cultural relations (including prejudice, discrimination, and violence), which seem to be more difficult for us to address openly.

Although intracultural traditions, norms, and values are important to family functioning, among the most important aspects of cultural differences are the types of prejudice and discrimination experienced by various groups in a given society (racism, homophobia, sexism, etc.). These factors affect families' access to resources and abilities to cope with the tasks of raising children. A main focus should be on how cultural groups manage their differences and how some cultural groups are positioned economically and politically to control other cultural groups in the society. Our focus on different cultural patterns and historical traditions *within* groups often obscures our understanding of the oppressive relations *between* groups.

Cultural, racial, and sexual orientation differences are *not* problems in and of themselves. Prejudice, discrimination, and other forms of aggressive intercultural conflict based on these differences *are* problems. This may seem too obvious to state. However, in the past, social scientists have done great damage by viewing certain minority groups' differentness as inherently problematic or pathological. There is a long history of researchers portraying minority group families—especially African American families, Native American families, Latino families, and gay and lesbian families—in very negative or pathological terms (Azibo, 1992; Green, Bettinger, & Zacks, 1996; Laird & Green, 1996).

For example, during the 1960s, the phrase "culturally deprived" was used to describe African American families—a term implying that Black culture was inferior to White culture, or even that Blacks were devoid of culture, as if White culture were the *only* good, true, and "cultured" culture (Duckitt, 1992). Then there were the long and continuing series of research reports showing that Blacks scored lower on IQ tests than Whites, without acknowledging that the tests were standardized on, and culturally biased in favor of, White middle-class children.

Even now, comparative research studies (i.e., studies comparing African American to White subjects) remain the most frequently utilized methods in research on African Americans, which tends to set White groups' results as the norm against which African Americans' are evaluated (Azibo, 1992). In this regard, Graham's (1992) 20-year survey of APA journals showed that 72% of research articles on African Americans were based on such race-comparative studies. It seems that researchers have been more concerned with how African Americans compare to Whites than with African Americans in their own right.

Furthermore, many of the comparative studies of the past did *not* adequately measure or control for socioeconomic status (Graham, 1992). Rather, they frequently compared middle-class white families to lower-socioeconomic-status African American families. This strategy hopelessly confounds social class and race, and yields a negatively biased picture of African American's functioning compared to Whites'. In addition, previous researchers often failed to take into account certain dimensions that seem to be uniquely important to the well-being of African American families: namely, greater involvement among extended kin; the importance of the church as a source of social identity and support; more fluid boundaries in terms of household membership and child-rearing roles; and ways of socializing children to deal with racial discrimination (Boykin, 1986; McAdoo, 1988).

Finally, researchers of the past tended to attribute the difficulties of African Americans to their cultural differentness from the majority group, rather than to the social oppression they face. I mean here that the amount of discrimination encountered by a minority group seems to be a larger factor in its functioning well than is the discrepancy between the minority and majority groups' original cultures. In this context, I would like to cite the work of John Ogbu (1978, 1989), a distinguished educational anthropologist at the University of California, Berkeley. In a review of cross-national studies of immigrants, Ogbu has shown that the social position of a minority group (i.e., the extent to which its opportunities are limited by the larger society) is the major determinant of that minority group's educational attainment.

In particular, Ogbu (1989) distinguishes between two types of minority groups. He calls the first type "voluntary immigrant" minority groups. These groups voluntarily came to the new country seeking a better life, sometimes to escape intolerable conditions in their countries of origin. Most European ethnics and Asians in the United States would be considered voluntary immigrants. Recent illustrations occurred on both the East and West Coasts of the United States during 1993, when ships carrying illegal immigrants from mainland China were intercepted, and it was discovered that many families had paid as much as $30,000 for the voyage to the United States. Ogbu calls the second type "involuntary caste-like" minority groups. These groups have a history of being enslaved or colonized by the dominant cultural group. For example, African Americans, Native Hawaiians, Puerto Ricans, Native Americans, and Mexican Americans would be considered involuntary, caste-like minorities in the United States.

In Ogbu's (1989) cross-national review, voluntary immigrant minority groups did as well academically as, or better than, the majority group in any given country. However, the involuntary, caste-like minority groups tended to be doing more poorly in school. To clarify, let me cite just a few examples from Ogbu's (1989) review.

Koreans have been studied in three locations: Korea, Japan, and the

United States. In Korea and the United States, Korean children are achieving very well in school. In Japan, however—where there is a long history of discrimination against Koreans—Korean children are performing poorly in school. Clearly, this implies that there is not something intrinsic to being Korean (such as higher IQ) or to Korean culture (such as placing a higher value on education) that leads to Koreans' higher achievement in the United States. Rather, there must be something in how Koreans are being treated in the United States versus Japan, or how Koreans view their situation in the two countries, that accounts for their better school performance in the United States than in Japan.

Similarly, the academic achievement of Finns has been studied in two locations: Sweden and Australia. In Sweden, which colonized Finland for centuries, Finns are performing very poorly in school. However, Finns who voluntarily immigrated to Australia are doing quite well in school. Again, the culture of origin does not, in and of itself, predict school achievement in these cross-national immigration comparisons.

Nor does dissimilarity between the culture of origin and the culture of immigration predict poorer school achievement. If cultural differences (i.e., between home and school) were the key, why would Koreans be doing more poorly in Japan (a more similar Buddhist culture) than in the United States (a more different Judeo-Christian culture)? Or why would Finns be doing more poorly in Sweden (a more similar Scandinavian culture) than in Australia (a more different Anglo-British culture)?

As a final example here, West Indians have been studied in Britain, Canada, and the United States. In Britain, which colonized the West Indies, West Indians are the *least* academically successful minority group, whereas in Canada and the United States, West Indians are doing well academically.

These cross-national immigration studies imply that language differences, economic differences, and culture-of-origin differences are *not* the primary determinants of differential school achievement by minority groups. Rather, a minority group's relative academic success seems related to its immigration history (voluntary vs. involuntary) and current status in relation to the dominant group. In particular, children from a given subcultural group will achieve more poorly if their group was colonized or enslaved historically by the dominant group (as was the case for African Americans, Native Americans, Puerto Ricans, and Mexican Americans in the United States; Koreans in Japan; Finns in Sweden; and West Indians in Britain).

Based on his findings, Ogbu (1989) concludes that a minority group's historical pattern of incorporation within a given society and the current level of discrimination it faces within that society are more important to its academic success than are its preimmigration *intra*cultural patterns, language differences, or other cultural differences from the majority. And from this, we family therapists might conclude that issues of oppression, racial discrimination, and their psychological effects (rather than *intra*-group cultural traditions) should be emphasized in our attempts to understand the long-term, multigenerational functioning of minority families in America. For example, in our research group's study of 95 African American inner-city families, we recently found that the amount of racial prejudice children experienced was significantly related to poorer academic achievement and to higher levels of problem behavior (Moore-McDowell, 1993).

We must keep in mind that members of a racial minority group have something more in common than just their traditional beliefs and family interaction patterns from their cultures or countries of origin. Despite the great diversity within a given minority group—whether its members are family therapists or computer operators, judges or nurses—the members of that group share a similar potential for experiencing racial discrimination, a similar vulnerability to discrimination. Regardless of their other characteristics as individuals, skin color constitutes a fundamental organizing characteristic of their lives and tends to structure their interactions with other racial groups in the society. And the same is true for Whites, although it involves racial privilege rather than racial discrimination. White skin color is a fundamental organizing characteristic of persons' lives, contributes to much of Whites' relative economic privilege, and structures much of their interaction with other races, including Whites' lack of interaction with other races.

I think that for members of the White majority group, it is very difficult to grasp emotionally a person of color's lifetime experiences in relation to prejudice—and, equally important, the anticipation of, and vulnerability to, prejudice. For example, I think that when Whites visualize racism, they tend to picture it primarily in terms of dramatic or violent instances of hatred and aggression (e.g., the Rodney King beating). But it is much more difficult for them to imagine the more common and cumulative acts of everyday discrimination, including subtle nonverbal cues and other, more ambiguous signs of prejudice that constitute a basic fabric of people of colors' experience. At the same time, I think it is difficult for members of the white majority group to see and to admit the extent to which they are privileged by virtue of skin color and the inequalities of race. It is sometimes painful for Whites to acknowledge that many of their opportunities for success in a competitive world are due to skin color and the many advantages that tend to go along with skin color, rather than to personal effort, talent, or other attributes of self or family.

Although I am stressing these overarching points about racial stratification and social class stratification in U.S. society, I want to make it clear that the family also has a role to play in the child's educational attainment and psychosocial functioning. Thus, even though racial discrimination is an important determinant of a minority group's relative achievement as a *group,* families within a given minority group still show great variability in their academic performance. Although the amount of societal discrimination may determine the relative academic performance of a one racial group compared to other racial groups, the family also makes a significant contribution to individual children's academic performance within each racial group or within each social class.

The findings described above suggest that researchers and clinicians should focus on two distinct processes: (1) how minority group families help their members cope behaviorally, emotionally, and cognitively with specific acts of discrimination and with institutionalized oppression of their group generally within U.S. society; and (2) how patterns of family interaction are associated with the variability of behavioral, emotional, and cognitive functioning of individuals within a specific ethnic/racial group.

MODELS OF SERVICE DELIVERY

In addition to focusing our thinking on both intracultural and intercultural patterns affecting family life, we in the field of family therapy need to develop more flexible, culturally attuned techniques and models of service delivery. There are large percentages of U.S. families whose members are in need of psychosocial help, but for whom the concept and quasi-medical trappings of "psychotherapy" are foreign and stigmatizing. Many people, especially those who are not of European descent, do not want to be associated with anything labeled "psycho-" or anything labeled "therapy," both of which signal medical illness or insanity. However, a much larger percentage of the population is open to such activities as interpersonal education, self-development, self-help, assertiveness training, parent effectiveness training, codependency groups, the various survivors' groups, immigration support groups, and other quasi-educational group activities. Quite simply, they can get help without labeling themselves, or being labeled by others, as "bad" or "crazy." This is no small matter. Despite the repulsion highly trained family therapists often feel toward certain self-help groups and their simplistic philosophies, it is clear that these groups are attractive to many persons who would not initially seek therapy, and that the groups actually provide a socializing experience, rendering help more acceptable to many participants.

Such families are much more likely to take part in community-based intervention programs that have an educational, support, or preventative orientation and are delivered through ordinary community institutions such as schools, religious organizations, primary care medical facilities, and workplaces. These programs include such activities as parent education; marriage preparation; and multifamily self-help or psychoeducational groups for a wide variety of physical problems, addictions, family transitions, and serious emotional disorders. Although professional roles in these kinds of community programs (e.g., family life educator, crisis counselor, community organizer, preschool consultant) have generally been viewed as relatively low-status among family therapists, we are going to have to rethink our patterns of office-based service delivery and our attachment to the "doctor" role if we are going to reach larger segments of the population that are at risk for emotional disorders.

The second arena toward which we should be drawn is prevention activities, especially: programs for pregnant teenage mothers; federal programs such as Head Start and Healthy Start, which are mandated to have family interventions components; programs like the family–school collaboration project of the Ackerman Institute (Weiss & Edwards, 1992) and like Comer's (1985) family–school interventions in New Haven; and programs currently going under the label of "family preservation" (see Schorr, 1989, for an overview of community-oriented family and child programs). These activities involve different professional tasks than does the "therapist" role, drawing us out of our offices and out of the one-to one mode, and into tasks more associated with the roles of organizational consultant, community psychologist, and family life educator.

Take, for example, the children in our research in Oakland, whose median achievement test score was at the 36th percentile on national norms. This means that half of the children in the sample were scoring *below* the 36th percentile. With the decline in the manufacturing and unskilled labor sectors of the U.S. economy, and the increased growth in the service sector, a child who is scoring below the 36th percentile is probably going to have a hard time later making it occupationally in the information age. These kids are headed for later emotional, health-related, financial, and behavioral difficulties—in other words, all the harsh effects that poverty and illiteracy have on self-regard, family relations, and access to health care and other services. Furthermore, many of their parents do not realize the implications of these low percentile test scores, because their children still receive passing grades in their classes and move up to the next level in school at the end of each year.

Few families in these circumstances would seek counseling to reduce the psychosocial risk factors their children face. Some of them view the trajectory of their lives and their children's lives as immutable. To almost all such families, therapy would seem ill suited to their problems because of social stigma (i.e., a treatment for mental illness), its cost, and, most important, its apparent irrelevance for solving their everyday life context problems.

We can either say "So much the worse for these families" or "So much the worse for therapy." I vote for the latter. That is, if we want to reach the bulk of poor families, we will have to abandon traditional notions of family therapy service delivery. We will have to start thinking in terms of family intervention with a healthy coping/prevention focus, with programs beginning early in the family life cycle, with programs offering multiple social/medical/educational/occupational services, and with programs that are available over many years in everyday settings rather than in mental health practitioners' offices. Head Start, with its family component, is a paradigmatic example of the kind of prevention programs I have in mind, although most Head Start centers are limited in terms of their availability over time and highly variable in their commitment to intensive parent involvement.

As we all know, there are many problems with family life in the United States that *we* would like to help change, even if families themselves do not consider those aspects of their lives problematic, or do not consider those problems suitable for therapy, or do not consider therapy suitable for *their* sort of family. Many of the social problems we are discussing here are caused by racism, sexism, homophobia, and other forms of prejudice, which are passed down over generations in families, but the families themselves do not perceive these aspects of their lives as problematic. To affect these family-linked problems, we will need to go to where the families are, rather than expect them to show up in our offices. The ways of reaching such families might include educational interventions in the schools, in churches, on television, and so on.

Sexism, racism, and homophobia, are partially learned in a family context and passed down over many generations in families, but clients do not ordinarily present themselves voluntarily for treatment of these problems. Victims of these forms of prejudice may seek treatment, but perpetrators generally do not. This, of course, is the case for many kinds of externalizing problems. The victims of the externalizer may seek therapy, or may even try to bring the externalizer for therapy, but the externalizer rarely initiates treatment and may remain resistant throughout. Therapy is essentially a context that draws and is suitable for persons with internalizing types of problems or those who are the victims of externalizers.

For example, if ever there was a family-linked problem, it is White racism, inasmuch as this problem tends to be passed down through the generations in families. I know of no White family that has ever requested help to change its racism. Nor is racism considered a mental disorder (although "racist personality disorder" was actually proposed at one point for inclusion in DSM-IV; see Hamlin, 1990). Managed care will not pay for treatment of family-linked White racism, unless it is associated with a DSM diagnosis. White racism is generally not a within-family problem, but might be better viewed as a problem between families or between families nested in certain communities.

Family therapy thus cannot treat problems of White racism very effectively, if at all. Family-oriented, community-based, educational interventions, rather than psychotherapy, will be necessary if we wish to reduce prejudice and discrimination based on race, ethnicity, social class, gender, sexual orientation, physical disability, and other minority statuses. If White family therapists wish to be of service to racial minority families, they will do well to spend at least part of their time initiating or becoming active in community efforts to reduce racism and to insure equal opportunity for all families. There are many, many ways for mental health professionals to help families besides family therapy.

CONCLUSION

What does it mean for us to be family therapists? Whom do we serve? Are we a part of the health care system? Are we a branch of applied anthropology, human ecology, family studies, or family life education—all of which now have some of their own doctoral programs? Will we continue only to huddle in our offices waiting for individual families to request treatment, or will we move beyond family therapy to include prevention, community intervention, and family social policy within our scope of practice?[2]

Speaking for myself, as a White family therapist who has been mainly a student and sometimes a teacher of multicultural issues, "there has been an alarming increase in the number of things I know nothing about" (Brilliant, 1992, p. 104). Many White family therapists are like immigrants in a multicultural land. We can cling to the old clinical traditions and delay the process of acculturation. Or, now that our monocultural illusions are crumbling, we can embrace a wider vision of our work.

ACKNOWLEDGMENTS

Portions of this chapter were originally presented as a plenary address at the 1993 American Family Therapy Academy (AFTA) meeting in Baltimore, Maryland. I am grateful to the California School of Professional Psychology, Berkeley/Alameda, for generously supporting a year-long sabbatical leave during which much of this chapter was written.

NOTES

1. This project involved a multiracial group of coinvestigators, including Julie Hagmann, Roxanne Okun, Jennifer Moore-McDowell, Uma Ratnam, Gerald Whitmore, and Marilyn Commerford Wilts. Also, many faculty members at the California School of Professional Psychology acted as consultants on one or more pieces of the larger study. See Green et al. (in preparation).

2. In this regard, a new family social policy organization has recently been formed by a group of prominent family researchers and family therapists—The Council on Contemporary Families, Washington, DC. It seeks to inform the public debate about "family values" by conveying accurate social science findings about families to the media and social policy makers. For more information, see their website at http://www.Slip.net/~ccf/.

REFERENCES

Ackerman, N. W. (1958). *The psychodynamics of family life*. New York: Basic Books.

Ackerman, N. W., & Jahoda, M. (1950). *Antisemitism and emotional disorders: A psychoanalytic interpretation*. New York: Harper.

Atkinson, D. R., & Hackett, G. (1995). *Counseling diverse populations*. Dubuque, IA: William C. Brown.

Azibo, D. A. Y. (1992). Understanding the proper and improper usage of the comparative research framework. In A. K. H. Burlew, W. C. Banks, H. P. McAdoo, & D. A. Y. Azibo (Eds.), *African American psychology: Theory, research, and practice* (pp. 18–27). Newbury Park, CA: Sage.

Bassi, V. (1991). *The genesis of family therapy: An oral history of the years 1945–1960*. Unpublished doctoral dissertation, California School of Professional Psychology, Alameda.

Bowen, M. (1966). The use of family theory in clinical practice. *Comprehensive Psychiatry, 345–374.*

Bowen, M. (1978). *Family therapy in clinical practice*. New York: Jason Aronson.

Boykin, A. W. (1986). The triple quandary and the schooling of Afro-American children. In U. Neisser (Ed.), *The school achievement of minority children: New perspectives*. Hillsdale, NJ: Erlbaum.

Brilliant, A. (1979). *I may not be totally perfect, but parts of me are excellent, and other brilliant thoughts*. Santa Barbara, CA: Woodbridge Press.

Comer, J. P. (1985). The Yale–New Haven Primary Prevention Project: A follow-up study. *Journal of the American Academy of Child Psychiatry, 24,* 154–160.

Duckitt, J. (1992). *The social psychology of prejudice*. New York: Praeger.

Goldner, V. (1988). Generation and gender: Normative and covert hierarchies. *Family Process, 27,* 17–31.

Graham, S. (1992). Most of the subjects were White and middle class: Trends in published research on African Americans in selected APA journals, 1970–1989. *American Psychologist, 47,* 629–639.

Green, R.-J. (1996). Why ask, why tell? Teaching and learning about lesbians and gays in family therapy. *Family Process, 35,* 389–400.

Green, R-J., Bettinger, M., & Zacks, E. (1996). Are lesbian couples fused and gay male couples disengaged?: Questioning gender straightjackets. In J. Laird & R-J. Green (Eds.), *Lesbians and gays in couples and families: A handbook for therapists* (pp. 185–230). San Francisco: Jossey-Bass.

Green, R.-J., Hagmann-Lasher, J., Moore-McDowell, J., Okun, R., Ratnam, U., Whitmore, G., Wilts, M. C., & Cooper, B. C. (in preparation). *African American inner-city families: Children's academic achievement and psychosocial functioning.*

Grier, W., & Cobbs, P. (1968). *Black rage.* New York: Basic Books.

Haley, J. (1977). *Problem-solving therapy.* San Francisco: Jossey-Bass.

Laing, R. D. (1965). Mystification, confusion, and conflict. In I. Boszormenyi-Nagy & J. L. Framo (Eds.), *Intensive family therapy* (pp. 343–363). Hagerstown, MD: Hoeber.

Laird, J., & Green, R.-J. (Eds.). (1996). *Lesbians and gays in couples and families: A handbook for therapists.* San Francisco: Jossey-Bass.

McAdoo, H. P. (Ed.). (1988). *Black families* (2nd ed.). Beverly Hills, CA: Sage.

McGoldrick, M., Giordano, J., & Pearce, J. K. (Eds.). (1996). *Ethnicity and family therapy* (2nd ed.). New York: Guilford Press.

Minuchin, S. (1974). *Families and family therapy.* Cambridge, MA: Harvard University Press.

Minuchin, S., Montalvo, B., Guerney, B. G., Jr., Rosman, B. L., & Schumer, F. (1967). *Families of the slums: An exploration of their structure and treatment.* New York: Basic Books.

Moore-McDowell, J. (1993). *Inner-city African-American families' achievement practices and children's experienced prejudice: Correlates of children's academic achievement and psychosocial competence.* Unpublished doctoral dissertation, California School of Professional Psychology, Alameda.

Ogbu, J. U. (1978). *Minority education and caste: The American system in cross-cultural perspective.* New York: Academic Press.

Ogbu, J. U. (1989). *Cultural models and educational strategies of non-dominant peoples* (1989 Catherine Molony Memorial Lecture). New York: City College Workshop Center.

Olmedo, E. L. (1994). Testimony of Esteban L. Olmedo to the Subcommittee on Health and the Environment, U.S. House of Representatives' Committee on Energy and Commerce. Reprinted in *CSPP Visions, 7*(1), 15–17.

Riemersma, M. (1995, September–October). Who is the typical MFCC in California?: 1995 CAMFT survey results. *The California Therapist,* pp. 7–9.

Schorr, L. (1989). *Within our reach: Breaking the cycle of disadvantage.* New York: Anchor.

Sue, D. W., Ivey, A. E., & Pedersen, P. B. (1996). *A theory of multicultural counseling and therapy.* Pacific Grove, CA: Brooks/Cole.

Sue, D. W., & Sue, D. (1990). *Counseling the culturally different: Theory and practice* (2nd ed.). New York: Wiley.

Vogel, E. F., & Bell, N. W. (1968). The emotionally disturbed child as the family scapegoat. In N. W. Bell & E. F. Vogel (Eds.), *A modern introduction to the family* (rev. ed., pp. 412–427). New York: Free Press.

Weiss, H. M., & Edwards, M. E. (1992). The family–school collaboration project: Systemic interventions for school improvement. In S. L. Christenson & J. C. Conoley (Eds.), *Home–school collaboration: Enhancing children's academic and social competence*. Silver Spring, MD: National Association of School Psychologists.

Wilson, L. L., & Stith, S. M. (1993). The voices of African-American MFT students: Suggestions for improving recruitment and retention. *Journal of Marital and Family Therapy, 19,* 17–30.

CHAPTER 8

Training Programs
GUIDELINES FOR MULTICULTURAL
TRANSFORMATION

Robert-Jay Green

Major advances in multicultural family systems theory and therapy are likely to follow from changes in the field's membership and leadership. Among the current barriers to such innovation are the institutional climates in training programs that perpetuate, in tandem with the larger society, the status quo dominance of majority groups and the exclusion and alienation of various minority groups (see Green, Chapter 7, this volume). Thus, much of our effort in creating in multicultural family therapy will have to be directed toward organizational change in our educational institutions.

For example, one of the most straightforward ways of improving mental health services for families of color is the training of graduate students who are themselves people of color. In a survey of graduates from the four campuses of the California School of Professional Psychology (CSPP—the nation's largest doctoral program in clinical psychology), Olmedo (1994) found that racial minority graduates had caseloads that included about twice as many clients of color as the caseloads of White graduates did. Also, minority graduates were much less likely to work in private practice settings than were all graduates (24% compared to 56%), which suggests that many more minority graduates are working in the public sector agencies that serve more families of color (Olmedo, 1994).

As I have written elsewhere (Green, 1996), I believe that five overlapping program elements are important for preparing students to work with different cultural groups:

> 1) *didactic training* (helping students acquire information through lectures and readings that are woven throughout the entire program);

2) *sensitization* (helping students develop a comfortable awareness of "not knowing everything" and an enthusiasm for learning about and forming multiple identifications with different cultural groups); 3) *personal contact* (helping students reduce their phobic and prejudicial responses, through cooperative interactions with members of different cultural groups); 4) *supervised clinical experience* (helping students acquire intervention skills that are culturally-attuned, under the guidance of supervisors and "culture-consultants" with expertise on specific groups); and 5) *modeling by means of organizational structure* (helping students become accustomed to seeking routine case consultation, personal guidance, and instruction from minority group professionals holding positions of senior leadership in the program). (pp. 390–391)

Expanding on these ideas here, I describe 11 guidelines for multicultural transformation of predominantly White, monocultural family therapy training programs. These suggestions derive from a campus-wide effort to transform our rather traditional clinical psychology doctoral program at CSPP's Berkeley/Alameda campus. The process has been led at various points during the last 10 years by Valata Jenkins-Monroe, Zonya Johnson, Patricia Canson, Diane Adams, Eduardo Morales, Peter Chang, and Derald Wing Sue.[1] Although we still have a great deal to accomplish and are dissatisfied with our own rate of progress, our training program has changed significantly during this period. Most tangibly, we have increased our enrollment of students of color from 8% to 22% (which is about twice the national average in the field of clinical psychology); and we have increased the percentage of full-time faculty members of color from 4% (1 out of 26) to 21% (8 out of 38).

GUIDELINES FOR MULTICULTURAL TRANSFORMATION OF TRAINING

Multicultural Competencies as Goals

The organization should define and distribute a set of multicultural competencies (in the areas of basic knowledge, attitudes, and clinical skills) toward which everyone in the organization can strive. These descriptions of multicultural competencies should be as specific as possible, with detailed behavioral examples of what would constitute each competency. The Association for Multicultural Counseling and Development (Sue, Arredondo, & McDavis, 1992) and the American Psychological Association (1991) both have produced statements of multicultural competencies for mental health professionals that can be adapted for use in family therapy training programs. Two examples from Sue et al. (1992) follow:

> ... Culturally skilled counselors are able to exercise institutional intervention skills on behalf of their clients. They can help clients determine whether a "problem" stems from racism or bias in others ... so that clients do not inappropriately personalize problems.

> ... Culturally skilled counselors are not adverse to seeking consultation with traditional healers and religious and spiritual leaders and practitioners in the treatment of culturally different clients when appropriate. (p. 486)

Outside Program Evaluation/Consultation

An outside, independent "authority" (e.g., a professional accrediting organization, or a group of consultants) should be utilized for preplanned, periodic assessments of the organization's progress toward multicultural goals. These accrediting agencies or external consultants may be used as leverage to help resolve the inevitable organizational impasses that arise. Rather than waiting for crises to occur, it is advisable to have preplanned assessments by outside consultants who are knowledgeable about multicultural issues and training programs in the mental health fields.

Multicultural Faculty Leadership

No single faculty member or subgroup should be made wholly responsible for multicultural teaching and transformation. Every faculty member in the program, regardless of his or her race, should assume some responsibility and leadership for its success. Faculty of color should not be concentrated only in the junior ranks of the faculty, but should also occupy positions of senior leadership. The typical attempted solution, in which a program hires one junior faculty member of color to initiate programmatic change amidst a more senior all-White faculty, usually leads to lack of support for multicultural efforts and to the margin–alization, burnout, and rapid departure of that faculty member.

Numerical Balance within the Faculty and within the Student Body

From a training standpoint, the program should contain a substantial proportion of people of color, at least representative proportionately to the general population. There *is* strength in numbers, and experience indicates that if the organization or group contains fewer than about 20%

people of color, these members may not feel empowered to express and assert themselves because they risk being personally blamed (scapegoated) when conflicts with the majority group occur. Thus, for the purposes of multicultural training, a minimum of 20% people of color at all ranks in the hierarchy is important to achieve, with a higher percentage being ideal. Some very useful guidelines for achieving these hiring aspirations are available in two reports—*Valuing Diversity: A Guide* and *How to Recruit and Hire Ethnic Minority Faculty* (Commission on Ethnic Minority Recruitment, Retention, and Training in Psychology, 1996).

Faculty Training

All instructors/supervisors should participate together in multicultural training as a prerequisite to continued teaching/supervising in the program. Faculty training activities can include lectures, workshops, ongoing peer case consultation seminars for faculty, a reading seminar, or a series of small-group discussions about how to include multicultural content in classes and supervision sessions. It is best if many of these activities have a collaborative format, with all program faculty members learning from each other as peers and grappling together with the difficult issues, rather than always being taught by "experts" from within or outside the program.

Coteaching of Intercultural Awareness

Wherever possible, intercultural awareness activities (such as workshops on racism or homophobia awareness) should be cotaught by leaders who are of different cultural groups and whose cultural affiliations are representative of the trainee group's cultural composition. The teaching of intercultural awareness should not be delegated to faculty of color alone.

Dispersion of Multicultural Content in All Courses

Multicultural content should be infused throughout all training activities and included by all instructors/supervisors. For example, it should not be compartmentalized into one or two elective or required courses on "cultural issues" taught by instructors of color. In addition to such specialized courses, every course in the entire curriculum should have a multicultural component. The program should require that all instructors explicitly state in course descriptions (syllabi) how they will include multicultural content in their proposed teaching activities. Instructors should be given advance help and feedback on their proposed coverage of multicultural issues.

Inclusion of Multicultural Content in Clinical Supervision

All individual and group supervision sessions (including supervision when the clients being discussed are White, middle-class, heterosexual, able-bodied, young adult, and Protestant) should involve an explicit discussion of multicultural factors in problem maintenance and the treatment relationship. This discussion should focus on: (1) how the cultural similarities/differences between a therapist and a client may be affecting the treatment relationship; (2) how the social norms of the client's cultural group may be contributing to the presenting problem; and (3) how intergroup relations (between the client's cultural group and other cultural groups in the society at large, or between the client and specific individuals or institutions representing other cultural groups) may be contributing to the presenting problem. Whenever possible (and particularly for "stuck cases"), input should be solicited from cultural consultants who are from the same culture as the client being discussed and who are knowledgeable about treatment of clients from that group.

Specialization of Faculty and Students

In addition to including multicultural content as a component of all training and supervision activities, there should be opportunities for specialized training experiences exclusively focused on minority mental health issues (e.g., a course on Latino families, lesbian and gay families, or families and immigration). Students and faculty members who wish to specialize in minority mental health work should be enabled to do so (e.g., a whole sequence of training experiences in multicultural issues).

Evaluation of Instructors on Their Multicultural Competencies

All evaluation forms filled out by students should include a section for describing how well the instructor or supervisor covered multicultural content and suggesting ways of improving the instructor's/supervisor's performance in this area. These evaluations should be used in decisions about merit raises, promotion, and retention. Instructors should also write yearly self-evaluations of their efforts to include multicultural content, outlining their strengths and plans for improvement in each activity.

Evaluation of Students on Their Multicultural Competencies

In all exams, assigned papers, and evaluations by supervisors, students should be required to demonstrate mastery of multicultural knowledge and sensitivity to the multicultural issues involved. Students' continuation in the training program should be contingent on adequate progress in developing multicultural competencies. The program should establish a set of remedial training experiences for students whose progress is less than satisfactory but who show promise of increasing their competencies to satisfactory levels.

CONCLUSION

It is essential for the success of any organizational change process that the administrators of the program support the change effort and its leaders. Also, it is inevitable that some faculty members will argue against change at some points along the way, but these conflicts will not derail progress unless the administration wavers in its support of the goals. Although general goals may be specified by the administration or a subgroup of the faculty, the entire faculty should bear the major responsibility for articulating those goals in detail and for designing a cooperative process for attaining them.

Multicultural transformation in predominantly White training programs (which includes almost all programs in the field of family therapy) is difficult and typically is characterized by a series of wrenching crises and ultimate resolutions. The process requires a long-term commitment to organizational self-examination. Like democracy itself, its survival requires continual vigilance.

ACKNOWLEDGMENTS

Portions of this chapter were originally presented at the 1994 Conference on Culture, Race, Class, and Gender, sponsored by the Family Institute of New Jersey. I am grateful to the California School of Professional Psychology, Berkeley/Alameda, for generously supporting a year-long sabbatical leave during which much of this chapter was written.

NOTE

1. For 3 years, this effort was supported by a grant from the Fund for the Improvement of Post-Secondary Education at the U.S. Department of Education. As part of this grant, extensive bibliographies on multicultural topics were compiled and are available upon request from Peter Chang, PhD, California School of Professional Psychology, Berkeley/Alameda Campus, 1005 Atlantic Ave., Alameda, CA 94501. Telephone: (510) 523-2300.

REFERENCES

American Psychological Association. (1991). *Guidelines for providers of psychological services to ethnic, linguistic, and culturally diverse populations.* Washington, DC: Author.

Commission on Ethnic Minority Recruitment, Retention, and Training in Psychology. (1996). *Valuing diversity: A guide* and *How to recruit and hire ethnic minority faculty.* Washington, DC: American Psychological Association.

Green, R.-J. (1996). Why ask, why tell? Teaching and learning about lesbians and gays in family therapy. *Family Process, 35,* 389–400.

Olmedo, E. L. (1994). Testimony of Esteban L. Olmedo to the Subcommittee on Health and the Environment, U.S. House of Representatives' Committee on Energy and Commerce. Reprinted in *CSPP Visions,* 7(1), 15–17.

Sue, D. W., Arredondo, P., & McDavis, R. J. (1992). Multicultural counseling competencies and standards: A call to the profession. *Journal of Counseling and Development, 70,* 477–486.

CHAPTER 9

The Dynamics of a Pro-Racist Ideology
IMPLICATIONS FOR FAMILY THERAPISTS

Kenneth V. Hardy
Tracey A. Laszloffy

As an African American male and as a White female, we have struggled with and grown through our efforts to forge a professional partnership dedicated to promoting racial justice, both in the world at large, and specifically within the context of family therapy. Our differences traverse the spectrum of diversity (i.e., race, gender, religion, age, professional status). And yet, despite these differences, for the past 6 years we have worked together most successfully. We believe that one of the critical factors associated with our success has been our relentless commitment to addressing and confronting the ways in which both our similarities and differences shape our relationship. Through this process we have learned a great deal about ourselves, particularly with regard to the dynamics of race, racism, and our racial identities. What follows is a discussion of some of the major insights we have gained about ourselves and about the process of promoting racial justice, both in our world and within family therapy.

DEFINING OUR TERMS

Through our interactions with others, one of our most compelling realizations has been that many people do not consider themselves to be racists; they think of themselves as "good people." They do not believe that race should be a basis for determining the types of opportunities or treatment that are afforded to individuals or groups. Because of their commitment to this premise, these individuals assume that their ideology and behavior reflect this ideal. And yet, despite the fact that many people are committed abstractly to racial justice, in concrete ways they lack racial sensitivity.

We define "racial sensitivity" as the ability to recognize the ways in which race and racism shape reality. It also involves using oneself to actively challenge attitudes, behaviors, and conditions that create or reinforce racial injustices. A salient dimension of achieving racial sensitivity involves identifying and resisting the pro-racist ideology that is an integral dimension of U.S. society. We define "pro-racist ideology" as a generalized belief that espouses and supports the superiority of Whites. This ideology reinforces the racial status quo whereby Whites are assumed to be more valuable than people of color. A pro-racist ideology also supports a system of opportunities and rewards that consistently privileges Whites, while oppressing and subjugating people of color.[1]

Support of a pro-racist ideology may manifest itself in comments or actions, but it can also be manifested through the tolerance of existing conditions that are inherently racist. Thus, when an individual tolerates a racist circumstance by not challenging it, her or his inaction unwittingly supports a pro-racist ideology. We believe that the more one challenges a pro-racist ideology, the more racially sensitive one is, and vice versa. We struggle with this phenomenon in our own lives. It seems that each day we encounter a comment or condition that appears to support a pro-racist ideology. As a result, we are faced continually with the dilemma of how to respond. It is exhausting and threatening to raise constant challenges to a pro-racist ideology. Because this type of vigilance can easily irritate and alienate others, such a stance is hard to maintain. One of the ways we remain focused on and committed to challenging a pro-racist ideology is by agreeing to hold one another accountable. In this way, our relationship provides a check-and-balance system that enables us to continue speaking out against manifestations of a pro-racist ideology, even when it seems easier or more expedient not to do so.

Another significant observation we have made is that many people are uncomfortable discussing race and racism. Their discomfort often results in the adherence to the myth that race is not important and that it is possible for one to be "color-blind." This myth seems to persist despite an abundance of evidence suggesting that virtually everyone sees color, and that our society is racially stratified in such a way as to favor Whites and disadvantage people of color.

We believe that one of the reasons it is difficult to acknowledge seeing color is the fear that it will automatically be equated with *discriminating* against another on the basis of color. Many people, Whites especially, live with the fear that they will be accused of being a racist. Because many of these same people believe themselves to be "good people" who are committed to racial justice, they find it difficult to acknowledge anything that might lead to the accusation that they are racist.

To circumvent the fear that is often associated with admitting that one sees color, we first emphasize that we do not assume that either seeing color or admitting that one sees color is the same as discriminating against someone on the basis of color. For example, in our relationship we often discuss our racial differences. Obviously, by doing so we are acknowledging that we see color. However, this acknowledgement has never been tantamount to either of us thinking about or treating each other in a derogatory or inequitable manner. We have been able to embrace our identities and explore our differences without attaching differential values to these.

Second, we draw a distinction between the terms "pro-racist ideology" and "racists." We prefer to refer to individuals as supporting a pro-racist ideology, rather than identifying them as racists. The term "racist" is a totalizing label that does not afford an individual the opportunity to be anything other than a racist. In contrast to this, stating that someone has acted in a way that supports a pro-racist ideology does not unalterably condemn the totality of that person's character. It leaves open the possibility that the individual can alter her or his behavior accordingly and thereby still be a "good person."

THE UNINTENTIONAL NATURE
OF PRO-RACIST IDEOLOGY

The notion that it is possible for individuals to say they believe in racial justice while acting in a way that supports a pro-racist ideology may seem contradictory. Yet we have found that an overwhelming number of pro-racist attitudes and actions are *unintentional*; that is, they occur outside the awareness of the perpetrator (Ridley, 1995). Therefore, it becomes possible to support racial justice verbally and ideologically, while being simultaneously unaware of the ways in which one's attitudes and behaviors perpetuate a pro-racist ideology. The following example shows how a well-intentioned school principal was able to commit a racial insensitivity and therefore support a pro-racist ideology without having any awareness of his actions.

A school had initiated a consultation with us because its personnel wished to address a number of racial inequalities that had been observed in the system. Although almost all of the teachers and staff members were White, the student population was 50% African American. During the many months that we worked with the school, the principal, who was White, demonstrated unrelenting support for all of the many difficult initiatives we had undertaken in our efforts to address racial inequalities and insensitivities throughout the school system. He undoubtedly was personally committed to promoting a racially tolerant and just climate in the school. Through our many interactions, we developed unwavering faith that he believed in the importance of eradicating racism. Moreover, it was clear that he worked hard in his interactions to act in a way, both personally and professionally, that supported his commitment. This brief background information provides an important context for understanding the events that transpired on the first day of the new school year during a school–parent orientation meeting.

During the orientation, the principal assumed his position at the microphone and began to talk with parents and teachers who were gathered. He spoke warmly about the school community and described how he saw it as an extended family. He then acknowledged that there were newcomers to "the family" whom he wished to identify so that they could be welcomed officially. He gradually worked his way around the room, pointing out new faces and extending welcoming words to new parents and teachers. Finally he acknowledged an individual who happened to be an African American male (one of the few in the room). He smiled at him warmly and then introduced him by saying, "This is one of our new parents, Mr. Adams. His son Tyler just started here in the first grade."

After a brief pause, a teacher jumped forward and said, "Oh, this isn't Tyler's dad. This is Mr. Johnson." Mr. Johnson, as it turned out, was a teacher's aide who had been working in the school for the past 4 months. There was a moment of tense quiet, and then the principal laughed nervously and said, "Oh, of course I know you, Mr. Johnson . . . yes, you are a great worker." At one level the principal's mistake did not appear to have anything at all to do with race, and yet on another level, it had everything to do with race.

In this example, the principal's behavior, albeit unintentional, lacked racial sensitivity and reinforced a pro-racist ideology. Confusing an African American staff person, after 4 months of service, with a new parent seemed to reflect the common stereotype that "all Black people look alike." The potential insult inherent in the situation was compounded by its irony. The principal had just finished talking about what a close-knit "family" the school was, and yet he was not able to differentiate between a staff member who had been a member of this "family" for 4 months and a new parent. Essentially, the staff person was invisible to the principal. He had no more awareness of him than he had of a virtual stranger. This invisibility was consistent with the devaluation and marginalization that Black people endure on a daily basis within a pro-racist society (Ellison, 1952; Franklin, 1993).

In the context of our own relationship, we have experienced the unintentional expression of a pro-racist ideology repeatedly. It is rare that we receive acknowledgment that our relationship is built on mutual trust, shared values, open communication, and a willingness to struggle with our differences. Instead, if is often judged according to old slavery-based narratives. During slavery the complex interaction between race and gender gave birth to a number of damaging stereotypes, some of which still persist today. One of the most common of these was that Black men regarded White women as idealized objects of beauty and status, while White women viewed Black men as brutish, mindless heathens who would revere and worship them blindly. This stereotype reduced the complexity of human experience to an absurd and grossly twisted depiction of Black men and White women. Both were objectified by this construction that merely served to reinforce the power and domination of White men over Black men, White women, and also Black women, who were no less marred by this construction.

The attributions and assumptions that cloud our relationship in the minds of others reveal the ways in which this slavery-based narrative festers in the unconscious and informs perceptions of reality outside most people's awareness. Those who make these racially based attributions do not usually perceive themselves as acting in a manner that is reinforcing a pro-racist ideology. Intentions aside, however, it appears that our relationship evokes a slavery-based narrative from some of our friends, colleagues, and onlookers. This construction denigrates the basis of our relationship and the complexity of our humanness, and it also serves to maintain White male supremacy.

As the targets of discrimination and prejudice, people of color incur the bulk of the burden of a pro-racist ideology. However, all individuals within society suffer from this ideology's inevitable erosion of the foundation that supports the establishment and maintenance of viable relationships. Such an ideology breeds hatred, mistrust, and callousness. It strips individuals and groups of the essentials of their humanity, and therefore compromises the health of all relationships at every level.

In family therapy, where the promotion of healthy relationships is central, the damaging effects of a pro-racist ideology are especially poignant. Relationships constitute the centerpiece of family therapy. Therapists must first establish effective relationships with their clients before therapy can occur. In addition, despite variations in style and theoretical framework, all family therapists strive to help their clients forge more healthy and meaningful relationships with each other. Unfortunately, however, when a pro-racist ideology remains unrecognized and/or unchallenged by therapists, it can infiltrate the therapeutic process in subtle but disruptive ways, thereby undermining the efficacy of the treatment process. The following example provides an illustration of this point.

The therapist, who was White, asked the client, who was African American, about her family of origin. During the conversation the therapist learned that the client had several younger siblings. Both she and her siblings were well educated and had established successful careers. The therapist responded to this information as follows: "Your parents must be very proud of you and your brothers and sisters, especially because I imagine it must have been difficult for a poor family to provide their children with all the resources and opportunities that supported your many accomplishments."

The therapist made several other comments while the client sat silently. After several minutes had passed, the client interrupted the therapist by stating, "I just have to comment on something that's bothering me. A few minutes ago, you made a statement about my family being poor while I was growing up. Why did you assume that? I never made any references to my family's economic situation. If I had, then I would have mentioned that we were financially well off."

On what basis did the therapist conclude that the client's family was poor while she was growing up? Is it possible that the therapist had unconsciously evoked the classic stereotype that all African American people are poor? More importantly, did the client believe that this was the explanation for the therapist's assumption?

The therapist in this example had good intentions. She was committed to racial justice and believed she was racially sensitive. However, her unconscious association between Blacks and poverty was an expression of pro-racist socialization that manifested itself outside her conscious awareness. Once she was confronted with her act of racial insensitivity, she was mortified and deeply embarrassed. She had never meant to offend or denigrate the client, and yet, despite her best intentions, she had committed an act of racial insensitivity.

In this particular case, the client commented on the offense; this made it possible for the therapist and client to engage in a racially candid discussion, and thereby to salvage their relationship. However, because of the defensiveness and criticism that racially candid comments tend to engender in mixed-race settings, many people of color learn early in life to censor such remarks while in the presence of White people. Therefore, although the client in this vignette risked confronting the therapist, it is more likely for clients in similar situations to remain silent.

Unfortunately, when acts of racial insensitivity remain unacknowledged in therapy, they tend to compromise the therapeutic relationship. If the therapist's act of racial insensitivity had remained unacknowledged, ultimately it would have sabotaged therapy. Moreover, since the racial dimensions of the case would have been outside of the therapist's awareness, she could easily have found a way to "blame" the client for being resistant, rather than recognizing the role she herself had played in undermining the relationship. This case highlights how the dynamics of a pro-racist ideology can infiltrate the therapeutic process.

Because of the toll that a pro-racist ideology takes upon relationships of all types, it represents a serious impediment to the treatment process—one that therapists must assume an active role in confronting and resisting. We have found that because many individuals are unaware of the existence and effects of a pro-racist ideology, the process of effectively challenging it is extremely difficult, both in and out of therapy. After all, one cannot actively resist a phenomenon to which one is oblivious.

Efforts to highlight the ways in which individuals may unwittingly support a pro-racist ideology often invite tremendous defensiveness and anxiety. Certainly this is understandable in light of the fact that such insight deeply challenges individuals' preferred views of themselves (Eron & Lund, 1996). Hence, when the external feedback persons receive about themselves contradicts their internal representation of themselves, a form of dissonance is created. This is especially poignant with regard to racial issues, because race is such a volatile topic in our society.

Helping individuals to begin to see and eventually resist the ways in which they may unintentionally support a pro-racist ideology is a painful and difficult process. If it is not pursued in a thoughtful and gentle manner, it can have the opposite effect. It can stifle those whose intentions and motivation would otherwise make them prime candidates for racial sensitivity. Furthermore, when the promotion of racial sensitivity is pursued too abruptly or harshly, it can generate levels of anxiety and defensiveness that can short-circuit the process of changing racial attitudes.

We live in a society where a pro-racist ideology is both pervasive and damaging. Unfortunately, many individuals are not consciously aware of this ideology and the ways in which it informs their lives. As a result, they are limited in their capacity to mount an effective resistance against it and its effects. As therapists who believe in the importance of promoting healthy and viable relationships between and among individuals and society, we are especially committed to the process of encouraging awareness of and active resistance against a pro-racist ideology.

STEPS TOWARD GREATER RACIAL SENSITIVITY: IMPLICATIONS FOR THERAPY

The following provides a map for how therapists can begin to enhance their racial sensitivity by learning how to defy a pro-racist ideology in their lives and therefore in therapy. Our approach challenges a traditional "cookbook approach" of teaching therapists the "1, 2, 3's" of how to be more racially sensitive in therapy. We do not believe there is a simple formula or a "knapsack" of techniques that one can employ. Rather, we envision this as a process that is rooted in how one lives on a daily basis. Because we believe that the line between therapy and everyday life is blurred, we find it impossible for therapists to separate who they are outside therapy from who they are inside therapy. Thus, the process of becoming racially sensitive begins with how each therapist lives his or her life. Once change occurs at this level, it is our belief that these changes will be manifested automatically within the therapy process.

Becoming Aware That Race Matters

Before one can commit to challenging a pro-racist ideology, it is necessary to acknowledge first that in this society, race matters. Despite the romantic myth that "race does not matter because we are all human," race remains a major marker of reality in all realms of society.

Recognizing the Existence of a Pro-Racist Ideology

After one acknowledges that society is organized around the concept of race, it then becomes necessary to recognize the ways in which the concept of race is used to structure vast and deeply entrenched inequalities between groups of people. Thus, the issue is not simply that people perceive racial differences, but that there exists an ideology that attaches differential values and rewards to these differences. As a result, all of us live in a society where a pro-racist ideology results in the privileging of Whites and the oppression of people of color. It is virtually impossible to become active in resisting a pro-racist ideology until one is capable of identifying and acknowledging its existence.

Enhancing Cross-Racial Experience

Once one understands that race is a central societal organizing principle, and that it shapes society through the lens of a pro-racist ideology, the next step toward racial sensitivity is increasing one's cross-racial exposure. It is only through consistent and direct contact with racially diverse people that one is challenged to learn more about oneself as a racial being—which is the next step.

Exploring One's Own Racial Identity

Interrogating oneself about one's racial identity is salient. Individuals need to ask themselves such questions as "What does it mean to be [whatever my racial identity is]?" and "What implications does this have for my relationships with others who are racially similar and different?" To take one of us (Tracey) as an example, part of examining my identity as a White person has meant facing the implications of my Whiteness, even when I do not intend such implications. An example that stands out for me occurred in a class when I challenged Sarah (an African American female) about a point she made regarding a particular family therapy theory. I expressed a lot of criticism, and she made it clear that she felt I was implying she was stupid. Eventually she acknowledged that our interaction had racial overtones for her. She was not free to interpret our interaction without considering that I was White and she was Black. She could never rule out the possibility that my criticism might have been informed by a pro-racist ideology whereby I had treated her disrespect-fully on the basis of race.

This incident was quite difficult for me, because I had to come to terms with the fact that two divergent realities were simultaneously true. On one hand, I knew in my heart that my criticism and my style of inter-action were not racially motivated. But on the other hand, from Sarah's perspective it *was* racial, and that reality was as true as my own. I had to find a way to embrace both truths. I had to be clear with myself about the basis for my interaction with Sarah. However, regardless of my intentions, I had to understand and take responsibility for the implications of my racial identity and behavior.

When therapists understand and can take responsibility for them-selves racially, this is an important therapeutic tool. Similarly, when therapists have limited knowledge of and access to themselves racially, we regard this as one of the greatest impediments to the delivery of effective therapy. The degree to which therapists understand themselves racially provides the foundation for taking the next difficult step of confronting the ways in which they may collude with a pro-racist ideology.

Challenging Pro-Racist Ideology First in Oneself and Then in Others

All individuals are socialized in a pro-racist society; therefore, to some degree, we all internalize some pieces of this ideology. As a result, the question is not "Do I manifest a pro-racist ideology?," but rather "*How* do I manifest a pro-racist ideology?" A common misconception is that it is only White people who can support a pro-racist ideology. All people are socialized in a society that espouses this ideology, and thus all people are vulnerable to absorbing and reflecting its principles. For instance, it is not only White people who have colluded with a pro-racist ideology by reducing our own relationship to slavery-based stereotypes.

In addition, one of us (Ken) has had to confront the ways in which a pro-racist ideology has made it difficult for me to accept other people of color who are not as racially conscious as I wish they were. As a result, I often want to disconnect from and punish them out of my frustration. But in my better moments, I realize that doing so would only reinforce the system I am committed to changing. Therefore, rather than rejecting or lashing out against those with whom I struggle, first I confront myself and try to understand the source of my frustration. With time I come to recognize that we are struggling in different ways with the same demons. This insight enables me to reach out and use myself as a basis for connecting with and eventually challenging those with whom I struggle. This illustrates that only through taking the initiative to confront ourselves first will we be appropriately positioned to begin challenging others in a similar way.

Persisting in Spite of Criticism or Rejection

Challenging a pro-racist ideology can be difficult because of the volatility associated with the subject of race. Moreover, such challenges often generate discomfort in others, who may not have come to terms with the existence of a pro-racist ideology and/or with the role they in perpetuating it. However, for those who have been diligent about exploring their racial identity and probing their relationship with a pro-racist ideology, it is possible to retain the clarity of vision and inner emotional resolve to persist in spite of others' reactivity and criticism.

CONCLUSION

In this chapter, we have discussed how a pro-racist ideology can be sustained through seemingly benign and unintentional actions (or inactions). We have also endeavored to illuminate the connection that exists between how one lives one's life on a daily basis and what occurs in therapy. Our hope is that all of us therapists will better appreciate the ways in which even the best-intentioned among us can unintentionally support a pro-racist ideology. Therefore, all of us need to undertake the difficult and sometimes painful task of confronting a pro-racist ideology in ourselves and in each other, whatever our racial identity, both within and outside of therapy. Only through this deliberate and consistent process can we begin to chisel away at the racial barriers that keep us divided.

NOTE

1. hooks (1989) uses the term "White supremacy" in a similar way.

REFERENCES

Ellison, R. (1952). *Invisible man.* New York: Random House.

Eron, J. B., & Lund, T. W. (1996). The 1990s: An emphasis on meaning. In J. B. Eron & T. W. Lund (Eds.), *Narrative solutions in brief therapy* (pp. 30–38). New York: Guilford Press.

Franklin, A. J. (1993). The invisibility syndrome. *Family Therapy Networker, 17*(4), 32–39.

hooks, b. (1989). *Talking back: Thinking feminist, thinking Black.* Boston: South End Press.

Ridley, C. R. (19950. *Overcoming intentional racism in counseling and therapy.* London: Sage.

CHAPTER 10

The Talking Oppression Blues

INCLUDING THE EXPERIENCE OF POWER/POWERLESSNESS IN THE TEACHING OF "CULTURAL SENSITIVITY"

N. Norma Akamatsu

This chapter focuses on a fundamental problem in the teaching of clinical practice across race and cultural difference: how to develop greater attunement to and facility in talking about power and the experience of inequality, especially among those in positions of privilege.[1] As I have listened to people of color and White people talking together about race, ethnicity, and culture, the conversation frequently diverges around the phenomenon of power (hooks, 1995; Pinderhughes, 1989; Sue & Sue, 1990).[2] Power differences are less apparent to the privileged, who can more readily accept a view of American society as classless and color-blind—the myth of "the level playing field." Such a view, however, ignores the unrelenting experience of inferior status, economic discrimination, marginalization, and injustice that many people of color and other oppressed groups encounter. The resulting social disparities can become brutally salient to some, while remaining veiled to those who are protected. The depth and breadth of this split in experience are captured in the title of one study on race relations: *Two Nations: Black and White, Separate, Hostile, Unequal* (Hacker, 1992).

When power differences are not addressed, the "two nations" remain irreparably disconnected. This was apparent in one project, for example, as a painful contrast emerged between White and Black college students.[3] In discussing stereotypes, a White woman argued energetically against "putting people into categories," insisting, "I want to be judged as an individual, not as a part of any group—which is exactly the way I relate to all other people, too!" Her friend told the story of two preschoolers, Black and White, examining their skin tones. The White child affirmed, "You know, we're the same on the inside." The extent to which such idealism falls flat for people of color—the privilege inherent in assuming that one can choose not to be racially categorized or can claim their common humanity—was not apparent until Black students responded. A young man used these measured words:

> If we're not born racist, what happens along the way? The real question is—does their *teacher* think those children are the same inside? I'm glad these White people say they are not prejudiced, but they're not running the government, and stereotypes are not the problem. It's when you have the ability to restrict me because of your prejudice. It all comes down to power.

Phrases like "multiculturalism" and "cultural difference" often obscure the linking of "different" and "less" in our society. This inattention to the experience of inequality can nullify attempts at "cultural sensitivity." "Not having to notice" is a privilege and noticing, not surprisingly, arouses much anxiety and defensiveness.

McGoldrick's (1994) account of the halting expansion of her own awareness is a candid illustration of the varying ability to perceive power, depending on one's own position:

> Over the years, I have been mystified by the reactivity of men to [feminist] issues. . . . Longtime male colleagues came up to me and said, " . . . Why are you so angry at men? Did you hate your father? . . . I'm not sexist. I've never mistreated a woman, so why are you blaming me for all this? Why are you saying we have the power? I feel quite powerless. We men have problems too, you know. After all, we're not allowed to feel." (p. 42)

> Within the past few years, I began to be confronted with race and racism and now it was "I" who was on the other side of the power imbalance. Suddenly, I wanted to say to others the same things men had been saying to me: "Why are you so angry? . . . I have nothing to do with racism, slavery or segregation. I've never mistreated a person of color. I would love to change things, but I don't have the power, either. White people have experienced oppression, too—let me tell you about it." (p. 42)

Romney (in Romney, Tatum, & Jones, 1992), from her vantage point as an African American professor, writes:

... I am always struggling as a teacher who is a member of a targeted racial group to understand the experiences of whites when they confront their own racism. In the last Psychology of Oppression class I taught, I shared ... that I could not fully understand why white students found it so upsetting to be called a racist. I explained that from an African-American perspective my thinking is that, of course, white people are racist. Racism is embodied in the culture.... Both I and the students of color in class began to understand that the term racism evokes for many whites an all-or-nothing feeling. ... (p. 103)

A biracial team of anti-bias educators (Ayvazian & Tatum, 1996) summarizes the situation:

Many people of color understand the power differential inherent in the three manifestations of racism: personal, cultural, and institutional. They view racism not as an individual issue but as a systemic problem. However, many white people still characterize racism as a virulent form of individual prejudice—they reduce the problem to ... "individual acts of meanness." They are unschooled in the systematic ways that racism has been institutionalized and are oblivious to the reality of privilege given automatically and invisibly to white people every single day. (p. 18)

"RACISM 101": FIRST LESSONS

Because of the embeddedness of racism in our society, White skin privilege is a camouflage for those who are not targeted. Not perceiving themselves as unknowing, they may never think, or may feel vaguely reluctant, to ask for information. In teaching, my colleague and I have found it most useful to begin with specific content describing how "invisible" power discrepancies operate.

Differentiating personal, institutional, and cultural racism is a crucial starting point. In our course, these distinctions are explained and clarified in the first class to prepare for that day's assignment: Students are sent in pairs to roam the surrounding New England town to compile a list of 20 examples of cultural racism, defined as "any message or image prevalent in society that promotes the false but constant idea that White is the standard, ideal, normal." Computer ads, monuments, magazine covers, greeting cards, museum portraits, cosmetics, baby products, and children's toys that only portray White people are frequently cited. The subtext of "White is intelligent, White is heroic, White is successful, White is beautiful, White is hygienic, White is cute" is boldly highlighted. Like a rap on the head from a Zen master, this exercise awakens White students to the pervasive ordinariness of a now-blatant cultural racism.

Basic information about systematic forms of contemporary racism, more subtle than the legal segregation of the past, is also presented at the outset. Some examples are discriminatory banking and real estate practices, or the corporate "glass ceilings" that limit promotion of peoples of color. Racism in educational systems and the considerable impact of attitudinal differences are also noted. Citing research that shows relatively depressed levels of achievement among African American students (including middle-class youngsters), the psychologist Claude Steele (1992) hypothesizes a process of disidentification from educational institutions. He attributes this to the power of negative expectations, an impact long considered in our field:

> Terms like "prejudice" and "racism" often miss the full scope of racial devaluation in our society. . . . in all of us, not just in the strongly prejudiced . . . even in blacks themselves. . . . Sooner or later it forces on its victims [the] painful realization . . . that society is preconditioned to see the worst in them. (pp. 72–74)

Finally, we invite students to use the Multicultural Organizational Assessment Inventory (Jackson & Holvino, 1988), which outlines differing types of organizational response to racism, to examine work contexts. The impact of exclusionary organizations (e.g., the Ku Klux Klan or country clubs) pales in comparison to the far-reaching effects of organizations with an attitude of passive compliance: "We meet all equal-opportunity criteria. Our doors are open, but 'they' don't apply!" The need for active restructuring and systemic change goes unrecognized. As an African American diversity trainer succinctly observes, "I'm less afraid of the men in white sheets than the men in blue suits" (Kenneth Jones, personal communication, June 1996).

RACISM AS DOMINANT DISCOURSE

Many White students begin to experience an uneasy puzzlement over their previous inability to notice these immense and pervasive systems of inequity. The framework of "dominant discourses," used by narrative therapists (e.g., Hare-Mustin, 1994; White & Epston, 1990; White, 1993), provides a theoretical perspective that makes sense of their predicament. Based on social constructionist principles, this perspective questions what we ordinarily regard as "neutral," "objective," or "common-sense" and reaches for the underlying values embedded within cultural norms. This analysis redirects our attention to the specific historical, social, economic, and political contexts that shape (and are in turn supported by) culturally approved beliefs. The subtle endorsement of particular arrangements of privilege and power is an especially important implication. For example, a Latino family therapist complained about a national family therapy conference brochure. The series of photographs of featured clinicians included only White people. This was met by the shocked dismay of a White colleague, who realized she hadn't even noticed the omission of people of color. The biases embedded within the dominant discourse are hidden by their very ordinariness, and this sense of "normality" functions to preclude questioning (White, 1993). "You first have to realize you're blind before you can try to see" (M. Pakman, personal communication, June 1995).

Previously applied to the problem of sexism (e.g., Weingarten, 1995), the construct of dominant discourses can be extended to the phenomenon of racism to investigate how unrecognized cultural assumptions inevitably envelop our clinical theory and practice. Deconstructive inquiry, a critical scrutiny of our own "taken-for-granted realities and practices" (White, 1993, p. 34), draws attention both to the shaping influence of larger social contexts and to the underlying values and biases that are enacted in therapy. The pedagogical efforts that accompany such an inquiry attempt to create a wedge of awareness that can help students "stand outside" their accustomed views.

PUTTING THE WORLD BACK INTO THERAPY

A family therapist once proudly described her approach to a racially and ethnically diverse caseload: "I treat them all the same." Much of our theory has shared this bias, which universalizes the experience and social context of the White middle class. By contrast, a social constructionist perspective reiterates the fundamental and long-standing position taken by many family therapists, especially those who have worked with oppressed populations, the absolute necessity of taking into account, and including in the therapeutic conversation, the impact of larger systems (see, e.g., Auerswald, 1968; Boyd-Franklin, 1989; Crawford, 1988; Goldner, 1985; Waldegrave, 1990). We ask students to consider the "mental health" implications of contingencies such as these:

- What if a family runs out of money for food by the third week of the month?
- What if a lesbian couple is raising a 14-year-old son in middle America?
- What if in one heterosexual couple, the man earns $65,000 and the woman earns $17,000?

- What if in another, the woman has a civil service position and the man can no longer find a job in the manufacturing industries that used to employ him?
- What if a 17-year-old Latino has no viable strategy for ever earning more than $12,000 a year?
- What if a 9-year-old is the only African American girl in her elementary school?

We then consider the implications of locating the effects of these problems *within* people, rather than taking broader social problems into account.[4]

WHITE IS HEALTHY: EUROCENTRIC THEORY

One student's list of cultural racism examples included these entries: "Band-Aids, Barbies, our theories" and was used to inaugurate a renewed appraisal of theory. Although initially very difficult for students to perceive, cultural biases are gradually discerned. Students make a start by recalling feminist critiques of psychological theory, with which they are usually more familiar, transposing from gender bias to cultural bias. Foucault's insight (cited by White & Epston, 1990) that power relations are embedded in and maintained by bodies of knowledge forms the basis of the critique. This analysis casts a more menacing light on clinical theory, and stimulates a renewed analysis of the political impact of ideas. In this way, the implicit endorsement of Eurocentric communicational styles, ways of handling emotion, and nonverbal behaviors, as well as the Eurocentric focus on the individual and on heterosexual, two-parent family structures, becomes apparent. (For fuller accounts of such bias, see other chapters of this book; Falicov, 1995; and Hardy & Laszloffy, 1994.)

Awareness of the Eurocentric tendency toward "you-have-ethnicity-and-I-don't" attitudes (M. White, personal communication, July 1994) also promotes a more critical perspective on ethnic differences (McGoldrick, Giordano, & Pearce, 1996). A deconstructive inquiry can move beyond a one-sided description of "them" and toward a recursive dialogue, in which students' own cultural and professional assumptions are also called into self-awareness and questioned.

Students are encouraged to become "transparent" (White, 1993)— that is, to make explicit how their clinical ideas and practices are linked to particular, meaningful personal experiences, values, or cultural contexts. They can invite their clients to do the same. For example, these questions can be used to engage immigrant mothers and their daughters in a conjoint deconstruction of their differing cultural premises about gender role (Akamatsu, 1995):

- What is the traditional role for women in your culture, as you understood that in your particular family?
- What was the impact of immigration or living in the United States on the traditional role?
- What aspects of the traditional role have the women in your family followed and what have they not followed, based on what experiences?
- Do you see yourself as similar to or different from your daughter/mother in this regard?

LOCAL KNOWLEDGE

The deeply entrenched tendency to ignore, disqualify, or pathologize the experience of targeted peoples requires our energetic attention and ingenuity to redress.[5] Various opportunities for recognizing local, "nonexpert" ways of knowing and problem solving can be considered—for example, the structural family therapy technique termed the "search for strengths." More specifically, acts of resistance can be identified and validated; the resilience required to manage oppression can be acknowledged; and the ethical implications of this struggle can be identified ("What does your tenacity say about what you are really committed to in your life?") (see Walsh, Chapter 5, and Hines, Chapter 6, this volume; White, 1993).

Therapists and teams can transform themselves into what L. Hoffman (personal communication, 1995) calls an "honoring community"—one that bears witness both to the painful realities of clients' oppressive situations and to the strengths that clients show, including the adaptive value of behavior that might easily be labeled "problematic" if the demands or influence of the social context are ignored.

Ayvazian and Tatum's (1996) "radical prescription" for developing more understanding about the experience of oppression is quite straightforward: "Listen and believe" (p. 18). They continue:

> Whites need to listen to the stories and struggles of people of color in their own or surrounding communities. Not judge, debate, defend, solve, or critique—but listen. Through the simple act of listening, the subtle and pervasive nature of "neoracism" . . . may become evident.

> However, listening itself will not reach hearts or change minds unless white people are encouraged to take another step that contradicts countless messages from their growing years, that is: to believe people of color. (p. 18)

Students or faculty members of color can offer their personal experience or critical feedback as a way to expand others' sensitivity to an unfamiliar existential territory. However, a recurring problem is that the burden of teaching is habitually placed on the oppressed; this often exacerbates the lack of initiative taken by those in power. Furthermore, discussing the impact of a subjugated status with people in a position of dominance is an inherently distressing step that renders a person immensely vulnerable. A student of color protested to us, "I am tired of being 'The Experience' for White students." Ayvazian and Tatum (1996) emphasize that people of color must feel such activities benefit *them,* and that clear guidelines and structures must be developed to safeguard the conversations. In the absence of such direct reports, there are many useful books, films, and videos that relate quite powerfully the experiences of oppressed people.[6]

There are other important reasons why it may be better to postpone face-to-face dialogue until after some work is done independently by each group. Those in the targeted group may simply wish to have the freedom to focus on their own needs and agendas first. For those in the dominant group, apprehending their own privilege—the benefits automatically bestowed, embraced, and relied upon—can be an identity-shifting awakening. It has been aptly labeled a "disintegration experience" (Helms, 1990), more complicated in racially combined groups, and often greatly discomforting for people of color to witness.

STANDING OUTSIDE ONESELF

Self-reflexiveness can be encouraged in those in a position of dominance, even in the absence of such dialogue. Taking the role of "emissaries," they can attempt to listen through the lens of a particular oppressed group for the relevance of theory and appropriateness of practice. Such a re-visioning has proved invaluable, for example, in discussing "family life cycle," frameworks which tend to institutionalize the "Ozzie and Harriet" ideal. The family experiences of gay men and lesbians, people of color, various ethnic groups, single parents, and childless couples have gained more prominence through the use of this device. Another very important aspect of this reflexivity is considering how members of dominant groups may themselves be perceived—"imagining others imagining you."[7] This is an exercise in subject–object reversals, in which seeing the "self" as "other" may facilitate seeing the "other" as "self." This imagining also tends to expose more of the "invisible" mantle of privilege. Some of the questions raised are:

- Considering specifically how you look, talk, dress, and so on, what stereotypes do you think people of color might hold about you?
- How might clients of color experience a predominantly White agency?
- How might social workers of color feel in these contexts?
- What might be useful in a dialogue between a White social worker and a client of color? That is, what do you imagine needs to be heard/experienced by this client in order to break the stereotypes?[8]

"MULTIPLEXITY"

In the process of teaching, these ideas and discussions help White students develop more awareness and knowledge. But managing their guilt or defensiveness about the advantages they enjoy involves articulation of other social constructionist principles, most basically the notion of multiple social identities. Falicov (1995) uses the term "ecological niche" to refer to the highly particular "combination of multiple contexts and partial cultural locations" an individual or family may occupy, "where views and values are shaped and where power or powerlessness are experienced" (pp. 376–377).

Theories of racial identity development for Whites and people of color (e.g., Helms, 1990; Tatum, 1992) are helpful, highlighting the relativity and context-dependent nature of our experience of our own race. Inevitable collisions can be analyzed and demystified, such as the mismatch between a student of color invested in networking with other people of color and a White student anxious to initiate cross-race connections.

One of the most important implications of our multiple social identities is the "multiplexity"[9]—that we may be disadvantaged in some contexts, yet privileged in others.

> In each form of oppression, there is a dominant group (the one that receives the unearned advantage, benefit, or privilege) and a targeted group (that is denied . . .). We know the litany of dominants: white people, males, Christians, heterosexuals, able-bodied people, those in their middle years and those who are middle or upper class. . . .

> We also know that everyone has multiple social identities—we are all dominant and targeted simultaneously. I am, in the very same moment, dominant as a white person and targeted as a woman. (Ayvazian, 1995, p. 17)

However, the underlying duality—the coexistence of one's own privileged and targeted positions—is not easy to apprehend emotionally. It requires a more complex view of identity, in which contradictory experiences of advantage and disadvantage form ragged layers. This demands a particular sort of "both–and" holding that relies on the ability to "contain opposites."

> The [both–and] metaphor embodies an intellectual, political and psychological ideal: the attempt to recognize the value of competing and contradictory perspectives and to tolerate the psychological experience of extreme ambivalence without splitting ideas and people into good and bad. (Goldner, 1992, pp. 56–57)

Foucault's perception (cited by White & Epston, 1990) that dominant discourses constrain both privileged and targeted groups can facilitate this understanding. I have reminded White students that they did *not,* upon turning age 21, march into City Hall and ask to sign up for "White skin privilege" to gain access to benefits systematically at the lifelong expense of people of color. This defines cultural racism as colonizing the minds of both people of color and Whites, who are inducted into their respective albeit vastly different positions.

LIVED EXPERIENCE

I have found that one of the most useful ways to approach the complicated issue of multiple social identities is through telling my personal story as a third-generation Japanese American. I have likened my growing-up experience to a checkerboard of disadvantage and privilege. Like a character in a Victorian novel, I was catapulted from "pauper" to "prince." I was one of the poorest kids, and one of the very few children of color, in an elementary school of predominantly well-to-do White children. From there, I went on to Booker T. Washington, Public Junior High School 54, where I was conspicuously advantaged as one of the most economically secure youngsters in a predominantly Black and Puerto Rican student body, with a high proportion of families supported by welfare. I first developed consciousness of race amid the still lingering anti-Japanese stereotypes of World War II; I came into adulthood during the Vietnam War years of "gooks" and "dinks"; and, in between, I was identified as a member of a "model minority." I tell the story of a road trip to the South in 1957, in which my then 11-year-old brother needed to make an emergency bathroom stop. My father pulled up to a roadside diner, where Johnny raced to the restrooms in the back, only to come careening out front to the car again: "The bathrooms have signs. One says 'White.' The other says 'Colored.' Where am I supposed to go?" And without skipping a beat, my mother told him firmly: "White. White. You go to the White bathroom."

This anecdote has come to symbolize my sense of participation in privilege. When I imagine how other people of color (people of other colors) might look at me, I would guess that despite its hazards, the social access conceded to Asians in this society is perceived as a "relative privilege."[10] Acknowledging the advantages that I can recognize in my life has eased my conversations with people of other targeted groups. A student pointed out, very importantly, how this acknowledgment simultaneously recognizes another's oppression and becomes an important form of validation.

THE PROBLEM OF COMPETING "-ISMS"

As political and economic forces increasingly threaten to divide and conquer some of us more than others, our connections become vital and tenuous. Our sense of oppression is a double-edged sword. The marginalization we have experienced, when unacknowledged, can polarize and divide us. Given a dominant discourse of "equality," these experiences are typically suppressed, so that we are all starved for validation. But the need for acknowledgment of the particular injustices we have endured can drive us into a symmetrical, mutually isolating competition to be heard. At the same time, these experiences, although different and unique, can provide a basis for coalition and a connecting arc/ark of mutual recognition when they are told, heard, and believed. Over time, collectively, we will have to learn to balance our need for validation with acknowledgment of our privilege and a readiness to validate another's suffering. A defensive holding on to our sense of disadvantage is likely to be experienced as denial of another's oppression. Ironically, we may only be released from our defensive posture by another's acknowledgment of our pain.

For their final assignment in our course, students are asked to inventory the dominant and targeted positions they occupy (in relation to racism, sexism, classism, heterosexism, anti-Semitism, abilism, and ageism), and to write something about "what personal experiences have brought the issue of racism to life for you." This formalizes an ongoing process, apparent in their journals, of connecting with the emotional truth of racial oppression through their own experiences of marginalization (of feeling "less than" or blocked by powerful social forces)—as women, members of the working class, lesbians, Jews, differently abled persons, and/or survivors of familial abuse.[11] The "both–and" process of journal-writing about these or other more idiosyncratic experiences, while increasing the awareness of privilege, is pivotal in the educational process. This exercise also addresses the confusion of those who enjoy a broad array of advantages. A heterosexual White male student noted his "triple dominance" with abashment, anxious that he had no basis for claiming an emotional connection to the experience of disadvantage. However, even as he developed an accounting of his privilege, he was able to identify areas of private suffering that constituted a personally meaningful basis for empathy, as well as those important in developing his commitment as a White anti-racist activist. Acknowledgment in the form of detailed and attentive written responses by both coteachers, who constituted a small "honoring community" for the students, further supported this development.

CONCLUSION

Some months after completing our class on racism, a student's letter was published in her local newspaper, registering her distress at the mistaken arrest of an African American woman on shoplifting charges:

> There's no way around it. If you grew up in this country you absorbed negative information about anyone who was not white. You were also fed negative information about anyone who was gay, lesbian, bisexual, overweight, old, with a physical or mental challenge, poor, or even female. No this is not your fault. You didn't ask to be born into this. But you were. If you're white, you might feel racism affects you, and it does; psychologically, spiritually, emotionally . . . but it's not the same as the daily grinding experience for people of color, who are systematically oppressed.
>
> The responsibility to dismantle racism and every other "-ism" belongs to each and every one of us.
>
> Passionately,
> Anna Gailitis

As practitioners/teachers who occupy positions of privilege and who choose to confront racism, we must stand ready to initiate dialogue about power and to demonstrate that we possess the "ears" that can hear these concerns. As we continue to learn more and talk together more openly about the lived experiences of privilege and oppression, teaching situations and the practice of therapy offer possible new sites of awakening, resistance, coalition, and connection.

NOTES

1. This discussion is oriented to the teaching of White students, with whom I have shared a unique learning experience. To educate myself more, I began coteaching a required racism course at the Smith College School for Social Work in 1995. Due to a student initiative to permit students of color to be grouped together, my sections have consisted exclusively of White students. I developed the "clinical applications" portion of a course designed by my coteacher, Andrea Ayvazian, PhD, whom I wish to acknowledge and thank for her inestimable contribution to the work discussed here.

2. Lee Mun Wah's documentary, *The Color of Fear* (1994), about an interracial dialogue among eight men, is a vivid and trenchant demonstration of this problem .

3. These perspectives were voiced by African American, Jewish, and White non-Jewish students as part of a project on "Black/Jewish/Other" Relations, organized by the Office of Human Relations, University of Massachusetts–Amherst, in 1995. A conversation was constructed through the exchange of videotaped discussions among homogeneous groups.

4. These questions were suggested by the work of Carter (1988), Crawford (1988), Waldegrave (1990), and White and Epston (1990).

5. We have used M. White's (personal communication, 1994) "Conscious Purpose and Commitment Exercise," which provides students with a direct experience of the contrast between a pathologizing description and a deconstructive inquiry. In this exercise, negative ascriptions about their choice of profession are recalled and then a brief history of actual experiences and ethical decisions is elicited that is acknowledging of the values and personal meaning inherent in the choice of a profession.

6. The video *True Colors* (Lukasiewicz & Harvey, 1991) is one example. A White and an African-American man posed as new arrivals to a Midwestern city and were secretly videotaped while searching for jobs, flagging taxis, hunting for apartments, shopping for cars, and so on. The chasm separating the "two nations" is conveyed with stunning immediacy by the literally split-screen portrayal of their unequal experiences, offering a unique basis for comparison and double description.

7. E. H. Auerswald introduced me to this approach in his design for a cross-cultural dialogue process among ethnically diverse high school students, which I facilitated in Hawaii in 1976. His idea of exchanging videotaped discussions among homogeneous groups was replicated in my later work with college students at the University of Massachusetts–Amherst.

8. A telling piece of feedback was student concern that these efforts would not be supported in the workplace. At the close of our 5-week course, students

felt they were now significantly more cognizant of the impact of racism than most supervisors they would encounter.

9. Cornel West's phrase, employed during a dialogue on Black–Jewish relations with Michael Lerner, October 1995, Mount Holyoke College, South Hadley, MA.

10. This is not intended to discount the reality of anti-Asian discriminatory attitudes. Chang (1995), for example, points out how the "model minority myth . . . renders the oppression of Asian Americans invisible" (p. 328).

11. Grillo and Wildman (1995) note the danger of presuming to understand one sort of oppression through personal experience with another. However, there is a subtle but significant difference between an uncritical substitution and the coming to life of another's experience through reference to one's own.

REFERENCES

Akamatsu, N. (1995). The defiant daughter and compliant mother: Multicultural dialogues on woman's role. *In Session: Psychotherapy in Practice, 1,* 43–55.

Auerswald, E. H. (1968). Interdisciplinary versus ecological approach. *Family Process, 7,* 202–215.

Ayvazian, A. (1995). Interrupting the cycle of oppression: The role of allies as agents of change. *Smith College School for Social Work Journal, 13,* 17–20.

Ayvazian, A., & Tatum, B. (1996, January–February). Can we talk? *Sojourners,* pp. 16–19.

Boyd-Franklin, N. (1989). *Black families in therapy: A multisystems approach.* New York: Guilford Press.

Carter, B. (1988). The person who has the gold makes the rules. In M. Walters, B. Carter, P. Papp, & O. Silverstein, *The invisible web: Gender patterns in family relationships.* New York: Guilford Press.

Chang, R. (1995). Toward an Asian American legal scholarship. In R. Delgado (Ed.), *Critical race theory: The cutting edge.* Philadelphia: Temple University Press.

Crawford, S. (1988). Cultural context as a factor in the expansion of therapeutic conversation with lesbian families. *Journal of Strategic and Systemic Therapies, 7*(3), 2–10.

Falicov, C. (1995). Training to think culturally: A multidimensional comparative framework. *Family Process, 34*(4), 373–388.

Goldner, V. (1985). Feminism and family therapy. *Family Process, 24,* 31–47.

Goldner, V. (1992). Making room for both–and. *Family Therapy Networker, 16*(2), 54–61.

Grillo, T., & Wildman, S. (1995). Obscuring the importance of race: The implication of making comparisons between racism and sexism (or other -isms). In R. Delgado (Ed.), *Critical race theory: The cutting edge.* Philadelphia: Temple University Press.

Hacker, A. (1992). *Two nations: Black and White, separate, hostile, unequal.* New York: Scribner.

Hardy, K., & Laszloffy, T. (1994). Deconstructing race in family therapy. In R. Almeida (Ed.), *Expansions of feminist family theory through diversity.* Binghamton, NY: Haworth Press.

Hare-Mustin, R. (1994). Discourses in the mirrored room: A postmodern analysis of therapy. *Family Process, 33*(1), 19–35.

Helms, J. (Ed.). (1990). *Black and White racial identity: Theory, research and practice.* Westport, CT: Greenwood Press.

hooks, b. (1995). *Killing rage/ending racism.* New York: Holt.

Jackson, B., & Holvino, E. (1988, April). Developing multicultural organizations. *Journal of Applied Behavioral Science and Religion,* pp. 14–19.

Lukasiewicz, M., & Harvey, E. (Producers). (1991). *True colors* [Video]. (Available from MTI/Film & Video, 420 Academy Dr., Northbrook, IL 60062)

McGoldrick, M. (1994). The ache for home. *Family Therapy Networker, 18*(4), 38–45.

McGoldrick, M., Giordano, J., & Pearce, J. (Eds.). (1996). *Ethnicity and family therapy* (2nd ed.). New York: Guilford Press.

Lee Mun Wah. (Producer). (1994). *The color of fear* [Video]. (Available from Stir Fry Productions, 470 Third St., Oakland, CA 94607)

Pinderhughes, E. (1989). *Understanding race, ethnicity and power: The key to efficacy in clinical practice.* New York: Free Press.

Romney, P., Tatum, B., & Jones, J. (1992). Feminist strategies for teaching about oppression: The importance of process. *Women's Studies Quarterly, 20,* 95–110.

Steele, C. (1992, April). Race and the schooling of Black Americans. *Atlantic Monthly,* pp. 68–78.

Sue, D. W., & Sue, D. (1990). *Counseling the culturally different: Theory and practice.* New York: Wiley.

Tatum, B. (1992). Talking about race, learning about racism: The application of racial identity development theory in the classroom. *Harvard Educational Review, 62*(1), 1–23.

Waldegrave, C. (1990). Just therapy. Social justice in family therapy. *Dulwich Centre Newsletter,* No. 1, 21–27.

Weingarten, K. (1995). Radical listening: Challenging cultural beliefs for and about mothers. *Journal of Feminist Family Therapy, 7*(1–2), 7–22.

White, M. (1993). Deconstruction and therapy. In S. Gilligan & R. Price (Eds.), *Therapeutic conversations.* New York: Norton.

White, M., & Epston, D. (1990). *Narrative means to therapeutic ends.* New York: Norton.

PART III

WHAT IT MEANS TO BE WHITE

Typically, discussions of culture and racism focus on the marginalized group as the "other." Re-visioning our field will require that we explore instead those who see themselves as the norm or who have established the norms. The chapters included in this section are attempts to deconstruct the dominant group. We have reprinted the late Horace Miner's classic spoof on the "Nacirema," an ethnographic study of "American" spelled backward, which makes fun of our cultural customs and turns the cultural lens of who is "other" upside down. This sort of turning the tables on the dominant versions of our stories seems particularly appropriate for the new vision we require. We often need to stand on our heads, flipping things upside down, in order to notice the most obvious facts. We have also included Peggy McIntosh's classic challenge to our "invisible knapsack" of White privilege, part of her series of articles that have helped us to begin re-visioning race as well as gender in the field of education. Ken Dolan-Del Vecchio has offered a critique of White male dominance—our effort to consider what must change so that White men can be collaborative partners with everyone else in families and communities in the 21st century.

"Whiteness" is a political descriptor of those who have unearned privilege in relation to others in the society. It is a characterization that exists because racism exists. Unfortunately, Whiteness is also something that defines and characterizes the practice of our profession. We cannot continue to train White therapists to work primarily with White families. Most family therapy training gives minimal lip service to cultural issues. Probably not even 5% of the faculty of most family therapy training programs and courses are people of color, and fewer than 10% of family therapists and psychologists are. Yet 25% of the U.S. population, and a much higher percentage of the families in need of psychological help, are ethnic minorities. As Hall and Greene (1994) have pointed out in their call for training in cultural competence as an ethical mandate of our times,

> The mental health professions [are] representative of the cultural norms and values of the dominant culture. Both African American and white therapists have been trained in institutions representative of the dominant culture's values, which for the most part embrace and support rather than explore or challenge the status quo. (pp. 24–25)

With its focus on deconstructing Whiteness, challenging White privilege, and working toward collaboration, Part III highlights a significant facet in the transformation of family therapy.

REFERENCE

Hall, R. L., & Greene, B. (1994). Cultural competence in feminist family therapy: An ethical mandate. *Journal of Feminist Family Therapy, 6*(3), 5–28.

CHAPTER 11

White Privilege: Unpacking the Invisible Knapsack

Peggy McIntosh

Through work to bring materials from Women's Studies into the rest of the curriculum, I have often noticed men's unwillingness to grant that they are over-privileged, even though they may grant that women are disadvantaged. They may say they will work to improve women's status, in the society, the university, or the curriculum, but they can't or won't support the idea of lessening men's. Denials which amount to taboos surround the subject of advantages which men gain from women's disadvantages. These denials protect male privilege from being fully acknowledged, lessened or ended.

Thinking through unacknowledged male privilege as a phenomenon, I realized that since hierarchies in our society are interlocking, there was most likely a phenomenon of white privilege which was similarly denied and protected. As a white person, I realized I had been taught about

Peggy McIntosh is Associate Director of the Wellesley College Center for Research on Women. This chapter (which appeared as an essay in *Peace and Freedom*, July/August 1989, pp. 10–12) is excerpted from her working paper (Center Working Paper No. 189), "White Privilege and Male Privilege: A Personal Account of Coming to See Correspondences through Work in Women's Studies," copyright © 1988 by Peggy McIntosh. The working paper contains a longer list of privileges and is available for $6.00 from the author. Neither paper may be duplicated without permission of the author: Peggy McIntosh, Wellesley College Center for Research on Women, Wellesley, MA 02181; (781) 283-2500. No excerpting is permitted. Proceeds from the duplication of either paper support the National SEED (Seeking Educational Equity and Diversity) Project on Inclusive Curriculum.

racism as something which puts others at a disadvantage, but had been taught not to see one of its corollary aspects, white privilege, which puts me at an advantage.

I think whites are carefully taught not to recognize white privilege, as males are taught not to recognize male privilege. So I have begun in an untutored way to ask what it is like to have white privilege. I have come to see white privilege as an invisible package of unearned assets which I can count on cashing in each day, but about which I was 'meant' to remain oblivious. White privilege is like an invisible weightless knapsack of special provisions, maps, passports, codebooks, visas, clothes, tools and blank checks.

Describing white privilege makes one newly accountable. As we in Women's Studies work to reveal male privilege and ask men to give up some of their power, so one who writes about having white privilege must ask, "Having described it, what will I do to lessen or end it?"

After I realized the extent to which men work from a base of unac-knowledged privilege, I understood that much of their oppressiveness was unconscious. Then I remembered the frequent charges from women of color that white women whom they encounter are oppressive. I began to understand why we are justly seen as oppressive, even when we don't see ourselves that way. I began to count the ways in which I enjoy un-earned skin privilege and have been conditioned into oblivion about its existence.

My schooling gave me no training in seeing myself as a oppressor, as an unfairly advantaged person, or as a participant in a damaged culture. I was taught to see myself as an individual whose moral state depended on her individual moral will. My schooling followed the pattern my col-league Elizabeth Minnich has pointed out: whites are taught to think of their lives as morally neutral, normative, and average, and also ideal, so that when we work to benefit others, this is seen as work which will allow "them" to be more like "us."

I decided to try to work on myself at least by identifying some of the daily effects of white privilege in my life. I have chosen those conditions which I think in my case *attach somewhat more to skin-color privilege* than to class, religion, ethnic status, or geographical location, though of course all these factors are intricately intertwined. As far as I can see, my African American co-workers, friends and acquaintances with whom I come into daily or frequent contact in this particular time, place, and line of work cannot count on most of these conditions.

1. I can if I wish arrange to be in the company of people of my race most of the time.
2. If I should need to move, I can be pretty sure of renting or pur-

chasing housing in an area which I can afford and in which I would want to live.

3. I can be pretty sure that my neighbors in such a location will be neutral or pleasant to me.
4. I can go shopping alone most of the time, pretty well assured that I will not be followed or harassed.
5. I can turn on the television or open to the front page of the paper and see people of my race widely represented.
6. When I am told about our national heritage or about "civilization," I am shown that people of my color made it what it is.
7. I can be sure that my children will be given curricular materials that testify to the existence of their race.
8. If I want to, I can be pretty sure off finding a publisher for this piece on white privilege.
9. I can go into a music shop and count on finding the music of my race represented, into a supermarket and find the staple foods which fit with my cultural traditions, into a hairdresser's shop and find someone who can cut my hair.
10. Whether I use checks, credit cards, or cash, I can count on my skin color not to work against the appearance of financial reliability.
11. I can arrange to protect my children most of the time from people who might not like them.
12. I can swear, or dress in second hand clothes, or not answer letters, without having people attribute these choices to the bad morals, the poverty, or the illiteracy of my race.
13. I can speak in public to a powerful male group without putting my race on trial.
14. I can do well in a challenging situation without being called a credit to my race.
15. I am never asked to speak for all the people of my racial group.
16. I can remain oblivious of the language and customs of persons of color who constitute the world's majority without feeling in my culture any penalty for such oblivion.
17. I can criticize our government and talk about how much I fear its policies and behavior without being seen as a cultural outsider.
18. I can be pretty sure that if I ask to talk to "the person in charge," I will be facing a person of my race.
19. If a traffic cop pulls me over or if the IRS audits my tax return, I can be sure I haven't been singled out because of my race.
20. I can easily buy posters, postcards, picture books, greeting cards, dolls, toys, and children's magazines featuring people of my race.
21. I can go home from most meetings of organizations I belong to

feeling somewhat tied in, rather than isolated, out-of-place, out-numbered, unheard, held at a distance, or feared.

22. I can take a job with an affirmative action employer without having co-workers on the job suspect that I got it because of race.
23. I can choose public accommodation without fearing that people of my race cannot get in or will be mistreated in the places I have chosen.
24. I can be sure that if I need legal or medical help, my race will not work against me.
25. If my day, week, or year is going badly, I need not ask of each negative episode or situation whether it has racial overtones.
26. I can choose blemish cover or bandages in "flesh" color and have them more or less match my skin.

I repeatedly forgot each of the realizations on this list until I wrote it down. For me white privilege has turned out to be an elusive and fugitive subject. The pressure to avoid it is great, for in facing it I must give up the myth of meritocracy. If these things are true, this is not such a free country; one's life is not what one makes it; many doors open for certain people through no virtues of their own.

In unpacking this invisible knapsack of white privilege, I have listed conditions of daily experience which I once took for granted. Nor did I think of any of these perquisites as bad for the holder. I now think that we need a more finely differentiated taxonomy of privilege, for some of these varieties are only what one would want for everyone in a just society, and others give license to be ignorant, oblivious, arrogant and destructive.

I see a pattern running through the matrix of white privilege, a pattern of assumptions which were passed on to me as a white person. There was one main piece of cultural turf; it was my own turf, and I was among those who could control the turf. *My skin color was an asset for any move I was educated to want to make.* I could think of myself as belonging in major ways, and of making social systems work for me. I could freely disparage, fear, neglect, or be oblivious to anything outside of the dominant cultural forms. Being of the main culture, I could also criticize it fairly freely. In proportion as my racial group was being made confident, comfortable, and oblivious, other groups were likely being made inconfident, uncomfortable, and alienated. Whiteness protected me from many kinds of hostility, distress, and violence, which I was being subtly trained to visit in turn upon people of color.

For this reason, the word "privilege" now seems to me misleading. We usually think of privilege as being a favored state, whether earned or conferred by birth or luck. Yet some of the conditions I have described here work to systematically overempower certain groups. Such privilege simply *confers dominance* because of one's race or sex.

I want, then, to distinguish between earned strength and unearned power conferred systemically. Power from unearned privilege can look like strength when it is in fact permission to escape or to dominate. But not all of the privileges on my list are inevitably damaging. Some, like the expectation that neighbors will be decent to you, or that your race will not count against you in court, should be the norm in a just society. Others, like the privilege to ignore less powerful people, distort the humanity of the holders as well as the ignored groups.

We might at least start by distinguishing between positive advantages which we can work to spread, and negative types of advantages which unless rejected will always reinforce our present hierarchies. For example, the feeling that one belongs within the human circle, as some Native Americans say, should not be as privilege for a few. Ideally it is an *unearned entitlement*. At present, since only a few have it, it is an *unearned advantage* for them. This paper results from a process of coming to see that some of the power which I originally saw as attendant on being a human being in the U. S. consisted in *unearned advantage* and *conferred dominance*.

I have met very few men who are truly distressed about systemic, unearned male advantage and conferred dominance. And so one question for me and others like me is whether we will be like most men, or whether we will get truly distressed, even outraged, about unearned race advantage and conferred dominance and if so, what we will do to lessen them. In any case, we need to do more work in identifying how they actually affect our daily lives. Many, perhaps most, of our white students in the U.S. think that racism doesn't affect them because they are not people of color; they do not see "whiteness" as a racial identity. In addition, since race and sex are not the only advantaging systems at work, we need similarly to examine the daily experience of having age advantage, or ethnic advantage, or physical ability, or advantage related to nationality, religion, or sexual orientation.

Difficulties and dangers surrounding the task of finding parallels are many. Since racism, sexism, and heterosexism are not the same, the advantaging associated with them should not be seen as the same. In addition, it is hard to disentangle aspects of unearned advantage which rest more on social class, economic class, race, religion, sex and ethnic identity than on other factors. Still, all of the oppressions are interlocking, as the Combahee River Collective Statement of 1977 continues to remind us eloquently.

One factor seems clear about all of the interlocking oppressions.

They take both active forms which we can see and embedded forms which as a member of the dominant group one is taught not to see. In my class and place, I did not see myself as a racist because I was taught to recognize racism only in individual acts of meanness by members of my group, never in invisible systems conferring unsought racial dominance on my group from birth.

Disapproving of the systems won't be enough to change them. I was taught to think that racism could end if white individuals changed their attitudes. [But] a "white" skin in the United States opens many doors for whites whether or not we approve of the way dominance has been conferred on us. Individual acts can palliate, but cannot end, these problems.

To redesign social systems we need first to acknowledge their colossal unseen dimensions. The silences and denials surrounding privilege are the key political tool here. They keep the thinking about equality or equity incomplete, protecting unearned advantage and conferred dominance by making these taboo subjects. Most talk by whites about equal opportunity seems to me now to be about equal opportunity to try to get into a position of dominance while denying that *systems* of dominance exist.

It seems to me that obliviousness about white advantage, like obliviousness about male advantage, is kept strongly inculturated in the United States so as to maintain the myth of meritocracy, the myth that democratic choice is equally available to all. Keeping most people unaware that freedom of confident action is there for just a small number of people props up those in power, and serves to keep power in the hands of the same groups that have most of it already.

Though systemic change takes many decades, there are pressing questions for me and I imagine for some others like me if we raise our daily consciousness on the perquisites of being light-skinned. What will we do with such knowledge? As we know from watching men, it is an open question whether we will choose to use unearned advantage to weaken hidden systems of advantage, and whether we will use any of our arbitrarily-awarded power to try to reconstruct power systems on a broader base.

CHAPTER 12

Body Ritual
among the Nacirema

Horace Miner

The anthropologist has become so familiar with the diversity of ways in which different peoples behave in similar situations that he is not apt to be surprised by even the most exotic customs.[1] In fact, if all of the logically possible combinations of behavior have not been found somewhere in the world, he is apt to suspect that they must be present in some yet undescribed tribe. This point has, in fact, been expressed with respect to clan organization by Murdock (1949, p. 71). In this light, the magical beliefs and practices of the Nacirema present such unusual aspects that it seems desirable to describe them as an example of the extremes to which human behavior can go.

Professor Linton first brought the ritual of the Nacirema to the attention of anthropologists 20 years ago (1936, p. 326), but the culture of this people is still very poorly understood. They are a North American group living in the territory between the Canadian Cree, the Yaqui and Tarahumare of Mexico, and the Carib and Arawak of the Antilles. Little is known of their origin, although tradition states that they came from the east. According to Nacirema mythology, their nation was originated by a culture hero, Notgnihsaw, who is otherwise known for two great feats of strength—the throwing of a piece of wampum across the river Pa-To-Mac and the chopping down of a cherry tree in which the Spirit of Truth resided.

Nacirema culture is characterized by a highly developed market

This chapter is reproduced by permission of the American Anthropological Association and of Agnes Miner from *American Anthropologist*, 58(3), June 1956. Not for further reproduction.

economy which has evolved in a rich natural habitat. While much of the people's time is devoted to economic pursuits, a large part of the fruits of these labors and a considerable portion of the day are spent in ritual activity. The focus of this activity is the human body, the appearance and health of which loom as a dominant concern in the ethos of the people. While such a concern is certainly not unusual, its ceremonial aspects and associated philosophy are unique.

The fundamental belief underlying the whole system appears to be that the human body is ugly and that its natural tendency is to debility and disease. Incarcerated in such a body, man's only hope is to avert these characteristics through the use of the powerful influences of ritual and ceremony. Every household has one or more shrines devoted to this purpose. The more powerful individuals in society have several shrines in their houses and, in fact, the opulence of a house is often referred to in terms of the number of such ritual centers it possesses. Most houses are of wattle and daub construction, but the shrine rooms of the more wealthy are walled with stone. Poorer families imitate the rich by applying pottery plaques to their shrine walls.

While each family has at least one such shrine, the rituals associated with it are not family ceremonies but are private and secret. The rites are normally only discussed with children, and then only during the period when they are being initiated into these mysteries. I was able, however, to establish sufficient rapport with the natives to examine these shrines and to have the rituals described to me.

The focal point of the shrine is a box or chest which is built into the wall. In this chest are kept the many charms and magical potions without which no native believes he could live. These preparations are secured from a variety of specialized practitioners. The most powerful of these are the medicine men, whose assistance must be rewarded with substantial gifts. However, the medicine men do not provide the curative potions for their clients, but decide what the ingredients should be and then write them down in an ancient and secret language. This writing is understood only by the medicine men and by the herbalists who, for another gift, provide the required charm.

The charm is not disposed of after it has served its purpose, but is placed in the charm-box of the household shrine. As these magical materials are specific for certain ills, and the real or imagined maladies of the people are many, the charm-box is usually full to overflowing. The magical packets are so numerous that people forget what their purposes were and fear to use them again. While the natives are very vague on this point, we can only assume that the idea in retaining all the old magical materials is that their presence in the charm-box, before which the body rituals are conducted, will some way protect the worshipper.

Beneath the charm-box is a small font. Each day every member of the family, in succession, enters the shrine room, bows his head before the charm-box, mingles different sorts of holy water in the font and proceeds with a brief rite of ablution. The holy waters are secured from the Water Temple of the community, where the priests conduct elaborate ceremonies to make the liquid ritually pure.

In the hierarchy of magical practitioners, and below the medicine men in prestige, are specialists whose designation is best translated "holy-mouth-men." The Nacirema have an almost pathological horror of and fascination with the mouth, the condition of which is believed to have a supernatural influence on all social relationships. Were it not for the rituals of the mouth, they believe that their teeth would fall out, their gums bleed, their jaws shrink, their friends desert them, and their lovers reject them. They also believe that a strong relationship exists between oral and moral characteristics. For example, there is a ritual ablution of the mouth for children which is supposed to improve their moral fiber.

The daily body ritual performed by everyone includes a mouth-rite. Despite the fact that these people are so punctilious about care of the mouth, this rite involves a practice which strikes the uninitiated stranger as revolting. It was reported to me that the ritual consists of inserting a small bundle of hog hairs into the mouth, along with certain magical powders, and then moving the bundle in a highly formalized series of gestures.

In addition to the private mouth-rite, the people seek out a holy mouth-man once or twice a year. These practitioners have an impressive set of paraphernalia, consisting of a variety of augers, awls, probes, and prods. The use of these objects in the exorcism of the evils of the mouth involves almost unbelievable ritual torture of the client. The holy-mouth-man opens the client's mouth and, using the above-mentioned tools, enlarges any holes which decay may have created in the teeth. Magical materials are put into these holes. If there are no naturally occurring holes in the teeth, large sections of one or more teeth are gouged out so that the supernatural substance can be applied. In the client's view, the purpose of these ministrations is to arrest decay and to draw friends. The extremely sacred and traditional character of the rite is evident in the fact that their teeth continue to decay.

It is to be hoped that, when a thorough study of the Nacirema is made, there will be careful inquiry into the personality structure of these people. One has but to watch the gleam in the eye of a holy-mouth-man, as he jabs an awl into an exposed nerve, to suspect that a certain amount of sadism is involved. If this can be established, a very interesting pattern emerges, for most of the population shows definite masochistic tendencies. It was to these that Professor Linton referred in discussing a distinctive part of the daily body ritual which is performed only by men. This part of the rite involves scraping and lacerating the surface of the face with a sharp instrument. Special women's rites are performed only four times during each lunar month, but what they lack in frequency is made up in barbarity. As part of this ceremony, women bake their heads in small ovens for about an hour. The theoretically interesting point is that what seems to be a preponderantly masochistic people have developed sadistic specialists.

The medicine men have an imposing temple, or latipsoh, in every community of any size. The more elaborate ceremonies required to treat very sick patients can only be performed at this temple. These ceremonies involve not only the thaumaturge but a permanent group of vestal maidens who move sedately about the temple chambers in distinctive costume and headdress.

The latipsoh ceremonies are so harsh that it is phenomenal that a fair proportion of the really sick natives who enter the temple ever recover. Small children whose indoctrination is still incomplete have been known to resist attempts to take them to the temple because "that is where you go to die." Despite this fact, sick adults are not only willing but eager to undergo the protracted ritual purification, if they can afford to do so. No matter how ill the supplicant or how grave the emergency, the guardians of many temples will not admit a client if he cannot give a rich gift to the custodian. Even after one has gained admission and survived the ceremonies, the guardians will not permit the neophyte to leave until he makes still another gift.

The supplicant entering the temple is first stripped of all his or her clothes. In everyday life the Nacirema avoids exposure of his body and its natural functions. Bathing and excretory acts are performed only in the secrecy of the household shrine, where they are ritualized as part of the body-rites. Psychological shock results from the fact that body secrecy is suddenly lost upon entry into the latipsoh. A man, whose own wife has never seen him in an excretory act, suddenly finds himself naked and assisted by a vestal maiden while he performs his natural functions into a sacred vessel. This sort of ceremonial treatment is necessitated by the fact that the excreta are used by a diviner to ascertain the course and nature of the client's sickness. Female clients, on the other hand, find their naked bodies are subjected to the scrutiny, manipulation, and prodding of the medicine men.

Few supplicants in the temple are well enough to do anything but lie on their hard beds. The daily ceremonies, like the rites of the holy-mouth-men, involve discomfort and torture. With ritual precision, the vestals awaken their miserable charges each dawn and roll them about on their beds of pain while performing ablutions, in the formal movements of which the maidens are highly trained. At other times they insert magic wands in the supplicant's mouth or force him to eat substances which are supposed to be healing. From time to time the medicine men come to their clients and jab magically treated needles into their flesh. The fact that these temple ceremonies may not cure, and may even kill the neophyte, in no way decreases the people's faith in the medicine men.

There remains one other kind of practitioner, known as a "listener." This witch-doctor has the power to exorcise the devils that lodge in the heads of people who have been bewitched. Nacirema believe that parents bewitch their own children. Mothers are particularly suspected of putting a curse on children while teaching them the secret body rituals. The countermagic of the witch-doctor is unusual in its lack of ritual. The patient simply tells the "listener" all his troubles and fears, beginning with the earliest difficulties he can remember. The memory displayed by the Nacirema in these exorcism sessions is truly remarkable. It is not uncommon for the patient to bemoan the rejection he felt upon being weaned as a babe, and a few individuals even see their troubles going back to the traumatic effects of their own birth.

In conclusion, mention must be made of certain practices which have their base in native esthetics but which depend upon the pervasive aversion to the natural body and its functions. There are ritual fasts to make fat people thin and ceremonial feasts to make thin people fat. Still other rites are used to make women's breasts larger if they are small, and smaller if they are large. General dissatisfaction with breast shape is symbolized in the fact that the ideal form is virtually outside the range of human variation. A few women afflicted with almost inhuman hypermammary development are so idolized that they make a handsome living by simply going from village to village and permitting the natives to stare at them for a fee.

Reference has already been made to the fact that excretory functions are ritualized, routinized, and relegated to secrecy. Natural reproductive functions are similarly distorted. Intercourse is taboo as a topic and scheduled as an act. Efforts are made to avoid pregnancy by the use of magical materials or by limiting intercourse to certain phases of the moon. Conception is actually very infrequent. When pregnant, women dress so as to hide their condition. Parturition takes place in secret, without friends or relatives to assist, and the majority of women do not nurse their infants.

Our review of the ritual life of the Nacirema has certainly shown them to be a magic-ridden people. It is hard to understand how they have managed to exist so long under the burdens which they have imposed upon themselves. But even such exotic customs as these take on real meaning when they are viewed with the insight provided by Malinowski when he wrote (1948, p. 70):

Looking from far and above, from our high places of safety in the developed civilization, it is easy to see all the crudity and irrelevance of magic. But without its power and guidance early man could not have mastered his practical difficulties as he has done, nor could man have advanced to the higher stages of civilization.

NOTE

1. *Editor's note*: Dr. Miner's use of "he" alone as the generic third person singular pronoun, and of "man" for "human being," reflects the academic usage of 1956—a time when male privilege was thoroughly embedded in formal discourse. Thus, this classic spoof provides food for thought in more ways than one.

REFERENCES

Linton, R. (1936). *The study of man.* New York: Appleton-Century.
Malinowksi, B. (1948). *Magic, science, and religion.* Glencoe, IL: Free Press.
Murdock, G. P. (1949). *Social structure.* New York: Macmillan.

CHAPTER 13

Dismantling White Male Privilege within Family Therapy

Ken Dolan-Del Vecchio

This fragile [American democratic] experiment began
by taking for granted the ugly conquest of
Amerindians and Mexicans, the exclusion of women,
the subordination of European working-class men and
the closeting of homosexuals. . . . The much heralded
stability and continuity of American democracy was
predicated upon black oppression and degradation.
Without the presence of black people in America,
European-Americans would not be "white"—they
would only be Irish, Italian, Poles, Welsh and others
engaged in class, ethnic, and gender struggles over
resources and identity. . . . Black slavery and racial
caste served as the floor upon which white class,
ethnic, and gender struggles could be diffused and
diverted.
—CORNEL WEST (1993, p. 156)

Denials which amount to taboos surround the subject
of advantages which men gain from women's
disadvantages. These denials protect male privilege
from being fully acknowledged, lessened or ended. . . .
I think white males are carefully taught not to
recognize male privilege.
—PEGGY MCINTOSH (1988, p. 1)

There is an increasing awareness these days of
insensitivity and injustice in therapy experienced by
women and cultural groups different from the
dominant one.
—KIWI TAMASESE AND CHARLES WALDEGRAVE
(1993, p. 29)

Most texts on the practice of family therapy, like most everything that has been published in the United States and other Western nations, are written by, about, and primarily for White people. This chapter focuses on White privilege itself, and, more specifically, on the profoundly significant ways in which our work with families is shaped by the social processes underlying the privileges that we who are White and male take largely for granted.

As a White man, I must legitimize my words on the subject of race and gender privilege by first noting that my awareness of this subject and all of my thinking about it have arisen through my connections to people who are racially and sexually different from me. I am grateful for the extraordinary patience and tolerance demonstrated by Rhea Almeida and other mentors (see the Acknowledgments at the end of the chapter) while helping me begin to move away from complicity with White supremacist culture, the foundation of my reality.

DOMINANT VALUES AND FAMILY THERAPY

> Ignoring the sociopolitical therapist–client, client–patriarchal interface creates the illusion of neutral practice. The multiple dimensions of power and privilege are obscured, limiting the options for empowerment and healing.
> —RHEA ALMEIDA (1993, p. 13)

Proponents of traditional theories that have privileged intrapsychic processes; those who believe in the medical model (DSM-IV; American Psychiatric Association, 1994); and, more recently, promoters of so-called "solution-focused therapies" argue that their approaches offer "neutrality" or "objectivity." In reality, however, what this means is that the values informing these approaches do not conflict substantially with widely held values and ideas regarding the optimal structure for family life and the meanings ascribed to life's difficulties.

For example, William O'Hanlon-Hudson and Patricia Hudson-O'Hanlon, in *Love Is a Verb: How to Stop Analyzing Your Relationship and Start Making It Great!* (1995), describe an approach to therapy with couples that never seems to question dominant values regarding relationships. Consider this case:

> Dave and Laurie were at an impasse . . . Dave wanted Laurie to be more adventuresome sexually. To Dave, being "sexually adventuresome" meant having anal sex. Pat suggested they look at the category "more adventuresome about sex" and find what other actions they

could agree upon. Laurie was modest . . . she decided she would be willing to be more adventuresome sexually by wearing a teddy, a garter belt, and hose. While this didn't completely meet Dave's desires, it gave him the message that she cared about his sexual desires and was willing to try some different behaviors to spice things up. (p. 49)

The "solution" supported Dave's objectified, pornographic imaging of his partner. He was not asked to describe the sexual activity that Laurie found most enjoyable and to imagine compromising in her direction. Dave was presumably never asked the question, "Have you ever performed any sexual act within this relationship that you were not 100% comfortable with?" (Most heterosexual men would answer no.) Instead, the "neutral" therapeutic context reinforced the larger societal context's attitude regarding the propriety of a man's sexual imposition upon his female partner.

In a second case described in *Love Is a Verb*, male values were again supported:

One couple Pat worked with discovered that they had completely different ideas about giving and receiving love. Jamal was very romantic and believed that love was demonstrated by things like surprise picnics and candlelit dinners. His wife, Denise, thought that Jamal could show her love by helping with the housework, arranging to have the wallpaper hung in the family room, and cleaning his whiskers out of the bathroom sink after he shaved. Once they accepted that neither of them had *the correct* view of what love really is, each could begin to give love to the other in a way that he or she recognized. (p. 37)

Jamal's notion of love is labeled "romantic" by the authors. Denise's is not characterized at all, but is left to be thought what—"mundane," perhaps? A more critical exploration by the therapist might have questioned why Jamal's visions of love were all about his own pleasure and Denise's were all about shared home responsibilities. Who did Jamal imagine would prepare the surprise picnics and candlelit dinners? What about this relationship (and about relationships between men and women in general) would have to be different in order for Denise's ideas about love to include visions of being given such things as surprise picnics and candlelit dinners? How was sexism contributing to the pattern of their different notions of love?

As these two case examples demonstrate, a therapist who assumes a "neutral" stance pretends that each partner in a couple relationship has equal power (i.e., that the relationship developed outside of any larger historical and relational context). In so doing, the therapist actually endorses the oppressive social processes, including sexism, racism, and homophobia, that contribute to the structure of all relationships in our society (Almeida, 1993, 1994, 1996; Almeida & Bograd, 1990; Almeida, Woods, & Messineo, 1993; Comas-Díaz, 1991; Dolan-Del Vecchio, 1996; Greene, 1993; Hardy, 1991; Hall & Greene, 1994; Laird & Green, 1995; McGoldrick, 1987, 1989, 1994; Tamasese & Waldegrave, 1993).

MY PHILOSOPHY AND VALUES

It is my belief that a therapy whose goal is to heal families is also a therapy directed by necessity toward healing communities, and ultimately toward healing civilization—such is the completeness and inescapability of our connections to one another. The century that is ending saw collective struggles against ancient practices of domination unfold in every realm of life and in every corner of the globe. Ours is an era when colonizers are finally being dislodged, when slavery is finally being outlawed, and when women are finally being made citizens in many (though still not all) places on the globe. With the unfolding of the labor movement, middle-class White women's movement for parity with White men, movements for social justice for men of color, and lesbian and gay rights movements in our own country, the times have borne witness to collective struggles against a multitude of institutional structures of domination. More recently still, social eruptions that challenge patterns of domination hidden within the privacy of home have emerged—that is, movements voicing the experiences and needs of incest survivors, adult children of alcoholics, and victims of domestic violence.

At the same time that structures of domination are being challenged, the dominant (White heterosexist male) discourse has produced no widely accepted notions of power aside from that of power as "domination over." Consequently, we White men tend readily to imagine that if other groups are gaining economic and political power, then we must be losing it (Lerner, 1995). Consider, for example, the emergence in this country of the mythopoetic and fathers' rights men's movements. These are backlash initiatives created by White men in order to counter the gains made by the White women's movement. Similarly, the "family values" crusade of recent decades vilifies alternative family structures, such as those constructed by lesbians and gays who are "out," in an effort to reinscribe the traditional, male-dominated/female-serviced family model as the only valid option. Within the "power as domination" paradigm, wherein any visible difference ignites a battle for supremacy, there is no place for "both–and"—no place for respectful and collaborative bridging across differences. As Audre Lorde (1984) put it:

We have all been programmed to respond to the human differences between us with fear and loathing and to handle that difference in one of three ways: ignore it, and if that is not possible, copy it if we think it is dominant, or destroy it if we think it is subordinate. But we have no patterns for relating across our human differences as equals. (p. 115)

Our civilization can no longer afford conceptualizations and practices of power built upon these "us or them" polarities, however, because of our unavoidable proximity to one another. We live in a world where miraculous advances in communications, travel, and information processing bring us together in ways previously unimaginable. In a civilization where difference, since the dawn of recorded history, has meant domination (Eisler, 1987), we are challenged to find new paradigms for connection if any of us are to survive and prosper. We have entered an era when—because the paradigm of dominance hierarchy will no longer hold, because of the new smallness of our world and our undeniable connections to one another, and because of our identification as healers—psychotherapy and struggles to end domination are joined.

SURVEYING THE FIELD: A LOOK AT THE CURRENT WORK OF WHITE MEN IN FAMILY THERAPY

Family therapist Ron Taffel acknowledges the oppressive realities for (White heterosexual) women and (White) children constructed by dominant prescriptions for family life. He notes in *Why Parents Disagree* (Taffel, 1995) that "after reading hundreds of psychological reports and listening to thousands of case studies, I have *never* seen a mother who is not explicitly blamed for her child's psychological problems" (p. 40). Taffel suggests that raising consciousness regarding the typical pattern of underresponsibility (but assumption of authority) by fathers and the resulting overresponsibility of mothers is often his first order of business in working with parents.

He also highlights the issue of physical violence as a matter for special and very serious concern. This distinguishes Taffel from most other male family therapy writers, too many of whom treat domestic violence as though it is simply another systemic family issue in which both members of a couple play a role, instead of characterizing it as a potentially lethal pattern that is the batterer's responsibility alone.

Supervising a case involving a husband who has frequently and severely beaten his wife, Jay Haley tells therapist David R. Grove in *Conversations on Therapy* (Grove & Haley, 1993):

> You described an incident that I bet is a metaphor for the history of
> their marriage. She leaves; 45 minutes later he leaves and she's waiting
> for him. I bet they have a pattern where she leaves and then comes
> back. She leaves and yet tempts him. That is part of the violence. (p.
> 77)

Another example of this kind of analysis, from Harville Hendrix's book
Keeping the Love You Find: A Guide for Singles (1992), follows.

> In many abusive families, there appears to be a victim and a
> tormentor. . . . the man who beats his wife and then children, while
> she cowers in the corner and silently comforts her children when it is
> over. It seems easy to fix the blame in these situations, but this is
> dangerously misguided. It takes two to create this warped ballet. What
> is rarely acknowledged is that the battered wife knows only one way—
> the way she learned from her own mother—to get attention, and that
> is to provoke her distant, silent husband with relentless, though perhaps
> subtle, criticism, complaints, and rejection—until he explodes. (p. 125)

In both of these cases the therapists, in reaching for what they would
probably describe as "fairness" or "neutrality" in their analyses, attempt
to assign to the woman partner part of the man's responsibility for choosing to use violence. Instead of acknowledging and countering the entrapment created by the spectrum of coercive tactics employed by men who
are abusive, this approach collaborates with batterers, reassaulting women
within the context of therapy (Stark & Flitcraft, 1995).

Robert Pasick's warm and engaging book *Awakening from the Deep
Sleep* (1992) includes a section on men's use of the spectrum of coercive
tactics in relationships with partners. Repeatedly acknowledging the debt
he feels men owe the women's movement, Pasick encourages a redefini-
tion of masculinity centered upon values of nurturing and respect for
difference. He also includes a section that strongly identifies the negative
impact of homophobia upon all men.

Although Pasick identifies his privilege connected to gender and class,
he never addresses how the privileges connected to being White and the
oppression experienced by men of color create different dilemmas centering around masculinity for each group. For example, I, being a White
man, felt right at home with what he was saying as I read his text the first
time. After discussing Pasick's work with a colleague who is a person of
color, however, I returned to his writing and was able to see that the
distinctions which might make visible the experiences of those men who
are racially different from White men are generally missing from his text.
For example, although Pasick delineates the particulars of the dominant
code of masculinity, including the importance of autonomy and success

measured by employment status and income level, he never mentions that these prescriptions interact with institutional racism to create intensified dilemmas for men of color (who have less access to high-level employment) and their family members. By not mentioning these kinds of distinctions, he subsumes the experiences of men of color under the experiences of the dominant group, White men, rendering the experiences of men of color invisible.

Michael Nichols, in *The Lost Art of Listening* (1995), proceeds as though the power dynamics of male–female relationships and gender-based inequities count for nothing and are not related to a man's inclination or disinclination to listen empathically and respectfully to women. He writes:

> I soon found out why Sheila hesitated to protest. Once she said, "Don't you think you're being a little unfair?" and Lenny flew into a rage. He started shouting at her . . . it was awful. . . . The same thing happened every time Sheila said anything critical to Lenny. . . . Others might say . . . Lenny's lashing out [is] typical of [his] gender. In fact these inferences are so general and judgmental as to constitute virtually meaningless clichés. For a more subtle appreciation of a person's overreaction we need to know its trigger. . . . Lenny was filled with deep and ugly fears of worthlessness. . . . (p. 90)

Collapsing the range of issues related to gender and thereby attempting to discount and trivialize them, Nichols constructs an intrapsychically focused hypothesis that privileges Lenny's "deep and ugly fears of worthlessness" over his accountability for the abusive impact of his "overreaction" upon Sheila and other family members.

Nichols presents the following as an example of successful communication:

> Wendy told Hank that she needed more help chauffeuring the kids to all their activities. He agreed. But Wendy went further and said, "I know you don't feel like it, otherwise you'd volunteer more often. When do you feel *least* like driving?" Hank really appreciated this consideration of his feelings. (Feeling like it's OK to say no made it a lot easier to say yes.) He said he didn't mind taking the kids places on weekends or early in the evening but he hated going out after nine on work nights. He also mentioned that it's a lot easier for him if he knows a day in advance that he has to drive them somewhere. (p. 143)

But why wasn't Nichols questioning the imbalance of power in this relationship? For example, why was it OK for Hank to say no, since, clearly, Wendy did not have that option? Why was the chauffeuring of the kids in the evening considered Wendy's job—a job for which the children's other parent, Hank, assumed no direct responsibility? Why was Wendy obliged to inform Hank of the children's planned activities a day in advance—in other words, why didn't Hank, who was also the children's parent, have any direct knowledge of their schedules? In choosing not to raise these questions, Nichols supported the power imbalance that was structuring this relationship.

Most disturbing of all in Nichols's writing is his use of humor to trivialize the inequities within heterosexual relationships:

> When I complain to my friends about my wife nagging me to take out the garbage, it's just because my wife doesn't understand why I don't always feel like doing it. Besides, if I tried to discuss this directly with her, we might get into tedious and unnecessary issues, like fairness and inequality and so on. (p. 205)

Frank Pittman, author of *Man Enough: Fathers, Sons and the Search for Masculinity* (1993), often uses sarcastic humor to embellish his formulations, and his statements are frequently denigrating to women and homosexuals.

> Most women realize their femininity is an act they go into to control men without scaring them ... Men who escape women, or seduce them, or silence them, or even beat and murder them are doing so not because they sadistically enjoy beating a woman—a feminist stereotype of men's motives—but because they feel weak, burdened with a sense of imperfect masculinity. (p. 33)

> Another way men have protected themselves from the power of women is to keep them too busy to stir up much trouble. (p. 242)

> The least a guy can do to pay back a gal who has down-pedaled her own career and tended to him and their kids, while letting him have all the fun of devoting himself to the selfish pleasures of work, is to make sure she gets to blow the money. If he can make her feel it is her money as much as his, she'll feel more nearly equal and will probably take better care of the money and better care of him. (p. 240)

Pittman describes a conversation he was part of while working out at the gym:

> One man said, "I've known homosexuals who were big and strong and could beat your ass." The other boys agreed that only heterosexuals could be real men, but they weren't too sure, and then they were sorry that such an unpleasant topic had been brought up. (p. 30)

This sort of joking from a heterosexual White man who is prominent within the field of family therapy can be very destructive because of the power he wields. He has the power both to validate and to demean the experiences of those, such as women, people of color, and sexual minorities, who are different from himself, because his voice (unlike theirs) is very much listened to.

Although each of the White male family therapists mentioned differs in his characterizations of the White women's movement and its impact upon men and family life, they all acknowledge the significance of this social phenomenon. Subscribing to Kenneth Hardy's (1991) "theoretical myth of sameness," however, none of the men unwraps the issue of race in a way that explores the fundamental manner in which racism structures all of our lives. Furthermore, none of the authors asks other White men to consider their collective responsibility for perpetuating the social order that supports our privilege. In other words, none of these White male family therapists issues a call to those of us who are all White men to acknowledge both our responsibility for transforming our own predicaments and, because we are the dominating class, our responsibility for working toward the liberation of women, children, and racial and sexual minorities.

THERAPY BASED IN LIBERATION CONSCIOUSNESS

Therapy based in liberation consciousness works to dismantle the hierarchy of power underlying white male heterosexual privilege (Almeida, 1993, 1994, 1996; Almeida & Bograd, 1990; Almeida et al., 1993). Two case illustrations follow.[1]

Josh, a White man of Eastern European Jewish heritage in his early 20s, was in a dilemma. Several months previously, during a 4-month period of time when Josh and Susan (his White, Jewish fiancée) had broken up and were not seeing each other, Josh impregnated a woman named Linda. Josh then ended the relationship with Linda and reconciled with Susan. With the support of advice from friends, his parents, and his brother, Josh kept Linda's pregnancy secret from Susan in an effort to "protect her." The baby was born 4 days before his initial consultation with me. Josh first told Susan about the child on the day of delivery. He was now considering terminating the relationship with Susan, because he felt her emotional response to the news of his newborn daughter was excessive and unpredictable. "Hey, I told her what's going on! Besides, the whole scenario's under control—I don't want anything to do with the kid, but I will pay child support . . . there's nothing to worry about . . . so I don't know what she's so freaked out about! Besides, I'm trying to start a new business, and that's where I really have to put my energy, not into this bullshit!" He presented this story in a tone I use too frequently myself—a style of voice common to us White men. It's a tone that suggests a solid belief in the correctness of our singular vision. I have heard Monica McGoldrick describe the voice of White male privilege as the voice of a person who presumes to "hold the truth of the universe within."

Josh believed that the issue he and Susan needed to address was their "communication problem," related mostly to Susan's excessive emotionality and difficulty understanding him with accuracy. He seemed to assume that my role would be to help Susan calm down, listen to reason, and help him "keep his eye on the ball" with his new business.

My hypothesis, however, centered upon Josh's decisions to keep Linda's pregnancy a secret from Susan and to invalidate her concerns and responses when she learned about the birth of his daughter. I saw Josh's entitlement and his emotional blindness as connected to our shared socialization into White manhood within this culture. Raising consciousness regarding patterns of socialization, I believe, shifts some life decisions from "inevitable and unavoidable" to the realm of deliberation and choice. For Josh, this would mean an exploration of the cultural and familial processes that convinced him to resign from most emotional connections with other human beings, disavow his accountability to his woman partner and to his child, and instead sacrifice his humanity to the ravenous masculine deities of work and financial success.

I began to ask Josh an array of questions designed to spark in him some awareness of how his current dilemma, including his vision of fathering and other relational responsibilities, along with his overall pattern of relational decision making, was connected to White heterosexist male socialization:

> "Where do you imagine you got the idea that it is reasonable for a man to try to 'protect' his woman partner from unpleasant or difficult realities that concern both of them? Would you consider it respectful to 'protect' a male friend or business partner in the same way? What rules within our society contribute to your belief that you have no responsibility at all to 'protect' the mother of your child and that financial support is an adequate contribution to the life of your newborn daughter? How would you imagine your average man would feel and respond if his fiancée concealed the fact of her child's existence? What are we White men taught are our primary responsibilities toward our children, and how do you imagine that the teaching women get on this topic is different? How do you imagine this

teaching and the pressures connected to it might be different in a family of color, where the prospects for men making big money are more remote due to institutional racism? What do you imagine, from your infant daughter's point of view, are the most important things her father can give her?"

The work included family-of-origin sessions with Josh's parents, and couple and individual sessions with his fiancée. After much directed questioning, Josh's father voiced a willingness to support Josh's developing something more than a monetary connection with this child if he so desired. The father was also guided toward reevaluating his view of Susan, whom he saw as demanding, childish, and unsupportive of Josh. I wondered whether he would be so negating of his child's partner's life and needs if this were his daughter and her partner was Josh. I also wondered whether he would so readily disavow his new grandchild if it were a grandson instead of a granddaughter. Josh's mother saw these issues in a more balanced way, but her voice was constricted by the presence of three males in her family.

Although a more traditional family therapist might have begun working with the couple by asking Susan to describe her issues with the couple relationship, I took a more directive approach. In order to gain a fuller understanding of the relationship while also orienting Susan's attention to the often hidden or taken-for-granted dimensions that form the foundation of heterosexual partnerships, I began to work with the couple by seeing Susan individually for a survey of power and control dimensions. Predictably, she related that Josh demonstrated a number of controlling patterns within the relationship, including characterizing Susan's emotionality as craziness while presenting a void of emotionality himself; regularly intimidating her by using a loud, belligerent voice; and consistently assuming that he would be the one to define shared realities. He demanded that his compartmentalized experience of relationships—a hallmark of male socialization—be the standard. For example, if Susan asked Josh a question about the status of the legal process regarding custody, he might angrily shut her down and then a half hour later feel baffled by Susan's irritability toward him when he invited her out to dinner. He might tell this story, starting where he asked her to go out to dinner, as evidence of Susan's bizarre moodiness and unwillingness to "open up to" him. Tying this kind of pattern together for Josh, and asking him to take responsibility for his control and intimidation, became a part of the work of therapy.

Family therapy based in liberation consciousness rebalances the traditional practice of blaming women through a process of inquiry regarding men's relational patterns and male socialization across multiple systems levels (Almeida, 1993, 1994, 1996; Almeida & Bograd, 1990; Almeida et al., 1993). Steven, a 17-year-old White male of Italian heritage, was brought to see me because of withdrawn behavior at home, punctuated by moments of explosive verbal and sometimes physical outbursts toward his mother. Donna and Al, Steven's parents, both believed that the core problem was between Steven and his mother. Many family therapists would be inclined to agree, hypothesizing perhaps that this "overly involved" mother was "enmeshed" with her son and that his violence toward her was an attempt to gain the space necessary for proper male development

In my formulation, however, this family's problem (as well as their idea of the problem) reflected the overly responsible role in which heterosexual women are typically cast by the parental irresponsibility of their male partners, as well as the ambivalence with which our society teaches us to view closeness between a mother and a son (and, more particularly, the assumption of authority by a mother over her teenaged son). Donna's position as the target of Steven's rage was probably more the result of her acceptance of parental responsibility than it was of anything as pathological as "enmeshment," and both her overresponsibility and Steven's rage and isolation were connected to Al's underresponsibility and distance. My hypothesis was aligned closely with the thinking Olga Silverstein presents in *The Courage to Raise Good Men* (Silverstein & Rashbaum, 1994). This book provides an essential reexamination of mother–son relationships within (White) families. Among the theories of the White male authors surveyed in the previous section, my hypothesis was most similar, perhaps, to the one that Ron Taffel might employ, and my interventions primarily investigated and challenged men's patterns of relationships.

Steven and I talked about what it takes to be respected as a man within high school culture. We talked about how power as physicality and as control over oneself and others is the standard, and stoicism and anger are the allowed emotions. We talked about the risks of being labeled a "fag" or a "girl" if a young man's actions differ from these prescriptions. We explored the implications of being labeled feminine or homosexual (i.e., how females and homosexuals are devalued). From there, we moved into an exploration of how Steven had seen the men in his family deal with conflict. He mentioned his father's abusiveness toward both him and his mother.

A private conversation with Donna revealed Al's long history of abusiveness. Although he had never been physically violent, Al had regularly abused and intimidated Donna by loudly screaming insults and foul names at her. After these explosive episodes, Al would sometimes not speak to

Donna for days. Because Donna assured me that she felt absolutely safe with my revealing the content of our conversation to Al, I opened a dialogue with him about his abusive actions. Al said that he was ready to do "whatever will help my son." In order to make his communication deliberate, comprehensive, and clear, Al was coached on writing a letter to Steven in which he apologized for his emotional abusiveness and distance in a way that claimed full responsibility for his behavior. Within this letter, he acknowledged that his abusive actions toward Steven's mother were the model for Steven's own abusiveness toward her.

The therapy with this family included an exploration of multigenerational legacies. During a meeting with Al and his father, Frank, we discussed how traditional White working-class family structures at the time of Al's childhood had contributed to Frank's absence from his son's life, and how norms of male stoicism had contributed to Frank's never acknowledging with his son the losses connected to that distance. We discussed the emotional and functional burden this structure had placed on Al's mother, Mary. Al was helped to see how the needs unmet by his father contributed to his demanding posture within his own marriage. Frank and Al readily agreed when they were encouraged to invite Steven into their conversation by taking him out to dinner and sharing much of what they had discussed.

CONCLUSION

Years of indoctrination into a relatively powerful and relatively blind place within the social order were challenged for me when I entered family therapy training under the supervision of Rhea Almeida and Monica McGoldrick. My experience since then convinces me every day that if we White men are to understand and intervene in a truly respectful and constructive fashion with families, we must engage in training relationships with women, people of color, and people who are gay and lesbian (if we are heterosexual), where we can experience a strong measure of accountability. Only if this occurs—only if we relinquish center stage and claim wholeheartedly the role of students relative to teachers whose gender, race, and sexual orientation locates them where they experience the impact of White male supremacy—will we remain reasonably conscious of the social realities that structure all of our lives, both publicly and privately. I believe, moreover, that the continuance of these kinds of connections throughout our professional careers is warranted, as the world is only too ready to reappoint those of us who are White and male to the position of unquestioned experts—and we, unfortunately, are too ready to accept these appointments.

ACKNOWLEDGMENTS

This chapter is presented in honor of such mentors as Rhea Almeida, Monica McGoldrick, Theresa Messineo, Rosemary Woods, Roberto Font, and Nydia Garcia-Preto, and also those who have helped me to open my mind and heart through their written words, including Alice Walker (1983, 1988, 1996, 1997), Audre Lorde (1984, 1997), bell hooks (1984, 1990, 1991), Cornel West (1993), Paulo Freire (1970, 1973), Ward Churchill (1996), Paula Gunn Allen (1992), Frederick Douglass (1845), Andrea Dworkin (1997), Carmen Vasquez (1997), David Becker (1997), Allan Bérubé (1997), Justin Chin (1997), William Mann (1997), Lillian Comas-Díaz (1991), Beverly Greene (1993), Michele Bograd (1984, 1991), Nathan McCall (1995), Ellis Cose (1993), Kenneth Hardy (1991), Kiwi Tamasese and her team (Tamasese & Waldegrave, 1993), Peggy McIntosh (1988), Beth Richie (1985), Kimberle Williams Crenshaw (1991, 1993, 1994), Phyllis Chesler (1989), John Stoltenberg (1990), Paul Kivel (1992), Michael Kimmel (1996), and Terry Kupers (1993, 1995). This work is also presented with mindful regard for all those whose names, talents, and contributions have gone unmentioned and uncelebrated; all those who have been silenced and made invisible by the institutions of white male supremacy.

NOTE

1. The case discussions depict an approach to therapy derived from the cultural context model, which was originated by Rhea Almeida. (See Almeida, Woods, Messineo, & Font, Chapter 31, this volume.)

REFERENCES

Almeida, R. (1993). Unexamined assumptions and service delivery systems: Feminist theory and racial exclusions. *Journal of Feminist Family Therapy, 5*(1), 3–23.

Almeida, R. (Ed.). (1994). *Expansions of feminist family theory through diversity.* Binghamton, NY: Haworth Press.

Almeida, R. (1996). *The cultural context model.* Unpublished manuscript.

Almeida, R., & Bograd, M. (1990). Sponsorship: Men holding men accountable for domestic violence. *Journal of Feminist Family Therapy, 2*(3–4), 243–256.

Almeida, R., Woods, R., & Messineo, T. (1993). *Integrating race and gender into the treatment of adolescents and children.* Unpublished manuscript.

American Psychiatric Association. (1994). *Diagnostic and statistical manual of mental disorders* (4th ed.). Washington, DC: Author.

Becker, D. P. (1997). Growing up in two closets: Class and privilege in the lesbian and gay community. In S. Raffo (Ed.), *Queerly classed: Gay men and lesbians write about class* (pp. 227–234). Boston: South End Press.

Bérubé, A. (1997). Intellectual desire. In S. Raffo (Ed.), *Queerly classed: Gay men and lesbians write about class* (pp. 43–66). Boston: South End Press.

Bograd, M. (1984). Family systems approaches to wife battering: A feminist critique. *American Journal of Orthopsychiatry, 54,* 558–568.

Bograd, M. (1991). *Feminist approaches for men in family therapy.* Binghamton, NY: Harrington Park Press.

Carter, B., & McGoldrick, M. (Eds.). (1989). *The changing family life cycle: A framework for family therapy* (2nd ed.). Boston: Allyn & Bacon.

Chesler, P. (1989). *Women and madness.* San Diego: Harcourt Brace.

Chin, J. (1997). Currency. In S. Raffo (Ed.), *Queerly classed: Gay men and lesbians write about class* (pp. 179–189). Boston: South End Press.

Churchill, W. (1996). Indians "R" us? Reflections on the "Men's Movement." In *From a native son: Selected essays on indigenism, 1985–1995* (pp. 367–408).

Comas-Díaz, L. (1991). Feminism and diversity in psychology: The case of women of color. *Psychology of Women Quarterly, 15,* 597–609.

Cose, E. (1993). *The rage of a privileged class: Why are middle-class Blacks angry? Why should America care?* New York: HarperCollins.

Crenshaw, K. W. (1991, November 15). Speech presented at the Forum for Women State Legislators, San Diego.

Crenshaw, K. W. (1993). Race, gender, and violence against women: Convergences, divergences and other Black Feminist conundrums. In M. Marion (Ed.), *Family matters: Readings on family lives and the law.* New York: New Press.

Crenshaw, K. W. (1994). Mapping the margins: Intersectionality, identity politics, and violence against women of color. In M. A. Fineman & R. Mykitiuk (Eds.), *The public nature of private violence.* New York: Routledge.

Dolan-Del Vecchio, K. (1996). The foundation for accountability: A linking of many different voices. *American Family Therapy Academy (AFTA) Newsletter,* No. 64, 20–23.

Douglas, S. F. (1845). *Narrative of the life of Frederick Douglass, an American slave.* New York: Anchor Books.

Dworkin, A. (1997). *Life and death: Unapologetic writings on the continuing war against women.* New York: Free Press.

Eisler, R. (1987). *The chalice and the blade: Our history, our future.* New York: Harper & Row.

Freire, P. (1970). *Education for critical consciousness.* New York: Continuum.

Freire, P. (1973). *Pedagogy of the oppressed.* New York: Continuum.

Greene, B. (1993). Psychotherapy with African-American women: Integrating feminist and psychodynamic models. *Journal of Training and Practice in Professional Psychology, 7*(1), 49–65.

Grove, D. R., & Haley, J. (1993). *Conversations on therapy.* New York: Norton.

Hall, R. L., & Greene, B. (1994). Cultural competence in feminist family therapy: An ethical mandate. *Journal of Feminist Family Therapy, 6*(3), 5–28.

Hardy, K. V. (1991). The theoretical myth of sameness: A critical issue in family therapy training and treatment. In G. W. Saba, B. M. Karrer, & K. V. Hardy (Eds.), *Minorities and family therapy.* Binghamton, NY: Haworth Press.

Hendrix, H. (1992). *Keeping the love you find: A guide for singles.* New York: Pocket Books.

hooks, b. (1984). *Feminist theory: From margin to center.* Boston: South End Press.

hooks, b. (1990). *Yearning: Race, gender, and cultural politics.* Boston: South End Press.

hooks, b. (1991). *Breaking bread: Insurgent Black intellectual life.* Boston: South End Press.

Kimmel, M. (1996). *Manhood in America: A cultural history.* New York: Free Press.

Kivel, P. (1992). *Men's work: How to stop the violence that tears our lives apart.* Center City, MN: Hazelden.

Kupers, T. (1993). *Revisioning men's lives: Gender, intimacy, and power.* New York: Guilford Press.

Kupers, T. (1995). The politics of psychiatry: Gender and sexual preference in DSM-IV. *masculinities, 3*(2), 67–78.

Laird, J., & Green, R.-J. (1995). Lesbians and gays in families: The last invisible minority. *Journal of Feminist Family Therapy, 7*(3–4).

Lerner, M. (1995). *The assault on psychotherapy.* Keynote address presented at the 1995 Family Therapy Networker Symposium, Washington, DC.

Lorde, A. (1984). *Sister outsider.* Freedom, CA: Crossing Press.

Lorde, A. (1997). *The collected poems of Audre Lourde.* New York: Norton.

Mann, W. J. (1997). A boy's own class. In S. Raffo (Ed.), *Queerly classed: Gay men and lesbians write about class* (pp. 217–226). Boston: South End Press.

McCall, N. (1995). *Makes me wanna holler: A young Black man in America.* New York: Vintage Books.

McGoldrick, M. (1987, May–June). On reaching mid-career without a wife. *Family Therapy Networker.*

McGoldrick, M. (1994). Culture, class, race, and gender. *Human Systems: The Journal of Systemic Consultation and Management, 5,* 131–153.

McGoldrick, M., Anderson, C. M., & Walsh, F. (Eds.). (1989). *Women in families: A framework for family therapy.* New York: Norton.

McIntosh, P. (1988). *White privilege and male privilege: A personal account of coming to see correspondences through work in women's studies* (Working Paper No. 189). Wellesley, MA: Wellesley College Center for Research on Women.

Nichols, M. (1995). *The lost art of listening.* New York: Guilford Press.

O'Hanlon-Hudson, W., & Hudson-O'Hanlon, P. (1995). *Love is a verb: How to stop analyzing your relationship and start making it great!* New York: Norton.

Pasick, R. (1992). *Awakening from the deep sleep: A powerful guide for courageous men.* San Francisco: HarperCollins.

Pittman, F. (1993). *Man enough: Fathers, sons and the search for masculinity.* New York: Putnam.

Richie, B. (1985, March–April). Battered Black women: A challenge for the Black community. *The Black Scholar.*

Rosen, E. J., & Weltman, S. (1996). Jewish families. In M. McGoldrick, J. Giordano, & J. K. Pearce (Eds.), *Ethnicity and family therapy* (2nd ed.). New York: Guilford Press.

Silverstein, O., & Rashbaum, B. (1994). *The courage to raise good men.* New York: Penguin Books.

Stark, E., & Flitcraft, A. (1995). Personal power and institutional victimization: Treating the dual trauma of woman battering. *Post Traumatic Therapy and Victims of Violence,* 115–151.

Taffel, R. (1995). *Why parents disagree: How women and men parent differently and how they can work together.* New York: Morrow.

Tamasese, K., & Waldegrave, C. (1993). Cultural and gender accountability in the "just therapy" approach. *Journal of Feminist Family Therapy, 5*(2), 29–45.

West, C. (1993). *Race matters.* New York: Vintage Books.

Vazquez, C. (1997). Spirit and passion. In S. Raffo (Ed.), *Queerly classed: Gay men and lesbians write about class* (pp. 121–134). Boston: South End Press.

Walker, A. (1983). *In search of our mothers' gardens: Womanist prose.* San Diego: Harcourt Brace.

Walker, A. (1988). *Living by the word.* San Diego: Harcourt Brace.

Walker, A. (1996). *The same river twice: Honoring the difficult.* New York: Washington Square Press.

Walker, A. (1997). *Anything we love can be saved: A writer's activism.* New York: Random House.

PART IV

CULTURAL LEGACIES

The attempts in this book and elsewhere to re-vision families and family therapy have led us to seek new, more inclusive ways to discuss our work. Personal narratives are a major part of this attempt to shift our paradigm. From Murray Bowen's first account of his own family at a 1967 research meeting, which stunned the field by breaking the rules of academic and professional discourse, we have gradually been stretching and transforming the boundaries of our dialogues to create more inclusive ways of thinking about our work. Clearly, the individualistic models of "scientific" discourse about therapy have proven inadequate to the realm of healing. These models are of limited relevance in a world where our lives are so profoundly interconnected. It is often through personal narratives that we may learn most about those aspects of our experience that have not fit into our theoretical and clinical models. These stories may be among the keys to liberating us so that we can strive for new visions of our work.

The authors of this section's chapters have focused on giving voice to those experiences that have generally been marginalized in the main cultural stories of our society. Elaine Pinderhughes explores the silenced history of White exploitation and internalized racism in her own Black and White ancestors. Fernando Colón's story is a remarkable example of the hidden oppressions of colonized groups and of the power of uncovering the cultural dimensions of one's history. In sharing aspects of my own story, I have tried to dissect the complexities of racial and class privilege in relation to gender and cultural oppression, as part of my efforts to find the meaning of the concept "home." Jayne Mahboubi and Ashburn Searcy have taken the daring step of exploring the intertwined threads of White supremacy and American subordination in their personal interconnectedness. Their own efforts to bridge the chasm between Black and White are an important model for the rest of us. John Folwarski's personal recollection of childhood in a Polish orphanage turns out to be a profound reflection of the effects of Polish subordination in European history, as well as a story of the impact of immigrant cultural disruption. All the chapters in Part IV highlight a reconnection with history, both personal and cultural, and provide impressive models of the power to challenge those who would deny us access to our history.

CHAPTER 14

Black Genealogy Revisited

RESTORYING AN AFRICAN AMERICAN FAMILY

Elaine Pinderhughes

The invisibility of African Americans in the recorded history of the United States has led to a pervasive ignorance for everyone, Black or White, about African Americans and their contributions to the building of our country. African Americans themselves have colluded in maintaining secrecy about their history. With no power to affect the writing of American history and few resources to disseminate our story, it has remained invisible or distorted by negative stereotypes, and we have until recently remained unable or unwilling to challenge the distortions, untruths, and omissions that have been accepted about our past. Sealing off the past has been a way of dealing with the pain, hardship, humiliation, and degradation that have marked African American history from slave times to the present. But we are coming to realize that knowledge of the past, even if painful, can nourish a people's strength. This realization has stimulated us to unseal these memories and reclaim the truth, no matter how cruel and shocking, so that the festering wound can begin to heal and so that we can better cope with the present and build the future. Only by exploring this painful history can we learn of the ingenious survival practices developed during and after slavery, which may guide us toward our own salvation as a nation. Many individuals have joined in the movement to search out their family odysseys, in order to see more clearly the struggle of our people to live with dignity and to find some sense of meaning and value, even as they have been dehumanized.

This chapter is part of my contribution to this effort. Discovering my repressed pride and love for my family has become an expansive experience for me. I value greatly what I have learned about my relatives' legacy of strength and endurance. It has enabled me to achieve a greater sense of integration and personal clarity within my family, along with a more fundamental sense of authenticity, rootedness, and continuity with history and time.

THE BEGINNINGS OF MY RESEARCH:
GAPS IN MY KNOWLEDGE

I began to research my family in 1977, and was able to trace two branches of my mother's family back to the 18th century. Growing up in a segregated, protected, and very supportive middle-class, African American community, I had thought very little about my family origins. Apart from some stories about my two grandmothers, there was minimal mention of our history by the family. All of my grandparents had died before my birth, and since my parents had left the other members of their extended families behind in Louisiana in their search for a better life in Washington, DC. I had little contact with them. My mother died when I was only 16, and it was not until my father died at age 88, when I myself was well into middle age, that my curiosity about my origins led to action.

I had always wondered how a family as impoverished as my father's had been—toiling in the bayous, harvesting rice, and battling snakes in the swamps—could produce such a bevy of high achievers. He became a dentist, and his siblings included a physician, a pharmacist, a nurse, and an undercover agent. (The agent was seen by the family as a "stool pigeon"; I later became aware that he had been the family scapegoat. We have learned recently of his heroic acts, as he was recognized for bravery in the line of duty.)

I was secretly more curious about my mother's family, but could not let myself admit this, for reasons that will become clear shortly. As I began my search, I ran into barriers in researching my father's family prior to 1880. However, the search for my mother's family produced knowledge that has had a profound influence upon my life.

Prior to my research, I knew only a few facts about my mother's family (see Figure 14.1 for a genogram reflecting my knowledge at this stage). I knew that my mother, Ollie Bourgeois, was the granddaughter of Lettie Bibbs Roberson, who had been born a slave. I had met Great-Grandma Lettie on several occasions when we visited Louisiana in my childhood. I also knew my mother's brother, Henry, and one of her sisters, Coralee. My grandmother, Cecelia, for whom my sister was named, had died when my mother was 16, just as my mother had died when I was 16. Whenever my mother had mentioned her mother's death, it was with great sadness. Although I knew my mother carried her father's name,

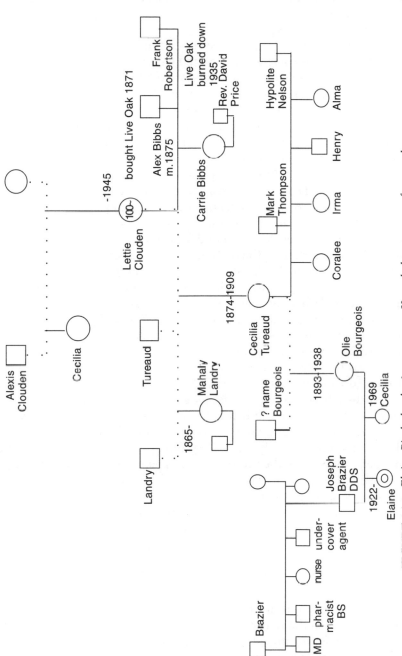

FIGURE 14.1. Elaine Pinderhughes's genogram: Knowledge at start of research.

Bourgeois (which I often wrote on documents when asked to give her maiden name), I knew nothing else about him and never dared to ask, although I was curious.

This side of the family was shrouded in shame for me as a girl. I knew that this was somehow connected with my mother's name and her appearance, which I suspected was related to her father's being a White man and not being married to her mother. Mother had always refused to discuss her father. I did not learn his first name, Adolph, until I procured a copy of my mother's death certificate. I also learned from my research that my maternal grandmother's last name had been Tureaud, and that she too had been fathered by a White man, whose name she bore.

As a child, I had known my grandmother Lettie's second husband, Frank Roberson. I had also heard stories about the warmth and caring of her first husband, Alec Bibbs, who, along with many other family members, had helped to raise my mother. Lettie had two other daughters besides my grandmother: Mahaly Landry, whom I learned had been named for her White father, and Carrie Bibbs, Alec's daughter. Mahaly, like my grandmother, also had a daughter, Mamie Armitage, by a White man.

When I was a girl, my mother had taken my sister and me to visit Live Oak, the farm in St. James Parish, Louisiana, where Lettie's family had lived for two generations. In 1935, when I was 13, Live Oak burned down in a tragic fire, and the family members living there were forced to move to New Orleans to live with friends and relatives. I learned also that Great-Grandma Lettie had also had a sister, Cecelia Grigsby. I was astounded to learn that the name of my sister and grandmother went even further back. Cecelia Grigsby's grandchildren turned out to have information about her and Lettie when they were children and slaves!

This was all I knew about my mother's family when I began, though I knew my father's family well. They often traveled from Louisiana to DC, perhaps because they were more affluent, and we had many visits with them. I remember now a certain pride and even arrogance among my father's relatives about the family and their achievements. When my father's two brothers visited, there was pride that *three* Drs. Brazier were together. My mother's family and their history were far less familiar to me.

THE RESEARCH

I began my search by trying to locate Great-Grandmother Lettie Roberson and her family in the census records. I started with the censuses of 1900 and 1880, preparing myself for the likelihood that I would not be able to trace her further back; census records before emancipation did not record slaves as people, but only by number as property of the owner, and I would have to find her owner (which wasn't very likely). Because slaves had no identity except as property, they could rarely be traced by name except through slave sale deeds and owners' wills. Legal documents of all other kinds were connected with the owner, not with the individual slave (Blockson, 1977; Herbert, 1976). To trace a Black family before 1870, one has to identify the slave owner. Thus, unless I could locate Great-Grandma Lettie's owner, my search would end before it even began. If I could find this information, I might trace the family through slave sales and probate records as far back as possible. If this worked, I could deduce from the information I gathered something about the family's values, roles, and behavioral interactions that might shed some light on my family's current lives.

The search for Great-Grandma Lettie's owner took 5 weeks of work. I hypothesized that her maiden name might be a clue to her owner. So I sought her marriage license, death certificate, baptismal record, and information from persons in St. James Parish who knew her. I spent over 50 hours just reading census records in the National Archives. I read books about slavery in Louisiana in general and in St. James Parish in particular. I studied the records and private papers of White members of the Tureaud, Landry, and Bourgeois families, hoping to find her owner. My search took me to the New Orleans Public Library, Dillard University, the Louisiana State Library at Baton Rouge, and Louisiana State University. I did title searches of property and slaves in courthouses in St. James Parish, as well as in Natchez, Mississippi and Woodville, Mississippi.

At first, most of my activity directed at finding Lettie's owner was unsuccessful. I traveled to cemeteries, only to find records burned up. I fought with clerks, who denied the existence of death certificates I knew were on file. After two skirmishes with the Louisiana Vital Statistics Office, I finally located Lettie's death certificate, when the librarian at the New Orleans Public Library found in a basement archive an undertaker's record book that listed a Lettie "Robinson" as age 74. Because I knew Lettie was close to 100 years old when she died, I almost discounted this information. However, on a hunch, I sent for the record. It turned out that Lettie had been "passing" for 74 because of insurance regulations. The 5 weeks it took to trace one generation into slavery may be compared with the 1 hour it took to track the White Bourgeois line back five generations to 1719!

Among the documents I eventually found were the following (see Figure 14.2 for a genogram reflecting the information provided in these documents):

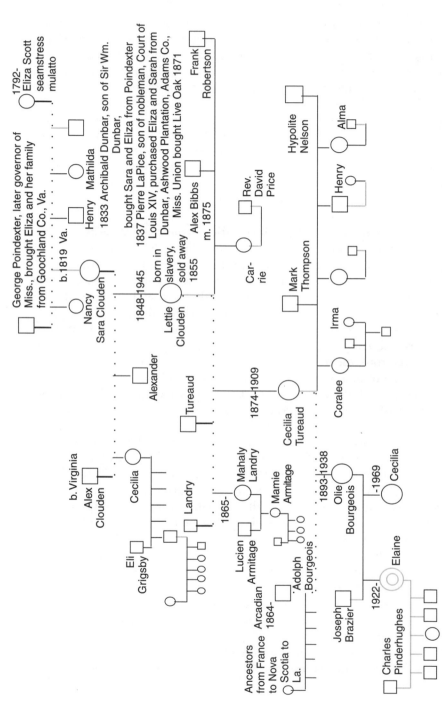

FIGURE 14.2. Elaine Pinderhughes's genogram with infomation from research.

- My mother's death certificate, signed by her sister, Coralee, which stated her father's name as Adolphe. I remember well the anxiety and pain I experienced upon first viewing this document.
- The census records of 1880, which listed Lettie, her husband, Alec Bibbs (then called "Alexander Bebe"), and her daughters, Mahaly and Cecelia. The records indicated that Lettie's parents were born in Maryland. Also listed in the household was a "Sara Clanton," who was identified as "mother." I assumed this to be Alec Bibbs's mother.
- The census of 1900, which listed Lettie (now calling herself "Lydia") and Alec with Cecelia Tureaud's children, Ollie, Eddie, and Coralee.
- The deed to the Live Oak property, which revealed that the property, acquired in 1871, is still owned by the family.
- Lettie's marriage certificate, dated 1875, which showed her maiden name as Clouden. I began to suspect that the "Sara Clanton," listed as "mother" in the 1880 census might actually be my great-great-grandmother, and that her name had been misspelled in the census record.
- Lettie's death certificate, which stated her father's name as Alexis Clouden.
- Cecelia Tureaud's baptismal record, which listed her as born in 1874, and named her godparents but not her father. It read: "Marie Cecilia, de Hattie Clouden. Le 27 September, j'ai baptisé Marie Cecilia, née le 9 Mai de Hattie Clouden. Parrain Camille Melancon; Marraine Coralie Lanoue."
- The census of 1870, which listed Lettie with her mother, Sarah Clouden, and her daughter, Mahaly. Listed adjacent to Lettie was Bergondy LaPice, a planter, who I soon discovered was the son of the family's slave owner.
- My grandmother's baptismal record, found at St. Michael's Church in Convent, Louisiana. Unlike her death certificate, this did not state her father's name. The birth record of my mother, who was also baptized there, was missing.
- Conveyance records in St. James Parish, which revealed that Lettie's owner was Pierre LaPice, the father of Bergondy LaPice. These records listed the property of the LaPice family and recorded the sale of over 200 Negroes in 1855, among whom were Lettie, Cecelia, and Sarah, all the right ages.
- Records of slave sales involving Sarah Clouden, Lettie's mother. These sales occurred in 1852, 1837, and 1833. The sale of 1837 listed Lettie's mother, Sarah, with a family group including her

brothers, sisters, and mother, Eliza Scott, a mulatto seamstress. Eliza was sold for $1,000, and it was noted that she could pick 140 bales of cotton. Sarah, who was sold for $1,200, could pick 160 bales. Pierre LaPice had purchased Sarah, Eliza, and her family from Archibald Dunbar of Adams County, Mississippi. Dunbar, in turn, had purchased them from James Poindexter of Wilkinson County, Mississippi, in 1833. Poindexter had come to Mississippi in 1808 from Goochland County, Virginia, bringing his family and chattel ("chattel" included animals and slaves).

I also received information from neighbors and friends who had known the Bourgeois family and Great-Grandma Lettie's family when they lived in St. James Parish. I was able to trace the ancestry of my grandfather, Adolph Bourgeois, back to 1719 in Nova Scotia, and was told there are data tracing the family from there back to France.

RE-VISIONING THE HISTORICAL CONTEXT

My research has shown how racism has operated in the lives of African American families. The domination and exploitation of African American have created conditions that have caused ignorance, gaps, and confusion about the realities of Black people's presence and existence—effects reflected not only in the difficulties of tracing Black people's lineage, but in psychological consequences that persist to this day.

Again, the sheer scarcity and inadequacy of information are remarkable in themselves. Although Blacks greatly outnumbered Whites in St. James Parish, far fewer data are available on Blacks. Lillian Bourgeois (1976), in her history of the parish, notes that "four thousand whites owned eight thousand Blacks." She says that the wealth of antebellum St. James was exclusively in land and slaves, but she devotes a mere four pages to slavery.

As noted earlier, the census records and other official/legal documents are also incomplete and confusing. I found that my family members, like others, were listed in pre-Civil War census records as numbers under their slave owners' names. It is often assumed that slaves took their owners' last names, but I discovered that this happened less often than has been assumed. The few slavery-era documents that did give names indicated that none of my family members took their owners; names tended to be related to them by blood or affection. I also found that in the census records of 1870, 1880, and 1900, many Black families had children with different last names, in contrast to White families, where the children usually had the same last name.

The confusion and ambivalence so typical of racism were seen also in the Catholic Church, which owned slaves and supported slavery, but at the same time mandated that slaves be well cared for and that "accurate" records be kept (Herbert, 1976). However, there were glaring omissions in these records as well. During slavery, slave children were listed as born of the mothers and belonging to the owners of the mothers. There was no mention of the fathers, or even of the fathers' owners. After slavery, fathers were listed only when the parents were married.

Black children's having many last names, and the omission of fathers from all slavery-era and many postslavery church records, are simply the most prominent reflections of the widespread exploitation visited upon Black families by the fact that children had many different fathers. Slave owners frequently forced slave women into cohabitation and pregnancy (Franklin, 1966). The cohabitor might be the master himself or a White overseer or a Black other than the husband—whomever the owner deemed suitable for fathering the babies he intended to sell. Whether the fathers were White or Black, fathers' names in cases of cohabitation were simply omitted from birth records, both during slavery and after. Obviously, there were several such omissions in my family. As I have noted earlier, my grandmother's birth record did not list her father's name, and my mother's birth record was missing from the records at the church where she was baptized. I do not know whether these omissions occurred because of the need to hide White paternity, but this would be a reasonable surmise. In any case, such a practice reflected the long-standing tendency in this country to nullify and neglect maleness in Black families. For all intents and purposes, the Black male was a zero; he did not exist.

As I pondered these findings—the absence of White fathers as well as Black fathers in the records—I came to the conclusion that the White man was the original abandoning father in this country. Throughout history, lower-caste women have been exploited by upper-caste men, who became the absent fathers of their children. These men were the models for the absent Black men in Black families. They persisted in having sexual relationships with Black women, while being protected by their society from acknowledging their paternity or taking responsibility for their behavior, though the society knew of it.

I found this fact to be all the more ironic when I learned during a research project we conducted in Nigeria in 1974 that among the Yoruba tribe—the group from which probably the largest number of slaves was taken—there was *no* illegitimacy (Pinderhughes, 1978). Whenever a man impregnated a woman, he married her. Although this custom was facilitated by the practice of polygamy, it meant also that at the time the slaves were taken from Africa, every mother had a husband and every child had a legal father. I also pondered the fact that under polygamy the children in one family had several mothers and one father, while under slavery and the conditions that have since prevailed in the United States, children in one family may have one mother but several fathers.

This precedent of abandonment is illustrated in my own family, where the absent and abandoning fathers were all Whites. The irresponsibility of such abandonment is compounded by the confusion, deception, and hysteria that have been, and are still connected with the reality of miscegenation. According to a White librarian I spoke with, New Orleans "is very nervous about birth certificates" because of the large number of Whites who have Black blood, and their extensive records proving Black ancestry are kept under lock and key. It is estimated that 80% of the Whites of French descent in New Orleans have Black relatives, and that 30% have Black blood of which they are unaware. Stories abound in the area about White politicians and well-known figures who have Black ancestors. During Reconstruction, many light-skinned Blacks in New Orleans altered records in order to identify themselves as White; however, copies of these records still exist unaltered. Exposure of the records validating the Black ancestry of one prospective bride led her to have a psychotic break. Another fled the country. The appalling fact is that in Louisiana until 1982, a person could only be considered legally White if he had no more than 1/64th "Negro" blood.

Thus, the pervasive domination, exploitation, and abandonment of Blacks by Whites massively influenced the psychology, personality development, and interracial behavior of all involved. A major effect for Blacks has been the fragmentation of identity. My research has sought to address and correct this in my own life.

RESTORYING THE FAMILY:
SEEING THE FAMILY IN CONTEXT

Restorying the family and placing it in the context of the times in which my ancestors lived facilitated my awareness of the cutoffs, secrets, fusion, and confusion caused by racism. I now understand that the abandonment by her White father, plus the poverty and desperation that followed the 1935 fire at Live Oak, were so painful to my mother that she could not mention them—and I did not dare ask.

I have learned via this research that there is much to be proud of in my mother's family. They were hard-working people with a strong sense of responsibility. I discovered that Alec Bibbs and members of 10 other families bought Live Oak in 1871. Live Oak was thus owned by a cooperative of families, and our family still has a legal claim to the property. Neighbors recollected the sharing that had characterized family and community interaction. The support among neighbors and extended family is well documented, especially in relation to the children. Although the White fathers were irresponsible and abandoned their children, other family members loved and cared for them. The household was well organized, and the farm flourished. Although life was harsh, these resourceful and competent people also had much love, abundance, and pleasure. I heard many stories of the efficiency of the farm, with its variety of crops and livestock; I also heard much about the warmth and good times, as well as hard times, that the family shared in the big old house with its encircling verandah. Neighbors still remember the wedding of Lettie's daughter Carrie in 1906 to a young minister, as they remember the hardworking and competent Lettie, my great grandma.

When Cecelia, my grandmother, died, leaving my mother a young teenager, others in the family provided nurturance and protection. After the fire in 1935, everyone rallied and worked to keep the extended family together. Families showed courage in naming their children after their fathers, no matter who they were. And they had pride, courage to survive, zest for life, and strong religious beliefs.

I found myself remembering many things I had forgotten: pleasant gatherings in the evenings at Live Oak, on the few occasions when my mother, my sister, and I visited; being taken for horseback and buggy rides; being loved and cared about by these gentle, caring people; and their togetherness and enjoyment of one another. I see this now in great contrast to the more lonely, isolated existence of our nuclear family in D.C. And I understand better my mother's eternal depression and longing for home, which she frequently shared with me. She greatly missed her family's humor, loyalty, and sense of working together. Also, the family showed dedication to improving the quality of life for its members. While Lettie and Mahaly were laborers (they farmed, cut sugar cane, etc.), Carrie and Ollie were educated to be teachers.

In exposing the family secrets and confronting the shame that entrapped the family, I have come to understand why they went to such lengths not to discuss the pain and humiliation of slavery and the sexual exploitation of women. But I have also come to understand that in trying to build a better life, and attempting desperately to forget the past, their defensive behavior only reinforced the secrets—rigidifying costly emotional cutoffs, fragmenting personal and group identity, and creating for individuals within the family a nonauthentic sense of self. Undoing the secrets and facing the shame have opened up the emotional cutoffs, freeing family members from their negative consequences. And recognizing the family's positive achievements has contributed to the healing as well.

HOW MY FAMILY ADAPTED TO RACISM

"Racism" is behavior, both individual and institutional, that is based on the belief in the superiority of one group of people and the inferiority of another because of national and ethnic origins (Pinderhughes, 1973). Family research can document some of the ways Black people have responded to the racism that has so dominated their environment in the United States. The slaves, when brought to this country from Africa, were forced to deal with Whites' definitions of them as lazy, dumb, evil, sexual, dirty, and so on. Although some slaves simply adopted these behaviors in the course of playing a role (to "trick" or placate the slave owners), others internalized these definitions. Probably those slaves who felt the most powerless assumed these behaviors in the most exaggerated form in an effort to turn their painful sense of powerlessness into some sense of power and initiative. (In many ways, this has continued into the present: For example, some individuals assume the pose of "superstud," or use manipulative, resistant, or oppositional behaviors, to convey some sense of control and counteract their sense of powerlessness. (See Pinderhughes, 1983, 1990.) Others reacted to their slave roles by identifying with the aggressor—by mimicking the values of the slave master as superior, entitled, and supercompetent. It was paradoxical (and also somewhat "crazy-making") for individuals who belonged to a group relegated to inferior status to perceive themselves as superior. This solution evidenced itself in a kind of elitism in my family, spanning generations right down to me.

The tendency to elitism among African Americans caused me pain more than once, when my family and I were seen by others as "stuck up." I have always been uncomfortable with an elitist stance within myself, which I realized distanced me from certain people. Since I was young, I found that when I least expected it, I had unintentionally offended someone. I was always disturbed by this, and I worked hard to cope with this tendency in myself. Until I researched my family history, I had attributed it entirely to growing up in Washington, DC, being the daughter of a well-known dentist, and attending Dunbar High School (that breeding ground of the old "Black elite"). However, understanding my family history has put me in touch with a more fundamental basis of elitism as a response to racism.

The story has an ironic twist, since my mother's family was the part of the family of which I was ashamed. It is true that, as discussed earlier,

I have come to view this family connection as a source of pride. However, it has also become clear that these strong, courageous, loving people were themselves racist and elitist—sometimes hating their Blackness, loving Whiteness, and feeling superior to other Blacks.

1. The first clue that turned up in my research was the fact that Great Grandma Lettie had been a "house nigger" and a "mammy." As her sister Cecelia's grandchildren said, their mother and Lettie were well treated. They told me that after her master's family ate, the "house niggers," almost all of whom were light-skinned, were allowed to have the pickings, whereas the dark-skinned ones were not. Cecelia was remembered as very loyal and protective of her White employers, to whom she once claimed to be related. She protected their secrets, ran to them when angered by her own family, and seemed "to love them more than she did us," as one of her grandchildren sadly stated. It was not rare that a Black child, whose parents' job it was to care for the children of White employers, would possess such a perception. I can recall two clients whose memories of maternal deprivation were connected with feelings that their mothers were more loving and accepting of their White charges than of their own children.

2. The second clue concerns the issue of skin color: Lettie, I was told, had definite preferences based on skin color. My aunt Mahaly's grandchildren, who knew her well, told of how she discouraged them from playing with dark-skinned children; the lessons of the "big house" had indeed remained with her. Regardless of the circumstances surrounding the origins of Mahaly and Cecelia, as well as Lettie's two biracial granddaughters, it appears that she highly valued their skin color.

3. The third clue was the discovery that Eliza Scott, Lettie's grandmother, had been identified in the slave sale record of 1837 as a mulatto and a seamstress—two characteristics that may have caused the family to regard themselves as special in those days. Indeed, on my visit back to St. James Parish, Miss Lavinia, who had been Coralee's childhood playmate and who knew the family well, remarked on what she perceived as the arrogance of the family.

4. I found a final source of such a response in attributes of the slave owners themselves. In my readings on plantation life in St. James Parish during and immediately following slavery, I became aware of the sense of connection, both in history and in attitude, that many people entertained in relation to French royalty and privilege. Pierre LaPice—owner of Lettie, Cecelia, and their mother, Sarah—was actually the son of a nobleman in the court of Louis XIV (*The Times-Picayune,* 1963). Archibald Dunbar, from whom LaPice purchased Sarah, her siblings, and their mother, Eliza Scott, was the son of a titled English gentleman, Sir William Dunbar. James Poindexter, Eliza's former owner (who, I believe, brought her to

Mississippi from Virginia), had been the governor of Mississippi. Here is ample evidence for such expectations of entitlement. Historians and others have pointed out how the identity and self-worth of slaves were often tied up with those of their masters: Those belonging to the wealthiest slave owners felt the most superior.

Embracing such "identification with the aggressor," which embodies self-negation and self-hatred, is only one example of the contradictions that characterized the lives of slaves as they attempted to cope. This identification was a consequence of the fused master–slave relationship that slave masters forged in the attempt to stamp out African identity, to create a slave identity, and thus to facilitate bonding to the masters. A dramatic example from *Roots* (Haley, 1976) was the slave master's attempt to force Kunta Kinte to accept the name of "Toby."

During our research sojourn in Nigeria, we found people whose identity and sense of themselves constituted very antithesis of such a slave mentality. We met the Oba of Ekeri-Iketi, who knew his lineage for 30 generations. Our research colleague, Dr. Akinsola Akiwowo, told us that when he was disobedient as a boy, his mother chastised him by reading his *oriki,* which was a recitation of his relationship to his ancestors back through time. The contrast here is extreme indeed between the clear and positive African identity and the situation in which slaves came to be known as "Mr. Henry's gal" or "Miss Sophie's boy."

As I pondered these interrelated issues, I wondered: Did my family adopt an orientation of identification with the aggressor? As I drove through Mississippi and saw the elaborate antebellum houses and Christian academies, I remembered my family's passion for large houses, including the one in which I was reared (and, I thought with irony, the one in which I now reside).

Another issue related to the family's sense of entitlement was my mother's outstanding beauty. No one ever mentioned her without reference to her beauty. Her beauty had been a major issue in my battle for self-esteem. I also knew the pain it had brought her, for she had often shared with me ugly incidents of rejection by others who envied her beauty and her fair color. I learned one source of her pain when her brother, Henry, told me this story: When their mother, Cecelia, married his father, Hypolite Nelson, a dark-skinned man, his relatives so abused my mother, Ollie, that she was sent away from her beloved family to stay with an aunt in a distant city. I had known that my mother, despite her unusual beauty, was often sad and depressed. I knew this well, for she was my first client, as she shared much of her sadness and depression with me. (I have often wondered whether through my becoming a "parentified child," as the family therapists label it, and listening to her pain and perpetual mourning, I may have saved her from a breakdown.) Clearly, Ollie's fair skin had led to rejection by and loss of her mother, stepfather, friends, and family.

I have also discovered that my grandfather, Adolphe Bourgeois, lived in the community and had a family, including other daughters, and that everyone knew him as Ollie's father. Ever since, I have tried to imagine how Ollie must have felt and been pained by the destructiveness of racism as it touched her life. Abandoned by her father because she was not White enough (or at least not White), and abused by her stepfather, in-laws, and others because she was not dark enough, she was in a poignantly tragic situation. She appeared to be the circuit breaker for the anxiety, hostility, and resentment of many others in the systems in which she was trapped.

My mother's full reality, however, was that, though envied and rejected by some, she was also admired and adored by many others. Her unusual beauty was both a curse and a blessing. Though they sent her away, she still remained special to her mother, grandmother, aunts, uncle, and siblings. Reared by her Aunt Carrie and Carrie's husband, the Rev. David Price, a district superintendent of the Methodist Church, my mother lived a fairly privileged life—such as privilege was in those days. Never the parental oldest child (as is usual in a large family), my mother was rather the special, idealized one, playing a role that stabilizes a family just as the role of scapegoat can. It is not surprising that she loved fairy tales, "Cinderella" being her favorite. Only now do I understand why. And she sent me messages that I should achieve for her, so she could live through me at the same time that I would be her therapist. This elitism and specialness—basic values in determining behavior in the family for five generations—entrapped me also, and further reinforced the partially nonseparate relationship I had with my mother. I worked hard to live up to her expectations.

Another of Mother's favorite stories was Longfellow's *Evangeline*, the story of French lovers in Nova Scotia who were tragically separated and, upon the banishment of the French to Louisiana, doomed to search for one another in vain. Only after learning that the Bourgeois family was Acadian, having emigrated from France to Nova Scotia and then (involuntary) to Louisiana, did I understand the appeal of this story for her. She never mentioned why this story of loss and sadness meant so much to her; nor did she ever speak of how it felt to see her father often, knowing who he was, but being unacknowledged by him.

The family expectation of entitlement may have had other sources as well. Many in St. James Parish confirmed for me that Lettie was the family matriarch. As a child, I both respected and feared her. As the initiator, decision maker, and authority, she held the power in the family;

others were dependent on her and less able to exercise initiative. When all the power in any group is invested in one person, the power relationship is not very different from that between master and slave. Understandably, relationships in the families of former slaves, who identified strongly with their masters, were characterized by authoritarianism, unequal power, and inbalanced interactions. Nevertheless, Lettie's superior power held the family together, keeping it functioning in support of its members. When Live Oak burned down and forced the family to move to New Orleans, living on friends, other relatives, and the state, Lettie suffered great humiliation and the family became disorganized.

Finally, the authoritarian nature of the relationships within the family can be viewed in terms of the male–female dyads in Lettie's generation. Lettie had two children by White men who took no responsibility. Her Black husband, Alec Bibbs, helped her rear these White men's children, and later the granddaughters as well. How did Bibbs feel about this? Did he feel exploited, overwhelmed, and undermined as a man, or was he loving and protective of his wife's children and grandchildren? Perhaps both. Whatever his feelings, the power and the sense of entitlement had belonged to his wife.

THE IMPLICATIONS
OF MY RESEARCH FOR THERAPY

Understanding my family's struggle to survive and thrive in a societal context of domination, oppression, mystification, and exploitation has been an act of liberation. It has enabled me to understand the residual effects of the past, which have reinforced the fragmented, often negative identity that has plagued African Americans. Through this experience, I was able to replace the shame, ignorance, and confusion that surrounded my heritage with pride, knowledge, and understanding—truly a transformative process.

As I have shared my experience with other therapists, many have had strong and immediate responses. They identify with different aspects— the sadness, the pain, the anger, or the guilt. My work both in my personal research and as a therapist has centered on the importance of being clear about who we are culturally. Whenever we find ourselves in the presence of the unfamiliar cultural adaptations and realities of persons who are different—whether that difference is one of race, ethnicity, gender, sexual orientation, or socioeconomic background—we need to try to understand and manage our responses so that they will not interfere with our work (Pinderhughes, 1989, 1995).

I have found two concepts especially helpful in this process. The first is the telling of one's story as a way of restorying the past (Laird, 1989; Griffin, 1992) and constructing a coherent narrative (Lifton, 1993). This highlights the significance of the meaning that people assign to their experience, both the past and the present, as reflected in their beliefs and perceptions. It can point the way to solving problems that have been created by the societal projection process. As Susan Griffin has put it, the restorying of our history involves

> ... moving beyond one's own family and explicitly merging our story with the larger themes of connectedness between the personal and the political, the private and the public, the individual and all of history. Through telling seemingly unrelated story fragments and brief scenes from history, we can overcome the bifurcating, reductionistic process that dominates Western thinking and alienates us from each other and from an intimate relationship with our surround. (1992)

Another idea I have found very useful is Murray Bowen's (1976) concept of the "societal projection process"—an expansion of his concept of the family projection process to the level of society. According to this concept, the dominant group in society may stabilize itself, relieving tension and anxiety for itself through the presence of a victim group, which it views as weak and less competent. Among the "victim groups" Bowen has identified are minorities and the poor: He says:

> These groups fit the best criteria for long-term anxiety relieving projection. They are vulnerable to become the pitiful objects of the benevolent, oversympathetic segment of society that improves its functioning at the expense of the pitiful. Just as the least adequate child in a family can become more impaired when he becomes the object of pity and oversympathetic help from the family, so can the "lowest" segment of society be chronically impaired by the very attention designed to help. ... They automatically put the recipient[s] in a "one-down" inferior position and they either keep them there or get angry at them. (pp. 444–445)

This societal process has grave implications for both beneficiaries and victims. As I have discussed elsewhere, Whites, upper- and middle-class people, males, and heterosexuals, as beneficiaries of the societal projection process, have been able to stabilize themselves and their communities by keeping large amounts of the tension, conflict, contradiction, and confusion of the larger social system confined to the victims (the poor, people of color, gays, etc.) of the projection process and their communities (Pinderhughes, 1989). I have questioned the impact upon both victims and beneficiaries of their entrapment in their roles and the consequences of these responses for their interaction with one another. I have also questioned the significance of these entrapped societal roles for the work of helpers, who are seeking to empower their clients. In cross-cultural treatment situations, practitioners who are White, male, and/or middle-class, or who are positioned in any other ongoing power role, are thus vulnerable to perceiving and handling clients who occupy subordinate societal roles (such as people of color, women, the poor, mental patients, or those positioned in any other societal powerless roles) in a manner that is largely beneficial to the practitioners themselves. These notions give substance to the issues and themes that have emerged from my family research:

1. The nonexistence of African Americans in the consciousness of the larger society. Not existing has serious consequences. This is especially significant, given the solid identity Africans had when they came here.

2. The nullification of the Black male. Even when the mother was named in birth and christening documents, the father was always omitted during slavery and often afterward as well. This was a systematic obliteration of his existence.

3. The vulnerability of slaves to development of a fused identity as a result of the enslavement process, which encouraged them to define themselves through identification with the master, the oppressor, the dominant one. This was an invitation to poor self differentiation. Thus does the "nonself" imposed by slavery and by the making of a slave (Elkins, 1976) become understandable.

4. The vulnerability of African Americans to emotional cutoff, due to their inability to claim the White part of their lineage and to the absence of the White fathers, which placed yet more emotional burden on the Black families. The consequence of such cutoffs was an intensification of the emotional processes within the families. (This factor was, of course, compounded by the systematic, intentional splitting up of African American families under slavery by selling family members to other White slave owners.)

5. The vulnerability of African Americans to the negative stereotypes of their masters (who perceived them as dumb, dirty, evil, sexual, etc.). They might develop a negative identity by internalizing these stereotypes, or spend enormous energy trying to maintain a positive identity. They might take the role of victim, struggling to manage an extreme sense of powerlessness, or try to achieve some sense of power through manipulation, passive–aggressive or oppositional behavior, striking back, or becoming dependent (Pinderhughes, 1989). At times, developing ex-

aggerated stereotypic behavior—becoming superdumb, a superstud, or superaggressive—has been a way to seize the initiative and thus to overcome feelings of powerlessness.

6. The vulnerability to responding to the pain of oppression by sealing off the pain, not talking about it, not asking, not trying to understand. This leads to secrecy, which can cause serious disconnection from one's self. As Stiver has put it, "Secrecy's pathological effects can have enormous ramifications for how one develops a sense of reality, understands and trusts one's own experience, and establishes relationships."

7. The tendency for a behavior I have labeled "not knowing" to become one's essential learning style. Child psychologists are more than familiar with children whose poor school performance and learning problems are linked to their efforts to keep hidden emotionally laden, overwhelming events of loss and abuse.

Undoing the negative consequences of these entrapped societal roles is an imperative for the mental health profession. In my search to give meaning to the facts I have learned about my own and my people's history, I was able to accomplish the following, which freed up enormous energy in the family and in myself personally:

1. To understand myself and my family in the context of history as well as the present. I was able to develop a sense of continuity with the past, which made me more connected in the present. That sense of continuity brought with it a greater sense of clarity and confidence about who I am and from whence I came. My "I-ness" is now more secure and integrated. I can see my family realistically, in all its complexities—strengths as well as weaknesses.

2. To label the complexities, contradictions, and gaps that, when unnamed and unidentified, have created confusion and entrapment for the family, becoming crazy-making and costly in energy. Filling gaps in information, and revealing secrets, have reversed the sense of disconnectedness, ignorance, and not knowing.

3. To identify the myths, misconceptions, and distortions that have reinforced both my own and others' stuckness in the family process, and our entrapment in societal processes that maintain people in contradictory, even paradoxical positions. An example of such a position is that of so-called "elite" victims—oppressed persons who are treated as special and different from their group, and who learn to seek solace in a perception of themselves as better than their fellow sufferers. I came to understand how people's responses to racism, which are used to cope with pain and shame, can create even more problems: identification with the ag-

gressor (elitism or domination of others), skin color prejudice, denial of family pain, cutoff from the family, and keeping secrets to deny the pain.

4. To undo the emotional cutoff from my extended family that was the result of poverty, racism, and shame. In learning about the strengths of my mother's people, and understanding their struggles, I could let go of the shame related to illegitimacy and poverty. In becoming more connected with them, I found that my present relationships became less burdened as well, because the intensification (fusion) of emotional processes caused by the cutoff was lessened.

For our work as helpers, I believe that what I have learned can enhance our understanding of personal emptiness, meaninglessness, depression, family cutoff, fusion, intensified emotional processes, maladaptive beliefs—all consequences of entrapping societal roles. It can also provide a basis for developing coping strategies.

All of us—African Americans, other people of color, and Whites too—must take responsibility for finding ways to tell our stories responsibly. We who have been victims must help others to understand the true context of our shared existence: our struggles in the entrapping roles in which we have found ourselves. We must identify our strengths, realize why we may have embraced negative stereotypes, and realize how we have coped with our status as victims in the societal projection process. This is our story and we must tell it. As the victims of the Holocaust have shown, not only can survivors and their descendants free themselves, but perpetrators (and their descendants) can also liberate themselves, when victims are allowed to tell their stories and be heard. Thus, when the stories of African Americans, descendants of those who were entrapped in slavery and its destructive aftermath, are listened to by those who have been "beneficiaries," the victims will really feel heard. And those who are beneficiaries must also tell their stories, examining how and why they may have been trapped in exploitative positions as beneficiaries, vulnerable to using the victims to relieve tension and reduce anxiety for themselves. In our work, this means that we must take responsibility for the way our personal need for the gratifying power role of helper, embodied in our aggrandized cultural group status in society, can make us doubly vulnerable to using our clients (who may well be victims in the societal process) to relieve our own anxiety or tension (Pinderhughes, 1989).

We must not let our society's pressure for cost containment, brief therapy, and partialized goals divert us from the importance of this task. Only when we deal with such connection to our context, clarifying our societal roles as well as our personal need, will we become truly effective in our helping endeavors with those who have been victimized by these roles. This includes not only African Americans, but indeed any clients we want to help toward self-empowerment. Only through bearing witness to this history and these narratives can we join our clients in their struggle to reinforce the functioning necessary for a genuine change in their victim status. Then we will really be ready to help them develop the networks and communities that will support and nourish them as families and individuals. Then and only then can the social system of which we are a part sustain them instead of undermining them.

Our country is rapidly becoming a mosaic of many cultures. Our readiness to receive them all, to honor their cultures *and* their histories, will determine whether or not our thrust toward pluralism in the 21st century will be for us all a tragedy or a triumph.

REFERENCES

Blockson, C. (1977). *Black genealogy*. Englewood Cliffs, NJ: Prentice-Hall.

Bourgeois, L. (1976). *Cabanocey: The history, customs and folklore of St. James parish*. Gretna, LA: Pelican.

Bowen, M. (1976). Theory in practice of psychotherapy. In P. Guerin (Ed.), *Family therapy: Theory and practice*. New York: Gardner Press.

Chasin, R. (1976). Lecture presented at Solomon Carter Fuller Center,

Elkins, S. (1976). *Slavery: A problem in American institutional and intellectual life*. Chicago: University of Chicago Press.

Franklin, J. H. (1966). *From slavery to freedom*. New York: Knopf.

Griffin, S. (1992). *A chorus of stones: The private life of war*. New York: Doubleday.

Herbert, D. (1976). Introduction to Black genealogy. *Southwest Louisiana Records, 13*(2).

Jones, C. (1995, April 2). Blacks seek catharsis by bringing slavery's long shadow to the light. *The New York Times*.

Laird, J. (1989). Women and stories: Restorying women's self-constructions. In M. McGoldrick, C. Anderson, & F. Walsh (Eds.), *Women in families: A framework for family therapy*. New York: Norton.

Litton, R. (1993). *The protean self*. New York: Basic Books.

Pinderhughes, C. A. (1973). Racism and psychotherapy. In C. Willie, B. Kramer, & B. Brown (Eds.), *Racism and mental health*. Pittsburgh: University of Pittsburgh Press.

Pinderhugnes, E. (1989). *Understanding race, ethnicity and power*. New York: Free Press.

Pinderhughes, E. (1995). The power to care.

Taylor, J. G. (1963). *Negro slavery in Louisiana*. New York: Negro Universities Press.

The Times-Picayune New Orleans. (1963, February). Sword's plunge introduced LaPice name to Louisiana.

CHAPTER 15

The Discovery of My Multicultural Identity

Fernando Colón

My sense of who I am has not come to me easily. My beginnings were shrouded by a mysterious tragedy that occurred at the time of my birth, the details of which were withheld from me for decades. I was raised in foster care, receiving only a handful of cryptic visits from my father and completely cut off from my mother. I was given no sense of who my people were, where I came from, or even what my racial and ethnic background was. The defining struggle of my life has been to find the racial, ethnic, and cultural aspects of my self; to uncover the truth of the events that transpired at my birth; and to integrate these discoveries into my sense of who I am.

MYSTERY AND CONFUSION: MY LIFE FROM BIRTH TO 17 YEARS

I was fortunate enough to land in the care of wonderful foster parents. "Mom" was a Swiss–German immigrant to the United States. At 19 she had fled an abusive alcoholic father and a long-suffering but courageous mother. Arriving in New York, she worked as a domestic, learned to speak Brooklynese English, married, and bore a daughter. After her husband, also an alcoholic, died of pneumonia, she met my foster father—a cab driver in Brooklyn who found her housecleaning jobs with some of his regular customers. He was of English heritage; he had previously been married and then divorced after the death of his only child, also a daughter. He was 15 years older than Mom.

"Dad" was a good man. He taught me the practical skills one needs to maintain a house. He and my foster mother built the house in which we lived, in spite of the fact that he had a stiff hip and a shortened leg from polio as a child. He read the newspaper and listened to the news on the radio every day. As I was growing up, he put together bikes and built toys for me. And at Easter he painted beautiful, European-style Easter eggs. He was a wonderful father figure and shaped my character in valuable ways.

Mom and Dad entered into what became a 25-year common-law marriage, which lasted until Dad's death at the age of 72. After Mom's daughter was grown and married, they began to take care of foster children. During the 15½ years that I lived with them, I had 10 foster brothers of different ages, gifts, and problems, who stayed with us for varying lengths of time.

Our diverse household was the context in which I first began to wonder about my racial and ethnic identity. Although I didn't yet know that my biological parents were Puerto Rican, I was well aware that my skin, hair, and eyes were darker than anyone else's in our home. Four of my foster brothers were German; three were English; one was Scotch, one Irish, and one a Jew. The contrast made me certain that I did not belong to my foster parents the way other children belonged to their parents.

The neighborhood was also quite diverse. An Irish Catholic family lived next door. Its members were morose and reserved, except for occasional alcohol-induced bursts of arguing. On the other side lived an extended Italian family. Three generations of Italians would gather on weekends to eat, laugh, drink wine, argue, play music, and have great family times together. I was fortunate to have these Italian neighbors, because their hearty way of life, expressiveness, and darker skin gave me a hint of who I might be. Growing up within a family where most of the other members were of Northern European origin was an ever-present source of confusion and uncertainty.

While I was being raised under Mom and Dad's care on Long Island, my biological father was a sergeant in the U.S. Army, stationed in New York City. Although his barracks were about an hour away, he visited me only occasionally during my childhood. I was confused by his visits, but filled with curiosity and respect for him in his impeccable uniform. Each of his infrequent visits brought up troubling questions about who I was, to whom I belonged, and what had happened to my mother. I had never seen her.

At about the age of 5, I began to ask some questions about my real mother, to which Mom and Dad had no answers. It may have been at their urging that my father visited for the particular purpose of telling me about my mother. I remember that he suggested we go for a walk around the block, possibly so we would not be overheard by my foster family. It felt like he was letting me in on a big secret. He told me that soon after I was born, my mother got a fever and died. I realized that I would never get to see her. I felt very sad on hearing this, and also smaller somehow—diminished and less complete.

Not long after that, I was visited by my father's youngest sister, her husband, and their daughter. They were very warm people and introduced themselves as my aunt, uncle, and cousin. I was thrilled to discover I had more family. Their skin, hair, and eyes were the same color as mine. Although the excitement of their visit was tinged with the fear that they had come to take me away, we enjoyed our time together immensely. Sadly, they never visited again, and those feelings were fleeting.

On another occasion, I was visited by some more dark-skinned people. An old man named Isaac, a younger man, and a boy arrived and asked to see me, but did not reveal who they were. It seemed as though they must be connected to me in some way, but they wouldn't give any indication of our relationship. We talked awkwardly as Mom served them coffee and little cookies in the living room. They asked to take some pictures of me, and I posed with my dog, Butch, in front of the house. They thanked us and left. The whole thing had a very strange air, and for decades it remained a mystery to me.

Meanwhile, I was enjoying school and getting along well with my peers, for the most part. Yet there were painful moments in elementary school that set me apart and deepened my confusion about who I was. When I was 10 years old, our music teacher decided my first name, Fernando, was too long. So he took it upon himself to give me a shorter, anglicized name: "Ferd." In front of the whole class, he announced that my name would now be Ferd. I was stunned. I couldn't speak to object as my name was wrenched away from me. From then on, the other teachers, my classmates and friends, and sometimes even my foster family called me Ferd. I experienced a deep sense of loss and shame, and, again, a feeling of being diminished.

Even though I had lost my Puerto Rican first name, I relished the Hispanic nature of my last name, Colón. During one of his visits, my father took great care to explain the importance of putting an accent over the last "o." If I didn't, he warned, people would confuse my name with the large intestine. I consider this one of the few gifts my father gave me: He instilled in me a sense of pride about my name. And every time I accented that "o," I felt a connection to him and a family lineage.

Another incident I vividly remember was being verbally abused in the sixth grade. I got into an argument with a classmate when we both wanted to sit in the same chair. We started arguing, and he ended it by calling me a "nigger." I was caught off guard by this, totally unprepared for such a thing. I never thought of myself as Black, but I knew I wasn't White. In addition to the fear and anger I felt at being hit with this loaded word, I was deeply ashamed. The incident reopened the painful and still very unresolved question of who I was. Was I Black, or White, or both?

The next defining incidents took place when I was 15. Out of the blue, my foster father suffered a massive stroke and went into a coma. We were able to care for him at home until he died, several days later. I was devastated by this loss and grieved for his death as though he were my real father. Dad had given me his love and been a guiding influence for me on many levels. I would miss him very much.

Later that same year, my father was discharged from the Army. There was a lot of discussion, which I was not privy to, about whether I would go to live with him or continue to stay with my foster mother. This was a pivotal point in my life. My connection to my father was rather thin. Although he had helped me to some extent with the question of who I was, he had not been present enough for me to feel really connected to him. On the other hand, I felt profoundly connected to my foster home, where I had received the love and continuity I needed. I don't remember talking to anyone about it, but I knew that I did not want to live with my father. I hoped he would stay nearby so that he might become more of a presence in my life, especially since Dad had recently died, but that was not an option.

My father decided that he would return to Puerto Rico and that I would stay in the foster home, finish high school, go on to college, and live "the good life" in the United States. I felt relieved and abandoned at the same time. It was a confusing time, but one thing was clear: My father's decision meant the end of what little connection I had to him and to a sense of family.

MAKING MY WAY IN THE WORLD: MY LIFE FROM 17 TO 33 YEARS

I graduated with honors from high school in June 1953. On September 3 of that year, I was "discharged to my own responsibility" from the New York City Child Welfare System. This meant that the financial responsibility for my care was over and I was "on my own." I was able nonetheless to go to college with a combination of savings from part-time work, a work–study program at the college, and scholarship assistance. The event of leaving home to attend college pushed my need to know more about my biological family back to the surface. There had been no discussion of or plans made for my continuing relationship with my foster mother, and I felt as if I were being cast off into the world with no formal ties to anyone. But Mom did a wonderful thing: She gave me the steamer trunk that carried her things from Switzerland. It was one of her prized possessions. With that trunk, she was giving me a part of her family, her history, and herself. This solidified our bond, and I knew we would stay connected even though I was officially discharged from her care. I stayed in touch with her for the duration of her life, and to this day I cherish that trunk.

After packing and shipping Mom's trunk to college, I set off for a trip to the west coast with two friends. We got a ride to Seattle and planned to hitch-hike our way back across the southwest to the college in Illinois. As we made our way through the deserts, my skin became increasingly tanned. I had noticed signs over bathrooms and drinking fountains designating "white" or "colored" and had been feeling uneasy. Things had gone relatively smoothly until just outside of Little Rock, when no one would pick us up. After several hours, we decided to split up and meet again in Memphis, thinking one person could get a ride more easily than three. One of us got a ride, the European American, and then another, the Italian. But no one would stop for me. Eventually I was picked up by the police. When they discovered that I had less than five dollars in my wallet, I was considered a vagrant and taken to jail. I repeatedly asked why they were detaining me, and requested a phone call, but they simply locked me away in a cell. The next morning, I was again denied a phone call and no one came to talk to me about the situation. On the third day, Sunday, a cleaning woman came through the hallway by the cells. I told her my story and she promised to get me some help. She must have succeeded, because on Monday morning I was released without question. Apparently they had been tracking a suspect when I was passing through the area. I decided not to hitch-hike and used my last dollars for a bus fare to Memphis. I made it to college without further incident, but I was deeply shaken by the incident.

Arriving on campus I endured further suspicion. Although I had had the chance to shower and clean up that morning, I looked less than my best in the clothes I'd been wearing for a week, and I was also deeply tanned. I felt myself being observed, sized up. Even the school's registrars were not at all sure that I was one of the matriculating students. Eventually, they checked the records and determined that I was in fact an incoming student. These experiences heightened my sense of being an outsider and renewed my racial uncertainty. But, eventually, I was able to settle into college life and make friends.

In the fall of my junior year, one of my friends introduced me to his cousin, a freshman named Lois. Lois was very attractive and receiving a fair amount of attention from other men on campus. So I decided I had to do something different, which was to pay her no attention at all. It worked. When she invited me to a Sadie Hawkins dance, we began a serious courtship. And at the end of that year, we married.

Our wedding was a mixed experience for me, as it brought our differing family backgrounds into sharp contrast. Lois's parents (of Scotch, Irish, French, and English descent) were there, along with her two sisters; several aunts, uncles, and cousins; and an abundance of Lois' long-standing friends from childhood, high school, and college. However, no one from either my foster family or my biological family attended (so the wedding didn't really bring Lois' and my families together). Two good friends from high school and five or six recent college buddies were there for me. I felt good about becoming a part of my wife's family, but I also felt a void where my own family should have been. For me, the day was both joyful and somber.

I went on to graduate school in clinical psychology. I had considered medicine and the ministry, but the idea of being a psychologist prevailed— perhaps because it was a natural extension of my childhood experience, in which I helped my younger foster brothers grow up. In the second year of graduate school, we had our first child, a beautiful brown-complexioned baby girl. It was an astounding experience for me, not only because I became a father, but because it was the first time that I felt part of an intact, biological family unit.

Throughout my high school and college years, my father and I hardly corresponded. Through his rare letters, I accumulated bits and pieces of information about my extended families. When I was 18, I learned my mother's first name, Margarita. When I was 19, I learned that both sets of my grandparents were farmers. This helped me to know myself a bit more, but it still seemed very distant and disconnected. In response to our announcement of our daughter's birth, my father wrote that he was the 4th of 14 children, 10 of whom were still alive. I was amazed to discover that I had such a large extended family. My father also said he knew very little about my mother's family, except that she had a sister who had three children.

In 1961, Lois and I had our second child, a son. His birth prompted me to write another letter to my father, in which I also asked more questions about my mother. In response, my father reported that after my birth, my mother got sick and was returned to her family in Puerto Rico. She was cared for on her family farm until she died, a year or so later. This was not what my father had told me when I was 5 years old, and it dawned on me that my father had been lying. I gradually became intent on finding some answers. I needed to learn more about my families, meet them, and reestablish face-to-face contact with my father. So, at the age of 33, I decided that it was time to visit Puerto Rico.

THE "IDENTITY SEARCH":
MY LIFE FROM 33 TO 37 YEARS

I made my first trip to Puerto Rico in 1968. Lois accompanied me, as did our children (we now had three, who were 10, 7, and 4 years old). By now I had obtained my PhD in clinical psychology, obtained a university position, and begun a private practice. It had been 16 years since I had seen my father, and I felt both elation and anxiety at the prospect of our meeting again. Upon hearing the news of our trip, my father wrote and informed me that he had remarried, and included a recent photo of himself and his new wife, Lydia. With the help of this photo, we were able to recognize each other at the airport and reintroduce ourselves to each other, as well as to introduce our wives and my children.

It was not a warm greeting, but the mood became more comfortable over the 3 weeks we were there. The children's natural warmth helped break the ice with my father; he even carried our youngest piggyback occasionally, a gesture of uncharacteristic playfulness. Despite my father's reserve, his family welcomed me warmly. On countless occasions, we would all pile into the car and set off to visit another aunt, uncle, or cousin. In particular, I reconnected with the aunt and uncle who had visited me when I was 6, and began what has become a close friendship with them and their daughter, Nancy.

The trip was not the vacation we had naively hoped it would be. It was a very stressful experience for Lois, especially because of the unfamiliar and intense mode of relating that is so characteristic of Puerto Ricans. But the intensity of their interactions matched the intensity I felt in finally finding my extended family. I was one of them, and I belonged. It was exhilarating.

During one memorable visit, Lydia talked to my father and aunt in hushed tones. There seemed to be something important going on as she urged him to grant a request. Lois and I had no idea what was being said. My father looked ominously at them, then at me. Then he sighed and said, "*Sí!*" My aunt hurried to get something, and I could tell from Lydia's excitement that they had something to show me. My aunt brought out a dusty sack and laid it on the table. Carefully, she slid out its contents and produced a photograph. It was my mother and father's wedding portrait. It was the first time I had ever seen a picture of my mother. I was dumbfounded. As I pored over every detail, it dawned on me that my face bears a striking resemblance to my mother's face. Lois, Lydia, and my aunt all wept. My father stood there and said nothing.

My aunt and uncle gave me the wedding picture to take home and copy. It felt as if they were palpably giving me a missing piece of myself, and I felt very grateful. For the first time, I felt a satisfying connection to my mother. Yet the wedding picture raised still more painful and haunting questions. Where in Puerto Rico had she lived? Was her family still there? What was she like? And if she hadn't died just after my birth, as I'd been told, why had she returned to Puerto Rico without me or my father? My attempts to discuss these issues with my father were difficult. He was tense, guarded, and evasive. He did reveal a few details: the name of my mother's home town, as well as the fact that she had an uncle named Isaac and a sister named Dominga, who had three children. He insisted that they had all moved to Washington, DC, but he didn't know their address. This made no sense to me—that my aunt, her children and her uncle would all move to the States and stay there. It just didn't ring true. But why would my father lie? The trip finally ended and we went home, but I resolved to continue searching for the truth about my mother.

By the summer of 1971, I had prepared for my second trip to Puerto Rico by brushing up on my Spanish. I decided to go alone because it would not be a vacation. Relations with my father were still somewhat tense, but an increasing bond grew between me and Lydia. Although she could speak no English and we could barely communicate, she was very sympathetic to my cause. Lydia was an orphan herself, and had grown up in very difficult circumstances. I understood later that her gentle prodding behind the scenes often prompted my father to share more information with me. Probably as a result of her insistence, my father gave me two more photos of my mother. Although he had told me the name of her home town on the earlier visit, he said when I pressed him on this occasion that he said he didn't know how to get there. I understood this to mean that he didn't know how to get there psychologically, and I realized I would have to go alone.

I borrowed my father's Volkswagen "bug" under false pretenses and headed to the western part of the island, toward my mother's home town. On the way, the weather suddenly changed and I found myself in a tropical rainstorm which forced me off the road. At first I felt blocked and frustrated. But then I thought, "No, this is it! Nothing, is going to stop me from getting to my mother's home town, *nothing*." When the rain was less intense, I drove on through the flooded roads. After a while, the VW's battery conked out, but I persevered. I was able to replace the battery with the help of two locals, a father and a son who refused to let me pay them for their labor. I sensed my luck had turned.

Before long I arrived at my mother's home town. I had no idea where to begin looking for any of her family; I merely had her name written on a piece of paper. I remembered my father's once mentioning that my mother was a Baptist, so I decided to begin looking at the Baptist church. Somehow the minister and I managed to communicate, he in his broken English and I in my broken Spanish. Unfortunately, he had only recently moved to town and did not recognize my mother's family name. He suggested that we go to the local hospital to see if there were any birth or death records on file. We did, but were unable to find any record of her.

Disappointed, we were about to leave when I happened to mention my great-uncle, Isaac—who was by now deceased, or so I assumed. The hospital clerk immediately recognized Isaac's name and directed us to his house. There I discovered that Isaac was still living at age 92, but was in a coma. He was being cared for by one of his adult daughters, who invited us in and chatted with us at his bedside. For some reason, I felt a sense of gratitude and a deep connection to him. Not knowing how else to express this feeling, before we left I leaned over and gave him a kiss on the forehead.

Isaac's daughter knew my mother's sister, Dominga, and gave us directions to find her. Dominga's house happened to be right across the street from the Baptist church. When we knocked at her door, Dominga answered. The minister started to introduce us, but Dominga's reaction interrupted him. Upon seeing my face, she gasped. Her hands flew to her mouth and she burst into tears, saying, "*La cara! La cara!*" ("The face! The face!"). She was seeing my mother's face in mine and realized who I must be. She and the minister exchanged words, and it seemed that yes, finally, I had found my mother's sister. All of this was happening so suddenly that it seemed almost too good to be true. I asked the minister to see whether there was any way she could prove that she was my aunt. He spoke quickly to her in Spanish. She ran into the house and returned with pictures of her adult children and other family members.

Dominga brought us into her living room and hurried to locate more pictures. She found one in particular and handed it to me, shaking with excitement. In it, I saw myself at age 6 on the front steps of my foster parents' house with my dog, Butch. This was the photo that those "mysterious visitors" had taken. I was amazed. And then the story came tumbling out. The whole family, she said, had been desperate to find out what had happened to Margarita's baby. Uncle Isaac had visited me, along with her cousin Jaime and her son Frank. They reported that I was doing well in the foster home and showed the family this picture of me. Now I knew why I'd felt such gratitude toward Isaac: He had been instrumental in bringing news of me to my mother's family.

After some time at Dominga's house, she took us to the family farm where she and my mother had grown up. It was now owned by another of Isaac's daughters and her husband. Excitedly Dominga introduced me to them and to their children and grandchildren. It was my first glimpse of the extended family on my mother's side, and the resemblance between these children and my own was striking. One of my second cousins was also named Fernando, and we even looked alike! Here, I felt I truly belonged—that I, too, had a place in a real, biological, blood *familia*!

At the farm, I also met Isaac's son Jaime, who had introduced my parents when he and my father were both in the Army. I was thankful that his fluency in English enabled us to talk freely. He said he had felt some responsibility to check on me while he was stationed in New York during those years. "Your mother was my favorite cousin," he said. He then told me what had really happened to my mother. After my birth she had become violently ill from the anesthesia. Although she got physically better, she then became emotionally depressed and started to hallucinate. She was transferred to a state psychiatric hospital on Long Island. When her condition did not improve, Jaime appealed to the welfare department for funds and made arrangements for her to return to the family farm. She stayed with her family for 9 months but could not emerge from the severe depression. Finally, she was admitted to a psychiatric hospital in San Juan, where she remained until she died—*25 years later.* She had died in 1962, from aspirating some food.

I was curious about my father's role in this. Jaime said that on one occasion, after my mother had returned to Puerto Rico, my father sent her some money; after that, however, the family never heard from him again. It was Jaime who later arranged to visit me in the foster home with Isaac and little Frank. Jaime said that my father had only agreed to it on the condition that they would not reveal who they were, that my mother would not be mentioned, and that I would receive no information about their family. Jaime believed that my father was afraid of my mother's illness, and that this was the reason he was never heard from again.

Jaime translated for Dominga, who said with tears in her eyes that my mother had always remembered me. Dominga had made the trip to San Juan to visit her every weekend, and during each visit, for 25 years, my mother had asked about me. Dominga believed that if my mother had been able to see me, her depression might have lifted.

Before I left, I called to let my father know that I was in my mother's home town and that I'd be back later that night. I thought he would be waiting up to talk to me when I returned, but he wasn't; he had gone to bed. The next day I told my father that I had found Dominga, met some of the family, and visited their farm. He did not seem pleased about this, and wanted to know exactly whom I had met. I told him, and conveyed their invitation for him to join me in a family reunion on the upcoming Saturday. He was quiet and didn't respond.

Despite his guardedness, I continued to seek out details of my mother's life. I visited the psychiatric facility where she was kept and succeeded with some difficulty in getting to review her voluminous twenty-five year record. Now I had the facts: names, dates, events and family information. The record corroborated exactly with what Dominga and Jaime had told me. I felt more grounded, it was beginning to sink in that I had found the truth about my mother.

On Friday night, my father said he'd decided not to go with me to the reunion on Saturday. He said he couldn't face Isaac. Although I told him that Isaac was in a coma and would not be there, he said, "No. They are all mad at me for not letting them see you. It has spread like a cloud through the family. No," he said, "get me Jaime's address. Then someday, on my own time, I'll go back, look him up and get him to talk to the family and make it right." I was frustrated by my father's decision. As I thought about it, I felt that he really had mishandled the situation. He had abandoned my mother when she, as he said, "went crazy." He had allowed her child to be taken away from her and hidden me from her family. He had lied to me about what had happened. And, finally, he hadn't even kept me with him. It was clear that he and I needed to talk.

The next morning my father and I sat down together. I hoped that if I openly shared with him what I'd discovered, he might be truthful too. I began by telling him that I'd discovered things about my mother that he didn't know, and I wanted to share them. I told him about her being in the psychiatric hospital until she died in 1962. His immediate reaction was anger. He felt I had been investigating him as if he were a criminal. I replied that although I could see why he might feel that way, I still had a right to know the truth about what had happened to my mother. Then he said, "I knew she was crazy. I didn't want to tell you because I didn't know how your mind would take it." When I heard this, his behavior and secrecy began to make some sense to me: He was afraid that her mental illness might affect me in some way, and wanted to protect me from it as best he could. He had truly believed it would be better for me to think that she was dead, and then he'd had to cut me off from her family to protect his lie. Now, finally, I had the whole truth.

I was deeply touched by the dilemma that he believed he was in, and with that knowledge I could begin to let go of my resentment and forgive him. Yet he still remained very reserved and quiet about the situation. Lydia later told me that after she and my father talked about all of these events, he wept.

I went on to spend the day with my mother's family at their farm. Before we arrived there, Dominga, Frank, and Evelyn (my cousin Frank's sister) took me to the cemetery where my mother was buried. It was an emotional experience for all of us. As we stood before her grave, my aunt and cousins wept. I had a strange feeling come over my whole being. I

didn't understand what it was, but I felt a sense of resolution: I had somehow reestablished my broken tie to my mother, and not even the reality
of her death could ever break it again. I felt complete, whole, and at
peace. It was a very sacred moment for me.

We went on to the farm, where Frank had prepared a feast by slaugh-
tering and roasting a young goat. About 30 people came for the day—
cousins, children, grandchildren, and some close friends who had known
my mother in her younger years. Beer and wine flowed freely, and they
all took great pleasure in introducing me to their family specialties: fried
plantains, spicy rice and beans, and an incredible flan made with tropical
fruits. We spent the whole day together, talking, laughing, and telling
stories. Each member of the family recalled for me experiences they had
had with my mother. It was their way of giving her back to me. Jaime
spoke to me again and said, "You know, Fernando—I had a feeling that
one day you would come and find us. I have looked forward to this for a
long time."

At one point, Dominga went into the house and found a family photograph. It was a group portrait of several families: Isaac with his children and grandchildren, Dominga and her children. Everyone in the picture was someone I had now met at this farm or heard stories about.
Dominga gave me a huge, radiant smile and gestured that the picture was
for me. Pressing it into my hand, she said "Tu familia," and then envel-
oped me in her arms. It was, without a doubt, a homecoming.

Upon experiencing the open warmth of my mother's extended family, I felt an even more complete sense of myself. I now had the fullness of
the other half of my identity, and could see, touch, and embrace my roots.
At last I would no longer feel painfully different from other people who
had close ties with their blood families. I would now be able to answer
the once painful questions about my family background without shame,
embarrassment, or confusion. My sense of self was now complete, and it
was a profoundly good feeling.

INTEGRATION: MY LIFE FROM 37 TO 60 YEARS

It took many years to integrate the pieces of myself that I discovered in
Puerto Rico. After the initial reunion with my mother's family, Jaime put
me in touch with his sister Connie, who lived in Washington, DC. Connie
proved to be a marvelous family resource and a kindred spirit. We spent
hours talking about my mother—what she was like as a child, what her
personality was like, and how joyful and energetic she could be. As she
got to know me, she told me that my personality was very similar to my
mother's. Connie told me many more specific details of my mother's life,

and in particular the details of her death. After my mother died, Dominga had had some difficulty in getting her body released from the psychiatric hospital. When the body finally came home, it was too late to organize a funeral. She was buried immediately, without any kind of service or gathering of the family. When I heard this, I knew what I wanted to do—to gather the family and have a memorial service for my mother.

Connie also had a deep sense that this was what I and the family needed to do together. She helped me contact members of the family and coordinate the service. We found that most of the women immediately connected to the idea and felt the need for it. The reaction from the men, on the other hand, was mixed. Nevertheless, they all attended the service that Connie, the minister and I arranged.

The memorial gave me and the family an opportunity to release the grief over my mother's tragic life and death that we'd carried for years. About 30 of us gathered at a small rural chapel near the farm. My cousin's husband, Miguel, a senator in the Puerto Rican government and a compelling speaker, gave an eloquent and moving eulogy. Connie wished they had thought to tape the service so that I could have received a translation. I, too, wished I could have understood the eulogy. And yet I felt I knew what was being said, in spirit if not in word. I will always be grateful to Connie and the rest of the family for having the courage and compassion to come together and share our grief. I will never forget that day and the tears we shared together.

I had invited my father to the memorial service; he declined the invitation, but told me he was glad that it was taking place. He could appreciate what we were doing, yet he could not overcome his reluctance to face my mother's family or his grief over the events that had occurred so long ago. A few years later, he did visit Jaime and some other members of my mother's family. Although it went well with Jaime, Dominga carried more anger. She and my father became very reactive to each other's emotional intensity, and some harsh words were exchanged. They were unable to achieve much of a reconciliation.

My father died in March 1990. When I received the news that he was near death, I made the trip to San Juan with my younger son, then 26. By the time we arrived at the VA hospital, my father had lapsed into a coma. It was a sad time, of course, but being in a hospital in Puerto Rico is truly a cultural experience. The visits on the ward were communal gatherings of families and friends of all ages. Fellow patients knew all about each other's families. We learned, however, that before my father lost consciousness, he had told the other patients on his ward all about me, my family, and my career in the United States. We also visited with Lydia and with the patients and families there, appreciating the camaraderie at my father's bedside. My father soon died of heart failure, a few days short of his 88th birthday.

The locus of our attention then shifted to a massive urban funeral home. My father's funeral was a particularly meaningful event for me because both sides of my family came to give their last respects. I was especially moved by the fact that members of my mother's family came in spite of my father's history with them. I believe that this in some way completed their relationships, after some 50 years of estrangement. Although we had not developed a close relationship in the 22 years I'd known him in adulthood, we had come to an understanding. We left no unfinished business.

Talking over these events with my foster mother helped me integrate the new material I had discovered about myself and my families. Mom and I had stayed in touch throughout these years. She had met Lois and our children, and we corresponded fairly regularly until her death at the age of 85. I was able to share with her my discoveries in Puerto Rico: how I found my mother's family, the details of her life, and the reasons for my father's secrecy and deception. She wanted to know because she, too, had sensed something was amiss with my father and had often wondered about my extended families.

Lois and I have been able to attend some family celebrations in Puerto Rico, which have deepened my connections to the island and the family. The most elaborate was the wedding of one of my second cousins. It was a Catholic High Mass in an ancient church, followed by a wonderful reception, where some 400 members of the community of all colors and social classes danced to traditional island favorites. During the waltz that formally introduces the new husband and wife, the families insisted that my wife and I take turns dancing—she with the groom, and I with the bride. I remembered my own wedding and how much I'd missed having family there. So being a part of this wedding was all the more wonderful for me.

In order to find out more about the island and my racial makeup, I researched the history of Puerto Rico. I learned that the indigenous people were wiped out by the Spaniards, who arrived in the early 1500s. Thereafter, the immigrants were largely Spanish colonists and African slaves; thus there probably flows both Spanish and African blood in my immediate family. Looking around at the various shades of skin color at family gatherings, I could see the mix of these racial influences. After doing this research, I wanted to explore aspects of my cultural and ethnic legacy further. So in 1985 I traveled to Spain for 3 weeks, visiting Madrid, Seville, Granada, Cordoba, and Toledo. I was delighted to find my name, Colón, everywhere—as the name of people, towns, hotels, and streets all over the country. It was impossible for me not to feel a connection to my Spanish heritage.

As the integration process progressed, I found myself revisiting a number of key childhood memories. One day, I awoke enraged at the memory of the music teacher and the experience of having my name arbitrarily changed. I decided to reclaim my given name, Fernando. It was a difficult thing to do, especially for my wife, who had fallen in love with me and had known me all these years as Ferd. But gradually my family and friends made the switch. These days, my grandchildren call me Nando, a common nickname for Fernando. I must admit it has a nice ring and a much warmer quality to it.

After reconnecting with both sides of my biological family, and understanding who I am racially, ethnically, and culturally, I feel like a whole person. I have a strong sense of being fully here, of having finally arrived. I am a living member of a blood family that extends into the past and future, over innumerable generations. I now know where my place is in the chain of humanity.

CHAPTER 16

Belonging and Liberation
FINDING A PLACE CALLED "HOME"

Monica McGoldrick

> We forget that we are history . . . We are not used to
> associating our private lives with public events. Yet
> the histories of families cannot be separated from the
> histories of nations. To divide them is part of our
> denial. All that I was taught at home or in school was
> colored by denial and thus it became so familiar to me
> that I did not see it. We keep secrets from ourselves
> that all along we know. . . . I do not see my life as
> separate from history. In my mind my family secrets
> mingle with the secrets of statesmen and bombers. My
> life [is not] divided from the lives of others. I who am
> woman, have my father's face. And he, I suspect, had
> his mother's face. There are so many strands to the
> story . . . I begin to suspect each strand goes out
> infinitely and touches everything, everyone. . . .
> Nothing stands alone. Everything has something
> standing beside it. And the two are really one.
> —SUSAN GRIFFIN, *A Chorus of Stones*
> (1992, pp. 4, 11)

There were many things about my privilege and about my oppression
that I grew up not knowing or not knowing that I knew—many issues
that were mystified, obscured, or kept invisible by my community and
my training. Society's invisible structuring of gender, class, culture, race,
and sexual orientation limited the relationships in my family, my schooling, and the communities in which I have lived. None of these issues was
ever mentioned during my childhood or adolescence, in my college or
graduate school experience, or in my study of family therapy. I think

---

The ideas in this chapter have been evolving over the past several years. I first presented
them at the *Family Therapy Networker* Conference in 1994, and they were published in
that organization's magazine the same year.

"passing" is what all people in the United States have been pressed to do: to accommodate, to fit into images, to keep invisible the parts of themselves that do not conform to the dominant culture's values. Historically, some of us have found our safety at the expense of others, mostly without knowing it. We must not seek safety that jeopardizes others or denies them their own sense of belonging and spiritual connection.

I have been wondering what will help us realize that, as Susan Griffin says, "our personal stories and the history of the world are all one story" (p. 8). How can we realize that somewhere within ourselves we know the secrets we keep from ourselves and from each other? I have come to realize that "home" is about much more than where we live physically. It is not just where we sleep, and it is not just the nostalgic home of our childhood or our wished-for childhood. It is a spiritual and psychological place of liberation. Home is a space where we could all belong, with each other—strengthened by what we take from those who have come before us, creating a safe haven for those who are with us in our time, and insuring that we leave a safe space for our children and all those who will come after us. I am coming to realize that I must work to create a safe place not just for my own child, but for the children of all of us, who are, as Jorge Luis Borges has put it, "our immortality" on earth.

My own notions of "going home" have been radically challenged as I have become aware of the constraints of class, culture, gender, and race on the structure of who I am. I have been coming to realize that "going home" means going to a place most of us have never been, since home in our society has not been a safe place for most people in our country—not for women, children, people of color, or gays and lesbians, given the pervasiveness of corporal punishment, child sexual abuse, the mistreatment and devaluing of women, and the appalling racism and homophobia of our society.

UNACKNOWLEDGED ASPECTS OF MY GROWING UP

I grew up quite blind to how gender, sexual orientation, class, race, and culture were structuring my life. My blindness existed in spite of the fact that I grew up in an interracial family, since my primary caretaker, Margaret Bush, was African American. Her role in our family was structured by her invisibility in the service of our becoming visible, and her race was never mentioned. Like most people in the United States, I also grew up in effectively segregated neighborhoods and went to *de facto* segregated schools. Even today the local school in my community is effectively segregated, as are the educational system as a whole, the government, and the mass media.

Although we also never mentioned gender in my family, my father was a visiting dignitary, while two women—one the servant of the other, my mother and my primary caretaker, Margaret—raised three girls in what was most of the time an all-female household. There were clearly different and preferential rules regarding men, but these rules were kept invisible. In addition, the influence of my Irish background would have been obvious to anyone who could recognize Irish behavior, looks, or names; yet I never knew that I was Irish. I think now that this was because my family was trying to "pass" for Anglo. Moreover, we were taught that class did not matter, though we learned implicitly who was above us and who was below us in class, and had a complete set of hierarchical prescriptions for our behavior (acceptable schools to go to, whom we could date or befriend, etc.). Though we were dimly aware of social stratification, class was never mentioned in my family, and we were led to believe that we lived in a class-blind as well as a color-blind family, community, and society. Yet at the same time we organized our relationships completely according to prescribed and biased rules of gender, class, culture, race, and sexual orientation.

I grew up not knowing that I had a cultural background at all. This, of course, was probably because I could "pass" for a member of the dominant group. Had I been Black or Latino, I would have known that I had a culture. As my mother put it when I began asking questions, "We're Americans now, Monica. Our ancestors were just peasants. What difference does it make where we came from?" It was not until the mid-1970s that I realized I was Irish. Through my interest in Murray Bowen's theory, I had begun to explore my own roots and inspired a trip by our whole family to Ireland. I was overwhelmed when I landed in Ireland by the feeling that I had come home. Everywhere I seemed to see my relatives, people who related in the same way my family did—using humor, teasing, and ridicule to keep others in line or to maintain distance in male–female relationships; failing to talk about the most important things that were happening; giving someone the "silent treatment." Suddenly patterns I had experienced all my life had a context: It wasn't that my family was "crazy," I was just Irish! It was a transformative experience that has never left me. I still think of Ireland as home in some deep way, and coming to define myself as Irish American has been an affirmation at the deepest level of my belonging. Much that I thought was strange or eccentric I now see has a meaning because of our cultural history.

It has been very reassuring to give a name to this and many other aspects of my life that were unacknowledged as I grew up. Of course, there is a problem at a certain point with any label such as this: It excludes those who do not belong, in ways that may not be helpful to our mutual sense of "home." Focusing on ethnicity or on any other group identity clarifies some things, but obscures others.

THREE UNSUNG "SHEROES"

I grew up hearing my mother and everyone else tell me how special my father was. My mother, on the other hand, I experienced as extremely intimidating, unaffectionate, and "difficult." Had my father had the same difficulty expressing his warmth that my mother did, I am sure I would have been less judgmental of that failing. Now I realize that nothing in my experience led me to have empathy for my mother's life or the difficulties of her position in raising us. She was a city person, extremely energetic, intelligent, and social, who for 8 years raised us in a country house to live out a dream of my father's, while he remained in the city— "the good provider" who was "making our dreams come true." My mother spent her life serving as our chauffeur and trying to invent things to do with her life, isolated from everything she had ever known. Much later, she admitted that she nearly went crazy wishing to be with my father and to have a career of her own again in New York City. Instead, she had to make the most of her enormous energy and ability in an extremely confining situation. She developed many home-related skills: rewiring lamps, painting, plumbing, and buying and fixing antiques.

My mother was also a great storyteller, though I now regret that I spent years not listening to her. Her family stories were primarily about the men in our family—her admired uncle, her beloved husband, and her beloved father. She did not talk about her mother, whom she hated for all of her life; who had an affair with a local priest (not the thing for an Irish matron to do!); and who had no patience for her three daughters, especially the youngest, my mother. Indeed, when my mother was small, her mother used to tell her not to come home from school because Father Egan would be there. She did not tell me that her mother was the first woman on Staten Island to drive a car; that she had an amazing eye for beautiful objects; or that, as my cousin put it, she was one of the early liberated women of her era.

My mother once commented that she had first been known as "Inspector Cahalane's daughter" and then as "Joe McGoldrick's wife." She ended by saying, "I was always somebody's something, just as now I'm Monica's mother. Just once I'd like to be known as Helen McGoldrick, who stands on her own two feet. But that's never going to happen, Monica."

The pain of my mother's always having to be "somebody's something" is a problem I have come to realize is mine as well as hers. Her history, fears, inadequacies, and struggles continue through me. Because of the time in which she lived, she was not able to be all that she could be. She, her two sisters, and their classmates at Barnard College in the 1930s were a privileged and exceptionally talented group of women who, for the most part, had to submerge their identities in those of the men and children in their lives. My mother had a successful career in public relations when she met my father, but she gave up her career and even her name to be Mrs. Joseph McGoldrick.

For years I resented her for what I saw as "bragging" and "covering up who we really were" by coloring stories to impress others with our accomplishments—where we went to school and so forth. When I switched fields from Russian studies to social work, my mother was embarrassed. She could not even bring herself to use the term "social work." It probably indicated to her a loss in her own precariously gained class status. She used to introduce me by saying, "This is my daughter Monica, who is doing psychiatric . . . at Yale." Now I feel shame about my anger; I realize that she did it because she was so unsure of her own status, and had been made to feel invisible and inadequate all her life. I have come to see it as my business that my mother was not free to be all she could be, and that we judged her so harshly for not being good at certain aspects of mothering. We did not validate or accept her for the great strengths she possessed. Her invisibility made our lives visible. I have come to realize it was not my mother who was inadequate, but the yardstick by which I measured her. As Ruth Bader Ginsburg said upon her swearing-in as a U.S. Supreme Court justice, "I would like to be the kind of woman my mother would have been, had she lived in different times."

There were several other unsung "sheroes" in my family. Aunt Mamie Cahalane, my grandfather's sister, was the only sister of seven brothers and a widowed father. The men in her family, fearing the loss of their caretaker, discouraged all suitors who came to call. So Aunt Mamie took care of her father and all seven brothers until they died or left home. She became the Santa Claus for five generations of our family, as well as for her whole court at 90 St. Marks Place on Staten Island. Yet she lived in poverty all her life ("on relief," as it was called then), because, not having the education for work that our culture sanctions with remuneration, she could not make ends meet. She taught me a great deal about what you can give others beyond your pocketbook—about humor and generosity of soul, as well as about sacredness that has nothing to do with physical beauty or great accomplishments of the sort that get rewarded in our individualistic, competitive, materialistic society. Her invisibility, like my mother's, made my life visible.

My primary caretaker, Margaret Bush, mentioned earlier, was another invisible "shero" of my life. Descended from slaves (in, I believe, Asheville, North Carolina), she was the person to whom I was closest both emotionally and physically from the time of my birth until her death, the year after I left for college. It was to her I confided my problems—about boyfriends, about teachers, and about my mother. She was always there for me, and loved me unconditionally. She had lost her twin sons and her first husband. She gave up living with her second husband, Joe, much of the time, to live with us—a common story for many African Americans, who were forced to sacrifice their own families for the White families they served. I miss her every day, and she, too, lives in my soul and made me who I am. When I speak, you hear her voice, her struggles, her silences, as they have filtered down to me, as you hear the others who loved and cared for me. And I know I have an ongoing responsibility to her to seek the right relations among things.

But how do I deal with the shadow side of my relationship with Margaret, who, like so many others, worked in the homes of White families, and gave to them love and care that deprived their own families? This is the story of racism. What I received is the complement to what my African American friends were denied when their mothers or fathers had to serve White families at their expense. And this is part of the unacknowledged benefit I have gotten from racism. It is painful to realize that my love and benefit have meant someone else's loss and deprivation, and that the two are intertwined.

I grew up thinking that I was innocent—that I had nothing to do with racism and certainly not with slavery, I did not recognize Margaret's white uniform as a symbol of her status within our family. I also did not grasp the significance of the fact that she did not learn how to read until after I did, when she was 50 years old. This too goes back to the history of slavery, when slaves could be killed for learning to read, as could anyone who taught them. It was incredibly ignorant of me not to know or sense anything of her dilemma. I realize that I am a part of all that came before me—that I have benefited from racism and benefit from it every day in the unearned White privilege I experience in terms of my safety and status in many contexts. These include the fact that most books are written for me as a White person, so that even when Margaret did learn to read, she was forced to read about white middle-class families with children Dick and Jane. No books were available for her about her history and her ancestors' courage to survive, which she would have found more gratifying and affirming subjects.

I am coming slowly and painfully to realize what it means that we who are White carry around, in Peggy McIntosh's terms, a kind of "invisible knapsack" of privilege (see Chapter 11). We cannot see it, but those who don't have one can.

BECOMING AWARE OF GENDER, RACE, AND CLASS: PROFESSIONAL AND PERSONAL STRUGGLES

Until recently, I never noticed how my professional education was structured in terms of gender, class, race, and other characteristics. As a young family therapist, I never noticed that the leaders of the field were virtually all men, and I certainly never noticed that they were all White heterosexuals and that a high percentage were psychiatrists, while the followers were largely women social workers. The major gurus, Ackerman, Haley, Minuchin, Bowen, and Whitaker, were all intimidating to me, but part of the gender problem was also, in Betty Friedan's (1963) phrase, a "problem that has no name." I remember being especially intimidated and put off by Nat Ackerman, whose objectifying and sexualizing of women and whose manner of confronting and discounting others were frankly scary. Salvador Minuchin also often seemed to disqualify or embarrass trainees, and Murray Bowen had an offensive way of responding to a question he did not like by saying: "Next question." I admired the leaders' intelligence and ability, but they left me feeling inadequate. I felt I could never do what they did, but the idea never crossed my mind that this might have to do with my being a woman, which would influence the response a family would have to me. I noticed how men on panels acted insulting to Virginia Satir, but I focused on how, amazingly, she never let herself respond with humiliation or defensiveness. Satir became the one I followed most closely; I never missed one of her workshops, no matter what. She had a way of validating each questioner, finding something useful in each question. I did not notice that gays and lesbians were never present or mentioned in the literature. Nor did I have any awareness of the absence of people of color in the field or in my life. I knew no African American family therapists. I admired Harry Aponte and Braulio Montalvo, but had no contact with them. It was years before this myopia was challenged, and I began to be uncomfortable with the Whiteness of the field, the maleness of the leadership, and the heterosexism embodied in it.

Gender

It was not until years after realizing that I was Irish that I first became aware of gender as an issue in my life and in our field—not until the 1980s. And when I did begin to become aware of it, it created more than a transformation; it created great turmoil in my personal as well as my professional life. With my Irishness, I could maintain a distance. I was Irish, yes, but that was just a certain part of my identity. And I could "pass" for "regular" in most contexts. I had also married a Greek, and my friends came from many different backgrounds. I could get away from it. Something different happened with gender, however: I could not escape it. Wherever I went, the rules for gender inequality still applied. When I left work, I went back to what I was coming to realize was a family pervaded by sexism, with a husband who thought he was helping me if he did *any* chores around the house. But then I realized I too was sexist because I felt grateful for his "help." Shortly thereafter we had our son, which put me even further in touch with patterns of patriarchy, as I saw that all aspects of child rearing in our society—from the structure of child care to children's TV, literature, clothing, and education—are pervaded by sexism and inequality. I could not get away from it. My mother felt sorry for my husband when I went away on business. My husband thought of me as "abandoning" him and going "on vacation" when I went to a professional meeting. I myself had to prepare days ahead of time for my absence and make up for it for days afterward. This was so different from my father's traveling when I was a child. Our whole family organized itself for his return, which was always a special occasion.

As I became aware of the unequal nature of my relationship with my husband, I struggled with how to address this inequality. I tried to be very patient, carefully judging just when I could bring up an issue, so as not to overload the circuits—not when he'd had a hard day or was in a bad mood. By the time I did raise an issue, I had usually been troubled by it for a very long time; yet my husband would experience me as ruining our relationship by starting the conversation. And a part of me believed this also. If I were just more generous or more worthy, or knew better how to express myself, I would be able to work things out with him more smoothly.

In my work as well, once I began to notice the patterns of gender inequality, I became aware (as my closest women colleagues were realizing at the same time) that they pervaded our field as well as every other aspect of our society. Commenting on these issues at family therapy meetings brought about powerful reactions. I remember that at the first panel on gender at a meeting of the American Family Therapy Academy, Virginia Goldner gave her incredible paper on gender and generation; she pointed out that of these two fundamental categories of human relations, family therapists had been raised to notice generation, but to keep gender invisible (see Goldner, 1989). I marveled at her clarity. What she said was so true. How had I not realized? But afterward, many men disparaged her; one of the leaders in the field even described her as "like Darth Vader." Another time, on the single occasion when a national family therapy conference program was planned with a strong predominance of women, many men within the organization were outraged. They felt betrayed and thought this represented the desire of the women to "kill off" the men. In the same year, many of the same men organized a major quadrennial meeting of the senior family therapy journal and were un-dismayed to have almost no women or minorities included.

I have been mystified over the years by the reactivity of men to these issues. No matter how carefully we tried to express ourselves—to say that feminism was about a new structuring of gender relationships as partnerships, not about women winning a competition against men—it was often virtually impossible to have conversations. People spoke of the possibility that the men would withdraw from the field if women didn't get off "this kick." One close male friend asked me after a year or so whether I wasn't ready to move on from "that fad." As cautious or care-ful as I tried to be, the feedback I got was frequently personally disparag-ing, defensive, and self-justifying:

> "Monica, you used to be so nice. What happened to you? Why are you so angry at men? Did you hate your father? Are you getting divorced? You are ruining our relationship. And anyway, I didn't do anything. I'm not sexist, I loved my mother, I respect my wife, I've never abused a woman—why are you blaming me for this? And why are you saying we have the power. In fact, I feel quite powerless. I don't have any power. What you're saying doesn't relate to me. We men have problems, too. We're not allowed to feel. We've lost our fathers. We're walled off." (And so on.)

Of course, it is the nature of patriarchy that men do not realize their power, because in a society where everyone is measured hierarchically, there is always someone ahead of you or just at your heels to take your place. But it seemed impossible to get men to envision a way of being that wasn't about winning or losing. This changing consciousness in the fam-ily therapy field began a very difficult time, when distrust increased be-tween men and women: Women feared that they would be sandbagged, while men feared that women were out to get them.

Race and Racism

After a few years, the issue shifted. We began to be confronted by col-leagues of color about race and racism. Here I fell on the other side of the power imbalance, so I heard the issues very differently. Suddenly I was the one who was defensive, disparaging, and self-justifying. I felt like saying to others the same things I had heard men saying about feminism:

> "You used to be so nice. Why are you so angry? You're being divisive. This will ruin our relationship. I had nothing to do with racism, slavery, or segregation. My ancestors were oppressed like yours were. I would love to change things, but I don't have the power either. We

have to deal with sexism first; then we'll get to racism. You must be talking about someone else. I'm not prejudiced. We have our problems too—let me tell you about them."

I was trying to exclude myself from the category of oppressor, just as I had heard men do so many times—defending their behavior by reference to their good intentions, their own victimization or powerlessness, or their kindness to women at a personal level. And as I heard my own reactivity, I gradually began to think that I must be part of the problem, or I would not be getting so defensive that I didn't even want to hear about it. Again, I remembered all the times I had heard men say, "We can't listen when you speak in that angry tone of voice. It makes us feel unsafe. If you would say it nicely, we would listen." And I realized that I had to start listening differently. I needed to really *listen,* and to believe what others described as their experience.

One day I got an insight about how to do this from my friend Paulette Hines as we were doing a school consultation. The principal was trying to get us to understand what he was up against with "those people" and their anger, "who just accuse you of being a racist no matter how hard you try." He described a mother who had come into school that morning, upset about the school's ways of handling lateness and absenteeism. She had finally blurted out, "I see this school is just as racist as it was when I went here 30 years ago!" Paulette quietly stopped him in his tracks by saying, "Do you have any idea what she was referring to?" Of course he didn't. But her idea struck me deeply. We "right-thinking" liberals react almost viscerally against being labeled "racist." But how can we not be racist, living in a racist society for all of our lives? What if we were to move toward comments about racism instead of running away by defending ourselves? What if we were really to *try* to understand what people mean when they say that to us? That is what we as women were saying to men for so long:

> "Just listen. Try to take in the pain of what we are saying, instead of thinking of the exceptions. When we speak of men's violence, for example, give some acknowledgment, rather than getting irate that we have not mentioned women's violence."

That is what we had wanted. But with racism the accusation is so painful. Most White people's image of racism extends only to lynching or the Klu Klux Klan, whereas when people of color use the word, they are often referring to such things as being treated as invisible, being ignored in a store, or the unknowing everyday microaggressions and insults that we who are White make through our ignorance of their history or expe-

rience. In fact, until recently, whenever I gave a presentation about culture, I prefaced my comments by talking about my fear that others would
hear my comments as prejudiced or racist, and appealing to them not to
think in those terms. That was when I still thought I wasn't a racist.

And it put the burden on the other to make me feel "OK." Subtly, if
the subject of racism did come up, I wanted the other person somehow to
make peace the issue by the end of the discussion, just as men often expressed the hope that gender problems would be resolved by the end of
the conversation. They hoped that their comments would somehow resolve the issue, so that women would no longer be upset. Such wishes
assume that the issues are small rather than pervasive, and that they can
be resolved by talk rather than by transforming our social arrangements.
More recently, I have noticed at family therapy meetings that if African
Americans experience frustration, anger, or pain, White people want to
get them feeling "OK" within a single conversation. Though I have done
this myself, I now realize that this is arrogant of me. What they are upset
about won't be taken care of in the space of one conversation. How can
we demand that their pain or anger cease, if the problems remain? I have
realized that my invisible knapsack of privilege must disappear before
such a conversation can be over. To men who said they were not sexist, I
used to reply: "Until you are actively working against gender inequality,
you are part of the problem." I realize now that unless my own life is
about overcoming racism, I am also part of the problem. My privilege
will not disappear of its own accord. I must work so that everyone is
entitled to those privileges, which we all deserve. Then we will all have a
home.

Many White people say that they cannot let themselves be very conscious of racism, or they get overwhelmed by guilt and shame. They feel
they will have to give up everything before their lives will become congruent with notions of "liberty and justice for all." And so denial becomes an easier approach. They move away from the issues, which is
very easy for us Whites to do, because our society is so very segregated
that we can generally live our lives quite oblivious to our connectedness
to people of color. We can walk away and pretend these issues do not
relate to us. We can do this as long as we do not think about who cares
for us when we are sick, needy, old, in hotels, or on vacation, or who
makes our shoes, our clothes, and the home products that keep us comfortable. But our denial will surely kill us in the long run. We need to do
what we can do to stay conscious of our situation, and for that we need
each other. Alone, we will get picked off; we will be mystified, silenced,
invalidated; we will burn out in the struggle. Together, there is nothing
we cannot do. So we must overcome our denial.

I have been trying to think differently about these issues—to listen, to attempt to learn about my ignorance, so that gradually I can overcome it. I am beginning to see the racism in a lot of my work. I spoke about couples or families, and didn't really mean Black couples or families. I spoke about women, and didn't really include women of color. In fact, in the mid-1980s when I coorganized conferences for women family therapists and almost no women of color came, I kept trying to figure out how to include them—how to get them to recognize the importance of the issues. One who did attend questioned how little reference there was to issues of women of color. I remember feeling irritated with her, because I thought it was so hard to think about the gender inequality that if we added race, we'd never "get it straight." Now I realize I had it wrong. The truth is that if we don't include race in the discussion of gender, we will never "get it straight." Women of color have been saying and showing clearly for a long time that they prioritize gender differently. They have been saying and showing by their absence and silence that the field of family therapy has not related too much to them. And we have thought it was *their* problem. We have thought we could go on with family therapy as usual, even though it was really White family therapy.

I also realize that telling only the stories of the positive values and actions of my family or my culture keeps me part of the problem. We need to realize that our family members may include Nazis, as well as victims of the Holocaust; members of the Ku Klux Klan and slave drivers, as well as victims of slavery and racial oppression. Any time I try to distinguish my family or my ancestors from the oppressors, I may be standing next to a person whose ancestors were slave owners, making this person's acknowledgment of that legacy even more difficult. I believe we need to create a crucible that can contain the history of us all. If we notice our connections to each other and help each other to acknowledge all of our history, then together we can all work to change our future.

Class

Without my knowing it, my whole life has also been organized by class hierarchies. The clothes I wear are a class statement, like the car I drive or would feel comfortable driving, my house, my furniture, and the pictures on my walls. The music I listen to is a class statement: If I say I like opera, it is a class statement (unless I'm Italian). If I say I like country and Western music, it is a class statement. The same is true for sports; bowling says one thing, tennis or golf another. The restaurants where we feel comfortable eating, or the places where we prefer to spend our vacations, are all about class (and race and gender, of course). Yet I never acknowledged any of this for a minute until recently, nor was it ever mentioned in my training. Everyone knows the class code for all the degrees in our field—MD, PhD, EdD, DSW, MSW, MA, and so forth—but we don't talk about it. We also know the complex hierarchy for rating colleges and universities: the Ivy League, the Seven Sisters, Duke, Berkeley, Georgetown, Notre Dame, Howard, Morehouse, Spelman, Michigan State. Class hierarchies are exquisitely comprehensive; they govern all our social interactions. How we celebrate life cycle rituals, such as death or marriage, is a matter of class (as well as gender, race, culture, and sexual orientation). In my family (at least since the early 1960s), it would be "declassé" to have a fancy wedding, with prescribed outfits, food, drink, and music. But for the classes just above and just below our family, these rituals are an absolute necessity.

I now realize how pervasively and how insidiously the rules of class influence our feeling of "otherness," of not being "OK" in one situation or another. I also realize how much we feel the need to hide who we are—whether to hide Anglo roots or money that would distance us socially in the mental health field, or to hide our poverty or working-class origins. In addition to the invisibility of class as an issue, there is the fact that most of us have changed class. We cannot change our race, our gender, our culture, or our sexual orientation; we can lie about them, but we cannot change them. However, we can—and most Americans do—change class frequently. My parents rose two classes from their parents, who rose one class from *their* parents. My generation (my sisters and I) moved down half a class, having less social status than my parents had because of my father's political and academic standing. Like most families, mine included various members who were in different classes, and the social distance this created was almost never dealt with directly.

Whatever we cannot acknowledge or feel we must keep secret about class—about how much or how little money we have, about class contempt and class elitism, about the pain of unacknowledged class distance from our family members—it all costs us. It keeps us from being free. I believe we should try to acknowledge these things. We should dare to put our prejudices on the table, to examine them, and to determine what they cost us. I believe we must radically change our family therapy training to help trainees have the courage to discuss these issues, as well as those pertaining to race, gender, culture, and so forth. A first step is to acknowledge how "half-baked" we are. It will help to acknowledge our prejudices and to know that we will make mistakes. We will blurt out racist comments, sexist comments, and other microaggressions or indicators of our prejudice without realizing it. If we are lucky, someone will draw this to our attention, and we will move along in overcoming our prejudice.

But these changes also require that those of us with privilege give up some of our privilege in the interest of social justice. We will feel individually less safe or secure, but empowered as a group by our awareness that we are in it together. We will need to realize that we will all need to feel secure for any of us to have true security. Our freedom and safety cannot be built on the backs of others. In the words of the Talmud, "It is not our job to finish the work, but we are not free to walk away from it."

REFERENCES

Friedan, B. (1963). *The feminist mystique*. New York: Norton.

Goldner, V. (1989). Generation and gender: Normative and covert hierarchies. In M. McGoldrick, C. M. Anderson, & F. Walsh (Eds.), *Women in families: A framework for family therapy*. New York: Norton.

Griffin, S. (1992). *A chorus of stones: The private life of war*. New York: Doubleday.

McGoldrick, M. (1994). The ache for home. *Family Therapy Networker, 18*, 38–45.

CHAPTER 17

Racial Unity from the Perspective of Personal Family History

WHERE BLACK AND WHITE ENTERED OUR FAMILIES

Jayne Everette Mahboubi
Ashburn Pidcock Searcy

> No man should blindly follow his ancestors and
> forefathers, Nay, each must see with his own eyes,
> hear with his own ears and investigate the truth
> himself in order that he may follow the truth instead
> of blind acquiescence and imitation of ancestral
> beliefs.
> —ABDUL-BAHA ABBAS, *Promulgation of*
> *Universal Peace* (1922–1925, p. 454)

We have written this chapter out of our deep commitment to the belief that it is only in facing the pain of our shared history that we can achieve multiracial peace and unity, which we see as the only hope for us all as human beings. Although we believe that all families have aspects that at times cause us to be less than proud, it is necessary to acknowledge these in order to face the pain and find ways to transcend it, so that we can be free to share our future. We all have the ability to become friends, and also to be honest about who we are and where we have come from. The two of us came to this perspective by divergent paths, with radically different yet strongly connected histories. We take turns in relating these histories in this chapter; shifts from one voice to the other are indicated by "I (Jayne)" or "I (Ashburn)."

One history is of a successful Southern White upper-class family of community leaders, written up in books and genealogies. I (Ashburn) am a member of the ninth American generation of this family—an anesthesiologist, raised with all the privileges of class and social standing, as well as love of family and community. The other history is of a Black family whose ancestors were brought to this country as slaves several hundred years ago to support the lives of southern White families, and remained so enslaved till a little over 130 years ago. They did not make it to the history books. Their stories have not been told. They were servants, the caretakers, nameless, forcibly kept illiterate, so that I (Jayne), a family therapist in Atlanta, Georgia, have had great trouble tracing the genealogy of my ancestors. The links between these two histories have created pain and shame for both our families.

OUR YOUNGER YEARS

> But always the violence was distant, the words vague
> and terrible, for we were protected children.
> —LILLIAN SMITH, *Killers of the Dream*
> (1949/1964, p. 166)

I (Ashburn) grew up in Thomasville, Georgia, about halfway between Moultrie, Georgia and Tallahassee, Florida, in the early 1940s; I was the second of five brothers, who were the children and grandchildren of privileged Whites. I initially shared the attitude of my family and class that slavery had not been so bad, and perhaps it was really a shame the South had lost the Civil War. Ours was a perspective reinforced by such books and movies as *Gone with the Wind,* which depicted a life of comfort and seeming importance for upper-class Whites, supported by gentle, caring, hard-working, and generally happy Black slaves. In fact, although *Gone with the Wind* describes a romanticized White viewpoint, some aspects of pre-Civil War Southern life still exist for those living at opposite extremes of the economic spectrum in my hometown.

Like many small Southern towns untouched by that war, Thomasville displays its share of antebellum homes, and in addition there are intact plantations, now owned and maintained by some of America's wealthiest families. The town of less than 20,000 is 50% Black. The few working in plantation homes appear to enjoy a sort of elite status within the Black community. When I was growing up, visiting the "colored" section of town (as we often did to transport a servant to or from work), with its unpaved, rutted streets and small, often poorly built and maintained homes, evoked feelings of depression and pity in me that people should have to live their entire lives so humbly and namelessly by comparison with ours. However, I accepted this as a fact of life.

I (Jayne) grew up in metropolitan Atlanta as the youngest of my parents' four children. It was during the 1950s and 1960s, when Atlanta was still segregated but changing. My family was "middle-class," which seems a funny description now, because in the Black community the determination of class was so different from the dominant standards. My father was a postal clerk, a job that during the 1950s many Black people envied. Not only was it steady work with good benefits, but it was work with the U.S. government—one of the few employers in the South that "promised" a Black fair treatment. For many Blacks in the South, this was one of the best employment opportunities other than preaching or teaching. Although we lived in the city, we still had a close association with the land. My maternal grandparents, who lived close to us, still farmed within the city limits.

There was never talk of or even acknowledgment of White people in my world, as I remember, until I was 7. Then a weird thing happened— they were everywhere. Once when the family was shopping and I wanted a drink of water, there were two water fountains, one marked "Colored" and another "White." To my knowledge, we had never discussed the difference at home. I pondered the thought of "Colored" water for a moment; it seemed intriguing, but I was too thirsty to experiment. "White" water it was. My mother, not isolated, must have noticed my approach toward the tabooed "White" fountain, and all I remember is being swooped up in her arms and drinking "Colored" water until what must have been the 1960s. As I recall, there was nothing particularly upsetting about this event at the time, but certainly it was significant as one of the most vivid of my childhood memories.

As I (Ashburn) moved into my teenage years, I began working for my father's canning plant during my vacations. One summer, I drove a blackberry-buying route deep into plantations south of Thomasville. I was shocked to discover family groups of 10–15 Black people of all ages, totally illiterate, with a language I hardly understood, living in two-room slave shacks with no running water or electricity and dressed in filthy rags. They were practically cut off from the outside world; their vestigial way of life was reminiscent of a bygone era. In such abject poverty and ignorance, where could they go? What could they do? They had few if any choices so far from civilization. I remember wondering what would happen if one of them was stricken with a severe illness or injury. Who would even know? Those dark faces, large and small, gathering to stare silently at me and the jeep as I weighed their berries to pay 10 cents a pound, made an indelible impression on me. At age 16, I did not think deeply about it; I just felt a little sick at what I saw. However, as time went on, a feeling of anger emerged in me that human beings could be allowed in 20th-century America to live in such humiliation, isolation, and poverty. It seemed inhumane, though at the time it was just a fact of Southern life.

From the time of my childhood, I (Jayne) knew that there were White and Black people and that somehow the latter had to struggle. I did not dwell on this reality daily; it was just a fact of life, and life went on. As I grew, however, my feelings emerged more consciously—mostly angry ones about racial differences as they related to privilege. I watched the Klan march in front of the local department store in support of preserving rules to keep me from using the bathroom next to them, eating next to them, or trying on clothes next to them. These men, dressed in peculiar white gowns and pointed hats, were scary—not because I had ever experienced an incident with them, but because somehow I just knew I should be scared. My family later told stories of Klan activity. My mother told us that her paternal grandfather was thought to have been killed by Klan members.

My high school years were almost free of racial incidents. I went to a segregated school and had a great time. I vaguely remember that I had a choice to attend the newly integrated, formerly all-White school not too far from home. I declined. I had always traveled at least 10 miles to school, so being closer was not significant enough to tempt me to go to the integrated school, which promised prospects of having rocks thrown at me, being jeered at, and being hated. All my friends were going to the Black school, and as a 13-year-old I found it a frightening idea to be thrust into the company of Whites socially and academically, when I had never even had a conversation with any.

As a high school student, I typed for a guy named Stokely Carmichael and a group named SNCC as a part-time job. That was the extent of my connection with the civil rights movement. My family was not involved in the movement, except for a brother who went to Morehouse College and was involved in some demonstrations. Later I felt shame about our family's lack of participation in the movement, growing up in the middle of it as we did. My father had always exhibited a sense of deference toward Whites that was a great source of embarrassment to us children. Perhaps my father's job as a government employee fueled his reluctance to get involved and his natural avoidance of confrontation with the White power structure, given his Deep South upbringing.

OUR MEETING THROUGH THE BAHA'I FAITH

> It is his life and no mere abstraction in someone's
> head. He must live it and try consciously to grasp its
> complexity until he can change it; must live it as he
> changes it.
>
> —RALPH ELLISON, *Shadow and Act*
> (1964/1994, p. 17)

The two of us met and became friends in the metropolitan Atlanta Baha'i community, having each independently discovered and accepted the Baha'i Faith. I (Jayne) experienced the turbulent campus riots of the 1960s at Fisk University in Nashville, Tennessee. As a Black college student, I struggled to move beyond self-definitions based on deference to White standards—to redefine myself, for myself, with pride rather than shame. However, I wrestled with pain, anger, sadness, and a sense of hopelessness that racial unity would ever be possible. Because I was so profoundly affected by the quest for definition as a meaningful contributor to the progress of civilization as an African American, I was led to seek consolation and meaning through a spiritual search. The Baha'i Faith appealed to me because of its fundamental valuing of diversity of the races—a transformational approach I had only dreamed of before. It asserted definitively that it was incumbent upon the races to unite with equal respect. I learned that the Baha'i Faith had a long history in this country of demonstrating its commitment to this principle. At last, I felt I was "Home."

   I (Ashburn) was introduced to the Baha'i Faith while in medical school, after disillusionment with my fundamentalist orientation and a frustrating search for meaning and relevance. As a Southern-born, Southern-bred White male, I gradually changed from wishing the South had won the war to an acute awareness of the sacrifice made by Northern soldiers to leave their homes, struggle, die, and be buried in Southern soil for the eradication of slavery and its erroneous misconceptions—the real function of the war. Changing was a difficult process (even though my maternal grandfather was a Northerner), so surrounded was I by Southern pride and racial prejudice, which were reinforced at school, at sports and cultural events, in the news media, and even at church. Nor can I claim even now to have completely eradicated all traces of racial prejudice, so subtle and pervasive is its influence.

   The gentleness and caring protectiveness of the Black people in whose charge my brothers and I were left as children were clearly evident. My perception of Black people's realistic approach to life, more free of illusion and fancy, than White people's, always intrigued me. Most important to my understanding of the true nature of the human race is Baha'u'llah, founder of the Baha'i Faith, about whom I learned as a second-year student in medical school. His teachings regarding the oneness of God and of humankind, the harmony of science and religion, the equality of women and men, and the absolute necessity to eliminate all forms of prejudice answered my questions about the reasons for existence and put in perspective the contradictions and inconsistencies of my upbringing. For example, how could African Americans, many of whom were among the most keenly intelligent and good-natured people I knew, be relegated to such a position of subservience and unimportance? If the churches sent missionaries to Africa to enroll these people, why were they not welcome as members in many of the churches supporting these missionaries? And why did Christian nations declare war and reduce each other to rubble during World Wars I and II? For that matter, why do people of different faiths behave so savagely toward one another when the purpose of religion is to establish peace and unity? I began to see that the economic success of people like my father and grandfather, who admittedly worked hard to achieve, nevertheless depended on the often backbreaking labor of an intelligent and talented people who happened to be born non-White and denied access to education. Moreover, I am deeply aware of the lasting influence on the lives of privileged Whites exerted by Black women, who of necessity neglected their own families to help raise them.

DISCOVERING OUR CONNECTED HISTORIES

> When we searched our hearts and found
> The quilted patches of their lives
> We knew they were ours to piece together. . . .
> —NAGUEYALTI WARREN, "Quilt Pieces"
> (1994, p. 236)

Thus, in the Baha'i Faith we both found fundamental answers to deep-rooted questions, which allowed the personal healing process from the effects of racism and the work toward unity to begin.

We had known each other for several years before we became close enough to discuss our family histories. We saw each other at Baha'i meetings and were cordial toward each other. Then we learned by chance that two of our parents, both in their 80s now, had known each other as children—clearly not as peers, but in the intimate, yet highly boundaried way that Black and White families in the South had come to live. The African American family knew a great deal about the history of the Anglo family, whereas the Anglo family had virtually no awareness of the life of the African American family, except as the African Americans provided service and the Anglos appreciated their care. Black and White were deeply intertwined, yet profoundly unequal in their relationships: patronizing regard for the "darkies" on the one side, "Uncle Tommish" deference on the other. Acknowledging our history and living our lives in the present have meant and still mean grappling with prejudice, hatred, ignorance, pain, rage, and denial.

Our parents (Jayne's father and Ashburn's mother) grew up in Moultrie, Georgia, soon after the turn of the century, about 45 years after the Civil War ended. They had played together as children at the tender ages of 6 and 5 years, respectively. My (Jayne's) father, at age 86, instantly recalled the circumstances of his meeting Ashburn's mother. She, a member of a family that was virtual aristocracy in Moultrie, was brought with her younger brother to be kept during the day at the home of a servant, who lived across the street from my grandparents' house. My father was fascinated in the present with the idea that I knew the son of his childhood playmate, and indeed that the two of us considered ourselves peers. I naively encouraged their reunion, which Ashburn and I would arrange. However, I soon questioned my decision when my father asked whether he should call Ashburn's mother "Miss Anna." I suddenly realized the distance between the families. A friend later, in an attempt to prepare me for what the reunion might bring, reminded me that Ashburn's mother was not a Baha'i, somehow suggesting that she might not fully share our commitment to the principle of the oneness of humankind. I was not present at the parents' meeting, but my father was apparently both nervous and excited to reminisce about home with "Miss Anna." Our parents visited for hours and talked nonstop about events, places, and people in Moultrie. The visit was one of the highlights of my father's last couple of years on this planet. He died a year later. He spoke fondly of it many times. For me, however, the thought of the reunion was riddled with feelings I had suppressed—anxiety, shame, anger, and hurt. I had to come to terms with the fact that Ashburn's mother could scarcely remember my father, although he appeared to have vividly remembered many aspects of her family's activities over the years. This blatant reality of my father's family's invisibility during that time hurt deeply, to my surprise.

After the reunion, and my father's subsequent death, I was able to interview Ashburn's mother and further reveal our families' connectedness. I was shocked by my overwhelming feelings of sadness for my ancestors as I listened to the stories of the life of privilege led by my friend's ancestors. The difference was so extreme. As noted earlier, Ashburn's maternal grandfather was a "Yankee"; with two brothers, he came to south Georgia from New Jersey before the turn of the century to help his father start a railroad. His marriage joined two of the most prominent families in the area. The bride's father, was a wealthy landowner, who established a textile mill, sawmill, extensive naval stores and farming operations, the Moultrie Banking company, and a competing railroad.

As a child visiting Moultrie, I (Ashburn) felt something like a celebrity, so well known were both sides of my mother's family. As in most small Southern towns, the Black people comprising a high percentage of Moultrie's population lived in less developed and less spacious sections of the town, and worked in homes and businesses owned almost exclusively by White. I (Jayne) remember some images of my father's homeplace in Moultrie: the small house on a sleepy, sandy street lined with palm trees, with talk of peanuts, watermelons, sugar cane, and cotton among the relatives. There was the house of Auntie, my dad's aunt—a very old woman who lived alone and wore strange clothes made from flour and feed sacks and a bandanna on her head, like "Aunt Jemima" of pancake fame. By contrast, Ashburn's family enjoyed life with one of the first motorcars in town, one of the first houses with electric lights, and summers in New Jersey to escape the heat.

My (Ashburn's) father's family members took pride that a great-grandmother was the niece of Alexander Hamilton Stephens, vice president of the Confederacy. By their forebears, my father and uncle were taught the importance of "keeping one's blood pure," and this side of the family kept detailed genealogies linking relatives with historically important Anglo-Saxon figures. Southern ancestors on both sides of my family had slaves. I struggle with the fact that they "owned" human beings; I know that they lived according to the ideas of their time, yet I am pained by the thought of the way of life in which they participated. I (Jayne) must sadly admit that at one time the fact that my ancestors were slaves embarrassed me, as perhaps it did (and does) some other Blacks. The particulars of slavery and of surviving it were virtually secret as I grew up. We somehow had the feeling that our enslavement as a people was the slaves' own fault. This generalized notion persists among some African Americans to this day. It was a lot easier to be ashamed of enslavement when we knew little or nothing of relatives who were in fact slaves. Sadly, the mystification of the institution of slavery continues, as the honest treatment of the issue receives little acknowledgment even today. The magnitude of its effects on our country is overwhelming.

Ironically, through my relationship with Ashburn, I have discovered more about my father's history than ever before. Since learning of my father's past association with his family, I have discovered that my great-grandfather was in fact born into slavery (a relative told me this after I began research for this chapter). He lived near Thomasville, Georgia. He ultimately gained his freedom and worked for the railroad owned by

Ashburn's family—so, again, our families were intertwined. He was known to be a hard worker and to be audacious about family members' standing up for their rights. His wife was also born into slavery, but lived with my great-grandfather as a freedwoman and worked as what is now politely termed a "domestic." She was called "Honey" for short, as her legal name, Sarah Luvenia Lois Jane Juliann Johnson Small, consisted of the seven names of her previous female slave owners, whom she had served before her marriage to my great-grandfather. My great-grandfather lost his leg while employed by the railroad, which gave him compensation for his loss, enabling him to buy his own farm property in the area.

My (Ashburn's) great-grandmother and Jayne's grandmother were similar: Both were devoted to their missionary work, and both greatly influenced each of us. My (Ashburn) great grandmother, although not a crusader for human rights as defined today, nevertheless sacrificed personal comfort and pleasure to support Southern Baptist missionaries in the foreign field—her way of reaching out to improve the world. My (Jayne's) grandmother, whose husband also worked for the railroad, used employee railroad passes to travel out of the Deep South to Northern cities for church conventions. Her passionate involvement with the African Methodist Episcopal Church resulted in her stressing education for my father as a way out of our family's slave-like existence in Moultrie. Once again, and in a more positive sense, our families were connected.

CONCLUSION

> Fix my voice on the machine so that my words come
> out clear. . . . I will tell my talk . . . but don't let the
> people I live with hear what I have to say.
> —NISA, "From *Nisa: The Life and Words*
> *of a !Kung Woman*" (1993, p. 637)

Today we find ourselves living in a society that often does not validate sincere efforts toward racial harmony. The sensational acts of extremist hate groups are only the most overt manifestations of racism; corpora tions and government institutions also quietly pursue racist policies. Moreover, little attention is given to overcoming the small hurdles—to combating family legacies of disdain and suspicion of differences. For us as clinicians, the necessity to own one's legacy, decide on one's journey, and accept another's similar challenge has become increasingly clear. Although this chapter speaks of transcendence and transformation, it does not promise that miracles will be encountered when we are confronted with challenges. The cliché "faith in the process" has to be appreciated and adhered to as we proceed. We are all moving, and if we are not

moving forward, then we are going backward; we never stand still. We
need to move toward unity and appreciation of each race's contribution
to the wholeness of humankind.

The contents of this chapter represent only a portion of the intense
feelings we two individuals have shared as we have attempted to transcend the bonds of racism. The difficulties in writing the chapter have
encompassed many feelings that we continue to discover about ourselves
and our families. Perhaps our most significant achievement thus far is
that we have agreed to be patient with one another concerning where we
are in the quest for racial unity and the abolition of prejudices, because
we are friends and in many ways family, in the spiritual sense, and we are
not willing to cut each other off.

Finally, we are aware that in facing our history and bearing witness
to its chains, we are breaking a silence that has implications for the other
members of our families as well, who may themselves be pained by what
we are saying here. We trust that in the fullness of time they will come to
know with what a strong sense of love and appreciation we are trying to
face these hard truths of our mutual history. We believe that facing these
painful truths is our best hope for freeing ourselves for a future that must
encompass all of us if it is to give meaningful dignity and peace to any of
us.

REFERENCES

Abbas, A.-B. (1922–1925). *Promulgation of universal peace*. Wilmette, IL: Baha'i
    Publishing Trust.
Ellison, R. (1994). Shadow and act. In S. T. Haizlip (Ed.), *The sweeter the juice*.
    New York: Simon & Schuster. (Original work published 1964)
Nisa. (1993). From *Nisa: The life and words of a !Kung woman*. In P. Rose
    (Ed.), *The Norton book of women's lives*. New York: Norton.
Smith, L. (1994). Killers of the dream. In S. T. Haizlip (Ed.), *The sweeter the
    juice*. New York: Simon & Schuster. (Original work published 1949)
Warren, N. (1994). Quilt pieces. In S. T. Haizlip (Ed.), *The sweeter the juice*.
    New York: Simon & Schuster.

CHAPTER 18

No Longer an Orphan in History

John Folwarski

Although I am aware that the phrase "illegitimate Polish Catholic orphan" is not exactly a Jungian archetype, it certainly was an abiding label for the personal and ethnic heritage that informed the way I viewed myself and the world from the time I was 4 years old. Even after I earned two advanced degrees, spent years as a college professor and later as a therapist, and raised two children (now in college themselves), the negative associations accompanying each of these words kept a strong hold on me. Not unlike flashbacks, the enduring power of those words would often invade and render unreal whatever was going on at any particular time.

At one professional seminar, for example, the presenter asked us to take a few moments to reflect on what the word "home" invoked. I thought of my current home (my wife, Helen; our children, Erica and David; our cat, Charlie); then, as frequently happened to me in situations like this, I had a strong impulse to hide. I wanted to excuse myself from the conversation on the grounds that, for starters, I am illegitimate; furthermore, I remember absolutely nothing about my first home (from birth to age 4), and my second home was an orphanage. However, I felt it was my professional obligation to share some warm memories and bear witness to how I had surmounted more disquieting images. I had often done exactly that, but for whatever reason, on this occasion the word "home" rocketed upward with more than the usual distress. My honest and immediate first reaction was an image of my sixth grade nun. She was well known for her abusive character. What frightened me was that I reacted spontaneously with unexpected warmth and longing, coupled with a need to hide from the secret we then shared.

In recent years, with effort and support, the "illegitimate Polish

Catholic orphan" label has been taking on a much more manageable shape. In coming to terms with the word "orphan," in particular, I have often been comforted by reading Eileen Simpson's (1987) book *Orphans: Real and Imaginary*. At one point, Simpson writes about a director of one New York orphanage who was having difficulties interviewing former "inmates": "Many whom they hoped to interview were as furtive about their past as if they had been in reform schools, and were unable to rid themselves of the feeling that they were somehow responsible for having been institutionalized. Others were afraid of being discriminated against professionally or patronized socially ('unfortunate little ones')" (p. 146).

MY FAMILY BACKGROUND

Most of what I know about my original family I have pieced together through arduous research over the past 35 years. Except for a few images and a few tactile memories (such as the taste of raindrops on an iron railing), I do remember nothing about my first 4 years. I now know that my maternal grandfather's name was Jan Folwarski, that he was a painter for a Chicago railroad, and that he died in the big flu epidemic of 1918. His wife's name was Julianna Gasior. She washed floors to support the family after his death and through the Depression. They had seven children (I had thought there were only four). Their death certificates listed Austria as the country of origin, and only a few years ago I discovered they came from two villages (Nowa Wies´ and Harklova Wies´) in the Austrian-occupied section of Poland. The four children who were around when I was born were my mother, Mary (Marianna); her two older brothers, Stanley (Stanislaw) and Frank (Franciszek); and her younger sister, Louise (Ludwika).

When I was 34, I got hold of my records from the Chicago Family Court, which told me the following: When my mother was 20, she had a relationship with a man named Tom Bieschke and became pregnant; he denied paternity. The family was poor and ashamed of the event, and petitioned the court, which decided she was to be placed in a mental institution as soon as a bed became available. I was left in the hospital. When I was 6 months old, the hospital notified the family members that the rules did not permit a longer stay. They then decided to bring me home, and received $6.90 biweekly from the Bureau of Family Welfare for my care. The records show that a few months before my fourth birthday, my grandmother died; the other members of the family were interviewed together and then separately, at which point my mother told the social worker "the truth." Stanley was abusive; they had no jobs and no money; the grandmother's dying wish was to place the child. My mother was committed (based on the original papers) to Dixon State Hospital, and I was sent to St. Hedwig's Orphanage. She was diagnosed as "feeble-minded" and was sterilized. An entry in the court records a few years later stated that the court-appointed social worker was "surprised that, other than to bring his clothes and toys, no one had been to see the child, believing that he would be better off that way."

When I was 11, the nuns told me to get cleaned up; my Uncle Stanley had died and I had to go to the funeral, which was right next door at St. Adalbert's Cemetery. I was allowed to bring a friend, Stanley Trzos. I got to ride in a car and got $2 from someone (Stanley got $1). I do remember the face of my Aunt Louise as she said from the back of the car, "Do you remember we used to call you Jackie?" I did not remember, but I said I did. At some point that same year, when I was returning from Confession, I walked downstairs and outside in what was a rather narrow space among three of our buildings. I had been there many times before. I had no idea what caused the feeling (because many things were going on that year), but suddenly I was seized with an overwhelming feeling of terror, which focused on wanting and needing to ask, "How can I know that these buildings will not fall apart and crush me?" I believed that if someone could simply explain how I could know for sure that this couldn't happen, I would be OK. But there was no one to ask. I have gone over this in my own therapy a variety of times, and have some answers. But it was one of those seminal experiences, like an awful nightmare that recurs throughout your life. Nonetheless, there was a time when I would have defined "home" as a place where, when you ask questions (large or small), somebody actually responds. Later, given what I believe is a universal feeling of kids in orphanages that there is never enough to eat, I came to define an ideal "home" as a place with a refrigerator and the conviction that you are entitled to open it and take whatever you want without asking.

Much later, when I was 20 and in the Air Force, I got a letter from a Mrs. Tobiaski (a generous Polish lady who took an interest in me and my mother after a chance meeting) that my Uncle Frank had been hit and killed by a bus, and that I should come to the city and bury him. I did. On the way back to the base, I stopped off in Cincinnati, got drunk, and got back 3 days late. A year later, when I was discharged, it never even occurred to me to go back to Chicago. A friend who had gone to San José State said I should go to college. So I got on a bus and went to San José. That was the start of repressing Chicago and acquiring a string of borrowed identities, mixed with periodic and increasingly frequent odysseys to Chicago in search of my roots. I did not revisit St. Hedwig's Orphanage, where I stayed until I was 16, until I was 30.

ST. HEDWIG'S ORPHANAGE

It was the age of ethnic/religious orphanages. During the space between World Wars I and II, churches took care of their own. St. Hedwig's Orphanage was Polish Catholic: The priests were Polish, the nuns were from a Polish order (the Felicians), and the children were almost all Polish. From the opening of St. Hedwig's in 1911 to its closing in 1959, more than 7,000 children were cared for there. The teaching nuns spoke both Polish and English and took care of the girls after school; the boys were in the care of nuns who spoke mostly Polish, as did the working nuns (bakery, farm, laundry, etc.). We gave money to support the Polish cause in World War II, and dutifully thought often of the "starving children in Poland" when we wasted food.

A sense of ethnicity, however, was not primary. The world was divided in our minds between Catholic and Protestant, as well as between orphans (us) and "city guys" (everyone else). During the war, we did have a shipment of war orphans from Poland via Mexico, who greatly enriched our sense of another world beyond our gates. I remember envying their fluency in Polish, their skills in soccer, and the great harmonies in which they sang Spanish music. We also envied the kids who came to us well past kindergarten age, who had more solid memories of their homes; who possessed more information about newspapers, telephones, clothes, foods, sports, and music; and who were not yet numbed by the rules of total obedience to authority that had become our way of survival. One girl, Rosie Rathnow-Killips (1994), remembers an early experience in the orphanage this way:

> I was 9 years old and scared. My mom and sisters were not with me. I felt all alone in that fourth grade. Even as I write this, I can recall the feelings of abandonment. When times got really tough at home, my mother would call us together and we would sing from "pluggers" (songs printed on colored cards). I wanted that feeling again, so I started to sing. All of a sudden, Sr. Tarcissus was standing over my bed. I kept on singing. She said, "We don't do things like that here." At that moment I made a decision that lasted for the entire time I was at St. Hedwig. I said to myself, "They have my body but they don't have my mind." (p. 12)

The new system became the new family. Actual parents were grouped for us under the heading of "visitors," allowed to visit twice a month. Monsignor Francis S. Rusch ran the show, assisted by two priests. The nuns wielded day-by-day parenting power. The various benefits and abuses of that power—the rules, roles, and relationships that developed—are part of our individual and collective memory. We were all, as Simpson (1987) has said of immigrants and siblings, "in the same boat."

THE IMPORTANCE OF THE CATHOLIC CHURCH
IN THE ORPHANAGE AND TO THE POLISH PEOPLE

Q. What do you wanna be when you grow up?
A. I wanna be a Holy Martyr and die rather than give
up my faith.
—A frequent exchange at St. Hedwig's

Underpinning and overriding everything else in the orphanage was the towering figure of the Catholic Church, Polish style. In that setting, something like martyrdom was a well-nourished daydream, a crowning goal of life if one were worthy and courageous; at times, it was as real a wish as wanting to be a fireman, a pilot, or a cop. The agony of St. Stephen and the ecstasy of St. Teresa of Avila, the litanies and lives of many Polish saints and martyrs, supported by daily rewards for being devotionally directed—all this, and more, shaped our most basic beliefs and our value system.

Of course, this is not uniquely Polish. Catholicism has its own life and detail in other ethnic Catholic cultures (Irish, Hispanic, French, Italian, etc.). I believe now that the uniqueness of Polish Catholicism lies in its historically greater fusion between ethnicity and religion—a fusion so strong that attempts to break it might better be called "fission." Trying to separate being Polish from being Catholic forebodes a nuclear explosion, metaphorically speaking; to the Polish, it can mean the death of personal identity. In his well-known novel *Poland*, James Michener (1983) wrote of the time when Communist power was entrenched: "Whereas many members of the government decried the Catholic church publicly in order to retain their jobs, they worshipped privately *to preserve their Polishness*" (p. 5; italics added)—a curious phrase, since he could have written "to preserve their faith." Poland as a nation, and Polish immigrants in particular, have depended on the Church to a far greater degree than any other Catholic culture. France and Italy, for example, have a continuous history (they were never "orphaned"). Poland disappeared from the map of Europe for 125 years! Continuity of identity rested with connection to the Church. Poles came to an America already dominated by Irish clery, and the need to preserve Polish identity resulted at one point in a full-blown schism with the formation of the PNCC (Polish National Catholic Church). The various ways in which fears of loss of identity worked their way into average Polish family life were, of course, diverse. In the orphanage, they were simply much more intensified than in even the most devout of individual families. For our time there, the Church was the family. All the patterns that govern family systems also governed the orphanage family, except that the mothers were nuns and the fathers were priests—certainly a peculiar psychic connection. Work

with clients who have spent time in religious orphanages needs to acknowledge the special power (positive or negative) of that connection.
"Losing one's faith" or learning to choose one's own—especially for those
who have no continued or restored connection with an actual family—
can run the risk not only of the usual eternal damnation, but the terror of
being excommunicated from the family (again) and perhaps reexperienc-
ing the original abandonment.

In the history of the Catholic clergy in America, the first Polish
American to achieve the status of auxiliary bishop was the Rev. Paul
Rhode (Chicago)—who, it turns out, was the original founder of St.
Hedwig's Orphanage. None of this, of course, was known to the kids in
this unique large family. Exploring this kind of ethnic information is liberating. And it may not be unlike unearthing family secrets, which can
explain a host of attitudes and behaviors that puzzlingly held one cap-
tive. Encouraging clients—especially the dispossessed, to whom most of
their birthright is a mysterious blur—to reconnect with their ethnic origins is indeed a way of helping them go home.

LATER CONTACTS WITH MY PARENTS

Once, in the seventh grade, I had a confusing option for a way out of St.
Hedwig's. Mrs. Tobiaski came for a visit and told me that my mother
was out of Dixon State Hospital and would come with her later to visit
me. For many years afterwards, I felt guilty for not wanting her out of
the hospital. What I knew consciously was that I would lose my status as
a "pure orphan" (kids who had no visitors and got special clothes and
presents from kindly Sister Aloysius); I was also aware that I did not
know her and did not know what to say. Mainly, I had some notion that
she was "crazy" and I would be called—as one girl called—"the kid with
the crazy mother." When Mrs. Tobiaski brought her over, she had bandages on her legs that I thought covered scars from shock treatments
(images from the *The Snake Pit*), and I feared for years, in addition to
everything else, that I had "insane blood." Of course, I never told anyone
about any of these fears.

I did "go to visitors" and try to make conversation with my mother,
on this and one or two subsequent occasions. I once asked her who my
father was, and she said he was a sailor who died in the war. I never
asked about him again, or about any of the other relatives. Years later, I
was told that my mother had been in a fight in a kitchen where Mrs.
Tobiaski had gotten her a job; she had left, and no one had heard from
her since. After many later searches of my own, I found out in 1988

through Social Security that she had died in a nursing home in Chicago in 1987. I missed her by only 1 year. When I visited that nursing home later, one lady, who said she had been on the staff for 10 of the years my mother was there, told me she had "never mentioned she had a son." That bothered me a lot. I felt somehow responsible for her dying in an institution. The last remaining relative was my Aunt Louise, and I sent a letter again through Social Security, but never knew if she got it, or if they really sent it. (I discuss my later search for her below.)

In the late 1960s, I pursued the search for my biological father. After an incredible amount of juggling, I found him in a suburb of Chicago and got him to agree to see me. I had all the pertinent facts from the court records. He told me he was married and had six children, none of whom were home at that moment. He looked like me; he showed me a picture of his eldest son, who also looked like me. In response to my story, he said, "I don't remember no girl named Mary." He then told me that he himself was adopted, and that he "knew a lot about this stuff." Since I was going to return to my home in Connecticut soon, he would be glad to check all this out for me—"but, of course, it would take a little dough." I did not go back to look for him until 1994. I didn't find him, but learned a lot more about him from various sources. I do regret letting that one go. As King Lear once said, "Readiness is all!"

RECONNECTING WITH THE ORPHANAGE AND THE FAMILY NEIGHBORHOOD

In 1994 I was ready to take my 17-year-old son, David, on his first trip to Chicago. He wanted to go to the top of the Sears Tower. We were hosted by two fellow Hedwigians, Tom Suchomski and Joey Popera, who had stayed in Chicago all those years. Tom scanned Chicago through the Sears Tower telescope and located the red brick buildings of the former orphanage. Later that same day we went up to the third-floor washroom at the old St. Hedwig's, and with Tom's binoculars we could see the Sears Tower. We traded stories, remembering how often we would be in that same spot at night, looking out toward the lighted top of the Wrigley Building. I remembered a frequent ritual: We would get into bed after saying our night prayers; the nun would say good night in Polish, and we would respond in kind; we would follow the clear rules (absolutely no talking, everyone was to start out facing the same direction, no getting out of bed unless a bathroom visit was urgently necessary). There were any number of occasions when the lights would suddenly flash back on. Someone had talked! We had various standard responses to this, one of which was to fall out of bed on our knees with our arms in the air (the way Moses prayed) and keep them up until the talker confessed. Barring such an episode, a period of time would elapse; darkness and silence would reign; then one was free to say, "Ah, now I can think anything I want!" And we did. After a safe period of waiting, I would get up out of bed, make my way to that third-floor washroom, stand on the urinal, stare out of that window, and listen to the night. In the summer, one could hear the faint strains of Polka music from Tromba's Grove, a Polish beer garden (where, rumor had it, one of the girls who ran away got a job). One could also listen to the screeching sound of the Milwaukee Avenue streetcar as it reached the end of the line on Newark Avenue (walking distance from the orphanage), where it would turn around and head back for the long run clear across the city, through the heart of the vast Polish neighborhood, all the way to the Loop. Such is the stuff that dreams are made of: Someday I would be a "city guy."

The only year I failed to carry out this ritual was the one year in the sixth grade when the reigning nun took me into her cell late each night, and sent me back very early in the morning. Off and on I have wrestled with the meaning of that relationship for almost 50 years, viewing her secretly as my "Evanngeline," since our relationship started one night in the dark gameroom as she showed us slides of that great poem and gently touched my forehead. I have no need to develop this story further here, other than to say that despite much effort, I have not been successful at "blaming" her. Only recently, however, have I become aware that her first touches had promised to replace what I had lost by coming to the orphanage. I think I am ready to stop waiting for Evangeline to return, and I am even readier to let go of the protective cover her special singling-out provided, so as to finally accept the original loss and see her behavior as her story, not mine.

Later on that same trip, I went myself to 1623 McReynolds Street (now LeMoyne), the house where I was born. I had carried for years some pictures that Mrs. Tobiaski had given me. The house was gone. On the corner, the sign that once read *Piwo* (Polish for "beer") now read *Cerveza* (Spanish for "beer"). I looked at the place where the house used to stand. I had a picture of my aunt and me at age 4, playing in the snow in front of those other neighboring houses, which still looked the same. A Latino guy said hello. I told him that I was born in the house that used to be there, and I showed him the picture. He told me, with great personal warmth, what he knew of the changing neighborhood. I believe the fact that I grew up there (proven by the picture), coupled with his natural, spontaneous Hispanic conviction that anyone's childhood is hugely important, erased our differences and turned on our connectedness. It legitimized beyond reproach my right to be there, to claim the neighborhood as my own. At least, that's what I felt. I felt entitled to stand and stare at the house—or the piece of ground on which it had stood—and at the neighboring ones, comparing them to my pictures. An elderly man came by and told me that if I wanted to find all the old Polish people who used to live there, I should go St. Adalbert's Cemetery. I did. I later learned that my grandparents had a plot there, but my time ran out before I could visit it. Almost all the Felician nuns who raised us are buried there, all with the same style and size of tombstone. In the middle is the tombstone of Monsignor Francis S. Rusch, at least 20 times as large. The "family" is together.

RECONNECTING WITH MY POLISHNESS

For myself, I cannot differentiate how much of which element (illegitimacy, being a *de facto* orphan, religion, being institutionalized) explains the abiding sense of not belonging that I always had, no matter what I did in my personal, social, or professional life. However, my being Polish is also far from irrelevant. Reconnecting with my Polishness made me aware of the "tenacity and depth of Polish ethnic self-consciousness" and convinced me that "shame is a central dimension of the experience of the Polish American family" (Folwarski & Marganoff, 1996, pp. 661, 665). I believe that Polish Americans, like orphans, have been members of a socially definable but disenfranchised class, with its sense of humiliation crystallized in Polish jokes and its deeper feelings of shame relegated for the most part to the realm of denial. The reconnection, however, also vastly enlarged my sense of home and family. This included a new sense of the Felician nuns. In the United States, unlike in Poland, the Felicians "were recruited from immigrant peasant families most of whom were strangers to life in industrial cities and who were strangers to the high Polish culture of the upper classes" (Radzialowski, 1975, p. 22). In the early part of this century, then, many Polish women faced a deck stacked against them: They were Polish, they were Catholic, and they were women. The order offered "social mobility . . . education, position, social status, travel" (Radzialowski, 1975, p. 22), not to mention family approval for their choice of "a vocation." Joining a religious order was one option for safety, purpose, and status. Re-visioning those caretakers as real young women in a real history also helps locate me outside the emotionally charged vulnerability of our mutual life at St. Hedwig's; it ameliorates my sense of the nuns' absolute authority and of the hypnotic magic of religion.

MY LAST RELATIVE:
THE END OF MY SEARCH FOR MY AUNT

The reawakening of my ethnic self in recent years went hand in hand with my continuing search for my family. In December 1994, I wrote another letter through Social Security to my Aunt Louise. I knew this time that she had changed her name (as many Poles did), to Louise G. ("Gerry") Fowler. I pictured her as a distraught Polish bag lady somewhere in Chicago, so I had the clever idea of enclosing a check for $100, figuring that at least I could trace the check. I wrote what I thought was a moving letter to get her to want to see me.

Months went by with no response, and the check was never cashed. So in the summer of 1995 I made another trip to Chicago; I spent more time examining records at the library, documents in the Polish Geneological Society archives, voting records, and so on. The very day I returned to my home (now in New Jersey), I got a call from a Maryknoll priest in San Francisco, asking who I was. He told me that Louise G. Fowler had died, and that he was the executor of her estate. He got my name from the county administrator's office. My letter and check were found in her safety deposit box. She had died in a hospital, where she would not tell anyone anything personal about herself. When the doctor needed authority to pull life supports, the administrator went through her apartment and found a copy of a will she had made out in 1965 (when she was turning 50), naming the Maryknoll Fathers as inheritors and executors. No copy of the will was in her safety deposit box. When I told the priest who I was, he said, "Are you a blood nephew?" and told me she would have a good Catholic funeral. I said I would fly out that night. By the time I got there, he had hired the law firm that wrote the will to represent the Maryknoll order. Neither the priest nor the lawyers told me when or where the funeral was, but a paralegal from the attorneys' office did give me a select bag of my aunt's things: old photo albums, costume jewelry, a baby tooth, old postcards, and various papers with notes she had made for shopping, reading, thoughts, and reflections. The priest was out of town, and there was no one to talk to. I felt as if I was 4 years old.

I went to the wake. No one else was there. The priest would meet me and the pallbearers at the church for the funeral. My head was spinning. I had never fully decided what I thought about ethnic burial practices. However, on this occasion I gave deep thanks for wakes. There is no way I can adequately describe the importance to me of finding her physical, actual body—looking at her, touching her, and in particular stroking her beautifully manicured, red-polished fingernails. I remarked on these to the funeral director. He, of course, had no way of knowing what all this meant to me, so he responded professionally, "Thanks . . . they weren't like that when we got them." I remembered a hymn from another very important time in my life, my years at Westmont College:

> This world is not my home/I'm just a-passin' through
> My treasures are laid up/Somewhere beyond the blue
> The angels beckon me/from heaven's open door
> And I can't feel at home/in this world any more.

I had always believed in my own way in this philosophy, as well as in biblical lines such as "Where your treasure is, there shall your heart be also," and "Be in the world, but not of the world." This occasion, by contrast, was the first time I felt like a fully three-dimensional, full existing person. I needed to see and touch my aunt's body, and now I felt at home in this world.

At the magnificent church, an attractive and beautifully dressed woman named Florence Popkin came up to me and said she had seen the notice in the paper; she had worked with my aunt 20 years before that. She was a Godsend. I met her after the funeral and had lunch with her and her daughter. I still write to her and to a woman named Elizabeth Carson-Garza, who had car-pooled with my aunt 30 years ago.

The priest sent me a letter explaining a variety of things and included congratulations on being the "fine, Christian gentleman" he saw at the funeral. I had decided I would sing "Amazing Grace" at the cemetery, consciously imitating the great bass voice of my college roommate, Paul Bergen. By the third verse, the stately, well-dressed pallbearers started humming and singing along. I was pleased. In the letter, the priest continued with appreciation of my accomplishments, considering that I "was a child of shame and disgrace"—words written with seemingly no awareness of their meaning, or discomfort that they were still a part of his emotional and doctrinal vocabulary. I was not pleased. I sent another letter to him and to his superior, in which I asked them, as executors, to consider our family history and award some small portion of my aunt's estate ($416,902.09) to my family or my children. That letter was never answered.

I have pieced together the events of my aunt's life as follows. It seems she left Chicago in 1944, the year of my Uncle Stanley's funeral, and joined the Merchant Marines. After the war, she ended up in California, where she worked for Standard Oil (Chevron) for 44 years (they could not release her personnel records), saved her money, and bought stock. She was a very private person. She gave small sums of money regularly to various charities (including the Maryknolls), and liked painting, jewelry making, and real estate. It seems she was abused by Uncle Stanley. One lady—a social worker who played a large part in convincing her to go to the hospital during her last illness—was the only one I talked to who was privy to one of her personal statements. She told me that my aunt had once told her in confidence that she was from Chicago; that her sister was once raped and had a little boy, whom the family had put in an orphanage; and that this "broke her heart." That *was* important. It makes me terribly sad to think that she and I missed out on a connection because of her anxiety that I might blame her for having abandoned me as a child—the furthest thing from my mind.

CONCLUSIONS

A colleague recently asked me, "What is the best thing about being Polish?" My answer on that day was something like "Passion and pageantry." Today, my answer is a little different. I think it was Milton Erickson who said, "Nothing can change until it first becomes what it is." So my answer now is, more simply, "The best thing about being Polish is that I *am* Polish!" An essential ingredient in mourning is to feel the loss, in denial is to feel the pain, and in rage is to feel the helplessness. In being an "illegitimate abandoned orphan," I have needed to feel all three, and then move on. Being Polish has involved acknowledging what might be called "ethnic shame," and recovering from what Gladsky (1992) has called "the loneliness of the long-distance ethnic" (p. 249). A common theme in my orphanage days was "going home" ("When do you think you'll go home? . . . do you think you'll ever go home? . . . Hey, What happened to Cesarz? Haven't seen him in a while . . . didn't you hear? He went home. . . . No kidding! Wow!"). For some orphans, and certainly for me, reconnecting with ethnic roots is a way to go home, to be legitimate—a way to cease to be blown about by the winds of fortune, but rather to be grounded in history.

In the spirit of reframing and reinventing myself, and claiming my inheritance and authenticity, I welcome the ambivalencies of Polish history and character. I feel the sense of belonging that comes from being part of a rich, legitimate history. I fully expect that from time to time, apropos of almost nothing, I can experience again the sudden terror of the walls that inexplicably come a-tumblin' down, but for now I can relish the notion that my "self" is as palpably real as the tombs of Kosciuszko and Sobieski, the lights of the Wrigley Building, the tracks of the Milwaukee Avenue streetcar line, and the bright red fingernails of my Aunt Louise. Incarnations can indeed take many forms.

In the absence of real bodies, living or dead, information (history) can be (and is) the furniture of home. In my search, each successive piece

of information mattered. Biographies need earthly details, and it is difficult to be a connected self with a disconnected history. In regard to children, taking them seriously and giving them information to explain what
is going on around them, in a caring, respectful way, are vital. This is not
to say that children will, or can, blithely survive traumatic events. But it
is to say that the chances of coping are greatly improved by honest information, respectfully given.

Although information itself cannot, of course, protect orphans from
what Simpson (1987) has called the "exquisite vulnerability" that makes
them "go numbly where they are told" (p. 157), it can help provide them
with a safe way to revisit and re-form their lives and to diminish the
numbing hold of a time when that vulnerability made them open to being preyed upon by needy caretakers, ambitious benefactors, and other
real predators (such as Al, the brother of one of our nuns, who seduced a
host of young boys by giving them goodies and rides in his car). Clinicians dealing with families and children (especially on issues having to do
with being orphaned, being placed in foster homes, and other displace-
ments) would do well to be not only informed listeners and informed
observers, but informed recorders of information, particularly positive
information. Later success in life are far from unimportant, but in my
experience they do not have the identity-affirming power of lines in the
Chicago Family Court records such as "The little boy was clever and
adorable," or "The family said that nothing could persuade them to give
him up" (R. Gordon, personal communication).

I do not view the Polish reconnection as a substitute for a family
that might have been, but rather as a discovery of the fuller, and hereto-
fore unknown, corporeality of the actual ocean of life from which I sprang.
On the other hand, to whatever extent substitute gratification is operative, let me say that it is not as good as finding a village of relatives happy
to see me, or finding my real live aunt. Still, as Robert Redford said to
Paul Newman in *The Sting,* "it's close!"

I suspect that for various orphans searching out their roots, dead
ends and disappointments are more likely than "miracle endings" to be
the norm. Nevertheless, next to spiritual transcendence, exploring the
body of one's ethnicity is a safety deposit box full of treasures—an earthy
"home" and a way to becoming more fully the person one is. I strongly
promote clinical, social, and political support for orphans, immigrants,
and other displaced persons seeking access to personal information. Eileen
Simpson makes some profound connections between this country as a
nation of immigrants and the concept of orphanhood, remarking at one
point: "The United States, which has been called the home of the perse-
cuted and the dispossessed, has been since its founding an asylum for
emotional orphans" (1987, p. 221). She also notes that many who have

assimilated by changing their names and foregoing their roots "have no way of estimating their spiritual loss" (p. 225). For myself, despite some heavy negative associations with my Catholic experience, I happen to like the basic idea that we all started out in paradise and that part of the explanation for the universal anxiety of humankind is that none of us is at home; we are all orphans, kicked out of the original household.

Ten years from now I will probably write this story differently. I acknowledge that for now, it is still difficult to let go of the need to find real live relatives, or the wish that they would want to find me. Meanwhile, 10 days from this writing I will again be in Chicago, this time for a reunion of Hedwigians. The old orphanage, which in 1961 became the Niles Seminary, has been sold, and condominiums are being built. The reunion was arranged by Rosie Rathnow-Killips, who for some years has been sending a quarterly newsletter to St. Hedwig's alumni—a remarkable gift of her time, money, and talent. I learned just yesterday that it will be held at Tromba's Grove (now called Przybylo's White Eagle). I don't know how many of my old "siblings" will be there, but I have no doubts that revisiting one's roots, although painful, is a terrific thing to do.

REFERENCES

Folwarski, J., & Marganoff, P. P. (1996). Polish families. In M. McGoldrick, J. Giordano, & J. K. Pearce (Eds.), *Ethnicity and family therapy* (2nd ed., pp. 658–672). New York: Guilford Press.

Gladsky, T. (1992). *Princes, peasants and other Polish selves: Ethnicity in American literature.* Amherst: University of Massachusetts Press.

Michener, J. A. (1983). *Poland.* New York: Random House.

Radzialowski, T. (1975). Reflections on the history of the Felicians in America. *Polish American Studies, 32*(1), 19–28.

Rathnow-Killips, R. M. (Ed.). (1994). *The Hedwigian II* (Vol. 13, No. 1). Blanchardville, WI: The Women and Men of St. Hedwig's Alumni Association.

Simpson, E. (1987). *Orphans: Real and imaginary.* New York: New American Library.

PART V

THERAPY WITH DIFFERENT POPULATIONS

The chapters in this section each attempt to focus on specific clinical issues for particular cultural groups. They are meant to be suggestive rather than comprehensive, indicating the subtlety and complexity of our cases when considered through a cultural filter. Each of the chapters in this section offers a re-visioning perspective by moving the subject under consideration "from margin to center," as bell hooks (1984) has put it. They use each group's own frame of reference for assessment and intervention, challenging our field's dominant notions of clinical practice.

This section opens with a chapter by Vanessa Mahmoud, which describes the ubiquitous double binds confronting African Americans in our society, and provides clear guidelines about how these "crazy-making" dynamics can be addressed in therapy. Nancy Boyd-Franklin and Anderson J. Franklin and Marlene Watson—focusing on couple therapy and on sibling relationships, respectively—discuss issues of relevance to work with African American families. Joel Crohn and Bok-Lim Kim both address the complex dynamics that arise with intermarriage, as well as the role of the therapist in working with a couple in which cultural differences are an inherent part of the relationship. Tom Johnson and Michael Keren, examining the much-neglected area of lesbian and gay family life, stress the need for therapists to understand the particular challenges facing those who live within a novel or marginalized family configuration. Finally, Nydia Garcia-Preto discusses the specific complexities of gender and cultural colonization for Latina women.

None of these groups have received the clinical attention they deserve in the family therapy literature in general. We hope that readers will use the ideas and insights offered here as a stimulus to reconsider their work with these and other subpopulations, so that we can develop a more inclusive field that listens to the voices of all our citizens and develops services to meet their many changing needs.

REFERENCE

hooks, b. (1984). *Feminist theory: From margin to center.* Boston: South End Press.

CHAPTER 19

The Double Binds of Racism

Vanessa M. Mahmoud

Iago: The Moor is of a free and open nature,
That thinks men honest that but seem to be so,
And will as tenderly be led by the nose
As asses are. . . .

Make the Moor thank me, love me, and reward me,
For making him egregiously an ass,
And practicing upon his peace and quiet
Even to madness.
—WILLIAM SHAKESPEARE, *Othello*
(1604/1974, I.iii. 399–402,
II.i. 308–311)

Four centuries after Shakespeare, African Americans are still subjected on a daily basis to the same exquisitely painful double binds to which Iago subjected Othello. The searing quality of the mystification involved in these double binds remains the same and creates an enormous clinical challenge for anyone who is working with African Americans in therapy. This chapter focuses on describing clearly what double binds are and how to help clients to escape and master them.

THE NATURE OF DOUBLE BINDS AND THEIR PERPETRATORS

A double-binding relationship is one in which a more powerful person tyrannizes and victimizes a less powerful person, communicating in a mystifying way that binds the victim and leaves him or her no room for safety. The mystification operates through subtle, covert messages that contradict the overt messages, but the victim can neither comment on the discrepancy nor leave the relationship. And thus, as Iago said, one can practice such techniques upon the unsuspecting other, "even to madness." Indeed, the term "double bind" was first developed to describe "crazy-making" communication patterns that appeared to lead the recipient into anxious feelings, doubt about his or her perceptions, and finally mental illness (Bateson, Jackson, Haley, & Weakland, 1968).

Carlos Castañeda (1984) has described those who inflict this kind of abuse as "petty tyrants":

> A petty tyrant is a tormentor . . . someone who either holds the power of life and death over warriors or simply annoys them to distraction. One that torments with brutality and violence. Another that does it by creating unbearable apprehension through deviousness. Another which oppresses with sadness. And the last, which torments by making warriors rage.

Such "petty tyrants" have usually learned their communication patterns early, from parents or other authority figures, and have become unconsciously aware of the power of this type of communication. Pimps, con artists, and gigolos, but also salespeople, attorneys, physicians, and others who hold power over the innocent, the ill, or the less privileged, may consciously use these patterns to take advantage of their victims. They may form groups or organizations that serve in part to maintain this power.

Narcissism figures prominently in the character and defenses of people who communicate in double-bind language. One is most likely to trigger such people's wrath when one contradicts or confronts disparities in their behavior, challenging their grandiose images of self. Upon confrontation, the persecutors may see themselves as the wronged parties and the real victims, and behave as if they have been misunderstood and maligned.

The double binds of slave times—when a master might say, "Haven't I always treated you well? How could you go against me by disagreeing with the system of slavery?"—are still all too operative or African Americans today. (Sexist relationships, too, are usually conducted with double-bind communication. Indeed, African American women have traditionally been subject to victimizing not only by European Americans, but also by African American men.) Often I have had African American clients tell me of double-binding situations that have been so overwhelming and "crazy-making" that they have suppressed the experience for long periods. At times, they may cry or become enraged as if the incidents happened recently, instead of years ago. These incidents retain their power and are replayed over and over in their consciousness. Most African

Americans have had a number of such experiences, lasting often for years at a time.

SOME EXAMPLES OF RACIST DOUBLE BINDS

Some of the double-bind strategies used in the service of racism are conscious and others are unconscious, just as any behaviors based on internally held values are apt to be. Such dynamics may produce intense emotional responses in their victims. As Charles Pinderhughes (1973) put it so well:

> Racism is a relatively constant pattern of prejudice and discrimination between one party who is idealized and favored and another who is devalued and exploited in a common relationship . . . involving an initiator and [an] adjusted . . . one who extends some thing of the self and one who adjusts to that . . . incorporating false belief systems aggrandizing the upper elites and denigrating the lower nonelites.

In this section, I provide some brief case examples that illustrate typical racist double binds. In the first example, a young light-skinned African American physician in his internship was subjected to racial slurs by his professors about his peers, who were darker-skinned and less successful in their studies. He was told repeatedly that he was "not like the rest of them." He was given preferential treatment, and his classmates resented it. They began to shy away from him and refused to socialize. He had no one to confide in. He also knew he had to continue working hard to maintain his scholarship. He began to experience unbearable anxiety and panic attacks.

This young physician was getting acceptance and favors from his professors for accepting their assertions that he was different from and better than his African American peers. There was a double message at work here, because they were actually saying, "We like you, but [subtext] we don't like most African Americans." In order to remain in favor, this young man had to seem to reject a conscious identification with his cultural group, which alienated his peers. Over time, a victim's emotional response to double binds such as this one is likely to become intense. The longer the victim is exposed to such a tyrannical relationship, the more severe the emotional damage will be.

Here is a second example. A little Black boy and his brother were the first to integrate their school. Every day they were chased home and often beaten by some of the White male students. The little boy, even though he was only 8, fought hard to protect his brother, who was only

5. He never mentioned this problem to his parents, because he felt they were so proud of him for being brave during the integration. Also, during this time his mother was very ill, and he felt he had to pretend everything was all right so that she would not worry. The school year ended without his telling them. Upon the start of the next school year, he took an overdose of his mother's sleeping pills on the bus ride to his first day of school. He was seen by a White psychiatrist in the hospital, but would not speak to him. He switched schools and did poorly in most of his classes. His teachers said he was "withdrawn, nervous, and angry," and had "low self-esteem and poor social skills with peers."

This little boy was suffering from posttraumatic stress disorder secondary to the tyrannical abuse he received from the group of White students, who were more numerous and larger than he and his brother. Despite the abuse, he felt as if he must continue going to school; this was the first double bind. In this case, the boy was also caught in the paradox of wanting to please his parents by being brave, courageous, and tough enough to handle the situation, and at the same time needing his parents to rescue him from danger. In addition, because of his experience with the cruel White children, the boy was suspicious of all White people. He found it hard to trust well-meaning people if they resembled those who had tormented him. He had a lot of residual anger with his parents for not perceiving his dilemma, which he internalized as well. He ended up feeling hopeless, with no way out except death. He felt he could not risk commenting on the situation in any other way.

It is characteristic of double binds that the recipient is prevented from commenting on the contradictory message she or he is being given. A victim who confronts the perpetrator with her or his true feelings runs the risk of consequences that are even more painful than the present situation. If the victim decides to take the risk of the painful consequences and to confront the perpetrator anyway, at times her or his perceptions may be disqualified and questioned. The perpetrator may say something like this: "That's crazy. There must be something wrong with you for perceiving the situation in that way. It has no basis in reality. You are too sensitive. You are fomenting disagreement and conflict where none existed before, and for that I will have to punish you."

The young physician in the first example would probably have been severely sanctioned if he were to say, "I feel you are judging my classmates on the basis of their race," when the professors made derogatory comments and judgments about his African American peers. A professor might have retorted. "This is not about race. It is about winners and losers, and I am only interested in winners. And I suggest you adopt my philosophy if you know what is good for you in terms of your future in this institution. You are being too sensitive and taking this all too personally." Many times, the victim of a double bind who confronts the perpetrator by voicing his or her accurate perceptions is set up for later harassment. Standing up to tyranny exacts a high price. It is one thing to risk punishment, receive that punishment, and be free to leave the "field of conflict"; it is another thing to have to return to it day after day.

In a third example, a little African American girl came home in tears from her private school in a Southern city. The school was to have an antebellum ball in which all of the students were to come in period dress. Her teacher suggested that she could come as a "pickaninny." When she asked what that was, she was told that it was a child slave, like Topsy in *Uncle Tom's Cabin*. All the other children started laughing, and the little girl began to cry. She was then told sternly by the teacher not to be so sensitive, as no one meant any harm by a little teasing.

The little girl felt that in order to be accepted by the rest of her class, she had to identify with the stereotype of a child slave. She had not learned how to pretend that she was not hurt and displayed her honest feelings. The double-binding messages to her were as follows: "You are just like everyone else. But your ancestors were slaves of our ancestors, and you should play a slave in our reenactment of those times. You should not have any emotional reaction to that, and if you do you will be excluded, censured, and blamed for your reaction." This child could have been excluded by the teacher from participation in subsequent activities and shamed further about her feelings if she confronted the teacher. Children are always vulnerable, having very little power to leave a classroom without severe consequences.

I remember that when I was a child, the humor I encountered in predominantly European American settings was often racist. Certain jokes were offensive to me as an African American. Indeed, it was a matter of folk wisdom in my community never to get too close to European Americans, because when they became too familiar, they were liable to try out these offensive jokes in our presence. The ability to discern the underlying meaning of a communication seems to be impaired by repeated exposure to double-bind situations. It is hard for many African Americans to tell whether a European American is sincere in humor, play, attempts at friendship, and so forth, because of their past experience of duplicitous communications. Native Americans have expressed their experience with this in the phrase that European Americans "speak with forked tongues." Michael Kimmel has described the double-binding interactions of European Americans with Native Americans as follows:

A simple pattern emerged: Appropriate their land and abridge their freedom because you see them as passive and helpless. This makes them passive and helpless, which then allows you to justify the whole thing by referring to the passivity and helplessness you have caused.

Hypervigilance, one of the symptoms of posttraumatic stress disorder, has become a cultural norm among African Americans. The reflective scanning of the environment for racist messages has been explained as a kind of double consciousness, which is an important survival skill. If a society has historically been hostile to a group's existence, it is important to know the signs of increased hostility and danger. African American people who do not know these signs or who drop this scanning defense may or may not be in physical danger, but they are surely in danger of emotional abuse.

Hypervigilance takes a great deal of psychic energy that would otherwise be available for other things. It also adds stress to most interracial relationships. When African Americans are watching TV or a movie or reading the newspaper, they engage in subconscious scanning for racist intent; such scanning is a part of their everyday lives. Hypervigilance tends to be more developed among African Americans than among persons of African descent who emigrate to the United States. The latter are sometimes at a disadvantage until they learn this "skill." They are often bewildered when they become aware of the need to guard themselves in this fashion, and are sometimes in awe of African Americans' ability to have existed in this cultural dissonance for so long.

African Americans, however, may also see benign situations as racist because of this defense. For instance, a mother confided in me that she had become concerned about her daughter's complaints about the way she was treated in her classroom. She was the only African American student, and she complained that she was never selected for certain activities, such as wiping the board, taking care of the pets, or passing out papers. She had a European American teacher who always seemed to call on the other children. The mother decided to confront the teacher. She was very nervous about it, because she did not want it to backfire on her daughter; she remembered when she had been treated the way her daughter was apparently treated. Upon talking to the teacher, however, she discovered that the reason her daughter had not been given those tasks was that she had been elected class president and had other leadership duties, such as leading the lunch line, leading the Pledge of Allegiance, and serving as teacher's helper. The mother realized that she had thought there was racist intent in the teacher's actions, but that, instead, the little girl was simply very eager to do everything in her class.

DEALING WITH DOUBLE BINDS IN THERAPY

In this section, I use the case of Eric to describe how to deal with racist double binds in therapy.

Case Background

Eric, an African American Vietnam veteran, was in a treatment center for detoxification and was placed in an all-African American treatment group. He maintained an aggressive stance toward most of the members of the group. He did not begin to become vulnerable until he began talking about his father, who was a sharecropper and who had been repeatedly shamed and humiliated by the landowner in his (Eric's) presence. Eric remembered his father crying after one incident, in which he was cheated financially by this man. He remembered the hurt and rage he felt at seeing his strong father reduced to tears; he also recalled feeling powerless to help his father.

Witnessing the abuse of another person can be traumatic for the witness as well. The overt tormenting of Eric's father was clearly a scene that played repeatedly in Eric's mind. It served as the template for every interaction that he had with White authority figures; it was also the source of a deeply held rage that would increase over the years, especially in Vietnam.

While in Southeast Asia, Eric was a leader in his platoon. He served in a Special Forces unit and did two tours of duty in Vietnam and Cambodia. He liked the power of a gun and found he could survive the jungles. In the jungles, an enemy could be killed. When Eric returned to the United States, he got a job in a manufacturing plant. He had a European American supervisor who became jealous of Eric's efficiency in performing tasks and popularity with other staff members. He began to criticize him and say demeaning things about him to the other workers, who were also African American. At one point, Eric was accused of stealing some money from a petty cash fund, and his supervisor had him arrested on the job. He was handcuffed and paraded before his coworkers. Although he was later cleared of the charges, he was unable to return to work, because he began to have panic attacks so severe and so debilitating that he was unable to drive or take public transportation.

On this job, Eric was in a double bind. At an overt level, the boss's message was "Do your job." But at a covert level, the boss was saying this: "Don't do your job too well, and don't say anything about my demeaning you, or it will go worse for you and I will humiliate you and set your coworkers against you." Eric was not free to leave his job, because jobs were hard to find and there was some stigma at the time in being a Vietnam veteran. One of the most toxic elements of his situation was the rage he felt at his supervisor, which led him to think of killing him, as he had been trained to do and rewarded for doing to his enemies as a soldier. But now he knew he would go to jail for such behavior. He also kept remembering his father's mistreatment. He tried to suppress his homicidal impulses, to ignore his supervisor, and to go on with his work. However, after the supervisor's tyranny culminated in his being arrested for something he did not do, he could no longer reconcile himself to working under the same conditions. His insurance company did not recognize his "job stress" as a reason for granting him disability pay, and he felt trapped. His flashbacks to the Vietnam War increased. His nightmares, hypervigilance, sleeplessness, depression, and social withdrawal increased as well. He sought relief in alcohol and was rarely able to leave his house without distress. Eventually he came to a local mental health center for assistance.

Ways of Escaping from a Double Bind

There seem to be only a few ways for people to escape from double binds:

1. *Passive acceptance.* By this method, feelings of powerlessness, anger, rage, hurt, shame, anxiety, and fear are repressed. However, the consequences of this repression are severe. Various symptoms of emotional distress—depression, anxiety attacks, obsessive–compulsive patterns, internalization of aggression, and so forth—are heightened by passively participating in such a relationship.

2. *Verification of the accuracy of perception by a powerful other.* If another person perceived as powerful verifies the accuracy of a victim's perception, there is considerable emotional relief. Many African Americans will use other African Americans as sounding boards to verify racist interactions ("Did he really say what I thought he said? Am I being too sensitive?") Therapists can sometimes serve as important validators of victims' experiences of racism.

3. *Physical escape from the field of conflict.* Physical escape provides significant relief. However, it does not guarantee psychological or emotional healing. The scars of the conflict, traumatic memories, depression, and rage often remain unresolved.

4. *Decision to risk punishment by direct confrontation.* Sometimes victims decide to confront perpetrators and risk the punishment that will be inflicted. They may choose this option because they can stand the situation no longer; they feel strong and healthy enough to be willing to risk punishment; or they represent a group of others who have experi-

enced similar treatment. After such a confrontation, even if a victim is punished by a perpetrator, the interaction between them may change.

Techniques for Helping Clients with Double Binds

How can a therapist begin to help a client like Eric? The usual methods pursued with such clients are to offer support, a safe place to ventilate feelings, antianxiety medication, and/or and referral to a veterans' support group. All of these can help, but many times oppression is not directly addressed. This means that a key dynamic in such a client's life and its concomitant pathology will be ignored.

In therapy with clients who have described such double-binding experiences, an effective technique is active exploration and diagramming of the communication patterns that have been causing the clients pain. It is important not to minimize their pain or to excuse the behavior of the perpetrators. Often it takes several sessions to explore all the layers of feelings that are triggered by a particular situation. It is crucial for a client to feel heard, understood, and reassured that his or her perceptions are valid. A therapist must convey an acceptance of a client's experience of events. By doing so, the therapist becomes a force of verification, bearing witness to the abuse and facilitating the client's relief.

It is also important not to send clients conflicting messages or to maintain an anxiety-provoking neutrality in therapy. Often at this stage clients see the perpetrators of the double binds as totally bad, and cannot bear the thought that there are any redeeming qualities in these persons. They need to be sure that the therapist understands that the perpetrators are trying to hurt them. This need is similar to the need of sexual abuse survivors when they reveal the abuse for the first time to another. In both cases, it is important that clients be believed. Not being believed after taking the risk of telling retraumatizes the clients and inhibits further attempts to seek help. Later in therapy, when a client has built a safe relationship with a therapist, the therapist can begin to "rehumanize" the client's perceptions of the perpetrator. Sometimes, however, a client is afraid to be angry with a perpetrator even in the privacy of therapy. Such clients have effectively repressed their angry to the point that they are not aware of it any longer; instead, they may project this anger onto others who are less threatening. This situation is particularly common in cases where clients' relatives have themselves previously projected bottled-up anger onto the clients in the form of double binds or other abuse, as I discuss in regard to Eric below.

People who abuse power do so in strategic ways. It is important for those who are targeted to understand these strategies, so that they can begin to empower themselves. When people understand how others manipulate or tyrannize them, they gain emotional distance, which helps them to avoid futile power struggles and free themselves.

It is important to explain to clients the process of double binds. Therapists should ask clients to observe the perpetrators and to count how many times in a day the perpetrators abuse their power or put the clients in a double bind. They also need to observe when this is most likely to happen. Next, they should begin to notice who receives similar treatment and who is spared. Clients usually report back with considerably more awareness about what is actually happening in such communications. They have begun the first steps toward empowerment. When I am doing therapy with such clients, we talk about strategies they might use to deal with these situations, and we explore options together. We become allies against oppression. We may talk in metaphors about armor, battle, or war; we also talk about spiritual transcendence, justice, honor, integrity, revenge, and hatred. We plot methods of escape (e.g., getting a new job, going back to school, starting a business). Finally, we talk at great length about others in their lives who also abuse power.

Often relatives in authority—parents, siblings, grandparents, aunts, or uncles—have subjected clients to double binds similar to those employed by perpetrators outside the family. Such double binds are even worse in some ways, because clients' relatives are the very people who are supposed to love and protect them. Clients with such experiences are extremely sensitive to double-bind messages from other authority figures. In Eric's case, we were able to identify various perpetrators of double binds: his boss, some of his officers in the service, and the landowner who had demeaned his father. However, it took longer for him to admit that his father, whom he had idolized, used to beat him with an extension cord. In addition to the physical abuse involved, this put Eric in a double bind because he was distressed at the way his father had been demeaned by the landowner and yet he was being demeaned in turn by his father. It took even longer for him to see the way he himself had tyrannized his wife and eldest son. During this time, Eric's rage and pain were so intense that he had to remain in partial hospitalization to contain him and keep him from hurting others. At times he was frightening to other patients and would avoid group therapy. The group he felt safest in was the all-African American therapy group, which he dominated at first. It was hard for him not to dehumanize people who disagreed with him, especially other men. Staff members would give him realistic feedback about how they saw him in the group. Though they maintained an accepting stance even when he voiced homicidal thoughts, they were firm about setting limits on his name calling and threats of physical intimidation or violence. The staff members had to work hard at not dehumanizing him in their own minds out of fear. They talked among themselves in supervision about the feelings he stirred in them. Slowly his outbursts became less frequent, and he began to show some empathy for others in the group. He did not seem to feel as pressured to dominate the group. He began to be more vulnerable, and people began to tell him they were not afraid of him any more.

If, however, the staff members had minimized the significance of his experience of oppression and prematurely put more behavioral constraints and expectations on him, his therapy would probably not have been as successful. If his bids for power in the therapeutic milieu had been met with power moves by the staff, the power struggle could have escalated the conflict, and he would have perceived the staff's suppression of his behavior and thoughts as yet another double bind ("Be honest about how you feel, but do not make us afraid of you, or we will punish you").

In individual therapy, Eric explored his feelings about work, about being an African American man, about his relationships with men and women, about racism, and about ways to take responsibility for his life. He and I talked about the effects of slavery on African American people and looked for evidence of those effects in his own family life. We found it in many ways, all of which had been triggers for his own violent and oppressive behavior—for which he now realized he had to take responsibility. We talked about how he felt about himself, what his strengths and assets were, and where he could improve. He began to seek out support in his group meetings, and he began to attend church with his family.

Summary of Techniques

Racism often involves double binds. For therapy to be effective with clients who describe racist, double-binding relationships, I suggest that therapists do the following:

1. *Verify the clients' perceptions of the relationships.* Clients should be encouraged to ventilate their feelings about the perpetrators as fully as possible. Therapists should not give clients the impression that they doubt their perceptions in any way, but should get them to clarify each problematic situation in detail. In a family therapy session, it is important to discuss the impact of a situation on the rest of the family. Frequently clients have had other abuse experiences, and as a result may be very sensitive to double-bind messages. They should be given ample opportunity to talk about other times they have been victimized and how they have responded. How do the present situations compare to similar situations in the past?

2. *Describe to clients what racism is and what a double bind is, as well as ways to respond to double-binding messages.* Therapists should

point out the conflicting overt and covert messages inherent in clients' situations. In a family therapy session, it is important to discuss whether a client has had similar problems with the way any other family member communicates. Also, a therapist who is of the same race as a perpetrator should ask whether this situation is difficult to talk about with this therapist.

3. *Double-check with clients that they feel their situations are correctly understood.* How do they feel about finding someone who understands and believes them? In a family therapy session, the family members can be asked to talk about how it feels to have a loved one victimized and how they have attempted to support the loved one.

4. *Contract and construct with clients an alliance that includes strategies for escaping racist relationships.* This may take more than one session. Family members should be allowed to make suggestions as well.

5. *Have clients do "research" by counting the number of times they catch the perpetrators sending double-bind messages.* This helps them gain emotional distance from their situations and allows them to delay their responses until these can be developed more fully in the safety of therapy.

6. *When clients are ready, have them begin to implement the strategies they have selected from the options already discussed.* The clients should report back on the outcome of their efforts, and therapists should continue to strategize and support them until they report adequate relief, leave their abusive situations, find themselves less emotionally reactive to the perpetrators, and/or feel empowered and not oppressed. Any progress should be discussed with other family members, who should be asked whether they have also felt a change in a victimized family member.

At worst, therapists can do incalculable harm to victims of racist abuse by perpetuating, exacerbating, and intensifying the victims' distress. Racist therapists have the power to create still more double binds with their clients, because of the power of the therapeutic role. Often even well-intentioned therapists are paralyzed by overt or covert racism, because they are unskilled in how to resist it, are afraid of it, or are in denial about its existence. Therapists working with people who experience racism in their daily lives are betraying them if they do not help their clients deal directly with the source of their pain. At a minimum, therapists should be powerful witnesses to the pain racist abuse causes. At their best, they can assist clients toward empowerment and autonomy.

REFERENCES

Bateson, G., Haley, J., Jackson, D., & Weakland, J. (1968). Towards a theory of schizophrenia. In D. Jackson (Ed.), *Communication, family and marriage*. Palo Alto, CA: Science & Behavior Books.

Castañcda, C. (1984).

Jacobs, H. (1993). Incidents in the life of a slave girl. In D. Mullane (Ed.), *Crossing the danger water*. New York: Doubleday/Anchor.

Pinderhughes, C. A. (1973). Racism and psychotherapy. In C. Willie, B. Kramer, & B. Brown, (Eds.), *Racism and mental health*. Pittsburgh: University of Pittsburgh Press.

Shakespeare, W. (1974). Othello. In G. B. Evans (Ed.), *The Riverside Shakespeare*. Boston: Houghton Mifflin. (Original work performed 1604)

CHAPTER 20

African American Couples in Therapy

Nancy Boyd-Franklin
Anderson J. Franklin

No issue in the African American community has generated more debate, pain, anger, anxiety, or conflict than that of male–female relationships. Many well-trained therapists who do excellent work with African American families find that they encounter unexpected difficulties when they are treating African American couples, or when the focus in family treatment shifts from child-centered to male–female relationships—a stage when many African American couples withdraw from therapy. To avoid such an unfortunate scenario, therapists must be helped to understand how racism and gender role issues affect male–female dynamics in Black couples today, and how family socialization practices in African American families have contributed to these dynamics. This chapter addresses these topics and their implications for family and couple therapy. Throughout the chapter, the terms "African American" and "Black" are used interchangeably. The term "couple therapy" rather than "marital therapy" is used, because many African American couples who present for treatment are not legally married and often come for treatment during a crisis that threatens their relationship. Although the couples discussed in this chapter are heterosexual, there is a small but growing literature on gay and lesbian African American couples (Greene & Boyd-Franklin, 1996).

RACE AND GENDER

Racism and sexism in the United States left both Black women *and* Black men "oppressed" (Jones, 1997). This is true even for those who have achieved middle-class status. Society's view of Black men and women has profoundly affected multigenerational messages about Black male–female relationships. Cross-racial treatment by therapists of different cultures can only be successful if such therapists understand that they cannot view African American gender roles and relationships as equivalent to those in their own cultures. To comprehend the difference in hierarchy and power between African American men and women, we must look first at their experiences.

Experiences of African American Men

Black men have been denied dignity throughout American history. They are often treated as objects of fear. Franklin (1992) has drawn upon Ralph Ellison's (1952) classic book *Invisible Man* to describe an "invisibility syndrome," wherein African American men are treated as if they are invisible except when they are perceived as a threat or challenge. Individual talent, ability, and contribution are rendered invisible when Black men are responded to stereotypically in terms of their race and skin color. This "invisibility pattern" has been embodied in societal institutions such as the welfare system, which has forced Black women to negate the existence of the men in their lives by "hiding" them.

Black male's conception of masculinity has attributes that both overlap and are independent of those held by White men (Franklin, in press). Both groups subscribe to the expectations of being a good provider, but Black men have to overcome racism to accomplish this goal. For example, when a Black man is assertive in protecting himself as a provider, that behavior may be misinterpreted as aggressive and may jeopardize his job. Yet a man who does not demonstrate sufficient assertiveness can be regarded by his partner as inadequate. This type of conflict can become the source of frustrating, angry outbursts by Black men. The consequences of the invisibility syndrome have a profound effect on the psyches of Black people and on the health and well-being of their male–female relationships.

Racist assaults are a daily reality for African Americans, regardless of class, socioeconomic level, education, and income (Cose, 1993; Hacker, 1992; Jones, 1997). Racism puts a tremendous additional burden on Black couple relationships that most White couples do not experience. A couple relationship must become a comforting and trusted place where each partner can "pull out the arrows" and heal the wounds inflicted by a racist society.

Experiences of African American Women

The complex interaction of racism and sexism can be seen in the very attempt of an African American couple to create a safe "homeplace" where these arrows of racism can be removed. Black feminist scholar bell hooks (1981, 1990) addresses the Black woman's role in this process:

> Since sexism delegates to females the task of creating and sustaining a home environment, it has been primarily the responsibility of black women to construct domestic households as spaces of care and nurturance in the face of the brutal harsh reality of racist oppression, of sexist domination.
> . . . This task of making homeplace was not simply a matter of black women providing service; it was about the construction of a safe place where black people could affirm one another and by so doing heal many of the wounds inflicted by racist domination. (hooks, 1990, p. 42)

Another part of the legacy of racism and sexism is that many African American women have grown up with negative messages from the media, schools, the mental health field, and sometimes their own families about their worth, intelligence, ability, and beauty. Although African American women have been described as suffering from the double jeopardy of racism and sexism (Comas-Díaz & Greene, 1994), American society has deemed African American women less threatening, in some instances, than Black men. African American women have learned self-reliance from their female role models, who have traditionally both worked and raised children (Giddings, 1984). The role of African American women in society is often complex and paradoxical.

Whereas African American men often fall victim to the "last hired, first fired" syndrome, African American women can often find work but are relegated to low-skill jobs and gender-stereotypical work (Giddings, 1984). To this day, Black women are often received and treated better in the world of work than Black men are. Combined with their resourcefulness, this means that they sometimes gain more and fare better in a White-male-dominated work world than African American men (Stone, 1995). This has led to a gender power balance between African American men and women quite different from that of their White counterparts, wherein African American women's expectations of African American men as partners are compromised. As a result, great tension often exists in the relationship of Black women to Black men.

The femininity and beauty of Black women have historically been denied in a society that imposes White features as the standards against which all are judged. In recent years, these standards have eased somewhat, but nevertheless the complex interplay of skin color, hair texture, body type, and the negative messages from society (as well as internalized racism and sexism) continue to cause many African American women a great deal of pain and anger. These emotions contribute to feelings of inferiority and low self-esteem, which the women often bring into their couple and family relationships.

Society's devaluation of African American women's appearance rendered them as "invisible" as Black men. Interestingly, however, sexual abuse and denigration were so rampant in domestic employment that African American families made education a priority for their daughters. However, even education offered limited alternatives to "domestic service" because of segregation and institutional racism. African American women continue to deal with condescension and maltreatment in the workplace. Both African American men and women have been victims of violence and abuse since the slavery era. It is an abuse perpetuated by many forms of prejudice and discrimination. The rage experienced by both Black men and women as a result of these situations has frequently been carried into couple and family relationships. It can be manifested in partners' frustration over the barriers of everyday racism and disillusionment with each other about individual, personal accomplishments (Franklin, in press). Such disillusionment can lead to poor communication and immobilization as a couple working in partnership. This situation is often presented in therapy as an argument between Black men and women about provider roles.

Socialization Differences by Gender

African American families often try to compensate for the negative and destructive messages that their male children are given by society (Boyd-Franklin, 1989; Franklin, 1993) by attempting to instill strong racial identity. Parents fear for the safety and well-being of their sons. Black males have been perceived in the African American community since slavery as an "endangered" group. Ways in which this endangerment manifests itself today include the disproportionate placement of Black male children in special education classes; high dropout rates; and the constant threat of violence against them—both from within their own communities, and from outside by law enforcement authorities (Hammond & Yung, 1993; Oliver, 1994). It is the contention of Kunjufu (1985) that by fourth grade, African American male children are often perceived as threats by their teachers or are more frequently labeled as "aggressive" or "hyperactive."

This can often lead to school failure. Unfortunately, in attempting to achieve balance, some African American families socialize their male and female children far differently, spawning the common belief that "we raise our daughters but love our sons." This does not imply that African Americans do not love their daughters, but merely that they often try to compensate for the intense discrimination against Black males in society by attempting to protect them within the family. This effort has many ramifications for African American couples. It has contributed greatly to the rage and pain that subsequent generations of African American women feel about male attitudes toward an equal partnership in a relationship. It also contributes to the complex victimizing messages that African American women and men receive while growing up, and it can result in excuses made for abusive male behavior in family and couple relationships.

Victimizing and Contradictory Messages

The messages given to African American men and women about each other are often conflictual, sexist, ambivalent, and potentially damaging to relationships. Black women are frequently given contradictory messages by their families of origin. One is a message of independence (e.g., "God bless the child who has her own"), with its implication that Black men cannot be trusted to stay with and provide for women; the other is a message that a woman's utmost goal is to find a Black man who will take care of her. This double bind often places Black women in difficult relationships with Black men or in no relationship at all.

Black men also receive mixed messages. On the one hand, they are often given the message that they must be "men"—assertive/aggressive, "productive" as providers, educated, and dominant. These are expectations consistent with White male gender roles. On the other hand, anxious parents afraid for their Black sons' survival will blunt this message with a caution such as this: "You are Black and you must not be too aggressive, too dominant, and so on, because 'the (White) man' will cut you down." Above all, Black males learn that they must be "cool"—that they must don a mask of utmost composure, no matter what is happening in their inner emotional worlds (Majors & Billson, 1992). These mixed messages create a "double bind" for African American men as well.

Complexity of Gender Roles

Given this interweaving of racism and sexism, gender roles are extremely complicated in African American families. A therapist must challenge obvious sexist behavior in a couple's relationship, but must also consider how racism may have contributed to the experience of a power imbalance in the home. When a man feels dehumanized, he may assert his power in sexist ways in order to compensate. Poussaint (1993), in an article in *Ebony* magazine, makes the following observation: "Although both Black men and women are victims in America, they are still victimizing each other. We have to stop inflicting more pain on each other by tearing each other apart" (p. 88). It is important to note that this does not just refer to physical abuse (in which women are more often abused by their partners), but to verbal and emotional abuse (which is often more mutual). Before we explore the presentation of African American couples in therapy, it is important for therapists to be aware of another force that can greatly affect messages about gender roles and treatment outcome in some cases—namely, extended family involvement.

Extended Family Involvement: Multigenerational Messages about Gender Roles

Many therapists have made the error of treating an African American couple or family in isolation, without recognizing the tremendous power that may be exerted by extended family members. Researchers and scholars (Billingsley, 1968, 1992; Boyd-Franklin, 1989; Hill, 1972) have documented the strength of extended family kinship networks in many African American families. Even though relatives may not live in the household, they can sabotage treatment. A careful genogram and the involvement of key family members in treatment may prevent such an unfortunate outcome.

The characters in the 1961 film *A Raisin in the Sun* powerfully illustrate the multigenerational transmission process of male–female relationships and socialization practices in many African American families. Although the play was written in the late 1950s, the issues resound for African American couples and families today. The adult son voices the rage and pain of other Black men when he gets down on his knees and says with intense anguish, "I am a man!", asking his family to recognize this in the face of a society he is convinced never will. The other members of his family compensate for this in a variety of ways; for instance, they put him forward as the family spokesperson to the "outsider." The sister embodies the pain of many African American women who were reared in families that "raise their daughters but love their sons" when she angrily says to her mother, who has defended her brother's actions, "Mama, will you be on *my* side for once?" The grandmother profoundly expresses the dilemma of generations of Black mothers in their response to racism when she says angrily to her daughter about her son, "You give him up for me like the rest of society. . . . Who gave you the right?"

PRESENTATION OF AFRICAN AMERICAN COUPLES IN THERAPY

Common Issues

The "healthy cultural suspicion" with which African Americans approach therapy is well documented (Boyd-Franklin, 1989; Grier & Cobbs, 1968; Hines & Boyd-Franklin, 1982, 1996). Many African Americans are hesitant to talk about their personal lives with strangers; this is particularly true of intimate couple relationships. As a consequence, a significant number of African American couples present a child for treatment initially, particularly in regard to school-related issues (Haley, 1976). In such a case, it is extremely important for therapists to address and resolve the presenting problem of the child within family sessions before moving to the couple's issues. This allows the therapist the opportunity to build credibility. An African American couple is more likely than a White couple to flee from therapy if the therapist is not sensitive to the timing of this intervention.

A second common complication that may arise in the treatment of an African American couple occurs when an appointment scheduled by the woman is canceled on the day of the session because the man "refuses to come." Refusal to see a member of the couple alone is often an error, as the therapist can begin with the woman and then work with her to engage the man in therapy. There are various strategies a therapist can pursue to get the man involved (e.g., sending an oral or written message with the woman, writing him directly, telephoning him), since it is important to avoid keeping African American men invisible in the treatment process. A pattern of withdrawing from treatment and then reappearing during a time of crisis is also typical of many African American couples, particularly in inner-city clinics. Flexibility is key with such couples and families, and therapists should be prepared to reach out and make home visits if the need arises.

The "Rage over Racism" Issue

African Americans struggle with the inequities of racism even at very high occupational, educational, and socioeconomic levels. Unfortunately, the rage about this is often misdirected toward family and couple relationships. The following case provides an example of this process.[1]

John (35) and Judy (36) were an African American professional couple with two children. They were both lawyers in major law firms until a year earlier, when John was dismissed by his firm—a dismissal he attributed to "institutional racism." He had not found another permanent job since, but was doing *per diem* work. Judy, however, was on the "fast track" for partnership. Over the course of the last year, John and Judy had become more angry and verbally abusive with each other. During an early session of couple therapy, John called Judy "lazy, a lousy house-keeper, and an inadequate lover," while she referred to John as "no good, lazy, and useless." When John also called her a "bad mother," Judy yelled that she was sick of carrying all of the financial, emotional, and parental responsibility for their home and family. She then began to sob. When the therapist asked John to pass her a tissue, Judy slapped it from his hand.

The therapist asked Judy to tell John what she was feeling. She told him she felt "damned if I do and damned if I don't." If she tried to support him, he told her she was condescending. If she tried to push him, he said she was a "castrating Black woman."

The therapist asked John to tell her how he felt. He said that sometimes he indeed felt "castrated"—by his former bosses, by Judy, and by others in their lives who "put me down." He added, "Why can't she [Judy] understand that it's hard for a Black man out here?"

Judy became angry at this and said that it was hard for her as a Black woman, too. She related a story about a social affair at which John had "put her down" in front of her colleagues at her law firm. John replied that he was sick of hearing about all her accomplishments. He stated that "they can take it from a Black woman, but they are threatened by me." He also reported another incident that occurred at the same social event: "Some woman thought I was a waiter earlier in the evening and asked me to get her coffee." The therapist explored how much of that feeling was underlying his anger and resentment of Judy. He talked about his experiences of racism and his sense that Judy just did not understand his pain.

Using the paradigm that they had introduced, the therapist (a Black female) told them this: She felt that they were both victims of racism, but that instead of uniting together to fight against it, they were tearing each other apart and letting racism win. This therapeutic reframe was designed to challenge their blaming definitions of the problem, and to provide common ground for them to begin to work on their relationship issues.

The reframe was a turning point. It allowed John and Judy to distance from their rage at each other and to begin looking at the messages they had each been given by their families of origin and in their communities about Black male–female relationships. Judy talked about the stereotypical socialization messages she had been given that Black men are "no good" and "lazy." She acknowledged her fear that John would not find another job. John, in turn, acknowledged receiving the message from other men that he should never let a Black woman get "too strong." The therapist helped them to see that they had both learned destructive, victimizing messages. The two were then able to begin to talk honestly about how painful this period had been. John shared his fears more openly with Judy, and she was able to share her insecurities with him. The therapist worked with them on their ability to "hear" each other, so that they could get beyond their anger to the deeper issues of their pain and hurt.

At this particular stage of treatment, the therapist focused on racism as a shared oppression that might be used strategically to bring John and Judy together. This should not be interpreted as ignoring the complex interaction of racism and sexism in their relationship. The therapist was well aware that Judy was being blamed by John for her success and his misfortune. The therapist's decision to use the racism reframe at this point was a question of the timing of the therapeutic intervention. It was her belief that only after the partners were forced (or shocked) into standing back from their mutual oppression could they find the "common ground" necessary to begin addressing the problems in their relationship. Later in treatment, the therapist was able to confront John on some of his own sexist assumptions that he would be earning more money and have the more prestigious job. If this had been done prematurely, the couple would have fled treatment.

Because Judy and John already saw some of their issues as related to racism, the therapist struggled with how to acknowledge racism—which today is far more subtle than it was during slavery and segregation—while preventing its use as an excuse mechanism for personal failure. The racial paradigm can be a useful reframe in helping African American partners like John and Judy, who introduced racism into the treatment process, to distance from their rage at each other and look at the larger context. Although it is not appropriate for every African American couple, it is a beginning, so that each partner may take responsibility for his or her part in their difficulties; understand victimizing messages from childhood, which exacerbate an already painful situation; and, if possible, challenge racism from a position of empowerment.

Middle- and upper-middle-class African American couples who believe that their problem has become one of "class, not race" react to incidents of racism with a sense of betrayal, disappointment, and often hopeless rage, which are then projected onto their loved ones. John and Judy's situation is reminiscent of the following statement by Poussaint (1993):

> African-American men and women alike face a difficult test in understanding the complexities of their dilemma because the gender issues, whatever they may be, are compounded by racism and the

subordinated roles of Blacks in American society. Sadly, Black men and women themselves harbor racial stereotypes about each other.

Both sexes are struggling for maturity in America where the rights of women are changing dramatically. White males, whose dominance has been based on female subjugation, must relinquish and share power with women. For Black males, who already feel subjugated by Whites, relinquishing dominance over women, especially Black women, is more problematic. (p. 89)

When some African American men feel threatened, they may assert their "manhood" in destructive, often sexist ways, through violence and/ or affairs. Or Black men may turn inward, leading to withdrawal and a profound sense of resignation or a "Why bother?" attitude.

The "Shortage of Black Men" Issue

Widely disseminated statistics indicate that increasing percentages of African American women are graduating from college, whereas African American men are dropping out of school and have high unemployment rates (one statistic that is frequently cited is that "25% of Black men are dead, on drugs, or in prison") (Butterfield, 1995; Hammond & Yung, 1993). This "conventional wisdom" has resulted in the belief that there are *no* good Black men available. Rodgers-Rose and Rodgers (1985) have described the "shortage of Black men" as one of the most damaging messages to African American male–female relationships. African American women are pessimistic about their chances of ever marrying, especially when the older female generations of their families have been unable to model lasting relationships (Tucker & Mitchell-Kernan, 1995).

The shortage of Black men can also cause Black women to stay in very destructive relationships. When this occurs, the therapist should never collude to explain this away by racism. Violence and use of power domination in a relationship can never be condoned. The following case demonstrates the interaction among racism, sexism, and domestic violence:

Laura (41, a school aide) and Arthur (38, a janitor) were an African American couple who came into treatment after living together for a year. Laura had a child, Keena (9), from an earlier relationship. She had been celibate between the time of her daughter's birth and the relationship with Arthur. The initial presenting problem was Keena's misbehavior, which had begun the year before, when Arthur moved into their home.

After a few sessions focused on Keena's behavior (which improved significantly), the work became more concentrated on the couple. In a family session, Keena had expressed concern about the angry outbursts between her mother and Arthur. Laura and Arthur were seen alone for a number of sessions to work on these issues. Arthur frequently arrived late or missed sessions and eventually stopped coming entirely.

When Laura became pregnant with his child, Arthur's angry outbursts escalated, and he became violent toward her. He accused her of having become pregnant to "trap" him. Laura insisted that he leave her home. In subsequent sessions, Laura revealed that Arthur had told her early in their relationship that he had badly beaten an earlier girlfriend when she had tried to "force a child on him." She excused his behavior by telling the therapist that he was a Black man who had lived a very tough life. She also told the therapist (a Black woman) that at least he had a job and was trying. She had been alone for almost 9 years since Keena's birth, and she was very aware of the shortage of Black men. The therapist explored with Laura how she was using racism and the shortage of Black men as excuses for his abuse of her. She told the therapist that she couldn't bear to be another "Black woman statistic" alone raising her kids.

Within several weeks, Arthur apologetically begged to return home. However, he refused to return for therapy, and Laura dropped out of treatment. The therapist, worried about the outcome for this family, contacted both of them a number of times to no avail.

After a year, Laura called the therapist in great distress to report that she had thrown Arthur out again after he threatened to beat Keena. She came in for a session with her daughter. Laura revealed a multigenerational history of battered women in her family of origin; in fact, her mother had encouraged her to return to Arthur. Concerned that Laura would go back to Arthur or fall into another abusive relationship, the therapist invited Laura to join a support group for African American women that the therapist also conducted. Laura learned in the group that she had a right to be treated with respect and that she did not need a relationship with a man to complete her life. The group members were able to acknowledge the role of racism, but challenged Laura's using it to excuse Arthur's abuse. Laura's story led the other women to explore times in which they had stayed in abusive situations and justified staying for these reasons. Discussions about the shortage of Black men are always lively in groups of Black women.

This example provides us with a look at the complexity of racism and sexism in the lives of Black men and women. Laura had internalized sexist messages that this relationship was all that she deserved. This was compounded by multigenerational messages from her own mother. On the other hand, racism was used as an excuse for his treatment of her. Both racism and sexism must be addressed if the domestic violence in a relationship such as this is to end.

COUNTERTRANSFERENTIAL ISSUES
FOR BLACK AND WHITE THERAPISTS

Therapists need to challenge both African American women and men when racism is used as an excuse for domination, intimidation, domestic violence, or child abuse. Groups provide a powerful therapeutic resource that can be used in conjunction with family therapy, particularly in regard to relationship issues. These groups are based on a therapeutic support model and borrow heavily on family systems concepts related to network building and social supports (Boyd-Franklin, 1987, 1991). They can often provide an opportunity to challenge the culturally conflictual messages given by families and communities as well as the racist and sexist messages given by society at large. The group members, because they are from the same culture, can be encouraged by the therapist to challenge each other on these assumptions and to empower each other to make changes.

The treatment of African American couples elicits a number of issues for Black as well as White therapists. White therapists often doubt their understanding of the deep-seated nature and complexity of the dilemmas African American couples face, and it may be difficult for them to identify either differences or similarities between the experiences of Black men and women and their own. Couple therapy can only succeed when a therapist understands the perspective of each member of the couple. If a Black man or woman is viewed only through the lens of gender issues, and racism is not factored into the assessment, a very distorted picture can result.

Black therapists (female or male) may become reactive in treating couples; the prevalence of these gender issues in Black communities has often affected the therapists' own socialization and family relationships. Good supervision is an important ingredient for both Black and White therapists in challenging culturally held beliefs and assumptions that have an adverse impact on Black couples. Peer group supervision with colleagues from diverse racial and cultural groups may also be very helpful. Finally, we need more research and clinical scholarship to help us understand the diversity that exists among African American couples and families.

NOTE

1. All names and other identifying information have been changed in order to protect the confidentiality of the clients.

REFERENCES

Billingsley, A. (1968). *Black families in white America.* Englewood Cliffs, NJ: Prentice Hall.

Billingsley, A. (1992). *Climbing Jacob's ladder: The enduring legacy of African-American families.* New York: Simon & Schuster.

Boyd-Franklin, N. (1987). Group therapy for Black women. A therapeutic support model. *American Journal of Orthopsychiatry, 57*(3), 394–401.

Boyd-Franklin, N. (1989). *Black families in therapy: A multisystems approach.* New York: Guilford Press.

Boyd-Franklin, N. (1991). Recurrent themes in the treatment of Black women in group therapy. *Women and Therapy, 11*(2).

Butterfield, F. (1995, October 5). More Blacks in their 20's have trouble with the law. *The New York Times, National Report,* p. A18.

Comas-Díaz, L., & Greene, B. (1994). *Women of color: Integrating ethnic and gender identities in psychotherapy.* New York: Guilford Press.

Cose, E. (1993). *The rage of a privileged class.* New York: HarperCollins.

Ellison, R. (1952). *Invisible man.* New York: Vintage Books.

Franklin, A. J. (in press). Invisibility syndrome in psychotherapy with African American males. In R. L. Jones (Ed.), *African American mental health.* Hampton, VA: Cobb & Henry.

Franklin, A. J. (1992). Therapy with African-American men. *Families in Society: The Journal of Contemporary Human Services, 73*(6), 350–355.

Franklin, A. J. (1993, July–August). The invisibility syndrome. *Family Therapy Networker,* pp. 32–39.

Greene, B., & Boyd-Franklin, N. (1996). African American lesbian couples: Ethnocultural considerations in therapy. *Women and Therapy, 19*(3), 49–60.

Giddings, P. (1984). *When and where I enter.* New York: Morrow.

Grier, W., & Cobbs, P. (1968). *Black rage.* New York: Basic Books.

Hacker, A. W. (1992). *Two nations: Black and White, separate, hostile, unequal.* New York: Scribner's.

Haley, J. (1976). *Problem-solving therapy.* San Francisco: Jossey-Bass.

Hammond, R., & Yung, B. (1993). Psychology's role in the public health response to assaultive violence among young African American men. *American Psychologist, 48*(2), 142–154.

Hill, R. (1972). *The strengths of Black families.* New York: Emerson-Hall.

Hines, P. M., & Boyd-Franklin, N. (1982). Black families. In M. McGoldrick, J. K. Pearce, & J. Giordano (Eds.), *Ethnicity and family therapy* (pp. 84–107). New York: Guilford Press.

Hines, P. M., & Boyd-Franklin, N. (1996). African American families. In M. McGoldrick, J. Giordano, & J. K. Pearce (Eds.), *Ethnicity and family therapy* (2nd ed., pp. 66–84). New York: Guilford Press.

hooks, b. (1981). *Ain't I a woman?* Boston: South End Press.

hooks, b. (1990). *Yearning: Race, gender and cultural politics.* Boston: South End Press.

Jones, J. M. (1997). *Prejudice and racism* (2nd ed.). New York: McGraw-Hill.

Kunjufu, J. (1985). *Countering the conspiracy to destroy Black boys* (Vol. 1). Chicago: African-American Images.

Majors, R., & Billson, J. M. (1992). *Cool pose: The dilemmas of Black manhood in America.* New York: Lexington Books.

Oliver, W. (1994). *The violent social world of Black men.* New York: Lexington Books.

Poussaint, A. (1993). African American couples. *Ebony,* pp. 88–89.

Rodgers-Rose, L., & Rodgers, J. (1985). *Strategies for resolving conflict in Black male and female relationships.* Newark, NJ: Traces Institute.

Stone, A. (1995, February 23). Educated Black women make biggest strides: Good, bad news found in census. *USA Today, The Nation,* p. 8A.

Susskind, D. (Producer), & Petrie, D. (Director). (1960). *A raisin in the sun* [Film]. (Available from Columbia Pictures Corporation, Burbank, CA)

Tucker, M. B., & Mitchell-Kernan, C. (Eds.). (1995). *The decline in marriage among African Americans.* New York: Russell Sage Foundation.

CHAPTER 21

African American Sibling Relationships

Marlene F. Watson

Sibling relationships are as powerful as parent–child relationships. They have significant implications for both individual and family functioning. Although siblings have received little attention in the field of couple and family therapy, siblings begin to affect one another from the moment they first lay eyes on one another. Our relationships with our sisters and brothers can help mold us as parents, partners, friends, and coworkers. This chapter specifically considers the importance of sibling relationships in African American families.

SIBLING BIRTH ORDER

Birth order is a primary factor in sibling relationships and directly influences each individual's personality. Firstborn children, by virtue of their position in the family, are usually credited with being smarter and more trustworthy than their younger brothers and sisters. Because firstborns are perceived as stronger and wiser by parents and siblings alike, they tend to feel more self-confident than laterborns (Sulloway, 1996). First-borns are also likely to feel that it is their birthright to be dominant in the sibship, possibly resulting in an exaggerated sense of self-importance.

Birth order is a formative experience, affecting one's perception of self, interests, and view of the world. For example, Lamont, a 28-year-old journalist, and Stephanie, a 26-year-old computer analyst entered therapy because of Lamont's low sexual desire. Lamont had an older brother who was a successful athlete in high school. Each night at the dinner table, the father would focus on athletics. Lamont, who was 5 years younger than his brother, felt excluded and began to worry secretly that he would never measure up to his older brother. Thus, he decided that he would stay away from sports. He refused to watch, read, or talk about sports, thus cutting himself off from both his brother and his father.

Lamont immersed himself in books and writing poetry. He did not date in high school and had only one girlfriend prior to Stephanie. In therapy, it became clear that Lamont had developed a poor male identity that affected his sexual desire. He feared being seen as sexually inadequate, and the way to protect himself from this fear was not to be interested in sex. Although Lamont outwardly showed disdain for sports, he had internalized the message that "real" men like sports. In addition, African American males tend to be validated for their athletic and sexual abilities, exacerbating Lamont's doubts about his manhood.

Lamont, as the youngest child, felt overshadowed by his older brother. He therefore tried to minimize the costs of having an older brother through quiet rebellion. He masterfully rejected both his brother and his brother's values by devoting himself entirely to something that represented the polar opposite of his brother, so that he could avoid any meaningful contact. The pain of living in his brother's shadow was enough to cause Lamont to cut himself off from the family.

THE EXTENDED FAMILY
IN AFRICAN AMERICAN CULTURE

African Americans are proud of their stance on family unity: In their view, the group is more important than the individual. This was the most precious gem that slaves could bring from the motherland, Africa. And so it was passed on to each new generation, giving rise to the extended family. Inherent in the extended family model is the notion of strong, unbreakable ties that bind members for life. Individual members inherit the permanent obligation to contribute to the well-being of the extended family; thus, individual needs are expected to be secondary. Later, in marriage, competing feelings may exist between loyalty to one's original family and the family of procreation.

In the aftermath of slavery, racism and oppression played a major role in African American families' retaining their extended family structure. For African Americans, survival depended on the sharing of goods and resources. Moreover, in a society full of barriers to educational and economic advancement for African Americans, it was (and often still is) necessary for families to rely on the pooled efforts of members to insure survival.

Another dimension of the extended family model that has been ob-scured by the greater emphasis on basic physical needs is the intense emo-tional need to belong. Slaves were forever separated from home and fam-ily when they were brought from Africa to America. Slave families were split apart, and individuals frequently lost all contact with their relatives. African Americans, of all the ethnic groups in America, are probably the only group whose members cannot trace their roots back to the specific villages or tribes of their original kin. Hence, loss is a crucial issue in the lives of African Americans and a hidden aspect of the cultural expecta-tion that family members remain loyal.

Because African American families have suffered tremendous loss, both physically and emotionally, it is not surprising for families to reduce the threat of loss by stressing familial relationships over individuals' needs and feelings. Given the greater value that is put on the family unit, both an individual and a family may attempt to conceal cutoffs. A brother or sister who in reality has left the family camouflages the cutoff through occasional visits "back home." The rest of the family, particularly the mother, tries to cover up the cutoff by making excuses for the son/brother or daughter/sister. And silence is the golden rule. No one speaks of the cutoff.

Because family loyalty is expected to supersede individual needs, African Americans have learned to disguise cutoffs when they occur. In the case described above, although Lamont kept mostly to himself, both he and his family could downplay his actions because he never expressed negative feelings toward his brother. In the book *Brothers and Keepers*, author John Edgar Wideman (1984) compellingly describes the process of cutting off his younger brother, Robby, who was the "bad seed" while he was the "good seed," by putting many miles between them. Through distance he was able to block out Robby's existence, thus suppressing the feelings of guilt that are likely to result when one sibling makes it out of poverty while others remain trapped.

Anger and resentment may also accompany the feelings of guilt, along with the successful sibling's desire to avoid the pain of knowing that he or she could have just as easily shared the fate of the brother or sister left behind. Conflicting feelings of individuals, coupled with the cultural myth that African Americans, unlike European Americans, are always there for one another, contribute to the family's collusion in regard to cutoffs. The actual cutoff between the Wideman brothers was masked because it was neither named nor talked about. For them, it took Robby's impris-onment for murder before they could genuinely and honestly examine their sibship and reclaim their brotherhood.

Sibling relationships are lifelong. Issues such as sibling rivalry, en-meshment, and disengagement do not simply fade away with childhood.

The tension between siblings is frequently carried into adulthood, becoming activated at various stages of the life cycle. Close sibling ties are forever for some, as evidenced by the Delany sisters, who after a century of life were still looking out for each other (Delany, Delany, & Hearth, 1993). For others, sibling fissures can result in permanent cutoffs once they reach adulthood.

Just as families must be seen in a cultural context, so must siblings. We African Americans have a unique history that colors all of our relationships, especially those with our brothers and sisters.

SIBLING CARETAKING

Sibling caretaking is a significant means of child care in many African American families. This form of caretaking has strong implications for sibling relationships. Caretaking by siblings can either enhance the sibling bond or lead to conflict. Although sibling caretaking is a major form of care for children in most societies (Weisner & Gallimore, 1977), this type of nonparental caretaking is intensified in African American families by the historical context of oppression.

Caretaking in general is a sensitive issue in African American families. Women were often forced to leave their children to the care of siblings or others while they cared for the children of White slave owners and later White employers. In addition, the pressures that parents experience due to the effects of racism will probably restrict the amount of support and supervision given to child caretakers. Hence, African American children may be more vulnerable to issues of abandonment, rejection, loyalty, anger, power/control, and competence when siblings are the caretakers.

Sibling caretaking in African American families can result in a rigid relationship, in which one sibling is the giver and one or more others are the takers throughout the life cycle. The lack of give and take in such a sibling relationship can set up an oppressive system that is analogous to the experience of African Americans in the larger society. It can restrict both a caregiver's and a recipient's sense of choice, influencing whether they pursue their interests and whom they become intimate with.

For African Americans, sibling caretaking is affected by two cultural expectations and values. First, the group is considered more important than the individual, as noted above; second, there is a strong emphasis on children. These two cultural messages can have a profound impact on a sibling caretaker, especially one who is female (as is often the case). The female caretaker may learn to deemphasize her own needs and elevate those of her charge. The caretaker child's role tends to become invisible within the family, while the dependent child's position is highlighted. In addition, the sibling caretaker may come to devalue himself or herself in relation to the sister or brother, who may be perceived as special (though this is not always the case). Three patterns of sibling caretaking are commonly found in African American families: "hierarchical," "mutual," and "pyramidic."

Hierarchical Caretaking

Hierarchical sibling caretaking is the most rigid and fixed pattern. In this arrangement, an older brother or sister is the caretaker and a younger child is the recipient. The flow of give and take necessary for the development of healthy peer relationships is absent in this pattern of caretaking.

A younger sibling may resent the perceived or actual authority of an older brother or sister. And the sibling caretaker may become bitter toward the dependent sibling, feeling burdened by having to care for this sibling. However, the younger sibling is more likely to express feelings of resentment than is the older child, who is more apt to hide his or her feelings.

The sibling caretaker's ability to acknowledge feelings of resentment openly may be determined largely by the family's emphasis on cultural expectations. Since African American families tend to place a high value on loyalty and responsibility to others (Hines, Garcia-Preto, McGoldrick, Almeida, & Weltman, 1992), parents may downplay or ignore the negative feelings expressed by the older sibling, while attempting to help the younger child deal with his or her resentment. Because African American parents tend to expect older children to understand their duty to the family, more time and energy are given to younger children and their feelings.

A younger sibling may counteract the authority of an older one by direct or passive–aggressive behavior, resulting in sibling antagonism and conflict. Such sibling conflict may even escalate into sibling violence (physically and/or verbally abusive acts).

The traumatic effects of institutionalized racism and poverty on African Americans leave them more at risk for violence as perpetrators, victims, and/or bystanders. The stress of racism also exposes African Americans unequally to other conditions, such as high blood pressure and substance addiction. African Americans often feel disempowered, unable to fight the forces of racism. It is therefore crucial for parents to encourage both sibling caretakers and those they are caring for to express their feelings and to develop ways of resolving conflict, since they will need these skills in later life for dealing with the effects of racism and oppression.

A case example illustrates the need for developing such skills. Bobby and Grace, both 34-year-old teachers, were court-referred, following a restraining order that Grace sought against Bobby. Grace described Bobby as a "good guy," as long as she did not express an opinion of her own. Bobby stated that Grace often disrespected him because she refused to accept his word for anything. Grace was the oldest of several sisters and had been responsible for taking care of her younger sisters. She was accustomed to her sisters' seeking her opinion. Bobby, on the other hand, was the younger brother of an older sister. He grew up resenting his older sister, who was the sibling caretaker. Bobby perceived the older sister as the favorite child, believing that she was their mother's favorite because of her lighter skin. He saw his sister as getting more, and he blamed her for life's not being fair. Since his sister could also discipline the younger children, she would physically punish Bobby when he misbehaved. Bobby did not openly express his anger as a child because he feared doing so; his sister was treated as special in the family, and she had power over him. Bobby eventually developed intense negative emotions against women, whom he perceived as trying to exert power over him. Feeling powerless whenever Grace expressed an opinion different from his, Bobby attempted to reclaim his power and manhood through physical abuse. At the same time, he was trying to overcome the sense that he had experienced injustice at the hands of his sister. Of course, what Bobby needed and wanted was to feel validated by his sister, in much the same way as a child seeks the approval of a parent. Thus, the marriage became the arena for acting out the unresolved conflict with his sister.

Hierarchical sibling caretaking generally leads to parentification of the child caretaker. Thus, the stress of caretaking for the caregiver can be overwhelming. Furthermore, it can be confusing to the dependent child, whose life can be complicated by the possibility of conflicting or competing rules. According to Boyd-Franklin (1989), the position of the parentified child in many African American families is functional as long as the parents remain in charge. It becomes dysfunctional when parents abdicate their role, placing a tremendous responsibility on the sibling caretaker, whose capacity for adult decision making has probably not been developed.

Hierarchical sibling caretaking can have negative consequences for both parent–child and sibling relationships. Children may have closer ties to the sibling caretaker than to the parents, possibly resulting in poor communication and detachment from the parents. Siblings may also become estranged because of the hierarchical nature of their relationship. Overall, hierarchical sibling caretaking can breed coalitions and cutoffs that are to the detriment of the entire family when problems are not addressed.

Mutual Caretaking

In mutual sibling caretaking, brothers and sisters care for one another. Because of the reciprocity inherent in this arrangement, it tends to leave children less vulnerable to negative feelings. Mutual caretaking is flexible, and everyone has some responsibility for the common welfare of the family. Responsibilities are usually age-based, but no one child is burdened with complete caretaking; therefore, no sibling feels overburdened. Mutual caretaking is exemplified by the Delany sisters (Delany et al., 1993), whose golden rule seemed to be "You watch my back and I'll watch yours." For over 100 years, they were together and committed to sisterhood, proving that a sister can be a friend forever when there is balance in the relationship.

Pyramidic Caretaking

Pyramidic sibling caretaking is an agreement whereby each child cares for the sibling next in line. Siblings, except for the "baby," share caretaking responsibilities. It is therefore the youngest child in this sibling caretaking pattern who is at risk for arrested development. He or she may become stuck in the baby role, with little or no expectation for personal competence.

As the baby of the family, this child receives lavish attention and is frequently not expected to be responsible. Older siblings are expected to be understanding and forgiving when the baby misbehaves. Given the permissive environment that surrounds the baby, she or he will probably not learn how to tolerate frustration or to delay gratification. Not only does this leave the baby ill prepared for adulthood, but this child will have missed out on two important lessons that bear directly on his or her ability to deal with the inevitable stress of societal racism.

Older siblings usually become resentful of the special treatment afforded to the baby, especially when the child is manipulative. The baby may therefore become cut off from the sibling subsystem because of his or her undesirable behavior and favored position.

Triangles can easily develop when parents assume an overprotective stance toward one child as opposed to the others, because the parents' behavior robs siblings of the opportunity to work out their own differences. Since parents are at the center of sibling conflict, alienation and/or tension often exists between the parents and the older children as well. Furthermore, the tension created in the family by this sibling caretaking arrangement is likely to last across the life cycle.

Childhood sibling conflicts resulting from pyramidic caretaking are particularly likely to reemerge in later life, when brothers and sisters are faced with caring for aging parents. As adults, siblings may express the anger and resentment that may have been held in check because of family loyalty. The baby, who is viewed as having lived the "easy life" because of parental favoritism, is now expected to do his or her duty in the family by caring for the elderly parents. However, the baby is ill equipped to do the job. It is important to note that the baby, especially if this is a male, may still be living at home with the parents when they become sick or too elderly to care for themselves. But the baby is likely to expect older siblings to provide care for the parents *and* him.

Although one might expect a daughter who is the baby of the family to be the likely one to assume the caregiving role for elderly parents, it is not guaranteed. If the daughter is still at home, she will probably inherit the job. If not, the sense of entitlement that was characteristic of her childhood may materialize, causing her to resist or refuse the job.

Caretaking is an essential component of sibship in African American families. Thus, sibling caretaking is a critical area to assess when treating African Americans. Moreover, African American siblings may have a greater impact on individual development than parents may.

SIBLING AND GENDER DYNAMICS

African American women have long been portrayed as "domineering" and "castrating." However, they have frequently lacked the nurturance given to males in childhood because of the cultural expectation that girls should be raised to be strong women—women who rely only on themselves. Thus, sibling caretaking by sisters places them at risk for not feeling entitled to have their own needs met and for overfunctioning with their brothers and in later couple and family relationships.

African American women often feel misunderstood by their men and by society. They also feel uncared for, because they are the ones expected to provide care in intimate relationships, despite being maligned by society and African American men. Since African American culture teaches kinship, unity, and responsibility to the extended family, girls may take pride in their caretaking role. But the caretaking role may also be devaluing and stressful. Without acknowledgment and support, the caring role leads to anger and resentment. And, again, it can lead to cutoffs in adulthood or to problems in male–female relationships.

A sister caretaker may expect either to transfer her role with a brother to a partner or to become the recipient of care by her partner. Depending on the partner's role in sibling caretaking in his family, the couple may be a perfect match or a case of mistaken identity, with each person trying to coerce the other to fulfill his or her expectations.

Boys frequently receive a lot of attention in African American families because they are generally more at risk for physical harm in a racist society. Although they suffer from the "invisibility syndrome" (Boyd-Franklin, 1989; see also Boyd-Franklin & Franklin, Chapter 20, this volume) in the larger society, males are very visible in African American families, where anxious females try to protect them. The extent to which brothers are visible and sisters are invisible in African American families has significant implications for sibling relationships. It affects how brothers and sisters relate to one another. Sisters may form a coalition against brothers that serves as the basis for cutoffs once they grow up. In addition, the resentment that began in the brother–sister relationship may be reenacted in the male–female relationship.

SIBLING TIES

According to Sudarkasa (1988), blood ties were (and are frequently still) valued over legal ties in African families because blood ties cannot be terminated. For African Americans, the extended family model encourages individuals to put a high value on blood relationships. Thus, individuals may involve siblings in decision making without consulting their partners. It is not uncommon for African Americans to invite siblings into the home as a way of helping them to get on their feet, or to contribute financially to their well-being, without asking for their partners' input. Siblings may also become caretakers for nieces and nephews if problems arise in the parent–child relationship or if a "better" environment is sought.

African Americans frequently assume that they have the right to assist their siblings without question from partners. Partners' protests may be silenced because their own siblings or other family members may need help at some point. Individuals may also be secretive about the help given to siblings because they fear interference from their partners. Therefore, issues of loyalty and problem siblings are likely to lead to conflict for African American couples.

On the other hand, siblings may also be a resource for couples. By assisting couples in times of need, siblings may help the couples to mediate their differences at various stages of the life cycle, thereby helping them to keep their relationships intact.

THE MYTH OF THE SAVIOR

Cultural myths have a particular theme and serve to explain the common needs, struggles, relationships, and aspirations of a people (Pillari, 1986). Cultural myths also help us to understand individual and family functioning. The "myth of the savior"—that is, the myth that a family, including brothers and sisters, must sacrifice for the sake of one member's success—is firmly rooted in African American culture.

The myth of the savior has profound and specific lifelong implications for siblings. According to Pillari (1986), culture is channeled through family myths from one generation to the next. Since family myths are frequently not discussed, members accept or passively resist the roles and status assigned to them by the myths in the family. Thus, siblings can become stuck in the roles prescribed by the family myths. Moreover, their behavior and interactions within the sibship are organized by the myths beyond childhood. Reactivity to family myths is often unconscious and therefore unchallenged.

Because African Americans exist in a racist and oppressive society, families need hope for survival and continuity. The myth of the savior carries the theme of hope and a belief that one member's success is the success of a family. This hope is usually placed in one particular child, who is expected to save the family. Since it is a child who is assigned the role of savior, the myth has a major impact on sibling relationships.

All family members, including siblings, are expected to sacrifice individual needs and desires whenever necessary for the savior. For their sacrifice, family members expect payback by way of financial aid, material goods, and mediation of problems. The savior is thought to be omnipotent. She or he is not expected to grow weary or to become tired. The savior carries a heavy burden because of the message "You must never forget those who helped you succeed."

Because the savior internalizes his or her debt to the family, conflicts are often experienced between the savior's needs and those of the family. The savior may become guilt-ridden and anxious about his or her debt to the family and may move far away, resulting in a functional cutoff. The cutoff is thus masked, and the family myth remains.

THE INTERACTION OF CLASS, GENDER, AND RACE DYNAMICS IN SIBLING RELATIONSHIPS

It is important to note that some of the issues described above may differ on the basis of class in African American families. However, upward mobility in African American families tends to ebb and flow according to economic trends (McAdoo, 1988) and to the persistence of racism and oppression. The majority of African American families will probably have brothers and sisters in different socioeconomic groups even if the parents were solidly in the middle or upper middle class. Brothers and sisters in middle-class families may have similar opportunities for educational achievement, but individual experiences and reactions to racism and oppression may result in a decline in social status for some.

Even when they have achieved middle-class status, many African American families rear boys and girls according to the old saying, "We raise our daughters but love our sons." African American males are still vulnerable to police attacks, despite their membership in upwardly mobile families. Sons are generally coddled more often because of a perceived threat to their well-being in a racist society, as the case of the P family illustrates.

The P family was an upper-middle-class family. Mr. P was a doctor, and Mrs. P was a librarian. They had two older daughters and a younger son. The two daughters were attorneys. The son had attended college but was floundering; he was without a job, and both his parents and his sisters were supporting him financially. In addition, they were setting up job interviews for him. The family members were extremely anxious about their son and brother's lack of ambition, and were working hard to help him achieve success. The second daughter remarked in a family session that their parents would not have allowed the girls to do what their brother was doing. Moreover, she expressed the belief that their parents would not pay for them to have a sports car and an apartment if they dropped out of school like their brother.

The P family was engaged in a dialogue about the impact of racism on parental attitudes and gender-specific behaviors. Mr. and Mrs. P were both from poor families in the Deep South. They had experienced overt racism while growing up and had heard stories of Black men being lynched. Although they rarely talked openly about racism, Mr. and Mrs. P were very much organized by their own negative racial experiences and the plight of Black men in America.

Mr. and Mrs. P wanted success for all of their children. Though they insisted that their daughters marry only accomplished Black men (the family discouraged interracial dating), Mr. and Mrs. P raised their daughters to be strong and self-sufficient. The cultural belief that Black women can't count on men, which was carried over from slavery and reinforced by racism and oppression, influenced Mr. and Mrs. P's authoritative stance with their daughters.

Mr. and Mrs. P were more permissive with their only son. They worried about his developing a positive Black male identity, especially with society's negative view of Black men, and tried to boost his self-esteem by giving him unconditional love. They rationalized his behavior instead of holding him accountable as they did their daughters, believing that more understanding and patience at home would buffer him against racism in the larger society. However, Mr. and Mrs. P's overanxious behavior toward their son had the opposite effect of what they intended: Instead of becoming a self-confident, successful individual, he was self-doubtful and tried to overcome his fears by not making life commitments.

Race was a hidden dimension in the P family's case. Since race is a guiding force in the lives of African Americans, it should be included as a key construct in therapy. Mr. and Mrs. P were unconsciously motivated by cultural beliefs and attitudes. Hence, they had failed to consider the wider implications of their permissive behavior toward their son. There is an inherent danger in parental and sibling overprotectiveness toward African American sons and brothers. African American males' self-esteem is threatened by society's negative stereotypes, and through expecting more of girls than of boys, families may inadvertently reinforce the notion that Black men are inadequate, lazy, and incompetent.

Siblings may experience guilt about their success or become resentful toward brothers or sisters who "make it." Cutoffs may be created by class differences. Siblings may limit their children's contact with aunts and uncles because they live in bad neighborhoods or because they fear that some of their siblings' values will rub off on their children. I have found this pattern to be present in a significant number of professional African American families. In one particular case, the daughter of two attorneys who was "protected" from the old neighborhood where aunts, uncles, and cousins still lived reacted by associating with streetwise young men with juvenile records. She was curious about her relatives and angered by what she described as her parents' "snobbery."

CONCLUSION

Since family therapy tends to follow the Eurocentric model, the sibling context is often ignored as a valid area of consideration in treatment. Therefore, family therapists frequently commence and terminate treatment without utilizing this important aspect of life in African American families. A focus on sibling relationships can give therapists a better understanding of individual and family dynamics for African Americans, resulting in improved treatment outcomes.

REFERENCES

Boyd-Franklin, N. (1989). *Black families in therapy: A multisystems approach.* New York: Guilford Press.

Delany, S. L., Delany, A. E., & Hearth, A. H. (1993). *Having our say: The Delany sisters' first 100 years.* New York: Dell.

Hines, P. M., Garcia-Preto, N., McGoldrick, M., Almeida, R., & Weltman, S. (1992). Intergenerational relationships across cultures. *Families in Society: The Journal of Contemporary Human Services, 43*(6), 323–338.

McAdoo, H. P. (1988). Transgenerational patterns of upward mobility in African-American families. In H. P. McAdoo (Ed.), *Black families* (2nd ed., pp. 148–168). Beverly Hills, CA: Sage.

Pillari, V. (1986). *Pathways to family myths.* New York: Brunner/Mazel.

Sudarkasa, N. (1988). Interpreting the African heritage in Afro-American family organization. In H. P. McAdoo (Ed.), *Black families* (2nd ed., pp. 27–43). Beverly Hills, CA: Sage.

Sulloway, F. J. (1996). *Born to rebel: Birth order, family dynamics, and creative lives.* New York: Pantheon.

Weisner, T. S., & Gallimore, R. (1977). My brother's keeper: Child and sibling caretaking. *Current Anthropology, 18*(2), 169–190.

Wideman, J. E. (1984). *Brothers and keepers.* New York: Vintage.

CHAPTER 22

Intercultural Couples

Joel Crohn

Like rival theologians, psychotherapists argue for the superiority and truth of their particular pathways to heaven. However varied their theoretical orientations, though, most clinicians who treat couples actually do have similar goals. Using a variety of techniques, couple therapists work to help partners in intimate relationships understand and empathize with each other's experiences as a way to enhance cooperation and compromise.

Some couples spontaneously focus on their cultural differences as a way of understanding their difficulties. Many do not, especially when the partners share common racial, national, and class backgrounds. Similarly, whereas some therapists use the lens of culture to help frame and understand couples' conflicts, many will not unless clients take the lead. In this era of discomfort and confusion surrounding issues of culture, religion, class, and race, together with the time pressures imposed by managed care, therapists increasingly focus on the "presenting problem" without attempting to understand couples' conflicts in a broader social and historical context. Superimposed on all of these issues are the dramatically changing roles of men and women, which enter into every couple's negotiation.

Ethnicity, religion, race, gender, and class *do* influence every aspect of how people view the world and what they consider "normal" or "abnormal" (for a more complete discussion of these issues, see Crohn, 1995). Culture molds attitudes toward time, family, eating, money, sex, and monogamy. Cultural norms affect how anger and affection are expressed, how children are disciplined and rewarded, how strangers and friends are greeted, and what roles men and women play. In cross-cultural relationships, contrasting norms may lead one partner to describe behavior as neighborly that the other sees as seductive. What he intends to be friendly disagreement, she may be just as sure is a threat; when he says he visits his parents "often," he may mean twice a year, but for her "seldom" may mean twice a week.

The potential value conflicts in an intermarriage involving different races, cultures, and/or nationalities can be dramatic. The normative gender roles of cultures have tremendous impact on men's and women's expectations of relationships. A Japanese-born man (raised in a nation where men, according to one report, average 11 minutes of family-related work a day) and an American-born woman (raised in a nation where men average 108 minutes of family-related work a day) are more likely to have difficulties agreeing upon what is "normal" than are partners from similar backgrounds (see *Newsweek*, 1993, p. 34).

A RADICALLY CHANGING WORLD

With massive migrations between nations; rapidly increasing rates of intermarriage; and religious apathy, rebirth, and conversions, the deconstruction and reconstruction of group identity have become the rules rather than the exceptions. Changes that used to occur over the course of several generations now take place in a single lifetime. Like computers "morphing" images together, individuals create complex and composite identities. All of these transformations make it much more difficult to tease out the influence of an individual's cultural history.

The changes in marital choice among White ethnic groups since the 1950s are but a few indications of how the fast the cultural tides have turned. Fewer than 10% of Jews and fewer than 20% of Italian Americans married outside their groups in the decade following World War II (Alba, 1985). During that era of low intermarriage rates, it was far easier to make meaningful generalizations about the values and norms of an ethnic group. Although the intermarriage rate in the United States among Jews remained less than 10% until 1960, today estimates range between 41–52% nationally (Cohen, 1994). The fabled solidarity of Italians was also a victim of the cultural revolution; as early as 1970, 80% of children under 14 who claimed Italian ancestry were the products of intermarriage (Alba, 1985).

World War II set changes in motion that radically affected not only the relationships between nations, but those between races, ethnic groups, and men and women. Who in the early 1950s could have predicted that by 1992, 65% of the children and grandchildren of the Japanese Americans who were interned during World War II for the crime of possessing Japanese ancestry would choose European American partners? By the time the U.S. Supreme Court struck down the last laws against interracial marriage in 1967, American society had already entered a period of rapid cultural change as the first postwar generation reached marriageable age.

A generation ago, few could have envisioned how quickly changing attitudes, behavior, and immigration patterns would literally transform the faces of America. Before 1960, about 80% of immigrants coming to America were from European backgrounds. Today the numbers are reversed: Of the over 1,000,000 legal immigrants a year entering the United States, over 80% of them are non-European. The greatest numbers are from Latin American, Caribbean, and Asian nations. And, without even waiting to assimilate, many of these immigrants are choosing to marry partners from other groups.

Intermarriage rates have been on the increase for almost all ethnic and cultural groups in America. There are now more than a million Hispanic–non-Hispanic marriages in the United States, more than double the number in 1970. And large numbers of marriages that are considered Hispanic–Hispanic are often cross-cultural marriages as well, bringing together partners from different nations all categorized as "Hispanic," but with significantly different cultures (e.g., Cuba, Mexico, Argentina, and Puerto Rico). For every 100 births to Native American couples, there are 140 births to mixed Native American–White couples. And to the surprise of many people both inside and outside Asian American communities, the great wall that formerly separated Asians from others is quickly being worn down by lovers who stream across it. The most recent statistics show that over 40% of all children born to an Asian or Pacific Islander parent also have a White parent (Population Reference Bureau, 1992; U.S. Bureau of the Census, 1993).

Although the legacy of slavery and racism makes Black–White marriage the most stigmatized, most controversial, and least frequent kind of mixed match, census numbers demonstrate that even among Blacks and Whites, significant changes are occurring. The number of Black–White married couples tripled over two decades, from 65,000 in 1970 to 231,000 in 1991; over that same period of time, the number of births to Black–White couples quintupled (U.S. Bureau of the Census, 1993).

BEYOND BLACK AND WHITE: COMPLEX CATEGORIES

Even in the legendary good old days of clear categories, intragroup homogeneity was more myth than reality. Southern rural, Northern urban, and Caribbean Blacks shared a common skin color, but the kinds of discrimination they faced were quite different. Also, they were very aware of cultural differences and competitive tensions within the confines of

color and culture. Hitler did not bother to discriminate among Ortho-
dox, Reform, agnostic, Eastern European, Ashkenazi, Sephardic, German, and Communist atheist Jews; however, Jews in Europe, Israel, and
the United States were always very aware not only of anti-Semitism, but
of the cultural, ideological, and behavioral differences and conflicts within
the Jewish group. Asians did not identify themselves as "Asians," but as
members of discrete and often hostile groups. From the perspective of a
postwar Chinese American parent who had family members in China
brutalized by the Japanese occupation, accepting the marriage of a daughter to a European American might be difficult, but a marriage to someone of Japanese ancestry would be impossible. Even in mythical Lake
Wobegon, Minnesota, it wasn't that long ago that "White" people were
not all the same and that the marriage of a Norwegian to a German
might raise the eyebrows and blood pressure of family members.

The complexity of all the intra- and intergroup contrasts, plus all of
the changes that have taken place during the last 40 years, make it increasingly difficult for psychotherapists to "place" anyone definitively in
a cultural category. This doesn't mean that therapists should conclude
that conducting a cultural history is irrelevant or impossible. It does,
however, require a flexible and creative approach to understanding differences between partners in a relationship.

GENDER AND MARITAL CHOICE:
MYTHS AND REALITIES

The question of which sex "marries out" more frequently among members of a particular cultural group is often very difficult to answer. The
fact that many unusually successful people from stigmatized groups such
as Jews and Blacks married out before intermarriage was common reinforced the view that love had far less to do with these matches than exchange of economic status for social status. But the reality of intermarriage gender patterns in America is far more complex.

Among African Americans, the intermarriage rate of men has consistently been two to three times higher than that of women. Census figures, however, undermine the notion of status exchange as being a primary motivator. In fact, it is the similarity in educational and class backgrounds of racially differing spouses that is striking. The 1970 census
found, for example, that White women married to Black men were the
best-educated group of White women, and that intermarrying Black men
were the *best*-educated group of African American men (Spickard, 1989).

The conventional wisdom about Jewish intermarriage may be similarly shaky. Jewish men, the argument went, having the economic advan-

tages of gender, had the means to find and marry Gentile women, whereas Jewish women, laboring under the burden of inequity, were far less likely to marry out. Many studies in the 1970s and 1980s supported this view. Recently, though, Egon Mayer, the foremost sociologist on Jewish intermarriage, has argued that the decades of statistics describing vastly different intermarriage rates for Jewish men and women are totally incorrect. Mayer has pointed out that much of the research was based on samples created by searches of surnames, and that since men seldom changed their names, their intermarriages were "discovered" by the researchers; intermarrying women, who were much more likely to adapt their husbands' names, simply disappeared from the researchers' view. Mayer's new research indicates little or no difference in intermarriage rates between Jewish men and women (E. Mayer, personal communication, 1996).

Claims of large gender differences in Asian intermarriage are similarly misleading. The most popular theory to explain the purported imbalances was the attraction of dominant-culture men to "submissive" Asian women, who could continue to support a male sense of power in the age of feminism. Although it is true that it was male soldiers in World War II who were bringing home Japanese war brides, more recent statistics indicate little gender difference in Japanese American intermarriage rates. By 1970, when members of the Sansei (the third American generation) were of marrying age, 43% of Japanese American men were marrying out, as were 49% of the Japanese American women. In Los Angeles in 1979, Japanese of both sexes married out at a rate of 49%. This trend toward equal gender rates of intermarriage has also been taking place among other Asian American groups (Spickard, 1989).

Male dominance and patriarchy in all societies, and women's heightened awareness of and desire for equality, can be important factors in the dynamics of intermarriage. Even as gender differences in intermarriage rates equalize, the subjective meaning of intermarriage *within* a particular cultural group may be very different. I interviewed a number of Italian American and Taiwanese American women who felt that their intermarriages were in part motivated by their beliefs about the gender norms of their cultural groups. They believed that marrying men from their own cultures would have resulted in less role flexibility and freedom than they thought they could find in marriages outside of their groups. Women from "traditional" cultures, in which the roles of women have been very constricted, may especially feel that intermarriage offers them a path to greater freedom.

When a strong preference for partners from outside one's group is combined with an intense dislike of the opposite-sex members of one's own cultural or racial group, it may be a manifestation of what psychologist and ethnotherapist Judith Weinstein Klein (1980) has labeled "ambivalent identification." Ambivalent identifiers accept their cultural label, but uniformly reject members of the opposite sex of their own cultural group. They project the dominant culture's negative stereotypes about their cultural group onto the opposite sex members of their own group. By placing the negative stereotypes onto the opposite-sex, the minority group member is unconsciously saying, "The negative stereotypes about us [Blacks, Jews, Asians, Hispanics, etc.] are true—but they are only true of the opposite-sex members of my group. I don't like them for the same reasons you don't. But my half of the group is OK. Accept us."

Love is the intersection where gender and culture collide in an era of change, confusion, and conflict about roles and relationships. Conflict in a relationship results when one partner finds attractive in the other perceived gender traits that are precisely what the other partner rejects.

For example, Lisa, an immigrant Chinese woman I interviewed, had believed that her marriage to a European American man meant that she would have more freedom as a woman than she would have had in a traditional Chinese marriage. However, Stan, her European American husband, had felt that the American women he had been raised with were too "entitled" and "demanding." He was aware that part of his attraction to Lisa was based on his fantasy that she would be more deferential to his male authority. Lisa had hoped for more autonomy through her marriage to an outsider; Stan was looking for a more clearly defined and traditional male role. During courtship, they were able to maintain their mutually satisfying fantasies of one another. After the birth of their first child, however, they each felt betrayed as they tried to divide up the increased demands of family life.

DEFINING FAMILY INDENTITY: CONFUSION OF CULTURE AND RELIGION

Intermarried couples often discover that they must grapple not only with different culturally shaped behavioral norms, but also with the nature of their blended families' cultural and religious identities. This process is often complicated by the fact that one or both partners may be confused or conflicted about their own identities and by the differences between religious and cultural identity. Although they traditionally overlap, culture and religion are not the same.

Modern life has fused and confused cultural, family, religious, and national loyalties in ways that make it difficult for many partners in mixed matches to understand and deal with the differences they bring to their relationships. When uprooted people reach back into their collective pasts in an attempt to create an identity, each person may reclaim different parts of the components of identity. Instead of striving for a balanced cultural/national/religious/family identity, some people emphasize religion, others their cultural or national roots, and still others their family roots. Often they end up having difficulty distinguishing among the different meanings of the elements of their identity collages.

This failure to clarify the meaning of these identity components can lead to conflict in relationships. Adam, a Jewish man who had not practiced Judaism since his adolescence, insisted that Mary, his fiancée, convert to Judaism. She was understandably upset by what she saw as the hypocrisy of his demand; at one point she asked him, "You never go to synagogue, never pray, and never talk about what it means to be Jewish. Just what are you asking me to convert to?" Adam's struggle to understand the meanings of his demand revealed a number of issues. He was worried about his parents' reactions to his marriage to a non-Jew. He also expressed his anxieties about anti-Semitism and his fears that if Mary was not Jewish, he might have difficulty feeling safe with her during hard times. Finally, he admitted that he had dreamed of having a Jewish son, even though his own connection to being Jewish was confused and tenuous.

Mary then told Adam about her own religious upbringing. She had felt a strong connection to the Methodist church her family belonged to as a child. Although she privately worried about how they might deal with the religious education of any children they would have, she had put off discussing the issue because she feared it would lead to conflict, and she wanted to protect her relationship with Adam until they had "built enough of a foundation."

Many couples attempt to deal with their differences by trying to forget the past altogether. Some couples use a kind of voluntary cultural and religious amnesia to ease the discomfort of living and loving together in relationships that defy tradition. For some, sacrificing the past and its traditions seems to be the price of creating a new and better future. But even when ties to tradition have eroded, the need to belong has not disappeared.

All of this taking apart and putting together of identities can create a lot of uncertainty. When partners in an intermarriage are unclear about the cultural or spiritual ground they stand on, it is difficult for them to negotiate any meaningful agreements. Both partners in an intercultural relationship need to work to clarify their cultural and religious values in order to work out their differences successfully.

One of the most difficult tasks for clinicians is confronting couples with the necessity of dealing with loss. "Suicide," "homicide," and "decide" all have the same root, "-cide," which is derived from the Latin *caedere,* meaning "to cut" or "to kill." The decision to raise a child in one culture or religion, in both, or in neither does kill other options. It is a difficult truth that even the best of decisions creates both risk and loss, requires compromise, and is never perfectly balanced. The American cultural delusion that "we should be able to create a compromise that makes us both perfectly happy" is one of the reasons why couples have difficulties making decisions. The therapist's job is to help couples puncture the myth.

THE LIFE CYCLE AS ALARM CLOCK: WAKING UP FROM CULTURAL AMNESIA

Cross-cultural couples are most likely to enter therapy when some life cycle event has disrupted a denial of differences in their relationship. Especially for partners who have minimized the importance of their different pasts, the reemergence of cultural loyalties—however confused or ambivalent—can lead to relationship conflict.

Steve and Betty entered therapy shortly after the death of Steve's mother. Betty felt very hurt by the way that Steve had treated her around the time of his mother's memorial service. After initially being defensive, Steve was finally able to begin to understand the ambivalent attachment he felt to his Japanese American identity—an ambivalence revealed by the loss of his mother. He wrote:

> My parents gave me a lot of mixed messages about being Japanese American. All of their friends were Japanese, but we lived in a neighborhood that was almost entirely Caucasian. They told me that it was important that I always remember that I was Japanese, but they didn't keep up any of the traditions at home. When we would visit my grandparents, I would watch my father go in and bow at the altar where they kept my great-grandfather's ashes in an urn, but they never included me in any ritual. I always pretended I hadn't seen him bow and felt vaguely embarrassed, as if I was witnessing something I shouldn't.
>
> When I started dating Betty, who is from a WASP background, I acted like being Japanese was of no real significance to me. We never talked about our backgrounds. When we did allude to our differences, it was usually to joke about how we had "recovered from our childhoods." I think we secretly prided ourselves on how we had transcended what we felt were our parochial cultural traditions.

But when my mother became ill and died last year, I was shocked by my own feelings—I suddenly started to feel very Japanese for the first time in my life. I couldn't believe that I felt guilty about bringing Betty to the funeral because she was White. I made up excuses to explain why I wanted to go to the funeral alone, and Betty got very upset and asked me if I was ashamed of being with her.

TAKING A CULTURAL HISTORY

It is very important to understand the differences—and similarities—between the cultural and religious milieus of the partners' families of origin. It is also crucial to assess how much each partner's identity has changed over the course of his or her life. Changes in nationality, class, religious belief and practice, and identity have a tremendous impact on how intercultural couples deal with their differences. The process of assessing these differences helps partners understand each other's unresolved cultural tensions, ambivalence, and oscillations in identity. Negotiating and dealing with differences are much easier when these kinds of issues are more clearly understood and acknowledged.

All identities are not created equal. Even when two partners in a relationship ascribe to egalitarian notions about the division of power and responsibility, the power of their feelings about their cultural and religious heritages may be very different. Asking each partner the following questions can help frame the discussion of identity:

- Born in another country?
  - If native-born, how many generations in country? Maternal? Paternal?
  - Ever lived in another country?
  - Speak a second language fluently? Which?
- Identify strongly with a religious faith as a child? Which religion?
  - Identify strongly now with a religion? Which religion?
  - Ever wished for a stronger sense of religious faith?
- Identify strongly with racial/cultural identity as a child? Which identity?
  - Identify strongly now with racial/cultural identity? Which identity?
  - Identified with more than one cultural/racial identity as a child? Now?
  - Ever wished for a stronger sense of cultural identity?
  - Ever felt burdened by racial/cultural identity and wished to assimilate more?

- Lived as a child in a culturally/religiously/racially diverse neighborhood? Homogeneous?
  - Neighborhood culture/religion different from your family's culture/religion? The same?
  - Lived in a cross-cultural family?
  - Urban, suburban, small-town, or rural environment?
- Ever experienced discrimination? By whom?
- Ever experienced racial/cultural religious stratification?
  - Which groups seen as superior? Inferior?
  - Overt and covert intolerance of family members of outsiders?
- Economic status of family of origin?
  - Family upwardly or downwardly mobile?

CLASS

Class functions as an overlay on cultural differences. Often the issue of class background is ignored in the assessment of a couple's conflict, especially when both partners in a relationship are similarly educated and currently middle-class. Like other differences in cultural background, the issue of different class origins becomes most obvious in child rearing. It can be just as misleading to assume that common educational and economic achievement indicate a common class background as it can be to assume that a common skin color connotes a common culture.

SEXUAL ORIENTATION

Intercultural relationships are increasingly common among gays and lesbians, just as in the larger population. I have conducted a number of intercultural couple groups that included both homosexual and heterosexual couples, and what was most striking was the *lack* of differences in the kinds of issues the couples discussed. Both gay and straight couples struggled with cultural and religious differences centering around celebration of holidays, child-rearing and identity issues, and contrasts in styles of emotional expression.

The one issue unique to gay couples in these groups was that of "coming out." A Cuban man, Roberto, and his White Protestant partner, Terry, had been involved in a committed relationship for over 10 years. They often joked about how much they conformed to the cultural stereotypes of the passionate, expressive Latin and the emotionally restrained WASP. When each of their fathers became very ill, they discovered that expressiveness and openness are not the same. Terry used his father's illness as a catalyst to finally reveal and discuss a fact that he had suspected his family already knew: that he was gay. Roberto, in spite of his greater expressiveness, felt that the Cuban American society in which his family was embedded could never accept his being open about being gay. When Terry's father died, Terry asked Roberto to travel to the funeral with him; when Roberto's father died, Roberto went to the funeral alone.

USING CULTURAL FOCUS TO DEPATHOLOGIZE DIFFERENCES

Conflict in intermarriage often occurs when partners take polarized positions on differences that were initially attractive. One way to help partners organize their understanding of their differences is to frame them in terms of the following categories:

> *Gender roles*: The division of roles of men and women in your [your partner's] family regarding work, power, money, housework, and so on.
>
> *Family cohesion*: The sense of concern, mutual involvement, and support in your [your partner's] family.
>
> *Emotional expression*: The intensity and nature of emotional expression in your [your partner's] family.
>
> *Cultural identity*: The manner and intensity with which your [your partner's] family expresses its cultural identity.
>
> *Religion*: The way your [your partner's] family expresses its religious beliefs. (These might include beliefs about the nature of the universe as well.)

When a couple is helped to discuss both the positive and negative aspects of these five dimensions in both partners' families, the partners can better assess the two-sided nature of differences. They often discover that the very differences they found attractive in one another are now at the core of their current conflict. When they are able to acknowledge this, they are better able to begin to look for ways to compromise and work on synthesizing their differences, rather than taking opposing positions. What often becomes clear is that both partners are ambivalent about the positions they are so fiercely defending.

PARENTING

There are no simple formulas for raising the children of intermarriage, because the best path for any particular child depends on so many variables. Children and families living in more tolerant environments face different issues than do those living in areas plagued by pervasive racial and social tensions. Wealthy families may be able to afford a lifestyle that insulates them from the harsher aspects of life, which families of more modest means may not be able to avoid. The concerns of single parents are different from those of parents with intact marriages. Stepparents and blended families may introduce even more complexity into a family situation, creating a rainbow array of cultures in one household. And while many children do better when they have a unified family faith, some children thrive without any organized religion or in families that practice a blend of religions.

Even though there is no one route to successful child rearing, there are a number of basic principles for helping children develop solid identities:

- Parents need to make working out their differences about their respective gender roles, as well as about the cultural and religious identity of their family, an ongoing process.
- Children need parents to listen to and try to understand their experiences.
- Parents need to see their children's ambivalence about their identity as a normal developmental process, especially for bicultural and biracial children.
- Children should be provided with positive cultural experiences that reflect who they are.
- Children need to be taught how to deal with prejudice.
- Parents cannot ultimately control the cultural/racial/religious identity of their children as they move through adolescence into adulthood.

CULTURAL COUNTERTRANSFERENCE: THE INDIVIDUALISTIC BIAS OF PSYCHOTHERAPY

Therapists must be aware of their own cultural and religious countertransference. The myth of therapist neutrality can make this difficult. As members of the secular priesthood, psychotherapists often have difficulty seeing their own relationships with faith, culture, and community as having an impact on how they approach helping couples. Although couple and family therapists often congratulate themselves on being "systemic," the extent of that broader perspective often stops at the boundaries of a couple's or family's relationship. The systemic perspective needs to be broadened to include an understanding of the clients' *and the therapist's* extended family, neighborhood, communal, and religious involvement.

Lacking objective criteria for evaluating family structure, therapists inevitably use the characteristics of their own cultures of origin as reference points in defining normality. It should come as little surprise, therefore, that what one therapist describes as an "enmeshed" family system, another may describe as "disengaged."

A therapist is particularly susceptible to falling into an individualistic trap when faced with partners who are dealing with familial opposition to their relationship. Although lack of family acceptance can destabilize a cross-cultural relationship, it can also have the opposite effect. Cut off from the usual sources of support, partners who feel exiled by their families are figuratively pushed into one another's arms. Resenting the judgments of others, they focus their anger on their families and may fail to experience normal ambivalence about their new relationship. Like citizens of a nation threatened by enemies from without, they close ranks and temporarily forget their own differences.

When dealing with a couple in this situation, a therapist may be tempted to frame the issue as simply one of incomplete differentiation from families of origin. As a result, she or he may fail to focus on unresolved conflicts within the relationship, as well as to assess the extent of each partner's ambivalent attachment to religious and cultural traditions.

To the extent that many couples' family difficulties are exacerbated by a lack of support from and connection with extended family and community, the individualistic assumptions of psychotherapy can exacerbate the very problems it seeks to alleviate. The therapist must help such couples recognize and deal with the importance of social support networks and help them to make difficult choices.

ACKNOWLEDGMENT

Portions of this chapter were adapted from Crohn (1995). Copyright 1995 by Fawcett/Columbine. Adapted by permission.

REFERENCES

Alba, R. (1985). *Italian Americans: Into the twilight of ethnicity.* Englewood Cliffs, NJ: Prentice-Hall.

Bernard, J. (1966). Note on educational homogamy in Negro–White marriages. *Journal of Marriage and the Family, 28,* 274–276.

Cohen, S. M. (1994, December). Why intermarriage may not threaten Jewish continuity. *Moment Magazine*, pp. 54–95.

Crohn, J. (1995). *Mixed matches: How to succeed in your interracial, interethnic, and interfaith relationships*. New York: Fawcett/Columbine.

Klein, J. (1980). *Jewish identity and self esteem: Healing wounds through ethnotherapy*. New York: American Jewish Committee.

Newsweek. (1993, May 24). The reluctant princess. pp. 28–39.

Population Reference Bureau. (1992, December). *Population today* (Vol. 20, No. 12).

Spickard, P. R. (1989). *Mixed blood: Intermarriage and ethnic identity in twentieth century America*. Madison: University of Wisconsin Press.

U.S. Bureau of the Census. (1993). *Statistical abstract of the United States*. Washington, DC: U.S. Government Printing Office.

CHAPTER 23

Marriages of Asian Women and American Military Men

THE IMPACT OF GENDER AND CULTURE

Bok-Lim C. Kim

Gender-based discrimination in the United States, with its concomitant results of unequal power and privilege, is now recognized to be as pervasive and toxic as racism. The impact and cost of both sexism and racism for individual victims and for American society as a whole have been studied and documented (Kramer, 1970). This chapter explores and discusses how racism and sexism intersect and affect the relationships of interracially and internationally married couples (Hardy & Laszloffy, 1994; Hare-Mustin, 1989). The chapter focuses on Asian women from South Korea, Japan, and the Philippines and on the American military men they marry. Implications for the assessment and treatment of these couples are presented.

Since World War II, marriage between Asian women and American military men has become a legacy of the U.S. military presence in Japan, South Korea, the Philippines, and Vietnam (Kim, Okamura, Ozawa, & Forest, 1981). I have worked with these couples closely as an advocate and therapist for the past 40 years.[1] Over this period, I have been most impressed by their undaunted courage and optimism about these marriages in spite of the many obstacles presented by language and cultural differences, as well as the absence of acceptance and support from either commanding officers and chaplains or from their families and communities in both countries. The Asian wife in particular carries the burden of cultural values that have severe penalties for out-marriage. Mere association with American military men brings instant stigma and shame for a young woman and her family. Marriage to such a man means that she can never live in her home country again with any degree of comfort. Another characteristic of these couples is a vast power imbalance, manifested in husband-dominant and wife-submissive positions.

CONTEXT OF INTERRACIAL AND INTERNATIONAL MARRIAGE

The legends of Oriental countries' allure and mystery, with their strange customs and exotic women who are self-sacrificing, docile, and eager to please, are immortalized in operas and plays such as *Madame Butterfly, The World of Suzie Wong, South Pacific,* and *Miss Saigon.* For centuries, the Asian woman has been either socialized or forced to be subservient and obedient. In reality, Asian women have dealt with their second-class position by acting docile and submissive (Kim, 1996). They have learned to conceal their own ideas about what they want for themselves and their families, and to use the very system that oppresses them to achieve some of their goals. Asian men have known this, but as long as they could maintain their dominant position and get the credit for the women's accomplishment, they did not object. However, many American military men stationed in Asia have been taken in by the outward appearance of Asian women's behavior and gender roles.

Although an increasing number of young Asian women now have access to higher levels of education and work, and aspire to gender equality, Asian women in general still occupy subservient positions on the job and at home. In particular, the Asian women who marry American military men generally have low-status and low-paying jobs, with neither job security nor prospects of advancement. The majority of them have suffered severe abuse, neglect, and poverty while growing up (Kim, 1972). Sexual harassment and economic exploitation in their workplaces are also prevalent. Their present life experience perpetuates that of their past in teaching them to see themselves as victims and inferior beings, deserving only subordinate positions and mistreatment.

Given the historically dominant position of the United States in relation to the Philippines (a former colony), Japan (a defeated former enemy), and South Korea (a country saved from Communist aggression by U.S. military intervention), American military men are in a very different position. For over half a century, the U.S. military uniform has symbolized superior military and economic power and affluence. This technology and affluence have been confused with American cultural superiority by many, and this conscious and unconscious assumption is shared by those Asian women and the American military men who marry them. Like these women, many of the men have life histories of abuse, neglect, and deprivation (Kim, 1972). However, joining the military has provided the men with needed structure, a sense of identity, and a unique opportunity to prove themselves.

Although the balance of power between these Asian nations and the United States is shifting to a more equal and collaborative mode, this change is not reflected in the relationship of the couples I see. Whether this stems from racism or sexism is unclear, but the cause is probably a combination of sexist expectations and cultural colonialism, a special form of racism. In any case, the husband's superior and dominant position in such a couple's relationship is affirmed and reinforced. The aphorism that the subjugated must adopt the language and customs of the dominant applies here too. No one seems to appreciate how important a knowledge of each partner's language and culture can be in overcoming miscommunication and misunderstanding and in establishing the marital bond (Falicov, 1995).

For a woman who comes to such a marriage with low socioeconomic status and low self-esteem, her dignity and identity are further diminished. Moreover, the arduous tasks of learning English and becoming acculturated to the American lifestyle are placed upon the wife, whereas the husband is nearly always exempted from learning his wife's language and culture. The couple's expectation that they will be returning to America, and the dictates of Asian culture that the wife must adopt her husband's way, all add to the pressure on the wife to become Americanized. The clear message to the wife is that her own heritage of language and culture is unworthy of her husband's attention or respect; this message further supports and reinforces the unequal and unbalanced relationship.

ROLE COMPLEMENTARITY

I have found that the idealization of partners lasts much longer among interracially and internationally married couples than it does among newly married couples sharing the same language and culture (Kim, 1972). Mutual discovery and exploration of each partner's background and personality, which replace idealization with a more truthful picture and understanding of each partner, occur very slowly if ever among intermarried couples. This is due not only to the absence of a common language and culture, but, more importantly, to the absence of expectations for such an exchange. Members of these couples show a conspicuous lack of curiosity about their own and their partners' motive for out-marriage. There appears to be a tacitly shared agreement that their past problems, failures, and difficulties will be filed away and that they can start with a clean slate. Each partner seems to have the fantasy that marrying a person from a drastically different culture will insure that the past can be protected from memory and scrutiny, and that earlier insults and deprivations will be magically resolved.

As long as a couple remains in the wife's country, and the partners' physical and material needs are met, they seem to be unaware of the limitations of their relationship. The spouses pursue work and friendship in their separate worlds: The husband continues to work and socialize with his peers on the military base, while the wife does the same with her friends who are also associating with U.S. military men.[2] The primary modes of communication are rudimentary English and the meeting of sexual and physical needs. Miscommunications and misunderstandings are common but tolerated. Usually, nothing in the experience of either partner has given him or her an appreciation for the kind of emotional closeness, understanding, and empathy that result in intimacy (Horst & Doherty, 1995).

STRESS AND PROBLEMS

When such a couple comes to the United States, hidden weaknesses in the marital bond and individual psychological vulnerabilities are revealed, and the outward appearance of role complementary dissolves. In particular, the wife is overwhelmed by the stress of immigration and the many aspects of acculturation. She must simultaneously deal with the loss of her support system and lifestyle while acquiring the new skills she needs to function in a foreign country with a vastly different culture and language.

The couple's problems are both practical and relational. The everyday tasks of managing a home, child care, and possibly even working, which the woman has successfully done in her own country, are rendered difficult or impossible by her limited proficiency in English and her inability to negotiate the systems governing daily life. The husband, who must bridge the gap between cultures by involving himself in what both he and his wife believe to be "women's work," often feels put upon. This new role of teaching and providing comfort and support with patience and empathy conflicts with his belief in what constitutes the "man's role" in the marriage. How well he helps his wife become Americanized often depends on his comfort with losing his "exotic Oriental wife" and, even more importantly, his dominant position. He can indeed feel threatened as he sees his Asian wife acculturating and simultaneously expecting to take an increasingly equal share in decision making and household responsibility.

If the marriage is to succeed, the couple must learn to function as a team by moving from dominant and subordinate positions toward a collaborative and cooperative relationship. The obstacles are many. Most obvious is the miscommunication caused by language barriers, as well as by the hitherto unrecognized misperception of each other's personalities. Another obstacle is the wife's helplessness during the early phase of immigration. The husband can exploit her helplessness and maintain his control by blocking her access to community resources through isolation, withholding of vital information, and provision of misinformation about the workings of American society. A common threat is that if the wife disobeys him, the husband will have her deported and keep their children with him; in truth, of course, he does not have this power.

For an Asian wife with limited education, writing a simple check can be a problem, and dependence on her husband is a practical necessity. The wife's level of innate intelligence is the key. No matter how well she learns English, she is vulnerable to confusion, uncertainty, and impaired reality testing unless she also learns about the sociocultural and economic context of systemic and interpersonal transactions. Something as ordinary to Americans as payroll deductions can be seen as the husband's holding back part of his paycheck for something he does not want his wife to know about. Finally, regardless of cultural differences, both partners need personal maturity (as manifested by empathy, self-awareness, trust, and respect) and appropriate role models if the marriage is to be healthy. Considering the complexity and enormity of the tasks they face, it is surprising that many intermarried couples complete this transition without developing major symptoms of family dysfunction.

In the following sections, treatment issues and strategies are discussed, and two case illustrations are provided. The families I see are mostly involuntary clients referred by hospitals, family services, child protective agencies, and public schools. The emotional and behavioral problems of the children of these couples, which reflect the marital discord of the parents, constitute too extensive a topic to be discussed in this context.

TREATMENT ISSUES

Many American service providers, including therapists, are hindered by their ignorance about Asian wives' sociocultural background and the special dynamics of this type of intercultural marriage. The therapists' own prejudices and assumptions about American cultural superiority can also interfere (Korin, 1994). Therapists often do not realize that it takes many more sessions than with American clients before they can accurately assess Asian wives and their problems. An Asian wife's limited English proficiency, along with uncertainty about what she is entitled to as an alien spouse, can also make truthful presentation virtually impossible. Because of the language difficulties, a therapist may use the husband as an intermediary and assume too readily that the husband and wife agree on the same version of the problem. Even when the English proficiency of these Asian wives is adequate, they do not expect to be understood or helped by Americans and are reluctant to share their feelings and problems. The desire to please and be polite to people in positions of authority is so strong that even after a therapeutic alliance has been established, these women will appear to agree with their therapists' suggestions and make promises that they cannot keep. It is common for treatment to continue for as long as 1 year before they feel free enough to reveal the extent of their hurt and pain.

The American military husband is equally guarded and shy about disclosing problems. He frequently presents his reluctance as concern for privacy, while in reality he is concerned about maintaining control over his wife. He is unaccustomed to asking for help and fears that his revelations will adversely affect his military career. Understanding, respect, and finding mutual solutions to problems are not what he has learned to expect.

By the time such a couple is brought for help, the problem is often so drastic that the therapist can understandably assume the presence of severe psychopathology when the symptoms may actually be a reaction to the severe stress of acculturation and an intensely toxic marital relationship. What an Asian wife frequently reveals is such extreme cruelty under such shocking circumstances that the therapist cannot help either wanting to rescue her or being repulsed. For example, a Korean wife found abandoned in a chicken coop was initially mistaken for an animal, because the only sounds she made were grunts. She remained incoherent for several days even after a Korean family took her in.

Up to this point, I have made no distinctions among Asian wives from South Korea, Japan, and the Philippines in terms of coping styles and reactions to immigration-related stresses and acculturation requirements. At the risk of oversimplification and generalization, some stylistic differences common to each group are offered; the reader is reminded that individual exceptions must be made. South Korean and Filipina wives tend to externalize difficulties, while Japanese wives tend to internalize their hurt and anger. The first two groups tend to blame, fight, and act out, while the third group holds in grudges, somatizes, and suffers from depression (Kim, 1972).

CASE EXAMPLES

Josey, a Filipina wife, was brought into the emergency room of a military hospital after ingesting a large dose of prescription painkillers. Josey was uncommunicative, and only very limited information was available about her, but it was established that her husband was away on a 6-month deployment. After 2 days, she was stabilized and discharged with a referral to me. Josey was guarded at first and repeated vague complaints about her husband's womanizing and selfishness. Her three children, aged 15, 13, and 7, seemed to be well cared for, and the school confirmed that their attendance and academic work were satisfactory. The house was always clean and tidy when I made home visits. Her English proficiency was adequate for shopping and talking with American neighbors and school personnel.

After a month of therapy, Josey began to verbalize her hurt and anger about her husband's constant put-downs, and to reveal her depressive symptoms and mildly paranoid ideas. A referral to a kind and culturally sensitive psychiatrist was made, but it took a month of repeated explanation and reassurance before medication compliance was achieved. By the third month, she disclosed daily conversations with a ghost she named Pat, who visited her when she was alone. Pat's visits were rendered harmless when Josey followed my suggestion to cultivate a friendly relationship with Pat. Within a month, Pat's visits as well as her depressive symptoms decreased. Josey then revealed the family's serious financial problems, which she had largely caused by overspending as a way of acting out her depression and retaliating against her husband. Help with money management and bill collectors lessened her general anxiety. Little by little, Josey disclosed childhood experiences of being hit regularly with sticks and chased by her enraged father with an ax, and witnessing his suicidal threats to jump from a tall tree while her mother and neighbors pleaded with him. She related these incidents without affect, as if she were talking about someone else. A few sessions later, apparently realizing that she had been acting somewhat crazily, she reasoned that her father (who had been so much crazier) must also have had a ghost he talked with. She was glad that her ghost was friendly and not like her father's.

Yoko, the Japanese wife of a Navy officer, was hospitalized after a serious suicide attempt. She slit the artery in one wrist and overdosed on sleeping pills after her husband asked for a divorce. Had the husband not returned a day earlier than expected, she would have died. She was furious with her husband for taking her to the hospital, and refused to see him. Her highly elevated blood pressure required a week-long hospitalization. She successfully concealed her persistent suicidal state and agreed to what appeared to be a safe discharge plan, all the while intending another suicide attempt. Only her commitment to honor a promise to a kind social worker that she see a therapist at least twice brought her to see me. She was clearly depressed and candidly admitted that she had no reasons to live, but a strong enough therapeutic alliance was established in these two visits to keep her in treatment.

Outwardly, these women had much in common: a serious suicide attempt, depression, abusive family background, and a domineering American military husband who was insensitive and emotionally abusive. Both had lived in America over a decade and half. Aside from cultural differences, what distinguished the two women seemed to be their innate intelligence and personal maturity. Yoko had obtained a high school diploma in the United States, ignoring her husband's derision, and got a steady job after her two children reached adolescence. Josey, on the other hand, could not read, write a check, or drive, and interpreted her husband's encouragement to go to English classes as a put-down.

TREATMENT STRATEGIES

Whenever possible, participation of the husband in therapy is essential, because he can undermine or sabotage his wife's treatment. But beginning with conjoint sessions only serves to reinforce the husband's dominance, despite the therapist's best efforts to block it. Ideally, the wife should be seen first; when this is not possible, therapy should begin with individual work with both partners, at the very least. The wife must be given the opportunity to present her problems without her husband's interference or intimidation, and to establish something of an alliance with the therapist.

Seeing the wife first conveys the therapist's confidence and respect for her, paves the way toward empowering her, and begins to unbalance the dominant–submissive marital relationship. It also prevents an American therapist from yielding to the temptation to turn to the husband for information and clarification when there are language difficulties or when the wife fails to articulate her concerns. Instead, the therapist's patient and persistent efforts to understand the wife, along with warm, empathetic listening and a nonjudgmental attitude, can transcend both language and cultural barriers (Hardy & Laszloffy, 1994). When the therapist expresses kindness and a sincere wish to help, his or her positive motives can have a beneficial effect on the wife, just as Yoko was touched by the kind social worker at the hospital.

Seeing the wife first also demonstrates to the husband that his wife's opinions are as important as his and should be respected. Seeing him individually serves to communicate to him that he has just as much responsibility for their problems as the wife does, and that, just like hers, his stress and pain are of sufficient severity to require professional help. After each partner resolves some of his or her individual issues, the final phase of conjoint sessions to help husband and wife learn how to collaborate as a couple can begin.

After the initial crisis management, priority must generally be given to practical problem solving. These families are frequently involved with a variety of agencies—hospitals, child protective services, courts, and collection agencies. Because the American husband is usually as inexperienced as his Asian wife in dealing with these, the therapist needs to function as a coach, advocate, and intermediary. This is an excellent way for the therapist to demonstrate his or her usefulness and willingness to help in a way that is meaningful to both husband and wife (Sue & Zane, 1987). The therapist is also empowering them by teaching useful skills.

Only after the practical problems are resolved can the relationship problems and individual difficulties be approached directly (S. C. Kim, 1985). The therapist needs to be sensitive to the couple's readiness for change. Very often the partners are quite satisfied with small changes in the relationship, along with clarification of misunderstandings and miscommunications. Many wives are happy when their husbands move from the role of dictator to that of benevolent though still domineering husband. Nearly three-quarters of the couples I have seen have terminated therapy at this point. Only about one-fifth are motivated to go on with treatment and seek further growth. Another small percentage needs continuing help with crisis management and small incremental changes. (This was true with Josey, whose emotional instability and psychological problems necessitated my ongoing involvement to safeguard against her decompensation.)

CONCLUSION

Gender-based discrimination and cultural forces promote inequality of power and privilege, which ultimately destroys self-esteem, isolates individuals, and prevents intimacy. Though these inequalities are seen throughout the world, Asian countries, with their emphasis on hierarchy and unquestioned male dominance, provide a particularly fertile breeding ground for extreme forms of inequality, which we can see played out in the relationship of many interracial couples who come for help. We can also see that the need for resolution of early childhood insults can be so strong that it takes precedence over the most powerful cultural forces.

The therapist needs to keep in mind not only that such a union may represent the partners' combined effort to resolve these traumas, but that this combined effort may also become the source of further growth.

NOTES

1. Since 1956, I have worked with Asian wives from Korea, Japan, the Philippines, Thailand, and Hong Kong who married their American military husbands overseas. In 1976, I formed the National Committee Concerned with Asian Wives of U.S. Servicemen. Its goals were to study the conditions and problems of this largely invisible population, develop educational materials for Asian wives in English and in their ethnic languages, educate and train American service providers about this population's unique needs and problems, and engage in advocacy activities. Many of the Committee's goals were accomplished: Information packets for the wives were developed, several journal articles were published, training materials and films were produced, and numerous 2-day workshops for the U.S. Navy, Air Force, and Army, and for Korean American clergy were held. Advocacy activities included providing expert witness testimony in criminal cases involving Asian wives (six cases so far), testimony before the U.S. Civil Rights Commission, and input to the rule making of the U.S. military family service provisions. For the past 17 years, I have provided direct services to Korean, Japanese, Filipina, Thai, and Chinese wives of American military husbands (active duty and retired) and consultation to service providers in the San Diego area.

2. In most of the Asian countries (South Korea, Japan, and the Philippines) where U.S. military bases have been established for any length of time, a local ethnic community (called Base Village) gets established with its own set of rules and norms which may be somewhat different from the larger ethnic community. Most of its members are directly and indirectly involved with the operation of the U.S. base and its personnel. Within the confines of such a base village, stigma for living or associating with American servicemen is minimal. If family members of the women also live within such a village, intercultural marriage or cohabitation is more likely to be accepted.

REFERENCES

Falicov, C. J. (1995). Cross-cultural marriage. In N. S. Jacobson & A. S. Gurman (Eds.), *Clinical handbook of couple therapy* (pp. 231–248). New York: Guilford Press.

Hardy, K. V., & Laszloffy, T. A. (1994). Deconstructing race in family therapy. *Journal of Feminist Family Therapy, 5,* 5–33.

Hare-Mustin, R. T. (1989). The problem of gender in family therapy theory. In M. McGoldrick, C. Anderson, & F. Walsh (Eds.), *Women in families: A framework for family therapy.* New York: Norton.

Horst, E. A., & Doherty, W. J. (1995). Gender, power and intimacy. *Journal of Feminist Family Therapy, 6,* 63–85.

Kim, B.-L. (1972). Casework with Japanese and Korean wives of Americans. *Social Casework, 53,* 273–279.

Kim, B.-L. (1996). Korean American families. In M. McGoldrick, J. Giordano, & J. K. Pearce (Eds.), *Ethnicity and family therapy* (2nd ed., p. 285). New York: Guilford Press.

Kim, B.-L., Okamura, A. L., Ozawa, N., & Forest, V. (1981). *Women in shadows: A handbook for service providers working with Asian wives of U.S. military personnel.* San Diego, CA: National Committee Concerned with Asian Wives of U.S. Servicemen.

Kim, S. C. (1985). Family therapy for Asian Americans: A strategic–structural framework. *Psychotherapy, 22*(2S), 342–348.

Korin, E. C. (1994). Social inequalities and therapeutic relationships: Applying Freire's idea to clinical practice. *Journal of Feminist Family Therapy, 5,* 75–98.

Kramer, J. R. (1970). *The American minority community.* New York: Crowell.

Sue, S., & Zane, N. (1987). The role of culture and cultural techniques in psychotherapy: A critique and reformulation. *American Psychologist, 42*(1), 37–45.

CHAPTER 24

The Families
of Lesbian Women
and Gay Men

Thomas W. Johnson
Michael S. Keren

Popular culture has long portrayed lesbians and gay men as eternal isolates—as disconnected souls living lives devoid of meaningful attachments,
moving from one failed relationship to the next. Movies and other cultural artifacts provide evidence of this, as exemplified by such films as
The Children's Hour, The Boys in the Band, The Killing of Sister George,
or *Cruising.* However, as the life narratives of lesbians and gays become
more and more visible in contemporary culture, the inaccuracy of the
isolate stereotype becomes clear. Lesbians and gays, like their heterosexual counterparts, maintain connections with their families of origin,
and many also create their own "families of choice" with partners, children, and groups of intimate friends.

More and more frequently, lesbians and gays are presenting at clinicians' offices for help with a variety of "family problems." Unfortunately,
many mainstream professionals are woefully unprepared for this work.
Well-meaning therapists apply dominant notions of relationship, out of
the assumption that, basically, "we're all the same underneath." There is
a grain of truth in this "sameness" position, but as some authors (Laird,
1993; Lukes & Land, 1990) remind us, lesbians and gays are "bicultural." Given that they are reared in the same dominant culture as heterosexuals, lesbians and gays operate under some of the same mainstream
cultural prescriptions; however, because of the unique experience created

by homophobia and by same-gender pairing, they depart from the dominant culture in a number of important ways. The aim of this chapter is to address these important differences in four specific areas: identity, gender, sexuality, and family construction.

IDENTITY

Family has long been seen as the main context for the development of personal identity. It is the family that conveys values, beliefs, and a sense of agency, as well as a model (both positive and negative) for relationship. The family is also the principal transmitter of mainstream cultural attitudes, as well as attitudes about those attitudes. Within the family, gay men and lesbian women struggle to establish a personal identity that runs against the grain of the family identity and family acculturation process in which they are embedded (Keren, 1993). This process of a distinct self-recognition, self-identification, and integration of a gay or lesbian identity is referred to in its totality as "coming out." Although the process was originally conceptualized as a staged developmental sequence in order to make it more understandable and more readily useful in clinical and research settings (Cass, 1979), it is better seen as a progression that moves back and forth along a continuum, influenced by feedback loops that include environmental, cultural, and emotional factors.

It is important for the clinician to understand that a gay/lesbian identity does not spring into awareness as an intact entity, but evolves through a developmental process that at times may be extremely ego-dystonic. Homosexuality may be an issue long before it is mentioned out loud, and it may be a secret identity for many years because of stigma and possible threat. Many gay men and lesbians report being told by well-meaning educators, clergy, and health care providers that their adolescent confusion about sexual orientation or their young crushes on same-sex chums were "just a phase you're going through." Often these words are muttered in an ill-founded attempt to alleviate parental fears. An important therapeutic task for clinicians working with lesbian/gay youngsters and their families is to create a more open and facilitating environment for the complicated and painful process of differentiating a lesbian/gay self. Given the cultural reactivity and censure, this task is easier said than done for all those involved.

It is important to remember that parents also have a parallel coming-out process as the parents of gay or lesbian children. This process also entails self-recognition, self-identification, self-disclosure, and integration of an altered identity. Clinical work with parents often involves challenging long-held cultural, religious, and family beliefs about homosexuality, as well as culturally embedded theories regarding its causes and manifestations. In addition, a gay or lesbian family member must be encouraged to be patient and to develop some empathy for the family's process.

Lesbians and gays of color experience additional struggles in grappling with a sexual minority identity (Chan, 1989; Greene, 1994; Greene & Boyd-Franklin, 1996; Morales, 1990, 1996; Savin-Williams, 1996). Since the family and/or the community may be the most crucial source of support in living within a hostile dominant culture, fears about loss of family support may seem to some too high a price to pay for coming out. In addition, the lesbian/gay component of identity may not assume as central a position for lesbians/gays of color as it does for their White counterparts. Moreover, the White lesbian/gay communities may represent yet another context of marginalization and loss of privilege for lesbians/gays of color (Font, 1997), and this may make identification with a lesbian/gay world more problematic (Morales, 1990).

An understanding of identity development is also important in clinical work with same-sex couples (Johnson & Keren, 1996). Individuals within couples may enter treatment at disparate points in development. This discordance may produce conflict, whether or not it is recognized by a couple. For this reason, we have found it clinically useful to have the partners tell their coming-out narratives as part of the assessment process. A careful listening can help partners remember and identify their own unique developmental processes, and can help them empathize with each other's developmental needs. Interracial, interfaith, and intercultural couples also often need help to understand how their individual identity development processes may differ as a function of their disparate backgrounds (Johnson & Keren, 1996). If an Asian man, for example, feels unable to come out to his family and include his partner, given various normative cultural scripts in his culture (Chan, 1989), a White partner may need help in understanding the key nature of the cultural influence, and in not dismissing his partner's concerns as neurotic diffidence about his identity.

GENDER

Clinical work with sexual minority families often entails a challenge to long-held gender narratives and myths. Despite volumes of postmodern discourse, which have clearly illustrated that gender, gender roles, and sex role behaviors are social constructions, the general population continues to believe and live as if gender is an essential given (Goldner, 1988, 1991; Hare-Mustin, 1987). It is precisely because the dominant culture subscribes to rigid ideas about gender, as well as to cultural myths equating homosexuality with gender nonconformity, that the culture finds homosexuality so threatening (Herek, 1984). These myths derive from the formulas that "gay male sexuality = passivity and femininity" and that "lesbianism = masculinity and dominance." These premises have influenced scientific pursuits, as seen in early experiments that looked for biological answers to homosexuality in estrogen and testosterone, the so-called "sex hormones."

Society, as reflected in the medical community, has been so threatened by gender nonconformity that it has been pathologized. DSM-IV (American Psychiatric Association, 1994) includes the category "gender identity disorder" as a mental disorder. One longitudinal study of so-called "sissy boys" has suggested that this gender nonconformity may be an early indicator of postpubertal homosexuality (Green, 1987). Indeed, clinical experience and other retrospective studies have identified that a large proportion of gay men remember behaving in nonstereotypically gendered ways. However, is their gender nonconformity a correlate of pathology?

At this point, the reader may well be confused. Are the assumptions about gender nonconformity and homosexuality myths or realities? The answer is a perplexing but resounding "Yes." Some gay men and lesbians do exhibit gender nonconformity, and some do not; some exhibit this behavior purposefully, while to others it comes naturally; still others, accepting a position outside the mainstream, refuse to play by essentialist assumptions and open themselves up to a range of gendered "performances" (D'Ercole, 1996). So bewildered clinicians must examine their own theoretical assumptions about gender and sexuality, and must be prepared to help families engage in dialogues about gender that may be the equivalent of "Mr. Toad's Wild Ride."

When clinicians are working with lesbians and gays in the family-of-origin context, initial parental concerns and homophobia often surface in questions about gender performance. Parents may feel guilty, and wonder whether they provided adequate role modeling of gendered behavior (Griffin, Wirth, & Wirth, 1986) or encouraged gender-appropriate behavior. In this regard, they wonder: Are they to blame? The emerging gay man or lesbian woman may also confuse his or her sexual orientation with gender nonconformity. Thus the adolescent boy may deny same-sex attractions by saying, "I can't be gay; I'm the star of the football team," or the young lesbian woman may deny her lesbian attractions by focusing on "feminine pursuits" or getting pregnant to prove her heterosexuality. Clinicians must help these families confront these sorts of gendered assumptions. One place to start is the genogram: Where did a family's gender assumptions originate? How have they been transmitted through the family? In what ways do members of the current family subscribe to or challenge gendered assumptions? Who in the extended network, both past and present, showed the ability to oppose successfully some of the dominant gender assumptions of their times?

Gay and lesbian couples also confront gendered assumptions every day of their lives. Stereotypically, a heterosexual couple can settle into proscribed norms for behavior, but a same-sex couple has no such luxury. This is both a confusing yet liberating challenge for the couples. Traditional gendered attitudes offer a map of sorts, but one with constraints that fit poorly with lesbian or gay life. Herein lies the opportunity for the creation of new norms, or new "gender performances." Still, lesbian and gay couples must confront the limits of gender stereotyping. For example, a male couple often needs to address how traditionally gender-scripted male competitiveness hinders the development of intimacy.

When the members of a gay or lesbian couple begin to consider parenting, they reenter the gender dialogue on a new level. Can same-sex parents provide both "mothering" and "fathering"? Are mothering and fathering functions gender-linked? Again, essentialist assumptions may be up for grabs in the face of reality. In this regard, a clinician must provide a forum for discovering or recreating new realities through dialogues on gender.

SEXUALITY

Nothing arouses more reactivity about homosexuality than the subject of sex. The gay male community's normative acceptance of nonmonogamy, recreational sex, and anonymous sex transgresses many important heterocentric norms and values. Similarly, in a lesbian context, the creation of a sexuality that does not necessarily and compulsively revolve around genital activity (particularly the phallus) and penetration confuses the dominant culture (Iasenza, 1995). In order to preserve the safety of mainstream role prescriptions, lesbian and gay sexualities are marginalized by means of silence and stigmatization. Fortunately, the silence has been lifted with studies like that of Blumstein and Schwartz (1983), which detail the sexual lives of lesbians and gay men. Although Blumstein and Schwartz's data may be somewhat outdated, given that they were collected and analyzed in the 1970s, at this point they are the only data we have for cataloguing the various sexual experiences of lesbians and gay men.

Blumstein and Schwartz compared the behavior of four groups of couples (married heterosexuals, cohabiting heterosexuals, lesbian couples, and gay couples) in three areas of couple life: money, work, and sex.

With regard to sex and male couples, they found that gay men had the highest frequency of sexual activity in the early part of their relationship, compared to the other three groups. However, gay men's level of sexual activity with their partners declined as time passed, even though their level of sexual interest was high. It is interesting that these gay male couples did not experience any decline in relationship satisfaction as the partners' sexual interest in each other declined. A frequent sexual outlet for these couples was "outside" sexual activity—an anonymous encounter, a fling on a business trip, or a one-night stand (referred to as a "trick" in the gay community). Blumstein and Schwartz's findings that male couples were less monogamous than other couples are consistent with those in other studies of gay couples (Carl, 1990; Peplau, 1991). In addition, Blumstein and Schwartz found, as did other researchers on gay couples (Kurdek & Schmitt, 1985–1986; Peplau, 1991), that this nonmonogamy was not deleterious to the couple relationship. The outside sex was reported to be just that—casual and recreational sex that had little significance in terms of intimacy and posed little threat to the primary relationship. However, not all male couples endorse nonmonogamy, and couples may shift back and forth over time on a continuum of sexual monogamy versus openness. We have found that male couples report a wide array of contracts concerning monogamy. There is also variety in how the outside sex is handled by the couple. Some couples set down rules, such as no affairs, only "tricking"; no disclosure about the outside sex; or full disclosure.

Blumstein and Schwartz found that lesbian couples had the lowest sexual frequency rate of the four groups. However, lesbian partners were more likely to rate their relationship as sexually compatible. Blumstein and Schwartz's findings and the dominant notion of lesbian sexual repression have since been critiqued by a number of sex researchers and sex therapists (Iasenza, 1995; Loulan, 1987). The revisionists claim that mainstream sex researchers like Blumstein and Schwartz use male-based and heterocentric norms and standards in measuring lesbian sexual behavior. As Iasenza (1995) notes, not all lesbian sexual behavior revolves around genital play and penetration. Iasenza (1995) also makes the claim that a sexual space that does not include men represents such a novel situation in the dominant culture that the landscape of this experience remains unnamed and uncharted. In this regard, the notion of lesbian sexual repression becomes the "myth of lesbian sexual repression."

The pictures of lesbian and gay sexualities painted above certainly do not represent a monolithic view of the entire gay and lesbian communities. It is crucial to remember that discontinuity and diversity exist in abundance. For example, the binary categories of heterosexual versus homosexual do not capture everyone's experience. Some people label themselves as bisexual and choose romantic/erotic relationships with both sexes. Some people may not label themselves as bisexual, and maintain a lesbian/gay identity, but periodically involve themselves in opposite-sex experiences. Clinicians need to monitor their own anxious inclination to categorize, and should stay close to the individual meanings people assign to their sexual behavior. Culture also plays a significant part in the meanings and names people attach to their sexual behavior. For example, among some Mexican men, if one maintains the "inserter" or "dominant" position in homosexual sex, one is not homosexual (Carrier, 1976). In addition, given cultural proscriptions about public assertion of one's sexuality, some Asian American gay/lesbian persons may not necessarily identify themselves publicly as gay/lesbian, even if homosexuality exclusively constitutes their private sexual practice (Chan, 1989).

FAMILY CONSTRUCTION

When it comes to the concept of "family," here again lesbians and gays are potentially bicultural. On one hand, whether or not they or their families are conflicted over their status, they are members of multigenerational families of origin that continue across time. On the other hand, some lesbians and gays stretch the definition of "family" to include some marginalized configurations.

As evidenced by the frequency with which lesbians and gays present with family-of-origin issues, and by the growing body of literature about this issue (Iasenza, Colucci, & Rothberg, 1996; Johnson & Keren, 1996; Krestan, 1988; Krestan & Bepko, 1980; Laird, 1993; Morales, 1990; Roth, 1989; Roth & Murphy, 1986),the family of origin is not an entity that fades away upon an individual's coming out. Lesbians and gays continue in reciprocally influential relationships with parents, siblings, and extended family members that span the life cycle. In addition, many lesbians and gays have had heterosexual nuclear families with children, and continue in these systems as well for the duration of their lives. And, as Bowen (1978) reminds us, membership in these systems persists regardless of distance or cutoff. Lesbians and gays are reared in the same dominant culture as heterosexuals and internalize the same sets of norms, values, and beliefs. However, as authors such as Slater (1995) and Siegel and Lowe (1994) remind us, lesbians and gays also reinvent and recast their notions of family in order to suit the idiosyncratic experiences of lesbian/gay life.

Slater (1995) provides a useful outline of the ways in which some mainstream constructions of family are not as relevant to the families formed by lesbians and gays. A primary issue appears in the basic definition of what constitutes a family. Dominant heterosexual definitions revolve around blood and legal ties. The research of anthropologist Kath Weston (1991) demonstrates that lesbians and gays often use broader criteria to define their families. She finds that often close friends are enumerated as family members, and that such individuals compose a "family of choice" or a "family of creation." This is not a new invention, since "fictive kin" have been a part of African American families for generations (Boyd-Franklin, 1989). However, a key question is whether chosen family members are accorded the respect and recognition they deserve as kin.

There is also variation in what constitutes a couple in the lesbian/gay world. This category might include committed couples who have never lived together (sometimes seen among older lesbians and gays, who lived in a more dangerous, pre-Stonewall era); couples with no sexual relationship (known historically, in the case of women, as "Boston marriages"); sexually "open" lesbian and gay couples; and ex-lovers who decide to spend their lives together.

In addition, Slater (1995) maintains that lesbians and gays often do not rely on family norms in traditional ways. For example, even though there is a lesbian and gay "baby boom," child rearing is not the primary purpose of family life (as it generally is for heterosexual families). Generativity concerns may also be addressed by lesbians and gay families through mentorship of younger members of the community or through social activism.

Finally, the invention and reconstruction of family norms have implications for the use of family-related language. There are no names for some of the aspects of lesbian/gay family life. But the language vacuum can also have a positive aspect, in that lesbians and gays can *choose* names that more closely suit their experiences.

CONCLUSIONS

The four areas addressed here are key dimensions by which to understand the variations in family and relational norms assumed by lesbians and gays. However, many more variations and exceptions exist, because there is not one monolithic lesbian/gay community, but in fact diverse communities. This chapter has provided only the briefest and most limited of introductions to this topic. The references provided can serve as a guide for those who wish to expand their knowledge.

REFERENCES

American Psychiatric Association. (1994). *Diagnostic and statistical manual of mental disorders* (4th ed.). Washington, DC: Author.

Blumstein, P., & Schwartz, P. (1983). *American couples: Money, work, and sex.* New York: Morrow.

Bowen, M. (1978). *Family therapy in clinical practice.* New York: Jason Aronson.

Boyd-Franklin, N. (1989). *Black families in therapy: A multisystems approach.* New York: Guilford Press.

Carl, D. (1990). *Counseling same-sex couples.* New York: Norton.

Carrier, J. (1976). Family attitudes and Mexican male homosexuality. *Urban Life, 5*(3), 359–375.

Cass, V. (1979). Homosexual identity formation: A theoretical model. *Journal of Homosexuality, 4,* 219–235.

Chan, C. S. (1989). Issues of identity development among Asian-American lesbians and gay men. *Journal of Counseling and Development, 68,* 16–20.

D'Ercole, A. (1996). Post-modern ideas about gender and sexuality: The lesbian woman redundancy. *Psychoanalysis and Psychotherapy, 13*(2), 142–152.

Font, R. (1997). Making sense of privilege and pain. *In the Family, 2*(3), 9.

Goldner, V. (1988). Generation and gender: Normative and covert hierarchies. *Family Process, 27,* 17–31.

Goldner, V. (1991). Toward a critical relational theory of gender. *Psychoanalytic Dialogues, 1,* 249–272.

Green, R. (1987). *The "sissy boy syndrome" and the development of homosexuality.* New Haven, CT: Yale University Press.

Greene, B. (1994). Ethnic-minority lesbians and gay men: Mental health and treatment issues. *Journal of Consulting and Clinical Psychology, 62,* 243–251.

Greene, B., & Boyd-Franklin, N. (1996). African American lesbians: Issues in couples therapy. In J. Laird & R.-J. Green (Eds.), *Lesbians and gays in couples and families: A handbook for therapists* (pp. 251–271). San Francisco: Jossey-Bass.

Griffin, C. W., Wirth, M. J., & Wirth, A. J. (1986). *Beyond acceptance: Parents of lesbians and gays talk about their experiences.* Englewood Cliffs, NJ: Prentice-Hall.

Hare-Mustin, R. (1987). The problem of gender in family therapy theory. *Family Process, 26,* 15–33.

Herek, G. M. (1984). Beyond "homophobia": A social psychological perspective on attitudes toward lesbians and gay men. *Journal of Homosexuality, 10*(1–2), 1–21.

Iasenza, S. (1995). Platonic pleasures and dangerous desires: Psychoanalytic theory, sex research, and lesbian sexuality. In J. M. Glassgold & S. Iasenza (Eds.), *Lesbians and psychoanalysis: Revolutions in theory and practice* (pp. 345–373). New York: Free Press.

Iasenza, S., Colucci, P. L., & Rothberg, B. (1996). Coming out and the mother–daughter bond: Two case examples. In J. Laird & R.-J. Green (Eds.), *Lesbians and gays in couples and families: A handbook for therapists* (pp. 123–136). San Francisco: Jossey-Bass.

Johnson, T. W., & Keren, M. S. (1996). Creating and maintaining boundaries in male couples. In J. Laird & R.-J. Green (Eds.), *Lesbians and gays in couples and families: A handbook for therapists* (pp. 231–250). San Francisco: Jossey-Bass.

Keren, M. S. (1993). Gay and lesbian issues in clinical work with adolescents. *New Jersey Psychologist, 43*(3), 26–28.

Krestan, J. (1988). Lesbian daughters and lesbian mothers: The crisis of disclosure from a family systems perspective. *Journal of Psychotherapy and the Family, 3*(4), 113–130.

Krestan, J., & Bepko, C. (1980). The problem of fusion in the lesbian relationship. *Family Process, 19*(3), 277–289.

Kurdek, L. A., & Schmitt, J. P. (1985–1986). Relationship quality of gay men in closed or open relationships. *Journal of Homosexuality, 12,* 85–99.

Laird, J. (1993). Lesbian and gay families. In F. Walsh (Ed.), *Normal family processes* (2nd ed., pp. 282–328). New York: Guilford Press.

Loulan, J. (1987). *Lesbian passion: Loving ourselves and each other.* San Francisco: Spinsters/Aunt Lute.

Lukes, C. A., & Land, H. (1990). Biculturality and homosexuality. *Social Work, 35,* 155–161.

Morales, E. (1990). Ethnic minority families and minority gays and lesbians. In F. Bozett & M. Sussman (Eds.), *Homosexuality and family relations* (pp. 217–239). Binghamton, NY: Haworth Press.

Morales, E. (1996). Gender roles among Latino gay and bisexual men: Implications for family and couple relationships. In J. Laird & R.-J. Green (Eds.), *Lesbians and gays in couples and families: A handbook for therapists* (pp. 272–297). San Francisco: Jossey-Bass.

Peplau, L. A. (1991). Lesbian and gay relationships. In J. C. Gonsiorek & J. D. Weinrich (Eds.), *Homosexuality: Research implications for public policy* (pp. 177–196). Newbury Park, CA: Sage.

Roth, S. (1989). Psychotherapy with lesbian couples: Individual issues, female socialization and the social context. In M. McGoldrick, C. M. Anderson, & F. Walsh (Eds.), *Women in families: A framework for family therapy* (pp. 286–307). New York: Norton.

Roth, S., & Murphy, B. C. (1986). Therapeutic work with lesbian clients: A systemic therapy view. In M. Aulte-Riche & J. C. Hansen (Eds.), *Women and family therapy* (pp. 78–89). Gaithersburg, MD: Aspen.

Savin-Williams, R. C. (1996). Self-labeling and disclosure among gay, lesbian, and bisexual youths. In J. Laird & R.-J. Green (Eds.), *Lesbians and gays in couples and families: A handbook for therapists* (pp. 231–250). San Francisco: Jossey-Bass.

Siegel, S., & Lowe, E., Jr. (1994). *Uncharted lives: Understanding the life passages of gay men.* New York: Dutton.

Slater, S. (1995). *The lesbian family life cycle.* New York: Free Press.

Weston, K. (1991). *Families we choose: Lesbians, gays, kinship.* New York: Columbia University Press.

CHAPTER 25

Latinas in the United States

BRIDGING TWO WORLDS

Nydia Garcia-Preto

> They stand on a bridge between two worlds, rejecting
> and loving, frightened and hopeful, screaming and
> praying, taking steps back and forth, learning to
> choose how much to change and how much to stay
> the same. They are learning to take care of
> themselves.

Latinas in the United States represent many different countries, races, cultures, and socioeconomic groups. Their adjustment to U.S. society varies, depending on why they come, the support systems they have here, the color of their skin, their level of education, and their fluency in English (Garcia-Preto, 1996; Vasquez, 1994). The stage of life they are in when they arrive is very significant, as is the place where they settle. The experience of a 15-year-old *mestiza* who settles in Washington, DC, with her parents after experiencing the trauma of war in El Salvador will be very different from that of a 34-year-old Black Dominican arriving with her 2-year-old son to live with her 40-year-old cousin who is raising four children by herself in the Bronx. However, whether we Latinas are wealthy, poor, professionals, laborers, housewives, or prostitutes, certain values are transferred down to us if we grow up in homes where our parents hold some allegiance to their Latin culture. Most of us are caught in cultural paradoxes as we struggle to shape our identities, from early in life onward (Comas-Díaz, 1994a; Garcia-Preto, 1994; Boyd-Franklin & Garcia-Preto, 1994; Gil & Vazquez, 1996). It is a lifelong process!

The process of Latinas adapting to mainstream American culture is always in flux, as new immigrants arrive and older generations dream of returning home. For most of us it is a process of selective adaptation, becoming American only to the extent that it feels safe. Sometimes while making our lives here, we lose our language and connection to the land and history that gave our ancestors essence. White skin and European looks, or Black skin and African features, make it easier to pass for "American," but always with a feeling of apprehension—of being found out and seen as impostors, second-class Americans. Marrying a blonde-haired, blue-eyed American may guarantee our children's passing, but the Indian and African genes of our ancestors will probably make our children look like beautifully tanned, almond-eyed Latinos. It is through our children's search for identity that we often find our roots and revel in the glory of our history, the pride of our people.

This chapter is about us Latinas as we find our place in the United States, make our lives, and live our dreams. Walking a tightrope, balancing at the edge of a cliff, we often live between two worlds. Stories about mothers and daughters—distant and close, rejecting and loving, learning from each other to fight, to dream, and to die—portray our struggles, pain, and liberation as we move through the life cycle negotiating cultural conflicts at different stages. Some of us hold on tightly to our Latina roots, afraid that if we step into the "American" world, we will fall into a precipice and lose ourselves. Others leap into the new world, rejecting our past and hoping to find a better place with more options. The therapeutic interventions I offer are intended to help Latinas build bridges that connect the two worlds, and to provide a safe place from which to choose what to keep from the old culture and what to take from the new. They provide perspective about the sociopolitical context in which Latinas live, and the ways in which prejudice and racism affect their lives. The goal is to encourage transformation and liberation of the spirit by validating personal strengths, maintaining family connections, and creating a sense of community and support.

GOOD LITTLE GIRLS

Traditionally, Latinas have been raised by their mothers with the help of grandmothers and other women in the family. In this country, where expectations of mutual aid cannot always be met, teaching daughters to guard their virginity and take care of themselves can become overwhelming and alarming for Latinas, who are often alone and isolated. At home daughters listen to their mothers' frustration, but often feel angry that they are expected to stay inside while "real American girls" go out to play with friends. Girls are expected to be obedient and respectful, and to behave in ways that are considered feminine.

As a therapist when I work with Latinas, I often hear them scream and yell at their daughters, "Stop acting like a boy. Don't climb on the couch like that—sit down with your legs crossed. Now be respectful to *la señora* when she speaks to you. Don't interrupt until she speaks to you." It all sounds so familiar. I remember being punished as a little girl for climbing trees and acting like a tomboy, and not being able to talk back to my mother because that was disrespectful. I have said to myself, and have heard other Latinas say, "I'm not raising my daughter that way"; I don't want my daughter to worry about *el que diran* (what people will say). Yet there is a part of me that worries about the strong emotions she shows, and about how people will view her if she is loud, aggressive, and competitive, and doesn't want to wear dresses with ruffles and lace. In my office, I gently put a stop to the mothers' yelling and screaming, and begin to address the care and love that mothers and daughters feel for each other.

Restrictions placed on Latinas usually increase as they get older, and sometimes limits and expectations imposed by parents are challenged by teachers and counselors at school. For example, 10-year-old Estela was referred to me by her school counselor after she had complained to her teachers about her mother's refusal to let her play sports, and about the strict rules at home in general. When I met with Estela and her mother, it became clear that Dolores, a 34-year-old Colombian, was trying very hard to raise her daughter in the best way she knew. As most Latinas do, she had the primary caretaking responsibility for her children, and was accountable to her husband for Estela's behavior. Antonio, a 36-year-old Ecuadorian, was strict and did not like Estela to go out of the house after school. After clarifying with them why the school had made the referral to me, I asked Dolores for permission to encourage Estela to talk about her unhappiness.

After listening to Estela's complaints about not being allowed to play sports or visit friends after school, Dolores explained that she didn't think playing sports was feminine, and that she worried about her daughter's getting hurt. She and Antonio wanted Estela to grow up to be a good, respectable young woman, and thought that girls who played sports were rough and wild. I asked Dolores if she had ever been to the after-school games or seen her daughter play. She hadn't. I told her that from what I have seen in this country, girls who play sports are usually good students and develop positive attitudes about themselves, which keep them from getting into trouble. I suggested that if she and her husband met with the teacher and counselor who referred them to me, they would all develop a better understanding of each other's concerns about Estela. I added that it would also give the parents a chance to ask questions about the sports program for girls. Apparently Estela had athletic talent, and the gym teacher was encouraging her to play and develop her skills. I offered to help arrange the meeting if they chose to do it.

Encouraging Dolores to ask Estela questions about why she liked playing sports, and which sport she liked better, began to make it easier for mother and daughter to talk to each other. I could see the proud smile on Dolores's face as she listened to her daughter's enthusiasm when she spoke about basketball and softball. Not only were they able to talk about sports, but the conversation expanded to friends, family, and different perceptions about how girls should act. The meeting with the teacher and counselor did take place; although Antonio was not able to attend, Dolores, with my help, asked questions about the sports program and was proud when she heard about Estela's athletic skills. The teacher and counselor also told her that usually girls who play sports stay out of trouble, because they have less time to hang around and get bored. The meeting at school, my introducing information about girls and sports in U.S. culture, and my facilitation of conversations between mother and daughter about their differences had the effect of transforming for Dolores the meaning of "good girl." A new dimension was added, which included some of the values that mainstream American culture offer to women. Estela was able to find a place for herself, while still remaining respectful of and close to her parents, which for Latinas is a source of validation and security.

WHERE HAVE ALL THE VIRGINS GONE?

Most Latinas go into high gear to guard their daughters' virginity, especially as they reach adolescence. It is as if we hear a call to respond to an ancient cultural myth about women and virginity that insures women safe futures in the hands of honorable men, but only if they are virgins. This myth emanates from the double standard about gender roles in patriarchal societies (such as those in Latin America and in the Caribbean), which limits the sexual freedom of women and gives men authority over them (Stevens, 1973; Comas-Díaz, 1991; Garcia-Preto, 1996; Gil & Vazquez, 1996). Although the double standard also applies to a lesser extent in the United States, women in U.S. society tend to experience greater sexual freedom than Latinas do in their countries of origin. The difference often creates cultural dilemmas for Latinas living in this country, especially during adolescence, and at a time in history when boys and girls seem to be engaging in sex earlier and earlier. According to the Carnegie Council on Adolescent Development (1992), 27% of U.S. girls and 33% of U.S. boys have had sexual intercourse by the age of 15, and 60% of these young people did not use contraception the first time.

In the United States, adolescent girls are given freedom to go out with girlfriends, sleep at their houses, talk with boys, and go on dates without chaperones. In contrast, Latinas tend to be supervised more closely when they go out with friends; dating doesn't take place until much later; and it is not unusual for chaperones to be present on dates. The emphasis is on protecting a girl's virginity and keeping her reputation unmarred. The responsibility for this task is given primarily to mothers. The extent to which Latino families living in this country hold on to these values depends on the length of time they have lived here, their level of education and social status, and the place where they settle. The greater the cultural gap between families and the new culture, the more likely it is for conflicts to erupt between mothers and daughters during adolescence around the issue of virginity, since children tend to adapt faster than parents to a new culture. The case of Magda, a 15-year-old, brown-skinned Salvadoran who had recently arrived in this country with her parents, illustrates this point.

Magda was referred to therapy by a bilingual social worker who ran groups at school for recently arrived Latino students. After one of the group meetings, Magda spoke to the social worker about the problems she was having at home. She was feeling trapped and frightened, and was thinking of hurting herself. She had lied about going out with a girlfriend, and instead had gone out to meet a boy; when her mother found out, she restricted her from going out of the house or speaking to friends on the telephone, and threatened to send her back to El Salvador with an uncle if she broke these rules. Magda felt that the punishment was extreme and unfair, and was angry with her mother.

When I met with them, Rosaura, Magda's mother, talked about feeling angry, betrayed, and unable to trust her daughter, whose future she thought would be ruined unless she supervised all her outings. She worried about drugs and crime, but her worst fear was that Magda would end up as she herself had done—pregnant and "having to get married." Her parents were very strict, but, like Magda, she had sneaked out to meet a boy—Miguel, her future husband. Her parents had not approved of him or his family, and had not allowed him to come to the house, but when she became pregnant at 16 they had made her get married. Rosaura was in love and wanted the baby, but as they struggled with poverty and lived through the war in their country, Miguel began to drink heavily and to distance himself emotionally. She wanted Magda to have a different life; this was why she had pushed to come to this country, in hope of a better future.

As she talked about her past in therapy, Rosaura stated clearly that she did not want to repeat the mistakes her parents had made. She had tried to compromise by allowing the boy to visit Magda at home, even though she felt uneasy about not knowing his family. However, he could only visit when she was present, and Magda could not go out with him unless she had a chaperone. Magda understood that her mother was trying to meet her halfway, but was embarrassed to tell the boy. Many of the Latinas she had met at school had been in this country longer and were allowed to go out with boys without chaperones. She envied their freedom and felt embarrassed by her mother's rules. As treatment progressed, Rosaura began to see more clearly that regardless of how hard she tried to protect Magda's virginity, her daughter was in control of her own sexuality. Instead of repeating her parents' mistakes by imposing rules that she herself had broken, she began to use her life experience as a resource to teach Magda how to value herself as a woman. We talked about the fallacy in the "virginity myth," and agreed that in reality women cannot rely on men to "take care of them."

Choosing what to keep from their old culture and what to take from the new culture became a therapeutic theme. Magda began to appreciate her mother's strengths as a woman, as she listened to Rosaura talk about her present goals with regard to Miguel, who had become more and more peripheral in their lives. His drinking had continued to increase in this country, where he felt alienated and powerless. He blamed Rosaura for pushing him to come here, and was verbally abusive toward both her and Magda. Rosaura was considering a separation, but needed financial stability before making a decision. We dealt with issues of safety at home, and debated possible strategies for getting Miguel into treatment.

Listening to Rosaura speak about possible options for her own life encouraged Magda to talk about her concerns, dreams, and goals for the future. Whereas guarding Magda's virginity had formerly been Rosaura's main goal as a mother, in therapy she became her daughter's ally, planning together for a future where they could both be independent. They could be loyal and respectful toward each other without losing the emotional connection that gave them strength, or feeling bound by the patriarchal legacies that keep women obedient and dependent on men and that sexualize their sense of self-worth. Virgins and martyrs go hand in hand in Latino cultures, and their glorification perpetuates male dominance and female oppression (Vega & Filippi, 1981).

WALKING A FINE LINE:
LATINAS LIVING INDEPENDENTLY

Traditionally, most Latinas have been expected to live with their parents until they marry, and to leave home only as brides dressed in white. Going away to college may be another acceptable way to leave home, but usually they are encouraged to go to school close to home. Moving out to live alone in an apartment is hard to explain to relatives, friends, and neighbors, and puts a woman's reputation at risk. Traditionally, having a good reputation has been necessary for a woman to have a good marriage and to be acknowledged in the community as a *doña* (a woman who is deserving of respect). Having sex before marriage, especially with more than one man; expressing pleasure about having sex; and/or living alone place women precariously on the edge of losing their good reputations and being labeled as *putas* (whores). For Latinas the cultural message has been that sex is for procreation, not for pleasure. The line between *putas* and *doñas* is very fine (Stevens, 1973; Espin, 1994; Garcia-Preto, 1990; Gil & Vazquez, 1996).

Claudia, a 24-year-old Cuban, came into treatment at the suggestion of her friend Cristina, a 27-year-old Argentinian I had previously seen in therapy. Claudia worked as a store clerk and lived at home with her parents. Recently she had begun to experience anxiety attacks, and was having difficulty leaving the house to go to work or to go out with friends. Cristina thought that the problems Claudia was having at home were probably the cause. While I was taking a genogram (McGoldrick & Gerson, 1985) and asking about the situation at home, Claudia said:

> "I don't mind living at home. My parents don't stop me from going out, and I can't afford to live alone. Anyway, I would be too scared to live by myself, and my parents' fear would be so great that they would die from a heart attack! They are constantly worrying, and advising me about friends and the men I meet. Cristina lives with another friend and would like me to join them, but my parents don't approve of her because she goes out with all kinds of men, and people talk."

Finding the right man had become a primary goal for Claudia, who felt that the only way she could leave home was through marriage. Her parents' approval was very important, and the man's acceptance of her obligation toward them was essential. Her parents had come to the United States in the 1970s, and had had problems adjusting and making a living. Now in their early 60s, they were thinking about retirement. They still held on to many of the traditional values that were part of their culture, and expected Claudia to be respectful, loyal, and protective of her reputation. She was the youngest of three children and the only daughter. The two older brothers were married and living busy lives with their families in nearby towns, which kept them less involved with their parents. Their absence increased Claudia's sense of obligation toward her parents, fitting with the cultural expectation in Latino families that women are the caretakers. It is not uncommon for Latinas who assume, or are assigned this type of caretaking role to remain single (Hines, Garcia-Preto, McGoldrick, Almeida, & Weltman, 1992).

In therapy, Claudia began to define more clearly her own values, attitudes, and beliefs about life, people, relationships, and sexuality. She spoke about her personal dreams and ambitions, and recognized that in order to feel freer to make decisions about her life, she needed to have greater financial independence. Her anxiety lessened, and with Cristina's help she enrolled in some college courses, which helped her gain confidence. The more clear she became about her personal goals, the less bound she felt by cultural expectations that limited her potential. For instance, she realized that she could be close to her parents and show them respect without losing her individuality or choice to exercise her rights as an adult woman. She felt more entitled to spend weekends away from home with friends, and to keep some of her relationships with men private, without feeling that she was being disloyal to her parents. The parents' fears didn't go away, but because Claudia felt more competent and confident herself, she was less frightened about moving on with her life. Unlike Cristina, who loved the freedom and anonymity she had in this country, Claudia had ties to the Latino community and wanted to keep these connections. She still wanted to share her life with a good man and to have her own family; however, she realized that making these the primary goals in her life had placed her in a powerless and helpless position, with little option for making decisions that promoted her well-being.

BREAKING ALL THE RULES: LATINA LESBIANS

Latinas who "come out" as lesbians break all the rules. They are openly challenging a culture where women have limited options, especially if they don't marry a man and have children. They struggle against beliefs that link women's femininity to the Virgin Mary, mother of God. To want a woman, to make love to a woman—these things mean assuming a position of power in a culture where men dominate and are free to express their sexuality in ways for which women would be condemned. Latina lesbians are perceived not only as rejecting the essence of being female, but as usurping male power; thus, they are a double threat to the culture.

When Ana, a 26-year-old Puerto Rican lawyer who was a closeted lesbian, spoke in therapy about her terror of coming out to her mother, I understood the spiritual desolation a Latina can feel for breaking the rules her mother lives by.

"Just the thought of telling my mother that I'm a lesbian makes me panic. She wouldn't be able to deal with it at all. I would lose my family. My mother believes that homosexuality is a sin, and it would kill her to know that I am choosing this lifestyle. One of my sisters knows, but she thinks that if the right man came along I would get over it. I want to move in with Vicky and not have to lie about our relationship to my family, but the fear of losing them is paralyzing. Sometimes I think God is punishing me."

Ana anticipated that her mother would be shocked, devastated, and furious at her for bringing dishonor to the family. She could hear her mother say, "How can you be so disrespectful to dare tell me such a thing? You were put on this earth to be a woman, to have children, to be a good mother and wife. You are going against God. How dare you disgrace this family?" The fear both of losing her family and of being punished by God kept her in the closet.

For Latinas, being lesbians means that they go against two moral prohibitions that the culture imposes, especially on women: sexuality and homosexuality. They fear rejection by their mothers, the culture, and the community, often hiding and denying who they are while feeling damaged and unacceptable (Anzaldua, 1987). I could hear Ana's fear and sadness as she envisioned her mother's horror; I was reminded of how, 35 years after her death, I still catch myself imagining the dismay of my dead mother's spirit at how I live my own life. I used the metaphor of the bridge to help Ana find a way to stay connected to her mother in Puerto Rico and the parts of the Latino world that still nurtured her, while also validating her life in this world. I was exhilarated when Ana was able to write a letter in which she came out to her mother, while also expressing her love and inviting her mother to visit. Although there was fear in her eyes, there was also the glow of liberation.

Cherrie Moraga, in her book *The Last Generation* (1993), talks about the active role that lesbians have played in the area of Chicana liberation (e.g., their work on sexual abuse, domestic violence, immigrant rights, indigenous women's issues, health care, etc.). Because of the marginalization and rejection that they often experience in both their families and their culture, lesbians are in a special position to address areas that need change in both contexts. Chicana lesbian writers such as Moraga and Anzaldua (Anzaldua, 1987; Anzaldua & Moraga, 1983; Moraga, 1993) have been among the first to explore how homophobia, gender roles, and sexuality are learned and expressed in Chicano culture. They have been pioneers in establishing a Chicana feminist perspective, which has influenced not only lesbians but heterosexual women who have been socialized in Latin American cultures. Their poetry and prose have given voice to the struggles that many Latina lesbians face when they try to integrate cultural values into their lives that deny their being. I have found sharing their work with lesbian clients helpful in promoting transformation and liberation in their lives.

MOTHERHOOD

Motherhood is probably the most important goal in life for Latinas, and the acclaim they receive when their first child is born is a great reinforcer, especially if the baby is a boy. Motherhood has been romanticized in Latino literature and music, and the associations made between mothers and the Virgin Mary have an explicitly religious quality. Having children both raises the status of women in society and is a rite of passage into adulthood, which confirms both the masculinity of the father and the femininity of the mother (Garcia-Preto, 1990; Gil & Vazquez, 1996). Becoming a mother, however, also implies that a woman must sacrifice herself for the children. This emphasis on motherhood and self-sacrifice creates dilemmas for women who cannot have children, who choose not to have them, or who have them but also work and have lives outside the home. Can they be respected and valued as women by their families and friends if they don't have children? And what price do they pay if they do have children, but must take jobs in order to survive?

Working outside the home is a necessity for many Latinas in this country, but it forces them to fulfill conflicting role expectations. According to official statistics in the late 1980s 50% of Hispanic women in the United States were employed (U.S. Department of Labor, 1989). Not being able to stay home to raise and protect their children places such women in a dilemma, especially when other women in the extended family are unable to offer support with child care. Mutual aid in the extended family has been a cultural pattern that provides support and flexibility for women, but for Latinas in this country it may not be an option. Often they have no female relatives here, and if they do, the other women may be too overwhelmed themselves to provide support. According to the culture, a good mother doesn't put her children at risk by leaving them with "strangers" (i.e., anyone outside the family). When confronted with conflicting role expectations, they are likely to choose their role as mothers, even when it causes problems for them at work.

Celia, a 34-year-old, Dominican "Lati-Negra" (Comas-Díaz, 1994b), was referred to therapy by an Employee Assistance Program counselor. She worked at a factory, and her frequent absences from work had become a problem. Even when she did make it to work, she seemed preoccupied; her level of productivity had diminished to the extent that she was on the verge of losing her job. Celia had recently arrived with her 2-

year-old son to live with a cousin. Unmarried, poor, and with little education, she came to the United States looking for a better life and future. Once here, however, she had to experience not only the shock of a new culture and language, but the prejudice and racism of a society that rejects Blacks.

Her 40-year-old cousin, Mercedes, had come to this country almost 20 years ago, shortly after her marriage; she was now divorced and struggling financially to raise four children on her own in a neighborhood plagued with crime, drugs, prostitution, and AIDS. She provided Celia with a place to stay and helped her find a factory job. However, because she was emotionally drained by her children's various problems, she had quickly felt the burden of two more people depending on her. Celia had started to work, and Mercedes was temporarily taking care of her son, but she knew that she needed to find a place to live and permanent child care. Her anxiety had escalated with the pressure of knowing that she would have to "fly solo" (Anderson, 1994) in this new world sooner than she had expected.

In therapy, Celia talked about feeling guilty and fearful whenever she left her son. She wanted to be a good mother, and the thought of leaving him with strangers or in a day care center frightened her. Even now that Mercedes was caring for him, she found leaving him intolerable. This was exacerbated by her son's fearful crying whenever she went out to work. However, she needed to work in order to make a life in this country, and missing work to stay home with him was jeopardizing her job. She was regretting her decision to come to this country, and considered the possibility of returning or of sending her son to Santo Domingo to stay with her mother. Framing her son's behavior as a normal reaction to separation at that stage of child development reduced some of her fear and guilt. Feeling less anxious about leaving her son, she began to look for child care; through a woman at work, she learned about a day care center in the neighborhood where other Latinas took their children.

Taking her son to the day care center helped Celia to connect with other women, and to feel less isolated and dependent on Mercedes. Initially, she had expected from her cousin the type of support that Latinas have traditionally provided for each other in their extended families, and she felt resentful and disappointed when Mercedes began to set limits. Inviting Mercedes to a therapy session helped strengthen their connection as they reviewed their family history in the Dominican Republic, their failed relationships with men, and their reasons for migrating. They laughed and cried while telling family stories, especially those that Mercedes remembered about Celia's childhood. Listening to her cousin speak about the problems she was having with her 18-year-old son, who lived at home and was addicted to heroin, and with her 16-year-old daughter, who had just returned home pregnant after running away with an abusive, alcoholic 20-year-old man, helped Celia understand why Mercedes needed to set limits.

Framing Celia's problems within a social context that is racist and prejudiced against Latinas, especially when their skin color is dark, helped her put into words some of the feelings of oppression she was experiencing at work. She had felt the looks, and even though she didn't understand English, people's tone and attitude when they spoke to her felt demeaning. Although Mercedes was trying to sponsor her, she was not yet a legal resident; this added to her anxiety, especially at work, but also whenever she had to seek medical care for herself or her son. Through our discussion, she stopped feeling personally responsible for the racist attitudes of people at work. Encouraging Celia to expand her network of connections helped her to learn about safe places where she could go for health care, and to find information about getting her immigration papers in order. As she got more in touch with her strengths, her work performance improved and she was able to offer more support to Mercedes, who no longer experienced her as a burden. She felt less pressured to move out right away, and less anxious about her son, who seemed to be adjusting well at the day care center. Although she still missed him, she no longer felt neglectful when she went to work. Instead, she felt that she was being a good mother by earning enough money to pay for good child care and to save for their own place. Motherhood continued to be the most important role for Celia, but it was no longer her only goal or identity. Taking care of herself and taking charge of her life became goals that enabled her to be both, a responsible woman and a caring mother.

ANSWERING THE CALL:
LATINAS CARING FOR RELATIVES

Answering the call to take care of old, poor, or frail parents or other relatives is deeply rooted in the soul and imprinted in the heart of Latinas; it is another rite of passage that defines womanhood. Not being able to meet that obligation stirs up incredible guilt in us Latinas and raises questions about our womanhood. My mother died at 48, and I, as the oldest granddaughter, felt the responsibility of taking care of her mother, who lived until she was 93. The problem was that she lived in Puerto Rico and I in the United States, and changing residence for either one of us would have been impossible. For some of her neighbors and relatives, however, the solution was clear: I should move back to the island. My grandmother had come to live with us in the States when my mother was still alive, and it had not worked. She didn't like the winters or the isolation of living in the suburbs. My mother couldn't stand the constant complaints and felt criticized. Fed up with their arguing, and feeling called upon to serve as a mediator, I couldn't wait to go to graduate school far enough away that commuting wouldn't be an option. To my parents, leaving home to go to college was an acceptable alternative to leaving home as a bride dressed in white.

Grandmother—fragile in health but strong in spirit—decided to return to the island, where she could keep the doors and windows open for neighbors to stop and chat, and could walk to the corner store without asking someone to go and talk for her because she didn't know the language. Sad and feeling like a failure, my mother worried about her mother's health, but understood that not everyone can adjust to living in this country (where neighbors stay in their homes, barely saying hello as they climb in and out of their cars or do their chores in the yard). Shortly after this, my mother died. It was now my turn to worry about my grandmother, and to feel disloyal whenever I would get a call from a relative to come visit because her health was declining. She held on for 10 years after my mother's death, and I traveled back and forth to the island—always feeling shame in my heart that I wasn't meeting my obligation, but knowing in my mind that I was doing as much as I could and still live my life.

CONCLUSION

Cultures don't remain static; they are always in flux. For us Latinas in the United States, a new reality evolves as we integrate two cultures. My personal knowledge of what it means to live between two worlds is a major part of what I offer Latina clients. It is what enables them to trust me with their struggles and to look to me for guidance. Even after living here for decades, some Latinas and Latinos are still struggling with cultural shock. My job is to help them understand, often for the first time, the cultural journey they are still embarked upon. What I offer beyond my skill as a therapist, my sociopolitical awareness, and my own experience of immigration is my optimism. Although it is never easy, I know it is possible to shuttle between these two worlds. I am able to share the metaphor of the bridge as a safe place to understand the world in which they grew up and the possibilities of the new world they have entered. When I help people construct the bridges they need for this journey between cultures, my own bridge becomes sturdier and wider (Garcia-Preto, 1994).

REFERENCES

Anderson, C. (1994). *Flying solo.* New York: Norton.

Anzaldua, G. (1987). *Borderlands, la frontera: The new Mestiza.* San Francisco: Aunt Lute.

Anzaldua, G., & Moraga, C. (1983). *This bridge called my back: Writings by radical women of color.* New York: Kitchen Table: Women of Color Press.

Boyd-Franklin, N., & Garcia-Preto, N. (1994). Family therapy: The case of African American and Hispanic women. In L. Comas-Díaz & B. Greene (Eds.), *Women of color: Integrating ethnic and gender identities in psychotherapy* (pp. 239—286). New York: Guilford Press.

Carnegie Council on Adolescent Development, Task Force on Youth Development and Community Programs. (1992). *A matter of time: Risk and opportunities in non-school hours.* New York: Carnegie Corporation.

Comas-Díaz, L. (1991). Feminism and diversity in psychology: The case of women of color. *Psychology of Women Quarterly, 15,* 597–609.

Comas-Díaz, L. (1994a). Integrative approach. In L. Comas-Díaz & B. Greene (Eds.), *Women of color: Integrating ethnic and gender identities in psychotherapy* (pp. 287–318). New York: Guilford Press.

Comas-Díaz, L. (1994b). Lati-Negra. *Journal of Feminist Family Therapy, 5*(3–4), 35–74.

Espin, O. M. (1994). Feminist approaches. In L. Comas-Díaz & B. Greene (Eds.), *Women of color: Integrating ethnic and gender identities in psychotherapy* (pp. 265–286). New York: Guilford Press.

Garcia-Preto, N. (1990). Hispanic mothers. *Journal of Feminist Family Therapy, 2*(2), 15–21.

Garcia-Preto, N. (1994). On the bridge. *Family Therapy Networker, 18*(4), 35–37.

Garcia-Preto, N. (1996). Latinos: An overview. In M. McGoldrick, J. Giordano, & J. K. Pearce (Eds.), *Ethnicity and family therapy* (2nd ed., pp. 141–154). New York: Guilford Press.

Gil, R. M., & Vazquez, C. I. (1996). *The Maria paradox.* New York: Putnam.

Hines, P. M., Garcia-Preto, N., McGoldrick, M., Almeida, R., & Weltman, S. (1992). Intergenerational relationships across cultures. *Families in Society: The Journal of Contemporary Human Services, 23,* 323–328.

McGoldrick, M., & Gerson, R. (1985). *Genograms in family assessment.* New York: Norton.

Moraga, C. (1993). *The last generation: Prose and poetry.* Boston: South End Press.

Stevens, E. D. (1973). *Marianismo:* The other face of *Machismo* in Latin America. In A. De Castello (Ed.), *Female and male in Latin America.* Pittsburgh: University of Pittsburgh Press.

U.S. Department of Labor. (1989). *Women and management* (Facts on Working Women, No. 89 4). Washington, DC: U.S. Government Printing Office.

Vasquez, M. J. T. (1994). In L. Comas-Díaz & B. Greene (Eds.), *Women of color: Integrating ethnic and gender identities in psychotherapy* (pp. 114–160). New York: Guilford Press.

Vega, A. L., & Filippi, C. L. (1981). *Virgenes y martires.* Rio Piedras, Puerto Rico: Editorial Antillana.

PART VI

MIGRATION

Immigrants, more than anyone else, experience U.S. society from a multicultural perspective. Their bicultural lens can be a model for the cultural flexibility we require as family therapists in the most culturally diverse nation that has ever existed.

Coming to terms with our diversity as a nation transforms our awareness of what it means to be quintessentially American. As Sanford Ungar (1997) writes of becoming conscious of the meaning of his family's migration for him, a great-grandchild of Eastern European Jewish immigrants: "I was no less American than ever before, of course, but now, in middle age, I had discovered my own immigrant consciousness. Indeed, in that sense, I could now feel more authentically American" (p. 18). Only by attending to the multiplicitous voices that have until now been silenced in the dominant story of many who we are as a nation, can we become "more authentically American." Although immigrants from the countries of Africa, Hmong refugees and other immigrants from Asia, and all those entering from the various "Hispanic" nations and territories have their own cultures of origin and particular experiences of migration and/or dislocation, they need equally to feel themselves included in the definition of "American."

The recent dramatic increase in immigrants in the United States is forcing us to come to terms with our multiculturality. At no time in our nation's history have so many people born abroad been residents of the United States (Roberts, 1994). And never before, despite previous waves of immigration, has our nation been so diverse. This is forcing us to challenge our unquestioned assumptions about who we are and what our values should be. The cultural richness and complexity of the immigrant generation, especially those whose cultures are most different from the dominant European American values of our society, offer us the greatest possibilities for re-visioning who we are and who we can be. Our diversity can become our greatest strength. When we instead fear our diversity, our prejudices and rigidities as a nation are highlighted. Our fears can result in the pernicious exclusion of others and the dehumanization of those who are not considered to "belong."

Family therapy has ignored this multicultural dimension of our society. We have developed models without accounting for their cultural limitations. We have failed to notice that families from many cultural groups never come to our therapy, or do not find our techniques helpful. It is we who must change to include them.

The three chapters in this section, by Matthew Mock, Carlos Sluzki, and Marsha Mirkin, address the profound disruptions of migration; describe the complexities of biculturality when families belong to more than one culture, as most families in the United States do; and suggest some of the larger implications of considering biculturality, difference, and acculturation. If we read them carefully, they can help us rethink the very nature of our identity (Tataki, 1997). Instead of measuring immigrants as "others," we will use their experience to re-vision our very notions of assessment and intervention.

REFERENCES

Roberts, S. (1994). *Who we are: A portrait of America based on the latest U.S. census.* New York: Times Books.

Tataki, R. (Ed.). (1997). *From different shores: Perspectives on race and ethnicity in America* (2nd ed.). New York: Oxford University Press.

Unger, S. (1997). *Fresh blood: The new American immigrants.* New York: Simon & Schuster.

CHAPTER 26

Clinical Reflections on Refugee Families

TRANSFORMING CRISES INTO OPPORTUNITIES

Matthew R. Mock

The Chinese characters that form the word for "listening" have greater relevance for the family therapist working with refugees. The written word for *Ting* or "ultimate listening" involves complexities of the "ear" (for taking in important information), "you" (the centered therapist), "eyes" (for observing and contrasting perspectives), "undivided attention" (oneness with the other), and "heart" (for being sensitive, being emotionally present, and conveying deep understanding).

THE CONTEXT: THE SIGNIFICANCE OF REFUGEE MOVEMENTS AND FAMILIES

Refugeeism is a global phenomenon that has existed throughout world history. In particular, the United States has been consistently characterized as a country composed of a constant influx of newcomers, many of whom are refugees. Since 1975, over 14 million people have been uprooted throughout the world and have resettled in America. Wars and other conflicts, as well as social, economic, and environmental turmoil, have led to an influx of displaced families. In fact, displacement and resettlement patterns have been so tremendous that the 20th century has been called "the century of the uprooted" (United Nations High Commissioner for Refugees, 1981). Major groups of refugees during this century have included survivors of World War II; Southeast Asians; victims of strife in Africa, the Middle East, Bosnia, and Central and South America; Cuban and Haitian expellees; and political and ideological opponents of various dictatorships.

Although the magnitude of refugee movements may seem to be on the rise, in actuality American history shows that many immigrant groups were themselves in many ways refugees. For immigrant families, there may be a "pull," or attraction to migrate; for refugees, there is a "push," or little choice but to leave in order to escape persecution or oppression. Refugees may be forced to leave their homelands because of their race, ethnicity, religion, social group, or political opinion (Nicassio, 1985; Mock, 1991). Refugee families are involuntarily displaced, often fleeing under conditions over which they have minimal or no control, and often moving from one country to another. The continual sense of physical, psychological, and emotional "homelessness" for family members may be profound. Refugeeism, or migration under ongoing stressors may be so disruptive that it is as though another stage, often of multiple crises is added to the life cycle (Carter & McGoldrick, 1988; Mock, 1994).

There has been growing interest in examining the psychological processes involved in the sequelae of abrupt, traumatic separation from one's "mother country" or "fatherland." The experience of culture shock and loss, with appropriate mourning, leads to extreme readjustment on both the individual and family levels. Several authors and therapists (Rumbaut, 1985; Akhtar, 1995; Mock, 1991; Cole, Espin, & Rothblum, 1992) have written about the repeated challenges refugeeism poses to an otherwise stable personal identity. In particular, individual recovery for refugees who have faced torture, starvation, rape, and/or other dehumanizing experiences is often extremely difficult.

The disorganizing circumstances of families forced to flee include multiple losses of homeland, significant family members, social status, cultural possessions, and other meaningful sources of identity and validation. Systemically, such profound losses constitute major transitions that can disrupt, distort, or stop life cycle patterns of family interaction (Carter & McGoldrick, 1988). Refugee families are thrown into chaos and disequilibrium. Previously agreed-upon norms and values may be immediately challenged and questioned. Family members of different life experiences, social backgrounds, and ages may have very different processes and rates of adjustment and acculturation. Cultural identity is powerfully intertwined with experiences of loss and mourning (Levy-Warren, 1987). Drawing connections between the current family problems and the experiences of refugeeism can be a powerful therapeutic intervention.

INDIVIDUAL AND FAMILY ASSESSMENT

The Therapist's Stance

In order to gain a clear picture of the dynamics both in refugees as individuals and in refugee families, a careful, in-depth evaluation is necessary. The stance of the evaluating therapist should be respectfully curious and open to cultural sharing. Cultural empathy without cultural stereotyping is essential to creating therapeutic rapport. A multicultural, multidisciplinary approach can be extremely useful in recreating the culturally familiar sense of "community." Cultural consultants and community workers can enhance a therapist's credibility and a refugee family's sense of being given to in the evaluation process; indeed, the participation of such consultants may be essential in the initial stages of building rapport.

The therapist's awareness that his or her own status is more stable and secure than that of the refugee family, and that he or she needs to learn about the family's status and perspective, helps guide the approach. Cultural sharing, soliciting stories, and asking for information about cultural norms can be extremely useful. The therapist can actually create openings to share previously shameful material of problems, conflicts, and solutions, as in this example. A young Afghani man in college gave up his studies in law for the arts. This formed the crux of dispute in the family, especially with his father. During one of the early family sessions, I asked the father to tell me what things were like in his homeland. He described how his brother, a judge, had been killed during the exodus, and noted that his son had been given a nickname in Farsi to honor the uncle. This was the first time the son had heard this, and it led to more open discussions about the father's hopes, dreams, and disappointments as head of a refugee family. Reinforcing these linkages to their culture opened up more communication between father and son.

Exploration of the Relationship between Refugeeism and Family Conflict

For refugees, who have encountered so many profound changes, acknowledging the connections between family conflict and their transition is often key. Developing a comprehensive transitional map that extends multigenerationally beyond the refugee generation can open up new possibilities (Landau-Stanton, 1990). In addition, outlining each current family member's life cycle stage, cultural origin, and present status; defining the impinging political, economic, and social forces; and establishing the continuity of past and present can all offer openings for future choices.

The individual and family assessment process can begin to create such openings. Assessment of the physical status of family members may be an important way to start, as many refugees have experienced trauma, torture, or injuries prior to their exodus. The impact of past experiences in refugee camps, such as malnutrition, parasites, or unattended illnesses, often extends into the present. Since somatizing is a common cultural expression of depression (Mock, 1995), attending to physical, concrete problems can strengthen the therapeutic relationship.

The following areas should also be assessed, via respectful questioning that proceeds from the family's initial responses. (For more details, see Lee, 1990, and Budman & Ponton, 1986.)

1. *Premigration history* (the foundation before the exodus)
   Family structure (untimely losses, survivors, roles assumed and expected, family members missing or unaccounted for, etc.)
   Socioeconomic status, including family members' occupations, rural versus urban residence, and the family's rank or caste in the homeland
   Stresses encountered prior to the exodus (losses, deaths, camp experiences, victimization, torture, other forced behavior.

2. *Migration history* (the uprooting and departure)
   Reasons why individuals and/or the family as a whole left (war, poverty, political differences, draft evasion, etc.)
   Circumstances of exodus: Was it planned or abrupt? Was it by choice or force? Is departure acknowledged to be permanent, or is there a fantasy about returning?
   Special roles of any family members: Was someone specially "chosen" to leave or to bring others? Did anyone stay behind (and, if so, was this by choice or force)?

3. *Postmigration history* (the process of adjustment)
   Current standard of living and family composition, including extended community supports
   Racism, discrimination, and oppression encountered in the United States
   Experiences of "culture shock"; conflicts between traditional and mainstream U.S. values
   Current sociopolitical context (anti-immigration laws, English-only legislation, normalized relations between the United States and the home country, public acknowledgement or apologies for injustices, etc.)

Other Considerations in Assessment

In cases where baselines are important, individual family members may be assessed through interviews. Such dialogue and reflections should usually concentrate on (1) distinguishing delusions from beliefs that give strength, comfort, and belonging; (2) differentiating strategies used for survival from maladaptive defenses (given the frequency with which refugees experience discrimination); and (3) distinguishing appropriate vigilance and wariness from paranoia. To assess individuals within their cultural view and knowledge base, the therapist should use culturally relevant proverbs and areas of information when testing thought processes.

Similarly, when formal psychological tests are used (especially for a child or elder), cultural bias should be accounted for. This is particularly important when the tester relies on the English language, and even translated instruments may not be effective. Thus, the examiner should try to use tests of performance whenever possible (Raven's Progressive Matrices, Bender–Gestalt, Tell Me a Story, Vineland tests, Draw-a-Person, etc.)

When individual diagnoses must be made, the therapist should be aware that there have been recent efforts to acknowledge culture in the presentation of psychological problems (Mock, 1995). The DSM-IV (American Psychiatric Association, 1994) now includes an appendix titled "Outline for Cultural Formulation and Glossary of Culture-Bound Syndromes" (pp. 843–849); this should be considered carefully in work with refugees and other patients within a multicultural context.

Medication may be tried as an adjunct treatment for individuals with severe problems. If so, the therapist should educate individuals about the medication and its potential side effects, and should also provide individuals with information about negotiating the U.S. health care system. In cases where herbal medicine or acupuncture is part of a culture's healing practices, the therapist should consider a combination of Western and traditional medical treatment. And, of course, the therapist should carefully monitor medication dosages and change these as necessary, depending on differences in biological responses.

Finally, a few points on planning for therapy are in order. Even when a therapist will be working with an individual alone, he or she should look for ways to form a therapeutic alliance with the family. The therapist should also bear in mind that cultural messages may conflict with changes in family dynamics occurring in the new context. In choosing a therapeutic modality, the therapist should consider problem-solving, solution-focused, or supportive therapy as opposed to insight-oriented approaches; in the latter, listening alone may be interpreted as a lack of caring, confidence, expertise, or competence.

MAJOR ISSUES IN THERAPY
WITH REFUGEE FAMILIES

Language: Finding a Way to Negotiate Old and New Worlds

For refugee clients, opportunities to express themselves in their native language are of great clinical importance. Even when clients are proficient in English, the nuances and power of their native language are clear. Language is one of the most enduring aspects of the original culture, extending into the new culture and even across generations. The deep emotional meaning of language is illustrated in this situation: A European American family therapist thought she could work with an acculturated Salvadoran mother and daughter who had been transferred to her. Although initially the mother spoke English, the more she spoke about her emotional traumas before arriving as a refugee, the more she reverted to her native language. This created a temporary impasse for the therapist, who wanted to validate her story with all of its nuances. The therapist used the opportunity to discuss loss of culture at many significant levels.

Language is also important to an understanding of changes in family dynamics that create role shifts and conflicts in family hierarchies. In cases where one or more family members have trouble functioning in a society with a different language, their need to rely on relatives who are more fluent in the new/language can create serious problems and role shifts. This can be effectively addressed in family therapy, as in the next example. An ethnic Chinese Vietnamese family sought help concerning the "acting out" of their daughter in high school. Although previously taken pride in her heritage and excelled academically, she had begun to have school problems in attendance and performance, and was "hanging out" with kids not of her culture. After a careful assessment of the family history, a caustic exchange took place in which the father, a real estate broker, berated his daughter because she was unable to translate a specific business concept for him in their Chinese dialect. Looking lost and frustrated, she explained that she could find no accurate way in English to convey the concept to her father. The father felt that she was thereby failing him and her family, and this led to his further devaluing of her.

Subsequent family sessions led to the father's discussing his loss of status in having his daughter speak and negotiate for him. Her proficiency in English had also been key in negotiating the family's departure from the refugee camps, but it had resulted in feelings of shame and reversal of dependency roles with her parents. The daughter spoke painfully of how she could never do "good enough"; she was aware of her parents' sadness, but "felt stuck," unable to ask them about it without arguing. Family sessions facilitated discussions about culture change and loss, the residual effects of shame, and the negotiating of appropriate roles.

Ideally, a family therapist should speak the dialect or provincial language spoken by a refugee family. When this is not possible, a translator who may also serve as a cultural consultant is extremely important. Using a more acculturated family member to serve as translator may only reinforce current difficult family dynamics underlying the presenting problem, as the case just described illustrates. If translators are utilized, they should be trained in the approaches being taken, and comments should still be directed to the family members.

If there is any obvious omission in the language exchange, more complete translation should be requested. The risks of not doing so are illustrated in the case of an elderly Cambodian woman referred by her young adult children for her emotional distress. When the family therapist conducted a family session aided by an interpreter, an exchange of several minutes occurred between the series of questions asked and the seemingly reasonable translation from the worker. Sensing an omission, the therapist asked for a verbatim, sentence-by-sentence construction of the woman's responses. The worker responded, "But if I did that, you might not understand, since her responses were jumbled, disjointed, and confusing!" The correct procedure that followed revealed that the woman, whom the interpreter also felt he had to protect, had a serious thought disorder with tangential thinking and possible Alzheimer's. After the woman's medical situation was stabilized, family sessions revealed differences in subsystem responses to the refugee transition. Attention to this led to critical changes in the children's involvement in their mother's care, renegotiation of boundaries, and formation of a more cohesive system.

A powerful intervention for the family therapist can be acknowledging the continuing prominence of clients' primary language even when the clients are bilingual, in order to reinforce cultural sharing, exchange, and facilitation of deeper communication between family members. A stance of credibility with respectful naiveté at specific junctures in the course of therapy can be useful, as was illustrated when an Ethiopian couple came into treatment with additional stressors brought on by the birth of two baby girls. The mother related feeling alone and left behind by the obviously faster acculturation of her husband, which was a great threat to the family. As the spouses discussed their travails, the therapist noticed that the wife was trying to use sayings and metaphors from her culture, but was having difficulty explaining their full meaning to the therapist. Taking a naive stance, the therapist facilitated the husband in working alongside his wife to assist her in making her meaning clear. In this way, the couple worked out some impasses in communication; the husband was able to work with his wife, and neither of them felt shamed by his doing so. In fact, the wife conveyed feeling pleased that her husband was helping her to cross a "cultural bridge," while he praised her devotion to the babies, carrying of cultural traditions, and attention to the family.

The Changing Cultural Identities of Family Members and Subsystems

The process of a family's uprooting itself to go to a new country can proceed through several stages. As Sluzki (1979) has described, there may be the following steps: (1) preparation; (2) the act of migration; (3) a period of overcompensation in the first several months of arrival, during which adaptive and survival mechanisms are optimal; and (4) a period of decompensation or storminess, during which there are conflicts, difficulties, and cultural dissonances. Each of these steps may be discrete, with distinctive characteristics. During the fourth step in particular, family conflicts and symptoms often arise, and family coping mechanisms may be brought into question. Long-term delays in the adaptive process may become apparent in subsequent generations. Therapeutic implications for these processes are significant. Linking a family's presenting problems to the uprooting and reestablishment process can be very meaningful in contextualizing and depathologizing family complaints.

Another important issue for the therapist to explore with members of a refugee family may be the changing identities of its individual members. The therapist's understanding and giving voice to these dynamic identities often helps family members to understand how the family system has been affected by the traumas of their forced migration. The different ages of family members may lead to differences in acculturation and assimilation (Wong & Mock, 1997).

Wang (1991) used several interesting sayings and paradigms to describe Chinese who have migrated from overseas. One of these, *yeluo guigen,* can be roughly translated as follows: "When the leaves fall from the trees, they return to the soil [or roots]." This may describe refugees abroad who feel compelled later in life to return to their earlier, more firmly rooted identity. Another saying, *luodi shenggen,* depicts the refugee experience as similar to "seeds planted in foreign soil taking root wherever they have emigrated." When there is little hope of returning home, the family members' sole option may be to restructure their existence, reshape their identity, and aim for a future as permanent residents in the United States. A third possible identity may be captured by this saying: "In order to get rid of unwanted grass, you can't just mow it; you have to pull it up from its roots." Family members to whom this saying applies retain an awareness of their country of origin, but may deny or totally suppress its present meaningfulness in order to cope with the pain of their losses. They may attempt to assimilate totally, in order to gain acceptance by the dominant culture. Contrasting with this may be those refugees "xungen wenzu," who are "planted" in America but desire to have stronger national and ethnic pride and consciousness. Such refugees may engage in pursuit of their roots and explorations of their origins in striving for biculturality. Lastly, there may be refugees who are totally cut off from their roots but are also unable to fit into mainstream U.S. culture. Such rootless wandering "shigen qunzu" can have a profound impact on a family and its functioning (Wang, 1991).

Using metaphors and cultural sayings such as these in work with families can serve several therapeutic purposes. It underscores the constant relevance of culture, and it can also indicate cultural awareness and sensitivity on the therapist's part. Perhaps most importantly, it can depathologize refugee families' presenting problems, which can instead be framed in the rich historical context of the migration of families worldwide throughout history.

Constructing a multigenerational genogram with descriptions of relationships among the generations helps to emphasize the dynamic process of individual identity in forming a family system and can lead to therapeutic dialogue. Identification of and education about the cycles of identity can help family members move toward forming a more cohesive system through understanding each other's perspectives. Recognizing conflicts as they are related to significant life transitions may be a key to helping families with members or subsystems at different stages of cultural identification, adaptation, and adjustment.

Acknowledging the Strengths and Resilience of Refugee Families

To help restore balance in refugee families, it is therapeutic to pay attention to the families' methods of coping and resilience amid stressors, in both the past and present (Mock, 1993). Because refugee families have been confronted by many events that are out of their control, and often are dehumanizing and disorganizing, appropriate reframing of behaviors can help them regain some semblance of control. Validation of cultural belief systems, family coping styles, and other strengths can open up new dialogue and possibilities (Mock, 1994). When issues of oppression and discrimination, are being discussed, reminders of successful coping can be encouraging and unifying for a family that feels discouraged or fragmented.

In a family study focusing on Vietnamese men (Mock, 1991), individual and family characteristics of hardiness and resilience corresponded with better adjustment, even when individuals had experienced multiple and prolonged stressors. Instead of turning away from or suppressing their painful stories of events that occurred during the Vietnam War and the exodus from that country, several men were able to share their stories and were honored to be acknowledged for their efforts. The discussion of survival strategies under trying circumstances may ameliorate refugees' grief amid profound and multiple losses (Lee, 1990; Mock, 1995). One client commented, "Thank you for allowing me to talk. I hope this helps my people back home [in Southeast Asia]." Another said, "Thanks for giving me a chance to answer these questions. This made me and others feel happy. All of these questions are useful to us and remind us of what we had been through." Several of the men asked to take the written questions home, in order to learn better English and to share them with their families!

Ting: The Ultimate Listening of the Family Therapist

Working as a family therapist with refugee families can be a deeply emotional, humbling, profound, and mutually triumphant experience. In a session with members of a refugee family, I once shared an anonymous poem that captures the fears of refugees and the sensitivity that is needed to hear their stories. This poem is condensed here as follows:

> Don't be fooled by me.
> Don't be fooled by the face I wear.
> For I wear a mask, I wear a thousand masks,
> masks that I am afraid to take off
> and none of them are me. . . .
>
> My surface may seem smooth, but my surface is my mask.
> My ever-varying and ever-concealing mask.
> Beneath lies no complacence.
> Beneath dwells the real me in confusion, in fear, in aloneness.
> But I hide this. . . .
>
> But I don't tell you this. I don't dare. I'm afraid to.
> I'm afraid you'll think less of me, that you'll laugh,
> and your laugh would kill me. . . .
> I idly chatter to you in suave tones of surface talk.
> I tell you everything that's really nothing,

And nothing of what's everything, of what's crying within me.
So when I'm going through my routine, do not be fooled by what I am saying.
Please listen carefully and try to hear what I'm not saying.

In clinical work with refugee families, the capacity for "ultimate listening" or *Ting* is greatly challenged. A therapist should listen to such a family with focused cultural empathy; should demonstrate compassion, heart, and sincerity in interacting with family members; and should be astute in observing how the family's current dynamics may be related to the upheaval of leaving the homeland. Refugee families in therapy may represent the dualities of fleeing from danger and endurance for a life of new opportunities. The ancient Chinese symbol for "crisis" has therapeutic relevance. "Crisis" is comprised of two parts "danger"—representing a person on the edge of a precipice, and "opportunity"—a symbol expressing dynamic transformation (Lau, 1995). When a therapist utilizes skills of listening amid refugee family "crises," powerful stories can be shared as forever memorable "gifts" in an ongoing process of such transformation.

Danger

and

Opportunity

REFERENCES

Akhtar, S. (1995). Immigration and identity. *Journal of the American Psychoanalytic Association, 43*(4), 1051–1084.

American Psychiatric Association. (1994). *Diagnostic and statistical manual of mental disorders* (4th ed.). Washington, DC: Author.

Budman, C., & Ponton, L. (1986, May 1). *A model for the psychiatric evaluation of the refugee adolescent.* Grand Rounds presented at the University of California at San Francisco.

Carter, B., & McGoldrick, M. (1988). *The changing family life cycle: A framework for family therapy* (2nd ed.). New York: Gardner Press.

Cole, E., Espin, O., & Rothblum, E. (1992). *Refugee women and their mental health: Shattered societies, shattered lives.* Binghamton, NY: Harrington Park Press.

Landau-Stanton, J. (1990). Issues and methods of treatment for families in cultural transition. In M. Mirkin (Ed.), *The social and political contexts of family therapy.* Needham Heights, MA: Allyn & Bacon.

Lau, T. (1995). *Best loved Chinese proverbs.* Needham Heights, MA: Allyn & Bacon.

Lee, E. (1990). Family therapy with Southeast Asian refugees. In M. Mirkin (Ed.), *The social and political contexts of family therapy.* Needham Heights, MA: Allyn & Bacon.

Levy-Warren, M. (1987). Moving to a new culture: Culture identity, loss and mourning. In S. Bloom & J. Bloom (Eds.), *The psychology of separation and loss.* San Francisco: Jossey-Bass.

Mock, M. (1991). *Life trauma, social support, and personality characteristics: Their impact on the psychological adjustment of Southeast Asians.* Ann Arbor: University of Michigan Press.

Mock, M. (1993, August). Hardiness and resilience of southeast Asian refugees. *Family Therapy News,* pp. 46–52.

Mock, M. (1994). Clinical perspectives on immigrant and refugee adaptation and coping. In J. Fong (Ed.), *Proceedings of the Asian American Psychological Association Convention, Atascadero, CA.*

Mock, M. (1995, October). Multicultural expressions of clinical depression. *Family Therapy News,* pp. 21–22.

Nicassio, P. (1985). The psychosocial adjustment of the Southeast Asian refugee: An overview of empirical findings and theoretical models. *Journal of Cross Cultural Psychology, 16,* 153–173.

Rumbaut, R. (1985). Mental health and the refugee experience: A comparative study of Southeast Asian refugees. In T. Owan (Ed.), *Southeast Asian mental health: Treatment, prevention, services, training and research.* Rockville, MD: U.S. Department of Health and Human Services.

Sluzki, C. (1979). Migration and family conflict. *Family Process, 16*(4), 379–390.

United Nations High Commissioner for Refugees. (1981). *Refugees: An historical view.* New York: Author.

Wang, L. L. (1991). Roots and changing identity of the Chinese in the United States. *Daedalus,* 181–206.

Wong, L., & Mock, M. (1997). Developmental and life cycle issues of Asian Americans: Asian American young adults. In E. Lee (Ed.), *Working with Asian Americans: A guide for clinicians.* New York: Guilford Press.

CHAPTER 27

Migration and the Disruption of the Social Network

Carlos E. Sluzki

Our personal social network—that rather stable but continually evolving interpersonal fabric woven of close and distant family members, friends, work and study connections, and relationships that result from informal and formal participation in community organizations (religious, social, political, health-related, etc.)—constitutes a key repository of our identity, our history, and our well-being (Sluzki, 1996). Countless research projects have evidenced the tight correlation between the quality of an individual's social support system and the individual's health and chances of survival (Berkman, 1984; House, Robbins, & Metzner, 1982; Schoenbach, Kaplan, Friedman, & Kleinbach, 1986). This correlation extends to a varied array of factors, such as frequency of myocardial infarction (Orth-Gomer, Rosengren, & Wilhelmsen, 1993) and recovery from that disorder (Medalie et al., 1973), tuberculosis (Holmes, 1956), accidents (Tillman & Hobbes, 1949), likelihood of rehospitalization after being discharged from a psychiatric hospital (Dozier, Harris, & Bergman, 1987), and many others.

The personal social network is a dynamic, evolving system. It affects, and is affected by, each of the normative stages in a person's life. In fact, most of the rituals that recognize life passages, from birth to marriage to death, include active network participation. It is also extremely sensitive to cultural and gender variables: Different cultures have different norms and expectations in terms of network involvement in people's everyday lives, and females and males show marked differences in network development, maintenance, and utilization skills.

In the increasingly mobile society that characterizes our industrial and postindustrial eras, relocation (within countries) and migration (between countries) are frequent, almost normative phenomena that unavoidably entail a major disruption in the social niche of an individual (Sluzki, 1979, 1992). Normativity notwithstanding, this disruption and its effects are seldom explicitly recognized by either the public or mental health professionals. As a result, people who migrate can do little to manage these processes (and, when they suffer the consequences of that disruption, they experience it as *their* failure); public policies and public practices can do little to help them; and, alas, therapists cannot do enough to help them unless they are themselves sensitized to these issues.

The purpose of this chapter is to illustrate the severe effects of the disruption of the personal social network during migration with a poignant clinical case,[1] and to use this case to underline some therapeutic stances that may contribute to ameliorate their effect.

CASE BACKGROUND AND INITIAL INTERVIEW

A family of Philippine origin came to a family-oriented family medicine clinic to seek treatment for a 14-year-old boy who had begun 2 months earlier to exhibit striking body tics, such as moving his arms as if to shoo flies away and intermittently uttering explosive clicking sounds or profanities. These tics occurred in the course of conversations or out of the blue, alternating with otherwise pleasant and appropriate behavior and speech. The youngster acted oblivious to the tics, and, when confronted, could not explain them. Their disruptive interference with the young man's daily social behavior had grown in intensity in the past few weeks—to the point that the principal of the junior high school he was attending informed his parents that their son's movements and explosive insults had become so disruptive that he had already been removed from his classroom, and he would have to be suspended from school until the problem was solved. The tics had acquired such predominance that the boy could no longer use public transportation, as fellow passengers took the insults he was muttering personally, and occasionally confronted him. The clinically astute reader will have already recognized in this description the traits of Gilles de la Tourette syndrome. Some specialists attribute this diagnostic category to a neurological base, others add it to the larger set of schizophrenias, and yet others define it as an independent diagnostic category.

During the interview, this slender, properly dressed, shy, and very pleasant youngster participated moderately. His utterances as well as his silences were punctuated by occasional noises, insults, and abrupt movements which occurred, so to speak, on another channel—parallel to that of the conversation, but criss-crossing it rather frequently. In fact, the boy expressed worry about his symptoms, but he seemed almost indifferent to their effect; they took place not only in parallel channels, but also in parallel worlds. When I would ask him, "What was that?", he would either deny those enactments or define them as puzzling for himself (his typical answers were "Nothing" or "I don't know"). The content of his contribution to the conversation was otherwise totally appropriate for his age, without any hint of additional "pathology" (by which I mean that the boy did not show any behavior or participatory style that could point me in the direction of schizophrenia or any other diagnostic category, beyond the already mentioned Gilles de la Tourette syndrome). Until he was suspended from school, his academic performance had been satisfactory.

His parents—a young, educated, elegant, and socially gracious couple, fluent in English—expressed their preoccupation and puzzlement about their son. A younger daughter, 10 years old, participated appropriately in the interview but added little further information. She had already "normalized" her brother's unusual behavior except in public situations, where it made her laugh and feel ashamed .

As the interview progressed, I explored everybody's theories about the boy's symptoms. The parents informed me that their family physician had made a provisional diagnosis of schizophrenia, but they did not understand very clearly what it meant. Neither the youngster himself nor his sister offered any theory or insight into the matter. In turn, I confided to them that I had not yet been able to produce myself any cogent explanation for the youngster's behavior, but that I supposed that, as frequently is the case with tics, it had to do with tensions and stress. This vague, tension-reducing statement seemed to satisfy the parents, at least at that point in the session. I informed them that I would recommend a temporary medication for the boy (specifically, haloperidol, a psychotropic medication recommended for this syndrome in the psychopharmacological literature). I also proposed to follow this meeting with one or two meetings with the parents alone, to explore with them additional elements of their life history, so that I could further familiarize myself with their predicament.

The decision to medicate (and, in general terms, my wish to keep myself up to date in terms of clinical psychopharmacology) represented my commitment toward maintaining a balanced biopsychosocial perspective in clinical practice, and my desire to avoid the risk of depriving patients under my care of the possible benefit of psychotropic medications because of my own ideological bias in favor of psychosocial interventions. However, this eclectic position contains an unavoidable drawback:

Once I have added the medication, I lose the possibility to discriminate the relative contribution of the psychosocial variables (and interventions) and the neurobiological variables (and interventions) to any improvement. In turn, the decision to interview the parental couple alone derived from my impression during the interview that they kept at all times a stance of "model parents" in front of their children—and, indeed, in front of me, if not of each other. This fit with my knowledge of the dominant value of "saving face at all expense" in people from various Asian/Oriental cultures.

INTERVIEWS WITH THE PARENTS ALONE

In the course of the two interviews with the parents only that followed, the family history unfolded. They both belonged to upper-middle-class traditional Philippine families. He was a lawyer, and his father had been a senator representing an opposition party. She, in turn, had a general college education and belonged to a family with connections to the establishment of the same political party. They had known each other since childhood, as their parents shared social circles and clubs. Almost predictably, they had begun their courtship as adolescents, married rather young with everybody's blessing, and had their two children within the large welcoming web of their two extended families. Their family and social life evolved in a sheltered and stable fashion, following class- and culture-outlined social pathways. However, after a military *coup d'état* that unleashed a political persecution of opponents to the new *de facto* regime, the husband's family was seriously threatened. The spouses, in an effort to protect themselves and their children, had migrated to the United States about 5 years ago. They received some economic support from both families, but not enough to live comfortably; thus the husband, and soon also the wife, started to work full-time and part-time, respectively. Since his credentials as an attorney were not valid in the United States (laws and judicial processes are fundamentally different in the two countries), he took a job as coordinator of a social center for the Philippine community, where he could use some of his prior training as a lawyer. In turn, she completed training as a dental hygienist at a community college and started working part-time during the hours when the children were in school. Both mentioned with a smile that their adaptation to the new circumstances hadn't been easy, but in what I understood as an effort to keep up appearances, they agreed that it had been a positive experience for them.

In my own remarks, I gradually introduced progressively the other side of the coin. I resonated to their descriptions with occasional comments about my own and my family's experience of immigration, about situations of cross-cultural misunderstanding and experiences of cultural dissonance, and about the family difficulties triggered by the unavoidable interpersonal overload of migration; in this fashion, I generated an empathetic echo about the most difficult aspects of their recent history. This had the progressive effect of normalizing their difficulties and legitimizing their experiences. Their shortcomings, instead of being signs of weakness or incompetence, could be seen as common if not unavoidable effects of difficult circumstances. My comments also modeled for them a stance of openness about one's own pain, which contributed to define the context of therapy as a safe one.

Progressively, the parents became more expressive and less defensive with me. And, even more importantly, they opened up to each other. Once and over again, when one of them would describe (almost confess) some specific area of difficulties, the other would respond with a surprised comment: "You never even mentioned that to us," or "I did not realize that you were having such a bad time." I eventually remarked, "Each one of you seems to have taken care of the other through minimizing comments about your own difficulties. But that may have had the unavoidable aftereffect of reducing your alertness to the other's signals." They found this comment very helpful. At one point the wife began to sob while expressing her isolation and feelings of loneliness, and the husband exclaimed with astonishment and tenderness that these were the first tears he had seen her weep since they arrived in the United States.

This rich unfolding of the spouses' individual and joint history also allowed me to glance at the vicissitudes of their social network in the course of this difficult transition. In the Philippines, each of them had grown up in an extended family, with a broad and rather dense net of relatives and friends (including many classmates and playmates from childhood, friends and teammates from adolescence, and workmates-turned-friends and conjoint [couple] friends from young adulthood). Even after their marriage, despite their getting along very well and loving each other, each spouse kept his or her own personal network of close friends, in addition to the shared friends with whom the couple would socialize. The wife could confide her emotional problems to her female cousins and friends, ask for and provide advice, and count on them for a range of functions. She could also rely upon and be relied upon by her siblings and her parents, and the husband could do the same in his family. In addition, he was a junior partner in his father's law firm. The spouses had thus never *needed* to develop a broad range of areas of intimacy; nor had they acquired the skills to do so, since many of these functions were consistently and nonconflictually covered by other members of their network. In addition, such intimacy was not prescribed by their culture (including their class culture), within which men and women kept many separate social relations, activities, and encounters.

Once the family migrated, the spouses' interpersonal net collapsed dramatically. They now lived surrounded by people with whom they had little in common. They were not skilled in developing new relationships quickly (a skill that is frequently developed, for instance, by members of military families, who have to move frequently from base to base). There was also a class difference between them and many people of their own community, and their own class bias made it harder for them to reach out to these others. This substantial social vacuum was, of course, within their awareness, but its full effects on them were not. One of these effects was that each one of them began to expect that the other would fulfill interpersonal roles and functions lost through their migration, as well as newly needed reciprocal support functions. Each spouse expected the other to become an unconditional soother, lover, confidant, companion, and sounding board, despite the fact that some of these roles were totally new for them within the couple relationship. And this was happening precisely during a period when each spouse was overloaded and needy, and therefore less open and accessible to the needs of the other. Besides, both were trapped by certain added constraints inherent to their culture in regard to behaviors that are considered acceptable and expected or not within a couple. These conspired against their ability to fulfill some of the functions previously covered by other members of their extended net work, and unfulfilled since the move. It was, in fact, difficult for them to lower the drawbridge of intimacy when some of the potential exchanges would risk lessening the face-saving quality of merely formal exchanges.

These difficulties, overloads, and pains of loneliness were explored and gently discussed with and by the spouses. An added step was taken when I introduced an idea that was rather novel for them: Perhaps the children were experiencing these same types of emotions and difficulties. Moreover, I suggested that perhaps their son's strange behavior was a way to demand attention—despite the inconveniences brought about by such a method. The spouses stated that a good part of their effort had been dedicated to making the transition less difficult for their children, but they acknowledged that their efforts had been focused more on practical matters than on providing emotional support. The husband commented that he was aware of having distanced himself a lot from the youngsters, particularly from the son. The wife added that since the move, she had noticed that her husband had been less expressive of his affection in general (thus gently implying that she had also been affected by this), although she quickly justified it on the basis of his work overload and the other family responsibilities he had assumed. The husband accepted her observation at face value, and reassured her that he would do his best to express all his affection for all three of them. In general terms, both partners acknowledged self-critically that they had been stingy in their support of each other; they vowed to increase their sensitivity toward each other's needs, as well as to be more open about their own needs, following relational pathways explored and experienced as safe in the course of both sessions.

Because I did not wish to sidetrack our focus of attention from the interpersonal processes, I explored only minimally how the son's symptoms were evolving, despite my curiosity about these. When I did ask, they mentioned that he was improving markedly. Indeed, in the course of the second session with the parents, they let me know that the boy had returned to school and no longer had difficulties in social situations or on public transportation. Also, at the end of that session and as if it were an afterthought, the father mentioned that there were signals of a drastic improvement in the political climate of the Philippines that might open up the possibility of the family's return there. He confessed that the only thing that kept him in the United States was a sense that to return without having "conquered America" would be tantamount to failure. His wife told him that she had already feared that such a sense of failure would trouble him, and that she hadn't mentioned the issue before for fear of offending him, because she knew how important success was for him. She showered him with praises for his success, especially considering the many difficulties entailed by their abrupt migration. The spouses also took advantage of this atmosphere of openness and intimacy to reveal to each other that they had kept private contact through mail with friends and relatives in their country. The conversation became even richer with the recognition that this secret desire had conspired against the possibility of developing a fulfilling social network in the United States: "Why should we make the effort to establish social contacts if we were thinking of returning to our country soon [a mythical "soon," since they had not spoken about this and had not defined their migratory experience as time- and context-limited or permanent]?" Both laughed, relieved that this topic could be discussed. I suggested to them that once they felt totally comfortable with the topic, they discuss it openly with their children, who might also bear some secret hopes—similar to or even different from theirs. This last comment worried the parents: What would happen if they wanted to return but their children did not? This second session with the parents alone closed with their expressions of gratitude, which I reciprocated by stating that I had also learned a lot from their openness.

FOLLOW-UP MEETINGS

I scheduled one follow-up interview one month later with the whole family, in which the parents described changes in the family climate—specifically, more closeness and warmth. They also mentioned that they were discussing openly the pros and cons of a return to the Philippines. The boy—who was continuing to take the prescribed medication and to function well in school—did not present any symptomatic behavior during the session.

At the close of that consultation, I suggested to the family members that we meet for a couple of follow-up appointments at 3-month intervals; they accepted this proposal. However, I saw them only once, after some 4 months, in an interview in which the patents commented that the young man's symptoms had vanished. They also informed me that the change in the political situation was making it possible for them to plan to return soon to their country without major risks to any of them. The first one to leave would be the son, so that he could prepare for the entrance examinations at the bilingual (Tagalog–English) secondary school that he would attend. He would live temporarily at his grandparents' house until the rest of the family returned. I commented that it is always wise to begin any moves by sending a scout in advance, to explore the territory and prepare "the locals" for the family reentry. Smiling at what they understood as a wise joke, the parents praised their son for his new potential role. Some 8 months after that session, at the end of the year, I received a postcard from the family, sending me Season's Greetings from the Philippines.

DISCUSSION

Even though the network disruption that follows a relocation is more readily explicit and salient as a theme for families belonging to cultures that favor close-knit, extended, family ties and are characterized by low geographic mobility, the active exploration of those variables—based on the assumption on the part of the consultant that such a disruption has taken place, regardless of the family's culture of origin—will show that these vicissitudes constitute a theme of almost universal appeal. This theme is one of those "strong attractors" that will organize the therapeutic conversation in a meaningful way, with powerful potential for transforming the collective experience.

In the rich tapestry of processes characterizing therapy with a family such as the one discussed above, I would like to highlight the following points:

• The vicissitudes of the experience of migration constitute a narrative that is readily accepted by all the participants—family and therapist alike—as a legitimate and meaningful theme of the therapeutic conversation. It allows for all the characters of the story to be placed in dignifying loci; it permits to define areas of conflict that do not hinge negatively on the intentions or competence of the participants; and it generates a background against which actions acquire a positive meaning, difficulties are legitimated, problems are redefined, and alternative solutions are developed. From that perspective, the theme of migration expands and reorganizes the description of the problems and the range of the potential solutions.

• Already within the content of the narrative, migration unavoidably overloads the members of any family, especially the parental couple. Many functions previously fulfilled by the members of the extended network—relatives as well as friends—remain unfulfilled; each member of the couple, experiencing this void, expects the other to fill in, regardless of the fact that the other may have never done so before. As these needs continue to go unsatisfied, complaints and resentment often ensue, which only escalate both partners' needs and unavailability.

• This increase in needs and reciprocal expectations takes place precisely when each partner is in turn most overloaded and least able to fulfill the other's needs.

• The dedication to fulfilling the children's needs is frequently a "smokescreen" to hide the needs of the adults. At the same time, the parents' need to concentrate on everyday survival may make them miss cues to pains and difficulties in their children, especially if these mimic those of their parents.

• A key component of the therapist's function as both cultural broker and legitimizer of the experiences of dissonance is that the therapist maintains an empathetic, contextualizing, and normalizing stance, with assumptions that competence and good intent characterize the participants' behaviors.

The explicit focus of the therapist on the vicissitudes of the process of migration is readily understood by consulting families, and has the powerful effect of both demystifying and depathologizing the therapeutic process. Symptoms and conflicts are thus not expressions of pathology or of incompetence, but the by-products of an intrinsically and unavoidably complex and painful process for which people are seldom prepared, and for which they have to develop new skills and new awareness.

NOTE

1. The clinical example used in this chapter has been previously discussed in Sluzki (1996).

REFERENCES

Berkman, L. F. (1984). Assessing the physical health effects of social networks and social support. *Annual Review of Public Health, 5,* 413–432.

Dozier, M., Harris, M., & Bergman, H. (1987). Social network density and re-hospitalization among young adult patients. *Hospital and Community Psychiatry, 38*(1), 61–65.

Holmes, T. H. (1956). In P. J. Soarer (Ed.), *Personality, stress and tuberculosis.* New York: International Universities Press.

House, J., Robbins, C., & Metzner, H. (1982). The association of social relations with mortality: Prospective evidence from the Tecumseh Community Health Study. *American Journal of Epidemiology, 116,* 123–140.

Medalie, J., Green, J., Snyder, M., Groen, J. J., Neufeld, H. N., Goldbourt, U., & Riss, E. (1973). Angina pectoris among 10,000 men: 5-year incidence and multivariate analysis. *American Journal of Medicine, 55,* 583–594.

Orth-Gomer, K., Rosengren, A., & Wilhelmsen, L. (1993). Lack of support and incidence of coronary heart disease in middle-aged Swedish men. *Psychosomatic Medicine, 55,* 37–43.

Schoenbach, V., Kaplan, H., Friedman, L., & Kleinbach, D. (1986). Social ties and mortality in Evans County, Georgia. *American Journal of Epidemiology, 123,* 577–591.

Sluzki, C. E. (1979). Migration and family conflict. *Family Process, 18*(1), 379–392.

Sluzki, C. E. (1992). Network disruption and network reconstruction in the process of migration/relocation. *Family Systems Medicine, 10*(4), 359–364.

Sluzki, C. E. (1996). *La red social: Frontera de la terapia sistemica* [*The social network: Frontier of systemic therapy*]. Barcelona: Gedisa. (*Note:* An English translation, under the title of *The creation of therapuetic alternatives: Social network in systemic practice,* is in preparation.)

Tillman, W., & Hobbes, G. (1949). The accident-prone automobile driver: A study of psychiatric and social background. *American Journal of Psychiatry, 106,* 321–330.

CHAPTER 28

The Impact of Multiple Contexts on Recent Immigrant Families

Marsha Pravder Mirkin

Even though I am the child of an immigrant mother, and the grandchild of four immigrant grandparents, I only recently began to look at the cultural and bicultural experiences that defined my family and shaped my childhood. Since I knew my father's parents well into early adulthood, I would like to share their experience, and particularly how it can guide us to understand what it was about their particular immigrant experience that promoted their resilience and relational capacity. From the perspective of dominant U.S. cultural values, one might well wonder how my father and his siblings would turn out. They were poor immigrants, living in a tenement where many families shared a single, cold hall bathroom. My grandfather worked nights and weekends in grueling dockside labor, leaving my father, who was by far the eldest sibling, to help his mother parent the younger children. My father lived at home until he married at age 40; that in itself would be enough to raise the eyebrows of traditional therapists. Yet my father and each of his siblings grew up to be loving, loved, productive adults.

If we expand the outline of this story, we can pull from it the ingredients of their strength. My grandparents came from the villages of Makava and Chichava, along the Russian–Polish border. These villages were poor Yiddish-speaking farming towns with no economic opportunity, the constant threat of religious persecution, and no opportunity for education in the larger Russian school system. My grandparents came to the United States at the turn of the century with their parents, brothers, and sisters. Although they experienced the loss of their old community and some members of their extended families, nobody in either immediate family was left behind.

My grandparents' families arrived in the Lower East Side of New York, a bustling although economically poor Jewish community. Their wealth was measured in educational opportunity and religious freedom: All the children were permitted to attend public schools, synagogues surrounded them, and Yiddish could be heard in the streets. The community not only built a synagogue, but its members assisted each other through the Educational Alliance, a combination of community-provided social services, recreational activities, and educational opportunities. The work on the docks was no harder than the work in the old country, and sharing an indoor "modern" bathroom was a step up from the facilities in the *shtetl.*

Within this culturally syntonic community, there was no talk about adolescent separation. Rather, my father was given a great deal of recognition in the family and among neighbors for being a good son who helped his mother and was well educated. He was honored, and his years at home promoted his self-esteem and earned him the respect from his younger brother and sister that was traditionally given to a father.

As I write this, I must also be careful not to romanticize my father's youth. Anti-Semitism peaked in the United States from the 1920s to the early 1940s. Many colleges and jobs were closed to the members of my father's family. Yet it was also a time when the City University of New York opened its doors to everyone, regardless of income and religious background, so the educational opportunity that they valued was never withheld from them.

Contrast this with the story of my childhood neighbors. They, too, were Jewish; the parents came to this country as young adults and had their children here. But the conflicts and problems they experienced were far more severe than those experienced by my father and his family. They were Holocaust survivors whose parents, sisters, and brothers had all been murdered in concentration camps. There were no goodbyes. Prior to the war, they had identified themselves more as Germans than as Jews. Synagogue involvement and religious comfort were never major parts of their lives in Germany. Where did they belong? What could they identify as the center, the anchor, of their personal and cultural world? They had led well-to-do lives, but all their financial resources were stolen by the Nazis, and they began their lives here as poor and later lower-middle-class Americans. The parents met each other in a refugee camp, drawn together more by trauma than by love. They moved to an English-speaking, acculturated community at a time when nobody in the United States seemed to want to hear their story. Everyone was celebrating the end of the war, and nobody wanted to be brought down by their bottomless grief. Depression and disconnection resonated in their household.

I would argue that the external circumstances surrounding the immigration experience—the context of the experience—can help us understand the degree of difficulty experienced by immigrant families and can give us a "road map" for working with immigrant families. In contrasting the two immigrant experiences I have described, we see that one family migrated intact, while the other was abused and witnessed the death of loved ones before migrating; that one family planned its migration, while the other could not; that one family experienced mild economic and significant educational gain, while the other experienced economic loss and loss of status; that one family settled in a community with familiar values, language, and religious and cultural beliefs, while the other settled in an acculturated, assimilated community. The family with more difficulty was cut off from discussing the trauma its members had experienced. Although both families experienced varying degrees of anti-Semitism and xenophobia, they also benefited from White privilege and did not experience the pervasive racism that immigrants of color often report.

Both families demonstrated many strengths and a great deal of resilience throughout the experience. Both found a way of leaving their old country and beginning anew with a new language and set of cultural standards; both integrated their country-of-origin values with their adoptive country's values as they raised their children; both countered the discrimination in response to their accents and names and provided economic stability for the family. Yet the cards were stacked against the second family. If we don't keep that in mind, we might start blaming the individuals in the family for their difficulties, rather than externalizing the difficulty and focusing on family strengths. So how do we begin to think about our work with immigrant families—work that could help us focus on their strengths, understand the many obstacles they face, and bear witness to the legacy they bring?

A RELATIONAL–NARRATIVE APPROACH

I have found it useful to conceptualize this work in terms of relational and narrative approaches (this approach is detailed in Mirkin & Geib, 1995, and is based on our collaborative work). Briefly, the goals and values that I bring to the work come from the relational model developed by Jean Baker Miller, Judith Jordan, Irene Stiver, Janet Surrey, and Alexandra Kaplan (1991). The model emphasizes that connection is central to healthy development, and that people strive for mutually enhancing, empathic, authentic relationships. When engaged in mutually enhancing relationships, people experience greater zest, an ability to act in and beyond their relationships, an increased knowledge of self and others, greater self-worth, and a desire for more connections (Miller & Stiver, 1991; Miller, 1988). The values of this model enable us to approach the therapeutic relationship more collaboratively, to pay attention to family strengths rather than pathology, and to identify and work to heal ruptures in family relationships. The model also acknowledges that because of our desire for relationships, we sometimes hide parts of ourselves that we think are unacceptable so that we don't lose relationships. By hiding these parts of ourselves, we lose authenticity and connection, and therefore at least partly lose the very same relationships that we were trying to hold onto and so desperately want and need. This is called the "relational paradox" (Miller & Stiver, 1991). It can be observed when immigrant family members hide parts of their prior experience, cultural rituals, and the like in an effort to fit in or to avoid rejection, but this very effort keeps parts of themselves outside of their relationships, resulting in feelings of isolation.

Often, when I consult with immigrant families and their treaters, I find that the families don't present with problems related to the immigrant experience. Instead, the presenting problems may focus on a child's misbehavior or a spouse's estrangement, at a point in time when empathy and mutuality have somehow become blocked. Narrative therapists (e.g., White, 1995) posit that families and individuals have created stories about their lives and about the problem situation—stories that have become so narrow and problematic that they lead to the same old solutions that don't work. A shift in the story can help individuals and families transform themselves and their relationships. For example, my family's story is that my father was a good, loyal, competent son. This promotes family strengths much more than a story labeling him and his mother as "enmeshed." All too often, therapy supports pathologizing, disempowering stories rather than ones that promote strength and resilience. Instead, we can help families expand narrow stories into ones that underline their strengths.

To change and expand the narrow story, Pamela Geib and I use a method called "expanding the context." Often family members blame each other for problems in the family. Rarely do they look at how larger societal expectations influence the family and the problems family members experience. Therefore, it is critical to generate some understanding of how the contexts of immigrant status, race, class, gender, ethnicity, religion, sexual lifestyle, and so on affect the family, the family's migration experience, and the ways in which the family members story their difficulties (McGoldrick & Giordano, 1996; Mirkin, 1990; Mirkin &

Geib, 1995). Because many of us are so entrenched in the dominant culture, some of its cultural imperatives are invisible to us. It is a challenge to us therapists as well as to our clients to recognize and verbalize these cultural imperatives, especially as they clash with the values and belief systems of the immigrant family.

To do this work, we as therapists must be able to bear witness and to send our clients the message that we can tolerate hearing their stories. We need to be humble: We can't possibly know as much about the client's culture of origin as they do. We need to listen carefully to each family's stories, and to learn as much as we can about migration history: loss, trauma, and "culture shock," as well as strength and resilience. We need to challenge ourselves constantly to see and hear the larger context—the context of race, gender, class—as we listen to each family's experience. We need to be able to take a proactive stance to connect families with the resources they need, whether these mean culturally compatible churches, advocates within the school system, or social services.

As we hear the stories of immigrant families, we need to pay attention to both the relational costs and gains of immigration, and to listen for both the places of disconnection and the places of healing and strength. We need to be aware of the "cultural fit" between the family and therapist, as well as between the immigrant and adopted society (Breunlin, Schwartz, & MacKune-Karrer, 1992, 1993; McGoldrick & Giordano, 1996; Mirkin, 1993). We don't know in advance where this road toward biculturality will lead. Each family's journey is unique, and different aspects and degrees of the old and new come together in the journey toward biculturality.

THE PREMIGRATION AND MIGRATION EXPERIENCE: TERROR AND MULTIPLE LOSSES

First, we need to look at the degree of trauma experienced before and during migration—the terror and multiple losses that were experienced by many immigrant families (Alvarez, 1995; Breunlin et al., 1992, 1993; Hernandez & Inclan, 1993; Ritterman & Simon, 1990; Lee, 1990). Why did each family leave the old country? What happened to its members before they left? Whom did they leave behind and why? How did they leave? What happened during the migration process?

Engaging in this work means being able to bear witness to the trauma experienced by many families before and during migration. For example, several Cambodian families I consulted with escaped the Khmer Rouge, but experienced terrifying traumas before their escape and in the refugee camps where they spent the time between their escape and their arrival in the United States. One adolescent silently ran in place for months, reenacting the years she spent terrified in Cambodia, watching those around her killed and trying to escape, only to face more terror and loss. Lee (1990) warns us that Southeast Asian families may not want to speak aloud about the trauma they experienced. It took months after entering a residential treatment program before this adolescent began to tell her story to her therapist, and her legs were able to be still.

Even when a family has not migrated to escape from terror, and the migration process has been fairly uncomplicated, it is important to gather the premigration information. This includes as broad a picture as possible of the culture of origin, and what each family member values from the culture. If family members disagreed about whether to migrate, it is important to hear how or by whom the decision was made, and what the repercussions of the differing opinions were within the family. Even when a family arrives intact, its members have still experienced the loss of friends, culture, neighborhood, schools, and way of life. It is important to pay attention to these losses, even if they feel less gripping and traumatic to us as therapists than the accounts of terrorized immigrants.

THE POSTMIGRATION EXPERIENCE

Racism and Stereotyping

Central to the experience of many immigrants of color are the racism and shortage of opportunity they experience in their adopted country. One Japanese American client, when speaking of her parents' experience, said to me:[1]

> "Think about it. First, even though they were so loyal to this country, they were treated as the enemy during World War II. Then, they became the enemy because of the Korean War. After all, many people here never bothered to distinguish between Japanese and Koreans. To most European Americans, Asian is Asian, period. Then they were the enemy because Communist China was supposed to be a threat to the United States, and finally we were the enemy because of the war in Vietnam. The racism and mistrust that my parents experienced left an indelible mark on them, and on me. The more they honor the old ways, and engage in Japanese customs, the more suspect they are. And we kids also feel under scrutiny because all of a sudden, Japanese Americans are supposed to be brilliant students, never cause any trouble, and get straight A's. The racism doesn't end."

Another client was surprised when I asked her about her experiences as a Mexican American. She felt that she stopped being Mexican American when she left her poverty-stricken family of migrant workers and got her law degree. Later, as she faced the racism that she had internalized, and as she discovered Mexican American role models, she chose a career that enabled her to offer free or low-cost legal services to Mexican Americans.

Class Differences

A second issue affecting the immigration experience is change in class. This can involve both financial and status changes. Members of immigrant families who are less financially stable in this country than in their country of origin clearly experience more stressors than those whose financial situation has improved since immigration. Yet at this writing all immigrants are at risk, since the federal government is attempting to take away the safety net of public assistance from legal immigrants. Many jobs are not open to immigrants until they speak fluent English. Many professional immigrants arrive to find that their licenses are not valid in this country and that they need to be relicensed—a procedure that takes time and is financially costly. One of my colleagues was a respected surgeon in his country of origin, but needed to enroll in a residency program here before he could practice in the United States.

Changes of status are often as traumatic as changes in finances. If someone was a well-respected professional in the country of origin and then loses that profession in this country, it can be damaging, whether or not the monetary difference in employment is significant. A taxi driver who once took me home from the airport told me of his training as an architect, and described how terrible it was to know that he could not have a job that is respected and valued in this country. A woman who advertised her housecleaning services had been a psychologist in her country of origin. Both people felt that their accents, their difficulty with English, others' negative stereotypes about their countries of origin, and U.S. licensing requirements made employees discriminate against them and made the obstacles to high-status employment insurmountable.

CULTURE OF ORIGIN, ACCULTURATION, AND BICULTURALITY

A primary issue facing immigrant families is the match between the culture of origin and the North American dominant culture: Are the central values syntonic? If we therapists were raised as members of the dominant culture in the United States, we sometimes assume that the norms we grew up with are universal. Yet, for immigrant families, some of the experiences they bring into therapy would not be as problematic in their culture of origin.

Several years ago, I consulted with a therapist who was working with a Cape Verdean family referred because the parents were beating their children. The parents reported that corporal punishment was regarded as useful discipline in their village. If they hadn't responded to their children in this way, they would think of themselves as negligent parents. They felt demeaned, disempowered, and confused by the Department of Social Services' intervention. In this case, it was helpful to look at corporal punishment not in terms of right and wrong, but in terms of U.S. law. We shared that this is a law based on ideas of raising children that are different from their beliefs and that might not make sense to them; yet, it is the law. We wondered aloud how we could be resources as the adults developed other ways of being responsible parents that wouldn't cause law enforcement agencies to intervene.

When our clients share ideas that are different from our own, and when they also come from a culture that is unfamiliar to us, we often attribute their belief systems to their culture of origin. Yet sometimes our clients had trouble in their culture of origin as well, and it is useful to find out whether a family's values and behaviors are representative of the culture of origin or whether they are idiosyncratic within that culture. To obtain this information, I try to involve as much of the extended family and friends as possible through my use of questions. This helps clarify not only the norms about behavior, but also the rules governing gender and generational family relationships. For example, Rosa's parents were very upset because the 16-year-old was wearing makeup, dating, and coming home after dark. In addition to hearing the family's perspective, I might ask:

> "What would Aunt Sylvia say if she knew that Rosa was dating [etc.]? What would Uncle Carlos say? If you were still living in Puerto Rico, who would make the decision about whether and when Rosa could date? Who made the important decisions when you [the parents] were teenagers? Have things changed in Puerto Rico since you were teenagers? Who is more likely to support those changes? Resist those changes?"

We also need to understand who is considered part of the helping system in the culture of origin. In the United States, we often look to mental health professionals for healing in a way that people in other cultures might look to a range of religious leaders and elders. Who are the healers in the culture of origin? What types of healers are shunned? Whom do we and the family then include on our treatment team? Very often, religious figures play a much larger part in the therapy than traditional treatment providers have assumed. Questions about religious belief and about persons the family wants included in the therapy from the religious community may be helpful. If a family is not identified with a spiritual community, I often ask whether it had been so identified at any time while in this country or in the country of origin. For example, a West African single-parent family presented with a depressed mother and a defiant older daughter. When asked about religion, the mother talked about how involved she had been with her spiritual community in West Africa, and how alone and isolated she had felt since she came here and joined her local church. A large part of the work involved helping the mother to find a religious community that was similar to the one she left behind. In another case, shortly before a Haitian girl was discharged, a staff member suggested that she leave a picture of herself for the residential program's "graduate photo album," without realizing that his suggestion made the girl panic because of her past experiences with voodoo.

Cultural Differences within Couples

There are times when couples seek treatment because of conflict between the partners that could be better understood as differences in the life style and values between their countries of origin. For example, Kliman (1994) presents an example of a Scottish American woman married to a man from a professional Yoruba family in Cameroon. They were in conflict because his relatives would come uninvited and stay for long periods of time. The collectivism, mutual obligation, and lack of distinction between immediate and extended family in the Yoruba culture were in conflict with the values of self-determination, privacy, and focus on nuclear family of the Scottish American culture. Clarifying and respecting the values of both cultures allowed for interventions that helped the spouses move out of mutual blame and into a more contextual framework.

Another couple came into therapy because the woman felt that the man was "too needy" and was placing excessive demands on her, while he felt hurt and angry at what he called her "unresponsiveness." As we explored his immigration history, we began to understand that he had lived in a tribal village where at least 20 family members were available for consultation and collaboration on issues as they arose. The discussion and advice seeking that was valued by his culture of origin and was once spread among 20 or more people were now focused on this one relationship. As a result, he was no longer labeled "needy"; instead, the focus was on seeking out a larger, more culturally syntonic support system for them.

Parent–Child Struggles

A frequent concern expressed by immigrant parents is conflict with their children. Sometimes the struggle can be traced to separation during the migration experience. For example, an angry, acting-out young man claimed to have no relationship with his father, whose attempts to control his behavior were backfiring. However, the father had recently immigrated from Cambodia, whereas the son had been here for a long time and was raised by his uncle. The father yearned for the day he could come here to parent his only child. The boy only saw a man foreign to him in almost every way who was trying to interfere with his life, as his father who had missed so many years with his son, tried to apply some rules that would have been more appropriate with a younger child. Expanding the context in such a case means looking at the effect of forced separation on the family members, normalizing their struggle, and contextualizing it in terms of forced separation and the migration process.[2]

A common cause of parent–child struggles is the difference in rates of acculturation (Montalvo & Gutierrez, 1990; Szapocznik, Rio, Perez, & Kurtines, 1986). To look at this issue, we can imagine immigrant parents coming to this country and raising children who have one foot in the dominant American culture and the other in the family's culture. Since the values may well be competing, this often leads to conflicts within the family. Evelyn Lee (1990) writes that Asian parents expect their children to be quiet, obedient, polite, and respectful. Yet North American values emphasize independence, assertiveness, and open communications. Conflict is often unavoidable.

While parents try to maintain the values of the culture of origin, children often learn English more rapidly and have greater exposure to the norms of the new culture through school and friendships. This leads to potential dilemmas. Without knowing English or dominant U.S. customs, parents may depend on children to navigate new living situations, which can result in the children's belief that their parents are not as competent and skilled as their friends. This also affects the parents' sense of self. Furthermore, as parents count on their children for tasks the parents used to do, the parent–child hierarchy gets reversed; many families from cultures with well-delineated hierarchies find this extremely difficult.

Parent–child struggle may intensify as children try to act like their peers and parents see these behaviors as turning against the family and its values. The children are bombarded with promises of a better life if they look and act like peers. Parents may see their children as misbehaving and disrespectful, while children see parents as useless in guiding their development. The two positions become polarized.

To exacerbate this dilemma further, immigrant families may find themselves in what I call a cultural relational paradox (see Miller & Stiver, 1997). Many immigrant parents, while craving relationships, find that their values and the values of the dominant culture are in conflict. They don't believe others can accept them for who they are, nor are they accepting of others with their foreign beliefs. If they want to make friends, they feel they must keep important parts of themselves out of connection, because of the fear that if others really know them, they will lose the relationships. Or, they avoid friendships and keep to their old ways of being, for fear that they will lose an important part of themselves if they have contact with others. This leads to a powerful sense of isolation.

Many immigrant children want to be close to their parents, but are afraid that if parents know of their new American ways, they will be rejected. Some children silence those beliefs in interaction with parents. Often the reverse is true: The children contrast the hardship that their parents are experiencing with the relative ease of their peers, and reject the old culture, getting into even more arguments with their parents.

Using a process they call "biculturality effectiveness training," Szapocznik et al. (1986) define the conflict not as between generations, but as between cultures. The family members are then asked in turn to specify what they value about the culture they are *less* identified with, thus valuing both cultures and redefining the conflict in a way that makes resolution possible.

CASE EXAMPLE

A therapist asked for a consultation, reporting that she was having difficulty working with a truant teenager and her mother. She said that the mother was never home to supervise the children and refused the suggestions she made. I learned that Mrs. B, 14-year-old Ana, and Ana's two younger brothers had immigrated from Mexico 2 years ago, not long after Mr. B's accidental death. The paternal grandmother had been living in the United States for the last 5 years. Mrs. B found a small apartment, and her mother-in-law began to live with them. Ana was responsible for caring for her siblings and grandmother after school while her mother worked, and in the evenings that her mother went to school. About a year later, Ana became truant, staying out very late without informing her mother where she was going. The school referred the family for therapy.

The therapist met with Ana and her mother, and recommended that Mrs. B give up one of her two jobs and her evening courses so that she could be more available to her family. She suggested that Ana was a parentified child, and that the caretaking burden be lifted from her. The therapist was looking at the family through a White, middle-class, Northwest European lens; Mrs. B's world was a very different one, and Ana was straddling the two worlds. I attempted to enter the mother's world, where daughters were expected to assume major household responsibilities at early ages. She didn't understand why this was so problematic for Ana. Mrs. B knew that she needed her jobs and courses to make a difference in her life and in the lives of her children. Yet the experts were telling her to give these up. She felt doomed. At the same time, Ana was in public school; she acculturated more quickly, and yet remained loyal to her family and her sense of duty and responsibility. When she stopped going to school, she maintained her household tasks, but also stayed out late to do what she thought American girls did.

The therapist's original recommendations were based on unchallenged assumptions and a traditional model of family therapy: She tried to restore the hierarchy, attempted to develop boundaries between the parental and sibling subsystems, and noted Mrs. B's "resistance." She also ignored the grandmother and placed the entire burden of the family on the mother. Instead, a culturally sensitive, relational family therapy would acknowledge the pull between the old and the new, and understand the mother–daughter struggle as a cultural clash, with an acknowledgment that the family was searching for a way of life that would incorporate both cultures.

In consultation, we looked at the relational picture, and at the isolation experienced by a family that had lost so much. We connected the mother and grandmother with a culturally similar community and with a church that was familiar to them. They could then begin to feel "part of" and not "separate from." From this community, Mrs. B received some of the help she needed, so that neither she nor her children were forced to do the impossible. Ana contributed to the household by being responsible for a kind of babysitting cooperative twice a week, which left her free from major household tasks the other days. On the other days, other families would watch Mrs. B's younger children. We also did not accept the ageist exclusion of the grandmother. Although the grandmother could no longer contribute to household tasks, it became clear that she was very central to the family, as both the banner carrier for tradition and a clear voice about child rearing.

Most important, we validated and respected the struggles of all family members, the major changes in their lives, and their attempts to cope while maintaining family integrity. The emphasis was on relationship (mourning their loss, affirming existing relationships, and developing new ones), restorying (not accepting the story that Mrs. B was resistant, Ana was rebellious, and the grandmother was insignificant, but rather developing a story that focused on strength, relationship, and resilience), and expanding the context (so that the immigration experience and the need to counter personal and cultural isolation constituted the foreground).

SUMMARY

Working with immigrant families challenges us to move beyond the cultural norms and imperatives that we take for granted, and to recognize the richness of other cultures and the strength and resilience of the families who carry those cultures. We need to understand the immigrant experience in its broadest context, which includes the premigration life of the family, the experience of the migration itself, and the benefits and obstacles families face in the adopted country. This involves exploring experiences of loss and trauma; it also means being able to look at the issues of racism, classism, and xenophobia, which cause pain to so many immigrant families. Finally, this involves understanding much of the conflict within couples, as well as between parents and children, as a clash between cultures that marks the beginning of the road toward biculturality. It is a privilege to accompany immigrant families along that road.

NOTES

1. All cases are composites, and quotes are used to illustrate points that I have heard from immigrants. These are not actual quotes, and composites are used to protect confidentiality at the expense of some of the authenticity.

2. Margarita Alvarez (1995) discusses the impact of separation on families in which a child has been brought up in the country of origin and then reunited with a parent living in the United States.

REFERENCES

Alvarez, M. (1995). *The experience of migration: A relational approach in therapy* (Work in Progress No. 71). Wellesley, MA: The Stone Center, Wellesley College.

Breunlin, D. C., Schwartz, R. C., & MacKune-Karrer, B. (1992). *Metaframeworks: Transcending the models of family therapy.* San Francisco: Jossey-Bass.

Breunlin, D. C., Schwartz, R. C., & MacKune-Karrer, B. (1993). Immigration and acculturation. In *AFTA resource packet: Honoring and working with diversity in family therapy.* Washington, DC: American Family Therapy Academy.

Hernandez, M., & Inclan, J. (1993). A conceptual framework for therapy with ethnic minority families. In *AFTA resource packet: Honoring and working with diversity in family therapy.* Washington, DC: American Family Therapy Academy.

Jordan, J., Kaplan, A., Miller, J. B., Stiver, I., & Surrey, J. (1991). *Women's growth in connection: Writings from the Stone Center.* New York: Guilford Press.

Kliman, J. (1994). The interweaving of gender, class, and race in family therapy. In M. P. Mirkin (Ed.), *Women in context: Toward a feminist reconstruction of psychotherapy.* New York: Guilford Press.

Lee, E. (1990). Family therapy with Southeast Asian families. In M. P. Mirkin (Ed.), *The social and political contexts of family therapy.* Needham Heights, MA: Allyn & Bacon.

McGoldrick, M., & Giordano, J. (1996). Overview: Ethnicity and family therapy. In M. McGoldrick, J. Giordano, & J. K. Pearce (Eds.), *Ethnicity and family therapy* (2nd ed.). New York: Guilford Press.

Miller, J. B. (1988). *Connections, disconnections, and violations* (Work in Progress No. 33). Wellesley, MA: The Stone Center, Wellesley College.

Miller, J. B., & Stiver, I. (1991). *A relational reframing of therapy* (Work in Progress No. 52). Wellesley, MA: The Stone Center, Wellesley College.

Miller, J. B., & Stiver, I. (1997). *The healing connection: How women form relationships in therapy and in life.* Boston: Beacon Press.

Mirkin, M. P. (Ed.). (1990). *The social and political contexts of family therapy.* Needham Heights, MA: Allyn & Bacon.

Mirkin, M. P. (1993). Some thoughts about cultural diversity. In *AFTA resource packet: Honoring and working with diversity in family therapy.* Washington, DC: American Family Therapy Academy.

Mirkin, M. P., & Geib, P. (1995). *Consciousness of context in relational couples therapy* (Work in Progress No. 73). Wellesley, MA: The Stone Center, Wellesley College.

Montalvo, B., & Gutierrez, M. (1990). Unevenness of cultural transition: Nine assumptions for work with ethnic minority families. In G. Saba, B. MacKune-Karrer, & K. Hardy (Eds.), *Minorities and family therapy.* New York: Haworth Press.

Ritterman, M., & Simon, R. (1990). Understanding and treating Latin American torture survivors. In M. P. Mirkin (Ed.), *The social and political contexts of family therapy.* Needham Heights, MA: Allyn & Bacon.

Szapocznik, J., Rio, A., Perez, Z. A., & Kurtines, W. (1986). Bicultural effectiveness-training: An experimental test of an intervention modality for families experiencing intergenerational–intercultural conflict. *Hispanic Journal of Behavioral Sciences, 8*(4), 303–330.

White, M. (1995). *Re-authoring lives.* Adelaide, South Australia: Dulwich Centre.

PART VII

NEW APPROACHES TO THERAPY PRACTICE

This final section of the book offers three transformative intervention models based on a re-visioning of families from a contextual perspective. The work of these authors is built around an acceptance of the need for social accountability. They attempt to integrate into their work the multiplicity of considerations that have been presented in this book, while avoiding the polarizing pitfalls we have alluded to. It is worth noticing here that although the emphasis in this book has been on conditions in the United States, two of the three models described in this section have been developed by therapists from other countries. International perspectives are invaluable in our efforts to move beyond therapy that is bound to traditional notions of culture, race, gender, class, and so on.

Nollaig Byrne and Imelda McCarthy have been developing their "Fifth Province" model in Ireland for some years, and here illustrate the creativity of their thinking and work with a complex and tragic case example. Charles Waldegrave and his colleagues in New Zealand have for some years been on the cutting edge of a re-visioning of our field in their "just therapy" model, an approach that attends to social justice in both thinking and practice. This model provides a profound challenge to traditional family therapy approaches by factoring in the impact of oppression on women, on different cultural groups, and on poor families, and by intentionally countering all these types of oppression in their ways of working. In his chapter, Waldegrave concentrates on cultural issues in describing his group's approach. Finally, Rhea Almeida, Rosemary Woods, Theresa Messineo, and Roberto Font offer a description of their extraordinarily creative approach to domestic violence and other family problems. Their approach, which they call the "cultural context model," starts by placing clients in cultural context through a socioeducational training program before they even describe their problems. Problems are thus contextualized from the first moment of assessment. Their program creates a new healing community to counter the dominant culture's oppressive messages; it also challenges the rules of privacy of traditional therapies, validated by our professional associations, which so often promote the status quo of oppressive relationships within families and for families in relation to the larger social context.

CHAPTER 29

Marginal Illuminations
A FIFTH PROVINCE APPROACH
TO INTRACULTURAL ISSUES
IN AN IRISH CONTEXT

Nollaig O'Reilly Byrne
Imelda Colgan McCarthy

> The word in language is half someone else's. It
> becomes "one's own" only when the speaker
> populates it with his own intent, his own accent, when
> he appropriates the word, adapting it to his own
> semantic and expressive intention.
> —BAKHTIN (1981, p. 293)

In the family therapy literature, a focus on multiculturalism has enabled practitioners to develop culture-specific practices for work with persons from ethnic groups other than those of the dominant culture (McGoldrick, 1996). Implicit in the term "multiculturalism," as a social orientation and concern, is the recognition of the potential for the silencing of marginal groups by the politically and culturally dominant. Therefore, as a requirement of justice, the value aspirations and needs specific to a particular cultural group are accorded moral recognition within a multicultural stance. However, a multiculturalism that produces an endless fallout of stories without acknowledging their interplay with the dominant cultural narratives with which they coexist will ultimately fail in its moral quest.

For the purpose of this chapter, "Marginal Illuminations,"[1] we are using an intracultural account to elaborate the particular story of one family living on the margins of Irish society. Like other welfare recipients, the members of this family are eminently vulnerable to state interventions.

COMMUNITY DEVELOPMENT AND
THE EMERGENCE OF A FIFTH PROVINCE APPROACH

In an attempt to redress this top-down stance of state services, community development and other associated projects, politically and spiritually informed by narratives of justice, speak to the possibility of an authentic cultural partnership with marginalized groups. The members of the "just therapy" group in New Zealand describe the ethical responsibility of dominant groups as one of entering into a decolonizing awareness, and the responsibility of practitioners as a sacred task to bring health and welfare to the people (see Waldegrave, Chapter 30, this volume). In their work, as in our own, the coauthoring of new stories (White & Epston, 1990) is addressed to the particular cultural experiences of the people we work with, while simultaneously remembering the overarching dominant cultural narratives that constrain them.

Since the mid-1980s, we have worked under the team name of the Fifth Province Associates (FPA). During this time we have collaborated with a colleague, Sister Jo Kennedy, who has taken a key role in forwarding community action/education/therapy projects in a deprived community (Kennedy, 1994). As an experienced professional, a family therapist, and a member of a religious community, she began to share housing with the people in a high-density public housing project. Her presence there was a sign and a witness to the inception of noncolonizing practices addressed to the dire needs of this community. Initially, as an "outsider," she had to sustain much hostility and suspicion from the community where she was now living. With time, her witness to the hardship of the people's day-to-day life made her an acceptable member of the community. In turn, we, the team, were given the opportunity by Sister Jo to develop a more refined, focused political and spiritual orientation for our own practice. We have learned much from her ongoing work, marked by the love implicit in commitment, creativity, and physical endurance.

Out of our many collaborative conversations with Sister Jo and her work in developing community initiatives and becoming kindred in that community, we have privileged to develop an "insider's" perspective drawn from the weave and tangle of many stories told to her, the events she has witnessed, and the advocacy she has articulated as a member of the community.

THE METAPHOR OF THE FIFTH PROVINCE:
TOWARD AN ETHICS OF IMAGINATION

The issues of intracultural diversity and silenced voices have been concerns for us since we began to work together in 1981. The story we tell in this chapter is the story of just one particular kind of intercultural marginalization: the story of a family living in poverty. Because of the processes of marginalization that occur in our society, those who are poor are socially excluded, and the stories of their lives on the edge are often silenced. Thus, listening to these silenced accounts becomes an ethical and political act of no small significance. Out of these concerns, we adopted the metaphor of the Fifth Province (Byrne, 1996; Byrne & McCarthy, 1995; Colgan, 1992; Kearney, Byrne, & McCarthy, 1989; McCarthy & Byrne, 1995; McCarthy, 1994).[2] The metaphor is taken from Celtic mythology and the work of two Irish philosophers, Richard Kearney and Mark P. Hederman (Hederman & Kearney, 1977). In the work of this team, the metaphor of the Fifth Province enables a re-view of the issues of power, justice, and language in relationships. It is in itself a metaphor for multicultural perspectives, as it refers to the possibility of holding together multiple stories and social realities in dialogue. For us, it is a province of possibilities, of imagination, and of ethics.

To imagine the life of an other is to adopt a stance of ethical responsibility toward the other. Placing such a stance within a therapeutic domain that features issues of social justice is a political act. Thus, a Fifth Province dis-position[3] in systemic therapies is, for us, about occupying a borderline territory between our own world and that of the people we are in conversation with. Richard Kearney (1996) has outlined an ethics of imagination, which is underpinned by three main principles. The first is the acceptance of the other. The second principle is the right of all to be heard and to have the testimony to their experiences witnessed. The final principle is the imagining of future possibilities. We incorporate these three principles when we utilize the Fifth Province metaphor. As a province of possibilities in language and imagination, it also becomes a province or domain of ethics. If those from marginalized groups are to be able to tell the stories of their lived experiences in a context where normative compliances are expected, then we must also recognize that there is a danger of subjecting them to silence and co-option (Byrne & McCarthy, 1995). We hold that imposing normative expectations on marginalized clients without reference to their contexts of adversity constitutes a colonial therapeutic stance that distances us from the subjugated other.

With a history of long periods of colonization behind us, we as Irish therapists want to honor our long oral tradition of storytelling of survival. We also imagine that life on the edges produces stories that may not reside comfortably within many of our normative discursive frames. As such, we hold strongly that it is the responsibility of therapists from Western traditions to reflect upon their own practices and theories, and not to expect clients to fit the norms of their professional practice. If this occurs there is a danger that both the therapists and the clients will blame the clients for the lack of fit. In culture-blind practices, therapists can become nonconscious oppressors in the guise of helping (Kearney et al., 1989; Byrne & McCarthy, 1995; Lorenz, 1994). Under such a regime, clients have little choice but to subjugate themselves further in order to avail themselves of help.

STORIES AND CONVERSATIONS
IN THE FIFTH PROVINCE:
A FAMILY–PROFESSIONAL NETWORK

In our collaboration with Sister Jo, we have had the opportunity to have conversations with families judged by an array of professionals to be incorrigible or inaccessible to services. In family–professional network meetings where Sister Jo's community alliance with the family has provided cultural safety for the work, it has been possible for families to assert their concerns and to reclaim responsibility for culturally fitting solutions. We as professionals, previously limited by an outsider's view, have sometimes heard for the first time stories that have proved crucial in a family's self-understanding. In these meetings, a family's account can be given without fear of correction or censure.

The work we re-present in this chapter included a paternal grandmother, Chrissie; a separated father, Joe; a lone mother, Mary; and Joe and Mary's six children—Tricia, 21 years; Brendan, 18 years; Jack, 16 years; Margaret, 14 years; Peter, 12 years (severely mentally and physically disabled, and not present at the interviews); and Joseph, 10 years.[4] Also included were a probation officer, a school attendance officer, Sister Jo, ourselves, and our FPA colleague Philip Kearney,[5] who conducted the family interviews. (Figure 29.1 illustrates the entire family–professional network.) Throughout the interview excerpts that follow, we highlight a Fifth Province dis-position in which a family's tale of outrageous and harmful acts, for which state censure was never far removed, was transformed.

Assembling the Family–Professional Network

Mary, Sister Jo, the school attendance officer, and the probation officer attended the first meeting with us. Mary explained that she had met with and listened to numerous professionals who advised her on the merits of controlling and supervising her children, all to no avail. Of immediate concern was the fact that Margaret and Joseph had absented themselves from school and would soon become subject to placement by the courts

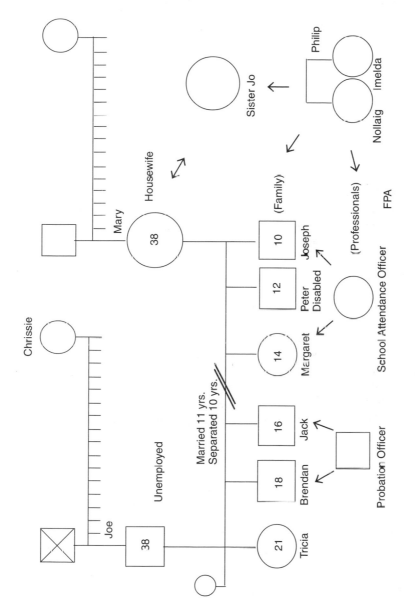

FIGURE 29.1. The family–professional network.

in a residential school. The older children, Tricia, Brendan, and Jack, were experiencing grave difficulties with drugs and violence. Peter attended a special school for children with serious intellectual disabilities.

Despite the inventory of difficulties as described by Mary, her status as protector of her children was not in question. The unambiguousness of her stance as she voiced her care and love for her difficult children was the familiar story of many mothers in that community, for whom Sister Jo was a resource person. Anchoring ourselves to this mother's concern made it possible for us to imagine the possibility of speaking to the children on her behalf, and not by way of her displacement and/or a societal insertion of authority. This professional acknowledgment of Mary's perspective provided an arena of cultural safety for the children, where they might not be constrained from speaking to a group of listeners about what most mattered to them.

We went on to suggest that the second network meeting might also include the children. Mary and Sister Jo agreed. To everybody's surprise, there was no difficulty in assembling them all (apart from Peter). Although their day-to-day lives suggested harmful activity, dispersal, and disconnection, it soon became clear that the possibility of family connection and continuity held a precious place in their lives. Using excerpts from the second meeting, we attempt to show how our inquiry—referred to by us as "questioning at the extremes"—threaded together a family narrative of tragic desperation, where forces of extinction and survival coexisted in an uncommonly close partnership. "Questioning at the extremes" is a mode of exaggerated inquiry whereby questions are directed toward revealing the extreme possibilities of a presented idea. As an example, when drug and alcohol abuse was mentioned as a frequent and dangerous activity for the children in this family, questions were then asked about who were the most likely ones to kill themselves. Killing oneself was the assumed extension of drug and alcohol abuse.

A Question of "Harmful" Extremes

The word "harm" was introduced by Mary in the first session as she expressed her ongoing concerns about her children's dangerous actions. It thus became the "motif," which proposed danger to, if not extinction of individual family members. As Mary's central concern for her children, it guided the inquiry to a place where the children could give an account.

PHILIP: Who is it that has taken overdoses in this family?

BRENDAN: Me and Jack.

PHILIP: Just the two of you?

BRENDAN: Yeh. Me and Jack, mostly.

PHILIP: (*To Tricia*) Have you taken overdoses?

TRICIA: I have.

BRENDAN: One.

JACK: Two.

TRICIA: I take a lot of tablets in the day.

PHILIP: Yeh, but have you taken deliberate overdoses?

TRICIA: Yeh. Twice.

PHILIP: Twice. You tried to kill yourself?

TRICIA: (*Looking confusedly to Mary, her mother*) No.

BRENDAN: No, he [Jack] is the only one who tried to kill himself.

PHILIP: He is the only one who has tried to kill himself (*Jack nods agreement*) . . . using tablets or what?

JACK: Tablets and drink.

What was surprising here was the willingness of the three older children to give first-person accounts of their involvement in acts of deliberate self-harm through drug and alcohol abuse. As seen in this segment, the children corrected a common professional assumption that overdoses are deliberate self-harming behaviors. They insisted on the distinction between intentional (Jack) and nonintentional (Tricia and Brendan) effects of self-harming behaviors.

The Risk of Suicide: A Mother and Son

PHILIP: (*To Mary*) And which of them do you think is most likely to harm themselves, through overdosing or whatever?

MARY: I think mostly Jack. He can be about the most depressed, in that . . . he is inclined to . . . Brendan will take tablets, but it might not be with the intention to kill himself—but he [Jack] would just keep on taking them.

PHILIP: So would you think that Jack is the most likely candidate for suicide?

MARY: Yeh.

PHILIP: And after Jack?

MARY: Brendan or Tricia, but I don't know if they would just take them at the moment, but not think that they are going to . . . not really wanting to kill themselves.

PHILIP: Would you say that your mother might commit suicide, Brendan?

BRENDAN: If we keep on going on the way we are, she will.

PHILIP: You think so?

BRENDAN: Yeh.

PHILIP: When did you first think of that as a possibility?

BRENDAN: The last 4 or 5 months.

TRICIA: I would say my mother would have taken her life long ago if my brother wasn't the way he is today. She knows he is depending on her, you know.

PHILIP: Which brother—Peter?

TRICIA: Peter, yeh. Peter is brain-damaged, too.

PHILIP: Yeh.

TRICIA: He can't walk or anything.

PHILIP: So you think if it weren't for him, your mother would have killed herself a long time ago?

TRICIA: Ah, yes, if it weren't for him she wouldn't be here today—or neither would we, you know.

PHILIP: I see. What would have happened?

TRICIA: She would either have killed herself or left us.

PHILIP: I see, yeh.

BRENDAN: And we would be after driving her to do it.

JOSEPH: And if she had died, we would have killed ourselves.

BRENDAN: Then if she died, we would have killed ourselves, and if she went, everything would have been worse and worse and worse.

JACK: And we probably would have followed her.

PHILIP: Yeh, OK . . .

JOSEPH: If she left us, there would be nothing left of the family.

The theme of suicidal risk was developed by Mary in response to Philip's question as she made distinctions among her children and confirmed declarations they had already made. Staying within the thematic frame of suicide, Philip raised the question as to whether Brendan, as oldest son and commentator on family issues, considered his mother to be in this risk category as well. What followed from the children was an acutely stark and condensed reply to an extreme question. This dialogue, which had the structure of a chorus, focused the question on the shared tragic experience of the family. Of cultural interest here is the fact that these barely literate children, with poor attention skills and much intragroup aggression and conflict, could produce in language a synchrony of voices of such dramatic structure and intensity.

From the children's point of view, Mary as mother, protector, and caretaker was the most tragically affected by Peter's injury, and this was the thread that maintained her tenuous presence in the family. This was the story that condemned and bound the children to a guilty stance toward both their mother and Peter. In addressing this interminable self-condemnation, the team through Philip referred to it as a "spell" cast over their lives, from which they must be released. To discuss their liberation from this "spell," we suggested a further meeting. At Mary's suggestion, the father and paternal grandmother, Joe and Chrissie, would also be invited.

Sacrificial Losses: A Father and Son

The following is an excerpt from the conversation that occurred in the third family–professional network meeting. As noted above, Joe and Chrissie attended, because Mary considered them to have a powerful influence on the lives of her children. As the session progressed, it emerged that Peter's disabilities and his place in the family related not only to the children's spellbound state, but also to Joe's sense of helplessness and desperation. Peter, when he was 2 years old, had fallen through a refuse chute in the tower block (i.e., government-subsidized apartment building) where the family lived. He was in the company of Brendan, then 8 years old. Joe wanted to wipe away the event by killing either himself or Peter. In recognizing Peter's importance to Mary, he decided to "give up everything that meant anything to me" and leave the family.

PHILIP: We talked a little the two previous times we have been here about other major events, like Peter's accident . . .

JOE: That was just . . . that was . . . I wouldn't even go into that now, you know what I mean? (*Voice breaks*)

PHILIP: It is too upsetting?

JOE: I think I would still be at home today if that had not happened to Peter, you know. Because I know for a fact, and she [Mary] knows as well, if I was to stay in that house for 3 days with that young fellow, I would smother him.

PHILIP: I didn't know that. (*To Mary*) Did you know that?

MARY: He came in one night, and (*to Joe*) you were drunk and I was putting Peter to bed, and you came up and you did say that to me.

JOE: I had the pillow and I was going to do it, and I was crying, and I said to her, "The only way I can . . . "

MARY: And I nearly lost my reason. . . . I have never really forgotten that, you know . . .

JOE: I mean, you are looking at a child who was perfect and running around. It was unfortunate that it had to be him that it happened to.

MARY: But he is so lovable.

JOE: Like you see kids now running around with their toys and everything. I know how wild he was, and seeing him now . . . I mean that . . .

PHILIP: Did you hear what Mary has just said, that he could be so lovable? Because I was very struck by your kids' talk about how important Peter is in the family.

JOE: I mean, Peter is everything—I mean, if anything happened to him now, I don't know, like, but there is no way I could live with the guy, you know. I couldn't live in the same house as him. I can't even bear to look at him. Don't get me wrong—every time I go up there and I see Peter, I think of the way he was. I cannot accept what happened to him.

PHILIP: Is that the hardest thing for you to accept?

JOE: Well, you put yourself in my shoes.

PHILIP: Sure . . . well, I can't even begin to . . . You have had many things to accept, I imagine.

JOE: I will never accept that. That is just one thing I will never accept. I was praying that he would not even come out of the hospital.

MARY: Well, I wanted him back, no matter what way I got him back. I just wanted him.

JOE: We did not get Peter back.

PHILIP: And you are saying that that is the reason why you are not in the house? That is why you left?

JOE: Well, that was really the breaking point between me and her. She took a nervous breakdown, and I ended up cracking up myself.

Philip: What happened?

JOE: Ah, well, I took a couple of overdoses (*voice trembles*) and that myself. Then I said to myself I would be better off getting rid of him rather than getting rid of myself. And I think I would have anyway.

PHILIP: And that is still the same for you?

JOE: Oh, yeh, I still feel the same way about it, yeh, even to the present day. I mean, I have talked to her [Mary] of this before.

MARY: No, I never heard those points so much before, I really didn't.

PHILIP: Which ones?

MARY: About Peter, regarding him dead and that. Just one night he did it, and I thought it . . . I overlooked it because I thought you were just drunk that night. You were crying and that. I think I said it to you, and I have never forgotten it.

JOE: Yeh, I know, yeh.

MARY: But I didn't think you felt that strongly. I thought it was because you were just drunk that night.

JOE: It is just like having a building, and you going away on holidays for a week and just looking, and your building is just condemned. I mean, it is the same way with Peter. I mean, Peter is going to need to be lifted around for the rest of his life. I mean, there is no way he is ever going to be able to live a life.

PHILIP: Has it anything to do with the circumstances of his accident?

JOE: How he got injured? There are still an awful lot of lies being told about how Peter got injured, and I don't think anybody has been able to face up to it. It has never really come out into the open, what really happened to Peter.

PHILIP: And who is most affected by that?

JOE: I don't know, to tell you the truth. I don't know.

PHILIP: I mean, is it the two of you, or is it the children, or is it . . .

JOE: Oh, I mean, I know she was broken up something terrible about it. I mean, I was broken up, but what could we do.

PHILIP: Who gets blamed for it?

JOE: Who gets blamed for Peter's accident?

PHILIP: Yeh.

JOE: Well, I always blame Brendan for Peter's accident, and I always will.

PHILIP: And how does that affect your relationship with Brendan?

JOE: It doesn't affect my relationship with Brendan now, because, I mean, he was only a child himself.

One of Joe's remarks above, "It is just like having a building . . . ," referred to an event in the family's history before Peter's accident. Years earlier, the family had lived in housing that was originally built as a barracks for the British Army in the 19th century. During the 1960s this housing was demolished, at which time the families living there were abruptly dispersed, disrupting their community identity and sense of place. The Peter who was remembered—the one who didn't come back, the one condemned to "uselessness"—was linked in Joe's mind with this family's historical experience of slum clearance. In cleaning up eyesores, did the official culture forget its obligation to the people who, for generation after generation, gave birth, lived, and died in this place? It was as if Joe was here reminded of that abrupt transition from a home to a useless and condemned building. However, in his telling, part of the responsibility for Peter's accident also resided within the family. It was this latter catastrophe that pushed him to further displacement. His leaving could be seen not only as a separation from his wife or abandonment of his family, but also as a sacrifice to protect Peter's life. This account drew together the "justice" exacted from Joe's "choices" in the family, and the pathos of failure and weakness in his exclusion. His self-justificatory appeal moved between lived experience and anticipated evaluative judgments. Joe's remark, "Well, you put yourself in my shoes," and Philip's rejoinder, "Sure . . . well, I can't even begin to . . . ," both acknowledged the incommensurability of discourses and the authentic distance of positions between the two speakers in this instance.

PHILIP: (*To Chrissie*) Which do you think was the greater loss for Mary: the injury to Peter—what happened to him—or Joe leaving?

CHRISSIE: The injury to her son.

PHILIP: Was more than her husband leaving?

CHRISSIE: Um.

PHILIP: You are very clear about that.

CHRISSIE: Um.

PHILIP: (*To Mary*) Do you agree?

CHRISSIE: Because I think more of my sons than I would of my husband any day.

PHILIP: Did I catch that right?

CHRISSIE: I think more of my sons than I would of my husband any day.

PHILIP: Yes, that is what I thought you said, yes. Would that be the same for you, Mary?

MARY: Yes, well, I brought them into the world, you know. He is part of both of us, really, but still I love them all. If it happened to any of them, I would have still felt the same way. It wouldn't have been important.

JOE: I think I would still be in the home today if that had not happened to Peter, you know.

Here Philip invited exaggerated comparison (a questioning at the extremes) between these two losses for Mary—that is, Joe's leaving and Peter's injury. Chrissie, the grandmother, by way of validation, was in no doubt about the greater loss: "The injury to her son." In this validation and her further statement, "Because I think more of my sons than I would of my husband any day," she cited the position of mother and child as central to the concept of "family." In a confessional autobiographical mode, Joe, Chrissie and Mary made manifest to a group of listeners the criminal and the tragic narratives that authorized their lives. The unity of this account presented a stark contradiction to the moral sensibility of normative conventions.

The Injured and the Innocent: A Connecting Narrative between Statutory Mandates and a Family's "Guilt"

From a position of distance and the expectation of normative evaluation, the team was called upon by the family's story to register a response beyond passive and (as the family thought) condemnatory listening. The image of Peter, everywhere evident in the family's account as the injured and the innocent, was the resonant key that opened the many-layered narrative of guilt and innocence. Peter's innocence pointed to possibilities for reauthoring, through which the family members and professionals might move beyond blame and counterblame, and in which the innocence of the family might be glimpsed by all. We in the team began to ask ourselves, "What is it that Peter might see when he looks at his family? What is it that Peter asks for?" He was the bearer of the most injury, and yet did not blame or accuse. We imagined that he saw the family members as they would wish to see themselves, if they were not blighted by adversity, failure, and self-condemnation. The following was our attempt to incorporate an ethical imagining.

The Team's Message

PHILIP: (*To Joe*) The story you have told us about Peter is absolutely central. . . . It seems that the family's possibilities . . . in a sense stopped with Peter's accident. That the possibilities of people in this family going on to a life of happiness and fulfillment stopped because of Peter's injury and his handicap. . . . It is as if when you look into his face that you say something like "I cannot enjoy my wife, my kids, my family because of what happened to you." It almost comes across that everybody in the family is under a spell. That because this child was injured and handicapped, "we are not free." In a sense, it is as if he has all the innocence . . .

JOE: (*Nods*) Yeh.

PHILIP: And everybody else has all the guilt. So that is what we now see as the spell your family is under, and that it is for you people to decide whether that is going to continue or not. Because if you don't, there is no doubt but that the outside society (*pointing to professionals*) will intervene.

JOE: Um.

PHILIP: And they will come and place your kids in care, and they will be doing it for the best reasons in the world. But somewhere in there, there is the possibility to change that for yourselves. We imagine that if we could see the world, see the family from Peter's eyes, we would see only the good side—of being taken care of, of people smiling at him, people doing things for him. I would say he would see an awful lot of good about the people in this family.

JOE: Ah, yeh. I would agree with that, allright, like if it was Peter looking out and like the way he is. Yeh, of course he would, yeh.

PHILIP: He had an extraordinary, powerful influence in this family. It is as if everyone is going around under a sentence since his accident, really.

JOE: Well, that is what the priest said to us. He said it to us . . . the priest in the hospital. "This is going to change your lives completely. When you walk outside the door now, after you know the news, you know how bad things are. It is going to be a completely different world out there. Even the road you walk on is going to seem different."

PHILIP: OK, well, I am saying that I believe it doesn't have to be like that always. . . . It seems to me that you have made a huge sacrifice since then. You gave up a lot.

JOE: I gave up everything that meant anything to me.

PHILIP: Yeh. I think Mary gave up a lot too.

JOE: She did, of course, yeh.

This was the team's acknowledgment that a professional stance is never "innocent" (McCarthy, 1991; Andersen, 1995). Most professional discourses are shot through with normative and professional judgments, which inevitably collide with marginalized personal accounts (Byrne & McCarthy, 1995). Mary's earlier remark, "I wanted him back, no matter what way I got him back," expressed this mother's valuing of a life, however disabled, as the deepest affirmation of an ethics of care. Joe, as the father and the bearer of guilt, was now addressed by Philip.

PHILIP: Maybe you have paid whatever dues have to be paid, and maybe for your kids' sake you need to . . . perhaps . . . stop paying them. I don't know, it is just a thought, because otherwise the kids may think they have to go on paying them for ever.

JOE: I know, yeh (*rubbing his eyes*).

PHILIP: And that is the way they are behaving.

JOE: I know what you mean, like, they feel guilty as well.

PHILIP: Yeh, and they may be think that the only way that they can be in the world is to continue to pay those dues, and they don't have to. (*Joe nods*) Because Peter is not asking it of them.

JOE: I know that, yeh.

In this inclusive move, Joe, reconnected himself with his children in their mutual but invalidating narrative of guilt and failure. These family members were the invalids beyond Mary's reach. Only Peter, standing outside condemnation, was able to recognize them and asked nothing of them except care.

CONCLUSION

To sum up the views we have expressed in this chapter, a narrative of a unique family or personal situation will remain exotic and incomprehensible if it is isolated from the larger social and cultural context that pervades it. Therefore, the contextual interplay between the personal stories of the marginalized and the larger narratives of injustice that penetrate their lives is constantly acknowledged. It is within this multilayered, resonating interplay—through speaking, inquiring, exaggerating, listening, and reflecting—that meaning is extended beyond the isolated words of both clients and professionals. What emerges, we believe, within this personalized and politicized cocreation is the possibility of an authentic emotional encounter.

In the years since this series of meetings, no one in this family has died, been jailed, been placed in care, or been hospitalized. The family for their part continues to exhibit its archetypal shape, although its members now hold themselves more aloof from professional intervention. Sister Jo remains a resource both to members of this family and to others in the community. Our conversations with her regarding the relevance of systemic practice to issues of justice and poverty continue (see Kennedy, 1994). The probation and school attendance officers reported a dramatic decrease in tension with the family, and experienced a release from the impossible double agendas of and contradictions between social control and therapeutic support.

ACKNOWLEDGMENTS

We would like to dedicate this chapter to Sister Jo Kennedy and to the family we describe here. We also acknowledge Philip Kearney, our colleague and dear friend of many years.

NOTES

1. It is a feature of Celtic manuscripts such as the 8th-century *Book of Kells* that major illuminations are placed in the margins.

2. The Fifth Province may have existed or it may not. There are many versions. Some say it was a province of imagination and possibility—a place that was other to the pragmatic concerns of the "real" world. Others site it as a druidic place at the center of Ireland, where the four provinces met and where kings and chieftains came to receive counsel and resolve conflicts through dialogue. Today its only remaining trace is in the Irish language, where the word for province is *coiced,* which means "fifth."

3. "Dis-position" is a term used by the FPA. It is hyphenated to illustrate movement between the taking of a position and the nontaking of one by a therapist. The term was first used by Seamus Heaney in the foreword to an issue of the Irish journal *The Crane Bag,* which was edited by Irish philosophers Richard Kearney and Mark P. Hederman (Heaney, 1977, p. 7).

4. The names of all family members have been changed.

5. Philip Kearney worked with us until 1995 and collaborated in the development of the ideas and practices outlined in this chapter.

REFERENCES

Andersen, T. (1995). Reflecting processes: Acts of informing and forming. In S. Friedman (Ed.), *The reflecting team in action.* New York: Guilford Press.

Bakhtin, M. (1981). *The dialogical imagination.* (M. Holquist, Ed.; C. Emerson & M. Holquist, Trans.). Austin: University of Texas Press.

Byrne, N. O'R. (1996). Diamond absolutes: A daughter's response to her mother's abortion. *Human Systems, 6*(3–4), 255–277.

Byrne, N. O'R., & McCarthy, I. C. (1988). Moving statues: Re-questing ambivalence through ambiguous discourse. *Irish Journal of Psychology, 9,* 173–182.

Byrne, N. O'R., & McCarthy, I. C. (1995). Abuse, risk and protection. In C. Burck & B. Speed (Eds.), *Gender and power in relationships.* London: Routledge.

Colgan, F. I. (1992). *The Fifth Province model: Father–daughter incest disclosure and systemic consultation.* Unpublished doctoral dissertation, University College Dublin.

Heaney, S. (1977). Preface. *The Crane Bag, 1,* 7–8.

Hederman, M. P., & Kearney, R. (1977). Editorial. *The Crane Bag, 1*(1), 10–12.

Kearney, P. A., Byrne, N. O'R., & McCarthy, I. C. (1989). Just metaphors: Marginal illuminations in a colonial retreat. *Family Therapy Case Studies, 4,* 17–31.

Kearney, R. (1996). Narrative imagination: Between ethics and poetics. In R. Kearney (Ed.), *Paul Ricoeur: The hermaneutics of action.* London: Sage.

Kennedy, J. (1994). Living and working in a poor community. *Human Systems, 5*(3–4), 209–218.

Lorenz, W. (1994). *Social work in a changing Europe.* London: Routledge.

McCarthy, I. C. (1990). Paradigms lost: Re-membering her-stories and other invalid subjects. *Journal of Contemporary Family Therapy, 12,* 427–437.

McCarthy, I. C. (1991). Colonial sentences and just subversions: The potential for love and abuse in therapeutic encounters. *Feedback, 3,* 3–7.

McCarthy, I. C. (1994). Abusing norms: Welfare families and a Fifth Province stance. *Human Systems, 5*(3–4), 229–239.

McCarthy, I. C. (1995). Serving those in poverty: A benevolent colonisation? In J. van Lawick & M. Sanders (Eds.), *Gender and beyond.* Amsterdam: LS Books.

McCarthy, I. C., & Byrne, N. O'R. (1988). Mis-taken love: Conversations on the problem of incest in an Irish context. *Family Process, 27,* 181–199.

McCarthy, I. C., & Byrne, N. O'R. (1995). A spell in therapy: It's between meself, herself, yerself and yer two imaginary friends. In S. Friedman (Ed.), *The reflecting team in action.* New York: Guilford Press.

McGoldrick, M. (1996). Irish families. In M. McGoldrick, J. Giordano, & J. K. Pearce (Eds.), *Ethnicity and family therapy* (2nd ed.). New York: Guilford Press.

White, M., & Epston, D. (1990). *Narrative means to therapeutic ends.* New York: Norton.

CHAPTER 30

The Challenges
of Culture to Psychology
and Postmodern Thinking

Charles Waldegrave

Subjecting the assumptions that underpin the social sciences to a cultural analysis can be a disturbing experience indeed. Such an analysis will confront the claims of the social sciences, and thus psychology, to knowledge that is independent, neutral, objective, and verifiable (Weiten, 1995; Habermas, 1971). Furthermore, a cultural analysis challenges the claim to an international body of knowledge that is intercultural.

Consider, for example, the language and the metaphors that are used in clinical psychology: the medical metaphors with their words like diagnoses and cures, the biological metaphors with their systemic focus, and of course social science itself, are metaphors modelled on the physical sciences and positivist thinking (Harré Hindmarsh, 1993). These all combine to create practitioners who search for objective diagnoses, objective causes, objective explanations, and objective cures. Many clinicians have become so attached, in fact, to the scientific metaphor that it is no wonder that psychiatry, psychology, and nursing, for example, often rely primarily on the so-called objectivity of chemical therapies to heal. They often diagnose only to sort out which chemistry to use. But even when therapy is not that of chemistry, it often relies on category diagnoses, such as those set out in the *Diagnostic and Statistical Manual of Mental Disorders* (DSM) published by the American Psychiatric Association, and the so-called scientific medical explanations and cures (Tomm, 1990).

Postmodern thinking in the European world has challenged all that (Foucault, 1971; Maturana & Varela, 1980). Of course there has always been skepticism outside the European world to the cold positivist metaphors. Maori and Pacific Island people in New Zealand have seldom voluntarily used the services of therapy. Normally, it was only when they were directed by the Departments of Social Welfare, Justice, or a psychiatric hospital, that they attended. On the whole, these processes have been imposed on them. Faith in the system amongst poor Pakeha (European) people has been rather questionable also. But the real challenge to the so-called objectivity of the scientific approach within the European world is with the postmodern developments and particularly critical postmodern thinking.

Postmodernism basically states that events occur in the physical world, and people give meaning to those events. In this paradigm there is no objective meaning and no objective explanation. For example, I could walk over to a Maori woman colleague and friend of mine and put my arm on her shoulder. We could take this as an event that has occurred in the physical world. Different people will give different meanings to that event. Some people might say it's a friendly gesture. Other people might say it's a patronizing gesture. Some might say it's a racist gesture. Another person might say it's cross-cultural camaraderie. Yet another could label it as violent and another person could say it's intrusive and sexist, and so on. The point is that there is no objective reality in terms of the explanations of events that occur in the physical world.

There are problems with this view, though, as it can suggest that all explanations are simply of equal value. But that is often not the case. The Jewish and Polish experience and explanations of World War II offer meanings quite different from the Nazi explanations and meanings of those same events, and we would want to treat them differently. Similarly, the victims/survivors of abuse often give different meanings to the physical events of their abuse than many perpetrators do; we would want to talk critically about the difference in those meanings.

So critical postmodernism talks about "preferred meanings" (Giroux, 1983; Waldegrave, 1990; Harré Hindmarsh, 1993; Tamasese & Waldegrave, 1993)—meanings that emerge out of values. For example, we would want to say that gender equity is preferable to male dominance, or that cultural self-determination is preferable to monocultural dominance. Whatever position we take flavors our view of the world. If there is no objective meaning, but simply explanations of meaning, then we have to start assessing our values and ethics in relation to these meanings—particularly when we work with individuals or with a family. The issue of our values becomes essential.

The contribution made by postmodernism is the view that all constructions of reality are simply that: constructions. And those constructions include the social sciences. In fact, we could go further and assert that the social sciences simply offer one cultural description of events that occur in the physical world. That particular cultural explanation springs out of a world view that centers around concepts of individualism and secularism, which are dominant values in Western Europe and White North America. There are, in fact, many other cultural explanations and descriptions of events. This perspective is a critical postmodern stance, and this stance is central to our work at the Family Centre.

Many people remember the days when both sexual and physical abuse were looked upon by psychologists and other therapists in clinical terms, within the old medical, biological, and social science metaphors. Causes were sought, and symptoms were treated, but the abuse itself was often ignored or considered outside the clinical arena. Numbers of women politicized the issue, however, and clarified the meaning they gave such events (Bograd, 1984; Goldner, 1985; Pilalis & Anderton, 1986; McKinnon & Miller, 1987; Kamsler, 1990). Psychologists and therapists can no longer act as they did before. The 'abuse' and the meanings we now give it have changed our practice and our explanations, not to mention the law. The tired old positivist metaphors were simply inadequate to the task. In fact, they contributed to a lot of unethical behavior. It was the change of meaning, to a preferred meaning, that made the difference. This was not discovered scientifically; it was the result of a political movement that created new awareness by drawing attention to the meanings we gave these events.

Bearing all this in mind, social scientists and clinicians should be more humble in their claims to knowledge. There is very little that we actually know. Take, for example, schizophrenia: We don't really know what it is or how to treat it, but we're very good at labeling people with it. In fact, we know very little in the social sciences about mental health. We have had few successes, in real terms; failure is more characteristic of our work in mental health institutions, as well as in prisons and in welfare. The record is quite appalling. It could be said that there is no evidence that exorcism, traditional healing, or faith healing is any less successful in its work within the communities embracing such practices.

With that backdrop, let us consider some of the issues that work with different cultures entails. Cultures are all about the meanings people give events. They raise issues that are critical for psychologists, such as identity and belonging. Our experience at the Family Centre—an organization that is structured along cultural lines, in the fields of family therapy, community development, social policy research, and education—has led to many new learnings. We do our work within three cultural sections, Maori, Pacific Island, and Pakeha (European); each section is staffed primarily by workers from that particular culture. The following are some of our learnings.

IDEAS OF SELF VERSUS FAMILY

All cultures carry with them history, beliefs, and ways of doing things. In particular, cultures carry meanings. We experience practically all the most intimate events in our lives within a culture or cultures. Within our families or intimate groupings, we learn the rules and the accepted ways of doing things. Public life is also determined by the meanings created by cultures. This is very significant; it indicates that anyone working with people from a culture different from his or her own requires at least a qualitative appreciation and informed knowledge of that culture. Normally, the only way people get such appreciation and knowledge is by being a part of that culture, or at least being extremely familiar with, and working under some supervision from, someone of that culture.

This is often misunderstood by White people. It is often misunderstood, because most of us in White cultures seldom reflect on our base values or consider how much our culture is permeated with the concepts of individualism. Most psychological theories, for example, have been developed in Western Europe, and White North America. In those cultures, as in Pakeha (European) New Zealand, individual self-worth is very important. Indeed, for practically all clinical psychological and psychotherapeutic theories, the primary goal of therapy is that of individual self-worth. That is because destiny, responsibility, legitimacy, and even human rights are seen to be essentially individual concepts. Concepts of self, individual assertiveness, and fulfillment are central to most of these therapies.

On the other hand, for people who come from a communal or extended family cultures, questions of self-exposure and self-assertion are often confusing and even alienating. I remember one occasion when I was involved in a project with the Family Centre's Pacific Island Section. We were talking about and debating the whole concept of self in psychotherapy and psychology. One of the workers said, "You don't realize what it is like for me as a Samoan, when I'm asked a question like 'What do you think?' about something in therapy. It is so hard for me to answer that question. I have to think, 'What does my mother think? What does my grandmother think? What does my father think? What does my uncle think? What does my sister think? What is the consensus of those thoughts? Ah, that must be what I think.'" That was how he described it. He explained that for him, "What do you think?" was an unnatural question, and an extraordinarily intrusive one.

Questions relating to self often alienate people in communal and extended family cultures; they crudely crash though their sensitivities. Within individually based cultures, such questions can be quite appropriate. Outside these cultures, however, the questions are often experienced as intrusive and rude, as my Samoan colleague's experience illustrates. They can rupture cooperative sensitivities among people, and destroy the essential framework for meaning, which should be drawn upon for healing.

Some examples from our own practice may help illustrate this. At the Family Centre, when the first Maori worker decided to develop a Maori therapy, I was invited to dialogue with him and other Maori colleagues in our community. Early in the project, a couple was referred from the Family Court in regard to child custody and access dispute. In those days at the Family Centre, there was one Maori worker, Warihi Campbell, who was working as a Maori consultant behind a one-way mirror. (That has all changed now, and there is a whole Maori Section that does all its own work, but these were the early days.)

Warihi and I worked behind the mirror. There was a Pakeha (European) therapist in front with the family. We had all met and been introduced before the interview. It became clear that the mother (and wife) in this family had left, and the father (and husband) was in the family home with their children. The issue of dispute centered around the mother's wanting to get back into the house with her children, and wanting the father out.

As we began to talk, it became clear that the father was quite happy for that to occur. Both of them had had a lot of experience in the parenting of the children, and both were considered responsible and capable in those areas. The therapist, after quite a long discussion, discovered that there was one hitch: The maternal grandmother wanted the children and the father to stay in the house together. As the discussion continued, the therapist—operating from a Pakeha, individualistic perspective—recognized the parents as the primary decision makers and said, "Well, if you two agree for this shift, then why don't you [to the father] just move out, and you [to the mother] can move in with your children? Then you can sort of explain it to your mother."

When the therapist made that move, Warihi became very concerned and tapped on the window to bring the therapist behind it with us. He stated that in Maoridom the primary relationship is traditionally between grandparents and grandchildren, not between parents and children, as in most Pakeha cultures. He continued: "If in fact you go against the grandmother's wishes—and she will have reasons for wanting this—then you run the risk of alienating this family from the extended family. She is not here to give her reasons. You must not do that."

We had agreed in this project from the earliest days that there would be no questioning of any cultural direction of this sort. So the therapist was sent in to say what Warihi had said. As soon as it was said, the parents agreed, because they understood the wisdom behind it. They were Maori, and it made sense to them. The custody–access situation was solved from that moment onward. In fact, in time things changed, and a year or two later the grandmother was quite supportive of a variation in that arrangement.

After the interview, we reflected on what had happened, and the psychologists among us realized that we had never been taught anything like this in our clinical training. We recognized that, had we gone against that grandmother's wishes, it would have been very disruptive for that family. It might well have alienated them from members of their *whanau* (extended family). We had never thought of that before. It would have caused much the same problems for them as if we had disregarded the wishes of a parent in a Pakeha (European) family, and simply agreed to a grandparent's view. In most Pakeha families, that would be experienced as extremely inappropriate and insensitive. We then began to think of how many times we must have made similar mistakes. If you're not part of the culture, you know nothing about such traditions, normally. If you are part of the culture, the traditions are quite natural.

We then began to think how many times this sort of thing must have happened in the Justice Department's psychological work, in the mental health area, and so on. How many times, with the best of intentions, these sorts of errors must have been made! This is because cultural knowledge has not been seen to be significant in clinical work (Waldegrave, 1985; Durie, 1986; Boyd-Franklin, 1989; Waldegrave & Tamasese, 1993; McGoldrick, 1994).

RESPECT, SHAME, AND SPIRITUALITY

Another aspect that has stood out in these projects has been the different notions of respect in therapy. I think that among most educated Pakeha people, there is a feeling that everyone is the same. There is a liberal approach. We actually don't treat everyone the same, but we try to in therapy. We often avoid attaching respect to status in an obvious way. For example, parents with teenagers or adolescents often come in for help, and the parents are really upset about what is happening at home or what the young persons may be doing. It is quite common in a Pakeha situation to hear the parents' concerns respectfully, and then to turn to the young person and say, "Well, Johnny or Jenny, you heard what your mum and dad have said. What are your views?" I have noticed whenever that same question is asked of Maori or Pacific Island young persons, they just lower their eyes and become silent. This is because they are being asked to comment on and evaluate what the generation above them has said. This individualizes them and discourages the respect they are taught to show to those in older generations. If a young person's opinion on these matters is wanted, there are different processes for gaining that information.

The whole issue of communal shame, especially in areas of abuse, is also a major issue. For example, the process of identifying a person who has been a perpetrator of abuse in a family is quite different in the Maori and Pacific Island cultures. If this issue is approached directly with a family, the whole *whanau* (extended family) experiences the shame, including the victim/survivor. As a result, the whole family often becomes silent. Although it can be quite appropriate to be direct in this manner with a Pakeha family, because it is acceptable to individualize blame, in a Maori or Pacific Island family it can further victimize the survivor of abuse. In cultures where identity is experienced collectively, the implications of many therapeutic probes are quite different. There are, of course, acceptable ways of addressing these issues with perpetrators of abuse, but the route is different.

Spirituality is yet another important aspect that stands out. Social science prides itself on being a secular science; it is suspicious of anything other-worldly. By contrast, Maori and Pacific Island families often share dreams, prayers, and numinous experiences that are important to family life and to the issues of health and wholeness. When violations are being talked about, there is often a need for spiritual rituals of protection. These things that are considered sacred are often totally disregarded by social scientists and psychologists.

EFFECTS OF THE PREDOMINANCE OF WESTERN FUNDAMENTAL VALUES

We often illustrate some of the significant differences between Maori and Pacific Island fundamental values on the one hand, and Pakeha fundamental values on the other, in the following way:

| Communal | vs. | Individual | Ecological | vs. | Consumer |
| Spiritual | vs. | Secular | Consensual | vs. | Conflictual |

From an ecological perspective, people's relationship to the environment is very different if they see Mother Earth in terms of who they are and where they stand, as opposed to an investment to be exploited or developed for profit. Although many Pakeha people are environmentally conscious, the values of consumerism predominate in Pakeha culture. Currently the pressures of consumerism and privatization are increasingly influencing our health services in New Zealand, for example.

In the Pakeha world, we often underestimate how confrontational the institutions of our society are. Our political party systems are set up so that one party puts up a thesis, and the others knock it down. The arrangements in workplaces between employers and employees are confrontational as well. This is quite different from Maori and Pacific Island consensual decision-making institutions and structures, such as the *marae* (the traditional gathering place for Maori).

The social sciences have been developed in an environment where individual, secular, consumer-oriented, and conflictual values are central. Naturally, these values permeate theories and training. Nowadays, nations and cultures that have quite different values are expected to qualify their clinicians and research personnel in the Western approach. In countries like New Zealand, most official health and welfare institutions still expect people from cultures that relate to communal, spiritual, ecological, and consensual values to gain academic qualifications that emphasize opposite values. This is quite absurd. It is particularly absurd when we consider that people in Western cultures are actually searching for many of the non-Western values themselves at the moment.

In most Western countries, people in indigenous and other cultural groups who wish to enter one of the helping professions are expected to gain a qualification in the social sciences to be recognized. Because of the dominance of White values in the social sciences, this often requires people to leave their own people and values to study under other people with different values, in order to be qualified to work with their own people again. This sort of learning process is quite disrespectful to other cultures; worse still, it may contribute to disabling indigenous and other cultural workers in their efforts to help their own. For social science to become consistently relevant to people of these cultures, it needs to be developed by them within their own cultural frames.

CONCLUSION: THE NEED FOR A "JUST THERAPY"

In summary, from our perspective at the Family Centre, the social sciences offer one cultural way of describing events. This is not meant to suggest that Pakeha people are never communal, spiritual, ecological, or consensual, but that the predominant values in most White cultures are individual, secular, consumerist, and conflictual. They are also patriarchal values. That is because until recently, men alone controlled the developments of science, technology, the markets, and the institutions of industrialized and post-industrialized countries. These are the values of the culture in which the social sciences have been developed.

Cultures differ greatly from one another. People from different cultures have different histories. They can have different experiences of immigration or war trauma. The languages of different cultures promote certain concepts and reduce others. Definitions of what is acceptable and unacceptable behavior differ from culture to culture. Associated concepts of respect and shame differ. Patterns of thinking and communication (linear patterns, circular patterns, etc.) differ from culture to culture. The degree of affirmation and the degree of subjugation that a culture has experienced also have a very strong influence on the feelings of belonging, identity, and confidence that the people of the culture have, and of course these factors vary among cultures as well. Family structures, boundaries, and decision making likewise differ from culture to culture. In short, culture is probably the most influential determinant of meaning that exists, because cultures express the humanity and cooperation of large groups of people over long periods of time. As such, they are sacred and worthy of the greatest respect.

Therapies and psychological practices that do not address cultural meaning webs in informed ways are racist. This racism may not be intentional, but the values of the group that controls all the other institutions in society predominate, in a manner that simply continues the process of colonization. These days, colonization is not carried out through the barrel of a gun, but through the comfortable words of those who change the hearts, minds, and spirits of people. Therapists and teachers have a huge responsibility here. Psychologists, especially those in clinical practice, need to be aware of the significance of their influence.

We in the social sciences should know this. We were taught that belonging and identity are the essence of health and human potential. It has been convenient for us to deny this, but the results of this denial have been tragic. Those most in need of the health and welfare resources in our societies come disproportionately from cultures that are dominated. They deserve, at the very least, what we at the Family Centre call "just therapy"—sensitive professional work that allows them to feel culturally safe.

After a workshop in New Zealand, someone once said to us, "You know, a Maori, if he or she wants to, can always learn to be a psychologist, but a psychologist can't learn to be a Maori." Cultural knowledge may or may not be accompanied by social science knowledge, but it can stand on its own. Those who possess it, and choose to work in the helping professions, have gifts our countries desperately need. Our organizations require such people, and they need to be properly resourced, to be given employment security, and to have control over their work. Other cultural work, away from our organizations, also requires adequate resourcing. Those doing such work can heal their own in ways that we will never be able to. Furthermore, they will almost certainly offer the field rich alternative metaphors and meanings, which can free us from the tired old medical, biological, and social science ones.

In fact, psychologists and other helping professionals have a unique opportunity at present to recognize other ways of describing events—in a manner that will lead to creative practices and enable the health and welfare resources to get to those who most need them, on their own terms. It would also enable workers from other cultures to develop new paradigms and new shifts in our field. This will not lead to the abandonment of social science, but it will enable that body of knowledge to sit appropriately alongside other realms of knowledge, such as gender know-ledge and cultural knowledge, without dominating. This will be a new experience for social scientists, but, I suspect, a liberating one!

REFERENCES

Bograd, M. (1984). Family systems approach to wife battering: A feminist cri-tique. *American Journal of Orthopsychiatry, 54*(4), 558–568.

Boyd-Franklin, N. (1989). *Black families in therapy: A multisystems approach.* New York: Guilford Press.

Durie, M. (1986). *Maori health: Contemporary issues and responses.* Auckland: Mental Health Foundation of New Zealand.

Foucault, M. (1972). *The order of things: An archeology of human sciences.* New York: Vintage Books.

Giroux, H. (1983). *Theory and resistance in education: A pedagogy for the op-position.* London: Heinemann.

Goldner, V. (1985). Feminism and family therapy. *Family Process, 24,* 31–47.

Habermas, J. (1971). *Knowledge and human interest* (J. J. Shapiro, Trans.). Bos-ton: Beacon Press.

Harré Hindmarsh, J. (1993). Alternative family therapy discourses: It is time to reflect (critically). *Journal of Feminist Family Therapy, 5*(2), 2–28.

Kamsler, A. (1990). Her story in the making: Therapy with women who were sexually abused in childhood. In C. White & M. Durrant (Eds.), *Ideas for therapy with sexual abuse.* Adelaide, South Australia: Dulwich Centre.

Maturana, H., & Varela, F. (Eds.). (1980). *Autopoesis and cognition: The realisation of living.* Boston: Reidel.

McGoldrick, M. (1994). Culture, class, race and gender. *Human Systems: The Journal of Systemic Consultation and Management, 5*(3–4), 131–153.

McKinnon, L., & Miller, D. (1987). The new epistemology and the Milan ap-proach: Feminist and sociopolitical considerations. *Journal of Marital and Family Therapy, 13*(2), 139–155.

Pilalis, J., & Anderton, J. (1986). Feminism and family therapy: A possible meeting point. *Journal of Family Therapy, 8*(2), 99–114.

Tamasese K., & Waldegrave C. (1993). Cultural and gender accountability in the "just therapy" approach. *Journal of Feminist Family Therapy, 5*(2), 29–45.

Tomm, K. (1990), A critique of the DSM. *Dulwich Centre Newsletter,* No. 3.

Waldegrave, C. (1985). Mono-cultural, mono-class, and so called non-political family therapy. *Australian and New Zealand Journal of Family Therapy, 6*(4), 197–200.

Waldegrave, C. (1990). "Just therapy." *Dulwich Centre Newsletter,* No. 1, 5–46.

Waldegrave, C., & Tamasese, K. (1993). Some central ideas in the "just therapy" approach. *Australian and New Zealand Journal of Family Therapy, 14*(1), 1–8.

Weiten, W. (1995). *Themes and variations* (3rd ed.). Pacific Grove, CA: Brooks/Cole.

CHAPTER 31

The Cultural Context Model
AN OVERVIEW

Rhea Almeida
Rosemary Woods
Theresa Messineo
Roberto Font

> My upbringing taught me that cultures are not
> isolated, and perish when deprived of contact with
> what is different and challenging. Reading, writing,
> teaching, learning are all activities aimed at
> introducing civilizations to each other. No culture, I
> believed unconsciously ever since then, and quite
> consciously today, retains its identity in isolation;
> identity is attained in contact, in contrast, in
> breakthrough.
> —CARLOS FUENTES (1988, p. 47)

The cultural context model describes the interplay of community/social factors and family/individual development. It places issues of race, gender, class, and sexual orientation in culturally diverse groups at the core of family intervention. Although its origins are in domestic violence, this model of therapy is applicable to a broad range of family problems, as the case histories later in the chapter will show,

DIFFERENCES BETWEEN THE CULTURAL CONTEXT MODEL AND TRADITIONAL MODELS

The cultural context model is based on more inclusive and expansive definitions of identity than those currently used in developmental and family models. Family theory describes structural, interactional, and intergenerational patterns of development within the interior of family life. Feminist family theory has added dimensions of power to this analysis, locating family life within the larger social context. The larger social context in this analysis, however, is often limited to gender and economic inequalities. Pulling threads from development theory, feminist theory, family theory, and cross-cultural studies to weave an integrated web, the cultural context model approaches the family from a multifaceted, community-based perspective that addresses gender, ethnic background, and socialization factors.

Traditional theories of identity applicable to mainstream U.S. culture have implied a compartmentalized self—a construct limited to specific dyadic relationships (e.g., mother–child, father–mother, or father–brother), typically within the boundaries of family life. As family therapists, we need to take seriously this restricted and compartmentalized concept of identity. Identity is not a static, self-enclosed concept, but rather a complex interweaving of different stages and states of being, both at once and in historical succession. Identity means connection with people, with home, with history, and with land.

Individual identity, then, is not only the steppingstone to a relationship; it is created through the context and interplay of a series of relationships. Developmental theory has been the basis on which inquiry, assessment, and intervention have been grounded. Current developmental theory, however, does not adequately address the richness of identity and the complexity of diversity. Assessment of children of color, like that of girls of all races, is based upon psychological theories derived from White androcentric ideals of development from the dominant culture (Freud, 1905/1953: Erikson, 1950, 1959, 1968; Kohlberg, 1969, 1981). These theories are based on hidden assumptions embedded in our cultural discourses, social institutions, and individual psyches, which privilege and perpetuate male power and oppress women, persons of color, and sexual minorities, therefore shaping our perception of social reality (Bem, 1983). Context and communication, which are central to a child's development, are neither acknowledged nor identified.

Child development, as historically described, relies upon images, symbols, and expectations created primarily for White male children. Rarely are children of color or different sexual orientations considered. The development of females is disregarded or treated only peripherally (Bem, 1983; Gilligan, 1982; Gilligan, Ward, Taylor, & Bardige, 1988; Broverman, Vogel, Broverman, Clarkson, & Rosenkrantz, 1972). Theories like Piaget's are not applicable cross-culturally. The current operative standards, which include idealizing individuality over human connections, logic over intuition, self-directed work over family life, and a general sense of entitlement, have left both privileged and disadvantaged children lacking. Traditional developmental theory has simply viewed psychological symptoms as indicating a delay in a child's progression through the normal stages of development. Traditional standards for defining healthy maturity have ignored the sense of emotional emptiness created by drastic expectations of autonomy and separation. The cultural context model, on the other hand, assumes that when a child presents as rebellious, depressed, anxious, or withdrawn, these symptoms reflect some personal dynamics, some family dynamics, and to a large extent the sociocultural factors affecting the family.

Some cross-cultural studies (Ainsworth, 1967; Ogbu, 1988; Tobin, Wu, & Davidson, 1989) that compare socialization patterns in Japan, China, Uganda, and the United States challenge American cultural biases and raise questions about U.S. child-rearing practices. These studies describe the importance of indulgence and protection of young children in the first three cultures; they also note the lower value placed on independent thinking, and the higher value placed on having a context of support and interdependence. In non-Western cultures, the values of loyalty and caring for others are esteemed above individual achievement. For example, 4- to 5-year-old boys from Asian Indian families often appear immature by Western standards, because they are pampered and permitted freedom of movement and language until age 7 or 8. Taken out of context, their behavior might be viewed as out of control. We offer a different perspective on identity as "self in context" (Almeida, Woods, & Messineo, 1998).

Culture pertains not only to customs, values, family patterns and religious beliefs, but also to the social and political forces that have shaped family life over time. For example, many Chinese families have worked in laundries and restaurants not because they are genetically more capable of these tasks, but because of racism and restrictive labor laws. These families have chosen businesses that have allowed them to offer a service directly to consumers without having to worry about hiring or firing practices. Asian Indian families have invested in convenience/grocery stores for similar reasons.

Some cultures require a high level of formal thinking, while others do not (Dasen, 1977). For example, mainstream U.S. culture requires that children be proficient in taking standardized tests; in other cultures, children may be required to pass essay tests, or to develop their skills through apprenticeship without tests at all. Yet current developmental theory often fails to consider these cultural differences, which we believe must be taken into consideration when one is evaluating an individual or family problem.

Feminist theory has its limitations as well. A theory of gender oppression alone is insufficient to explain the multiple levels of oppression that occur in family life. Gender oppression must be viewed in the context of other oppressions with which it is embedded: racism, colonization, classism, heterosexism, and homophobia. Social class evolves in distinctively different ways across these intersections (Almeida, 1993, 1994; Havighurst, 1976). Thus we need to illuminate multiple levels of oppression, including the privileging and power of some men over other men, some women over other women, and heterosexuals over homosexuals.

Also, although the feminist analysis has taught us many different ways of accessing family life while addressing power inequities, the social context in which these services are offered has generally gone unexamined. Yet the context in which human services are provided is almost always patriarchal in structure, with rules more suited to patterns of domination than of liberation. For example, the scriptures of mental health have historically emphasized confidentiality as a form of protection for people experiencing family or personal problems. Privacy, which often serves as a patriarchal method of enforcing domination, is a deeply cherished value in mainstream U.S. culture—one that previously has not been challenged, despite its destructive effect on women and on families living on the margin. Privacy, as a major organizing rule of patriarchy, has informed the ethics of confidentiality and autonomy. There are no guiding distinctions that inform social analysis in ways that determine when confidentiality and autonomy actually hinder the development of individuals; within this context of patriarchy, gender role socialization is a powerful organizer of family life (Maccoby, 1990).

The cultural context model of human development attempts to break through these barriers. Using gender as an embracing context, we reexamine privacy in a number of ways, along with notions of the cultural self (Almeida et al., 1998). For example, a woman who is battered and receives a diagnosis of posttraumatic stress disorder (PTSD) is also a member of a culture, a family, a community, and a workplace. We not only treat the PTSD, which is only a fragment of her identity, but also address her experiences as a woman of a particular race, religion, and so on, in a family with a culture perhaps characterized by loss and trauma. A man who has battered his wife is challenged to expose the abuse to a group of community sponsors as well as other clients. Dissolving barriers of privacy in this way makes him accountable to his peers for his behavior, and enables the community to take responsibility for helping to change it.

COMPONENTS OF THE MODEL

The reexamination of privacy, family theory, developmental theory, and feminist theory have all been instrumental in developing the cultural context model of family therapy. As noted earlier, this model, which is accountability-based, has its origins in domestic violence work but is now used for all types of family therapy. It encompasses many forms of gender, racial, and class oppression in family life.

The cultural context model includes several components (see Figure 31.1 for a flow chart of the program and all its components), which we describe here in detail. After this, case examples illustrate the ways in which they are used in the course of the therapeutic process.

Sponsorship: Men Holding Men Accountable

We use "sponsors" (Almeida & Bograd, 1990) to counter the framework of the private psychotherapeutic encounter. Sponsorship builds a bridge across the social values of privacy and autonomy in the family, and examines male rites of passage organized around themes of violence and devaluation of women. These sponsors were originally men from the community who volunteered to help other men deal with their problems. These days the sponsors are primarily men who have been through our program, and who want now to give back to others and to stay clear on their own issues.

Our sponsorship model, though comparable in some ways to the Alcoholics Anonymous (AA) model, is conceptually different in several ways. Our sponsorship arrangement is more fluid. Our clients do not have a single sponsor with whom they have an ongoing agreement. Any sponsor may serve the role of mentor at a particular meeting for one or several clients who are in need of help. Furthermore, we use sponsors to support men, while simultaneously holding them accountable for abusive patterns of behavior in their intimate lives. In contrast to AA sponsors, whose sponsorship is focused on a person's sobriety, our sponsors have a broader focus of helping other men to be accountable to the others in their lives. In addition, though our sponsors share common male bonds with those they are sponsoring, they may not have perpetrated violence in their own lives (although some have). Matching sponsors with clients of different backgrounds is designed to help challenge the problem definitions so prevalent in mental health, while helping men form alliances with other men who may be different in age, class, race, or sexual orientation. However, sometimes links of similarity are encouraged to ensure connection to the therapeutic community.

In the initial contact, we use film clips and other visual aids (see below), and have clients talk with sponsors in order to help them rethink issues of gender and racial oppression. The sponsor can gently challenge ideas regarding the institution of marriage that include subtle definitions

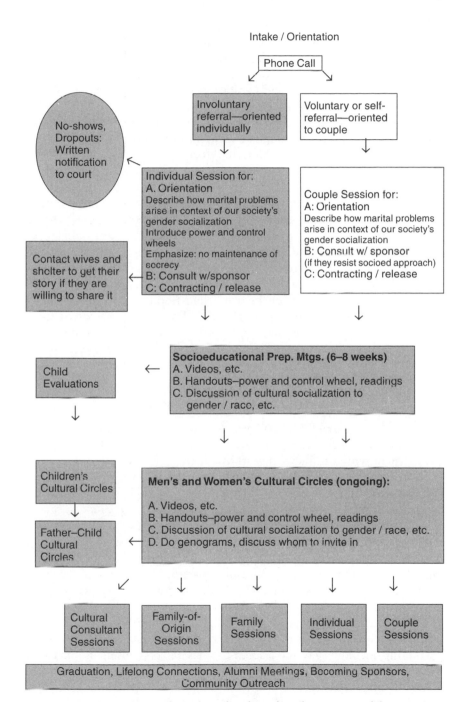

FIGURE 31.1. Flow chart for the cultural context model.

of patriarchy and euphemisms for cultural models of domination. For example, a Muslim man may say that in his culture a good wife will teach her daughters to dress "modestly." An Asian Indian man may say that it is good for his wife to work outside of the home and have her own money, but that it is also good to share their money with his family of origin. A man from the Caribbean may try to justify his violent actions by explaining that in his culture women are expected to respect their husbands and that his wife did not consider this significant cultural value when she chose not to respect him; therefore, he was "forced" to hit her. We may seek therapeutic solutions from such a client's cultural context, by asking an elder or community leader to speak with the couple about family difficulties. These community consultants must have an advanced gender and racial consciousness. Solutions are then customized within the larger therapeutic context, through a rethinking of power imbalances across gender, race, sexual orientation, and class lines. If a sponsor from the client's cultural background is not available, we may try to show a film that speaks to particulars of the client's cultural and social context. For example, for a Muslim client from the Middle East, we introduced clips from the documentary film *Morning Voices* (see the list of films provided at the end of this chapter) to provoke discussion about clashes between Islamic and Western religions, constructs of marriage, roles of women and men in family life, and methods of discipline for children.

Socioeducational Orientation

Various film clips and readings are used to raise the consciousness of men, women, and children regarding gender, race, class, and culture, providing them with a framework within which they can link their experiences to a larger social context. The emphasis is on dismantling rigid roles of masculinity, femininity, and sexuality, as well as racial and cultural biases. Although this orientation phase is largely didactic, every effort is made to engage the clients on a personal level and to connect them with others through discussion and sharing of experiences and ideas.

Film clips, articles from the popular press, and songs may be presented to show the ways in which issues of gender, race, class, and culture are handled in the mass media. These clips and articles are carefully selected to challenge traditional gender roles, as well as hidden dimensions of class, race, and sexual orientation. Conversations are aimed at deconstructing the institution of marriage as well as other forms of partnering, including gay and lesbian couples and cohabiting, nonmarried couples. For instance, we review the violence of movies and music cross-culturally and discuss the emphasis on male entitlement. Additional film clips are used to spark discussion of the institution of marriage in our culture, addressing the ways it has been shaped by outdated social structures and values, despite the gains made by many women in income' job status, and reproductive planning. Other topics addressed with clips from various feature films include racial oppression (*The Color Purple, Jungle Fever, Mississippi Masala, Stand and Deliver, Boyz N the Hood*), domestic violence and intimidation (*The Great Santini, Straight Out of Brooklyn, Beauty and the Beast*), sexism (*Pretty Woman, The Little Mermaid*), and the gendered and cultural aspects of loss (*Steel Magnolias, The Joy Luck Club, Heaven and Earth, Corinna, Corinna*).

A variety of instruments such as the Traditional Male Norms (Green, 1991) and Power and Control Wheels (1994) are used to assist women and men to examine the misuses and abuses of power they may have experienced at home, and to encourage clients to place these in the perspective of the larger social context. We have found that a great many women who initially say, "I've never been abused," or "He only hit me once, and that was quite a while ago," are brought into powerful awareness of the experiences of intimidation, threats, and abuse they have encountered when they examine this wheel of relationships. For men, the wheel helps them become aware of the pervasiveness of their power moves in their intimate relationships, as well as of the need for accountability in developing equitable relationships.

Separate Cultural Circles for Men and Women

"Cultural circles," which are open-ended groups that meet weekly, are run with a therapist and staff team behind the one-way mirror to insure member accountability and gender–racial balance. Individuals enter a larger, ongoing culture circle once they have completed the socioeducational orientation. Sponsors often participate in this context, which addresses a number of relationship issues, including family-of-origin and couple relationships, parenting, work, and friendships. Family therapy as we know it occurs here and in separate family sessions.

The cultural circles are structured differently for men and women. (Children have their own cultural circles as well, but these are discussed in a later section.) Men's groups emphasize personal accountability to others rather than to self. In our experience, one of the most common problems men have is overfocusing on "self" and the "resolution" of their own feelings. As soon as they begin to acknowledge abuse against someone else, they tend to translate their guilt into premature requests for forgiveness and then want to move on. We help them take time to attend to their impact on others. Even concentrating on their guilt and shame may overfocus them on their own feelings and inhibit their attention to the feelings and experiences of those they have abused. The common assumption therapists make is that guilt is something to help men overcome. But from the social accountability perspective, moderate amounts of guilt are important to a sense of moral consciousness. The cultural circle helps them instead remain with the experience of what they have done, by bearing witness to the injustices they have perpetrated against others. This process helps men not to compartmentalize their issues, as they are often wont to do. The cultural circle emphasize men's relationship responsibilities over the privileging of their own desires.

For women, on the other hand, the therapeutic intent is to empower them and to increase the range of felt and expressed emotions—in particular, to sanction anger as an appropriate emotion and form of social justice. Their typical pattern of overfocusing on their guilt is discouraged. They are encouraged to take less responsibility for the overall well-being of their families. Contributing to family life in more balanced ways also helps them modify the intensity of their guilt and responsibility for others.

Since the cultural circles are open to new members and include men and women from different stages of the life cycle, men and women can view aspects of their own lives from new perspectives through the stories of both old and new members.

Couple, Individual, Parent–Child, Sibling, Whole-Family, and Family-of-Origin Sessions

Individuals and various types of dyadic and family sessions are always orchestrated with at least one sponsor, especially in the early stages of the process. This facilities the handling of sensitive issues and helps when hidden issues of power and domination are being confronted. Parent–child negotiations are always done within the context of cultural circle support. For example, an adolescent who wants additional privileges will be coached with other siblings and provided with an adolescent sponsor to help in negotiating with the parents. Similarly, a parent who describes experiencing problem behavior with a child or adolescent can either resolve the problem in the cultural circle, without needing to meet separately with the therapist and child, or rethink the problem and consider new solutions in preparation for a parent–child meeting.

Work with Children (with Adult and Child Sponsors)

The cultural context model places children's behavior and problems in a larger social context. For example, a Puerto Rican male adolescent referred by the school for poor grades and depression may be viewed within a traditional model as having low motivation and not having achieved "appropriate" independent learning skills. Perhaps some investigation into possible drug or alcohol use and "appropriate" parenting will be suggested. Our model expands the definition of the problem to explore its social roots, which may include an absent father, who sends money intermittently but has not seen his son in years. Father absence is explored both as it relates to men's frequent absence within families, and in terms of the particular dilemmas it creates for the remaining family members in terms of work and family choices. If connecting with the father himself is not possible, we may facilitate a session with another Puerto Rican father who can bridge the conversation about fathers, sons, and loss with a conversation about mothers who are faced with carrying family responsibilities on their own. The focus is on rebuilding connections to the boy's family heritage and making him aware of the difficult job his mother faces daily, rather than on autonomy and separation. Requests by the adolescent to be like his peers are nurtured with conversations about his location in the sphere of multiple contexts.

Problems between the mother and son are addressed as part of this larger context, rather than focusing on the dyad alone. When the problem is redefined in this way, the intervention takes on a nontraditional structure. Some of these nontraditional interventions include evaluations of children in family sessions, in their homes, in individual sessions, in the children's and adolescents' cultural circles, or in sessions with adult sponsors. College students who received treatment as adolescents occasionally drop by to share their experiences with newer members. The fluidity of these connections helps to break down the walls of privacy that typically surround family difficulties, and to expand the context within which families evaluate their problems. We expand the context through videotapes, literature, activities, stories, drawings, and role plays. We also involve sponsors and other clients in "communal" discussion of problems, intentionally challenging societal rules of individual privilege and privacy to empower clients within the natural healing context of a community of support.

In their own cultural circles, children are encouraged to describe their perceptions of issues of race, gender, culture, and (for adolescents) sexual orientation, and to articulate their particular dilemma within this larger context. Group composition is mixed by ages (3–7, 7–12, and 12–18), to dismantle the rigid ways in which age defines the expectations for social and academic performance in our society. Children are divided by gender for half of each group session, and then joined together for the remaining half. Adolescents, however (12–18) are brought together in mixed-sex groups intermittently. Ideally, there should be a natural sharing among the children, and wisdom and experience should be passed from the older to the younger children, regardless of gender. We also try to teach children the value of respect for elders.

In family sessions, therapists request that the older family members permit the children to discuss concerns and problems openly. After the older members describe the problems children are asked separately for their perception of family issues, away from the possible influence or intimidating presence of the parents or others (especially the father, in cases of domestic violence). Each child's safety is also assessed.

We conduct father–mother–child groups. Parents, fathers in particular, participate in the groups with their children to help teach them about equitable forms of nurturing, listening, discipline and control. By means of a "bug-in-the-ear" device, similarly parents are coached by therapists and sponsors (who are parents themselves) behind a one-way mirror. They are taught to resolve conflict using appropriate language instead of violence.

Boys and men plan and serve food in groups and attend to young infants in the group when necessary. Girls are asked to assist both with nurturing and with instrumental tasks, such as leading the group or choosing an activity. Everyone is encouraged to resolve issues of conflict directly.

Graduation

"Graduation" is a transition from treatment to other forms of connection within the community. Unlike the traditional therapeutic termination, which consists of a review of problems and solutions, we make this an important stage of connections and a chance to give back to the community. These connections are designed to put the therapeutic ideas initiated in our treatment into action. For example, we have forged a link with the National Organization of Men Against Sexism, which allows clients (men in particular) to further develop ideals of nonviolence and egalitarian values in family life. Many possibilities evolve for women, such as new work choices. Both men and women are encouraged to do community work to educate various segments of the community (e.g., schools, police departments, hospitals, and business groups) about racial and gender equity.

Community Outreach

Like all the components of this model, community outreach is fluid and overlaps with other components. Our central themes of "sponsorship" to mentor others continue throughout the community. Although the idea of community coordination is not new to public agencies, the cultural context model defines boundaries of service altogether differently. Community coordination within our context revolves around forming coalitions with sponsors as part of the team and taking these men and women into professional meetings and court services; this dismantles the barriers of privacy in a way that redefines notions of power, privilege, invisibility, and visibility (Almeida, 1993, 1994). Our sponsors remain actively involved in the community, giving back to others while strengthening their own inner commitment to an equitable and just family and community life.

A CASE OF CULTURALLY SANCTIONED VIOLENCE BROUGHT HOME BY A POLICE OFFICER

Michael, a police officer, and his wife, Sharon came to our program after 14 years of marriage, during most of which Michael had been violent toward Sharon. The couple had two daughters, ages 12 and 3. Sharon was referred by the local domestic violence shelter. She had tried to obtain a restraining order, but received insufficient response from the police, since Michael was an officer. Although Sharon was seeking temporary protection from Michael, she also wanted to try to salvage the marriage, without the violence. Michael walked out of the initial intake session, put off by the one-way mirror and therapy team.

Sharon remained in treatment, meeting with female sponsors who attempted to help her see that her panic attacks and severe depression were directly linked to the abuse she had encountered throughout her marriage. Michael finally agreed to come back a few months later, after a conversation in which a sponsor asked him to return to "help" his wife work through her issues. This solution came out of his complaining about her depression and lack of attention to him. The sponsor suggested that he come in and "help her," if he was invested in their family. He remained angry and uncooperative during the first several months of therapy, however, and tried repeatedly to convince the team that his wife was completely crazy.

Michael was clear, in charge, and charming most of the time, except when it was suggested that he might have contributed to his wife's mental state. Sharon vacillated from rage to depression and suicidal thoughts. Her previous psychological treatment had included years of medication, hospitalization, behavioral regimens for her panic attacks, and therapists who kept searching for pathology in her family history. Sharon had been repeatedly told in therapy that her greatest task was trusting her own judgment and clarity. Michael, on the other hand, felt totally entitled to power and authority at home, since he was the "breadwinner."

During the socioeducational component, the couple was shown clips from films such as *The Great Santini,* discussion of which centered around the military context of the film, in which violence and power exercised in a work context spill over into the home. In Michael's case, work in group and couple sessions centered around the issue of his abuse of power. We also showed clips from an episode of the ABC-TV newsmagazine *20/20* on pornography, and used these to discuss the objectification of women's bodies and lives and its impact on Michael's numerous affairs and avoidance of intimacy. Since Michael's father was Italian and a police officer, we used an older Italian man as a sponsor. The sponsor was himself a former abuser who had been resocialized through the program.

In sessions with his own parents, Michael confronted his father about the ramifications of being taken to a prostitute at age 16 as an "initiation rite" of manhood. He spoke of how this rite, until now, had separated the experience of intimacy from sexuality, and described his affairs as a extension of this rite. He spoke of the violence towards Sharon as a continuation of the loyalty towards his father and mother and their traditional arrangement of gender, marriage and child rearing. His parents were shocked by the stories of violence, especially his father, who insisted he had never laid a hand on Michael's mother.

In time and with the help of several sponsors, his men's group, and family-of-origin sessions, Michael came to see how he had been socialized into entitled, abusive, self-centered behavior in his marriage and other relationships. He realized also that the "macho" values of his police department were racist and heterosexist, and fed into his pattern of abusing his wife when she did not obey his wishes. He has become a very different kind of police officer, father, husband, and son, working to help others overcome their prejudices as he continues working to overcome his oppressive behaviors in his intimate relationships.

Meanwhile, Sharon's work revolved around the meaning of gender roles within the institution of marriage and family. Early in therapy she needed to attend to her mother's impending death, the result of long-denied alcoholism. The alcoholism and neglect that had plagued this family for generations, along with general issues of loss and regret, were addressed in the mother's home. In the presence of a sponsor, Sharon reflected upon her childhood, including the many traumas and the few good times. Her bedridden mother smiled, hugged her daughter, and thanked her for being brave enough to speak to her honestly. This visit, along with her work in the women's group, helped Sharon to redefine her concepts of marriage, intimacy, and parenting.

Michael spent many hours both with his own children and with children from other families, describing his story of violence and control, while maintaining a position of remorse and justice. Other activities with children included watching films like *The Little Mermaid* and *Beauty and the Beast* with his daughters, and pointing out rigid male–female norms in the movies. In *The Little Mermaid*, Ariel will lose her voice to get her prince, aided by a dark, ugly, overweight, but strong woman. In *Beauty and the Beast*, Belle is chided by the active community for not responding to Gaston's marriage proposal. His dismissal of Belle's "mind" is obscured because of his status as an eligible bachelor.

A CASE OF "GASLIGHTING"[1]

Tim and Mary, married for over 25 years, entered treatment to deal with Tim's long history of extramarital affairs. Their adult children were Kathy, 20, and Jason, 24. Most recently, the family had been in therapy on account of their daughter's anorexia nervosa. Tim, in his initial session, avowed strongly that Mary had abandoned him both sexually and emotionally. She countered that she suspected him of having an intense relationship with her best friend, who lived a few houses away from them. He vehemently denied this, attributing it to Mary's "vivid fantasy life," and insisting that her mother's death had left her unable to nurture him. To address issues of loss, both Tim and Mary were shown clips of *Steel Magnolias* in separate dyads with same-sex sponsors. The process engendered was one of addressing issues of loss and mourning as related to culture and gender. Other movies they were shown included *Pretty Woman* and *Jungle Fever*. These two movies expanded their awareness of the different forms of entitlement open to men from different racial and economic backgrounds, as well as the different forms of oppression experienced by women in various racial and economic contexts.

After talking further with Mary in separate sessions, the therapists were quite certain that Tim was in fact involved with Mary's friend. Tim was then paired with a man who had been in the program for a while, to help him address his ability to rationalize the ways in which he exploited his partner. The sponsor introduced the idea that perhaps Tim's privileging of his own desires in the marriage, to the exclusion of his partner's and children's, might be the first order of business to address. Tim, appalled by this suggestion, threatened to leave and find a "more responsible" therapist. He was confronted by the fact that he had in fact been in a number of therapies over the years. It was suggested that perhaps the problem was not the therapists, but Tim's reluctance to confront issues and share information. Tim grudgingly agreed to stay.

He still had difficulty sharing in culture circle sessions, however, because he firmly believed in privacy regarding personal matters. The therapists supported the sponsors in urging Tim toward a position of personal responsibility that would both hold him accountable and sustain the emotion of guilt for hurting his partner. The truth emerged that Tim had, in fact, been having an affair with Mary's best friend. The therapists confronted Tim, asking him to tell Mary and the family. Initially he balked at telling the children, but eventually agreed to do so. First, however, he wrote and mailed a letter officially terminating the affair. Although understandably upset, Mary was also relieved to hear the truth at last and learn that she hadn't been crazy or overly suspicious of her husband.

In her group, Mary spent many hours confused over her responsibilities in the marriage and at work, as opposed to Tim's exploitation of her at home and at work (the couple owned and managed a printing store, with Tim assuming responsibility over Mary and the staff). Slowly, she became aware of the many, seemingly insignificant ways in which he kept her subordinate to him both at work and at home. Tim, in his group, realized for the first time the ways in which he had abused his privileges, assuming Mary would be there for him without ever expecting to nurture her in return. Although Tim and Mary's children were too old for the children's group, we planned a few sessions for each child and parent. Same-sex sponsors were used with Mary and her daughter in an initial session, where Kathy vented her anger that her mother chose to stay with her father in spite of the horrible way he had treated her. Later, she was better able to begin to understand her mother's choices, while differentiating the choices (she would make if she were in a similar situation. Tim, in the end, really began to enjoy his sponsorship role and the camai derie of the men's groups. Mary, in the meantime, was better able to clearly define her own role and limitations as a wife, mother, and woman. Eight years later, Kathy brought her partner to our center. She was very much in love with him, but feared that his predisposition to "gaslighting" in subtle forms might become a major problem if unattended to. He is currently enrolled in our men's program.

CONCLUSION

The cultural context model takes as its underlying foundation the challenging of traditional gender and social roles, which allows for the creation of a more equitable partnership and family system. The model veers away from traditional methods of addressing issues strictly on an individual, couple, or family level, centering instead on multiple relationships and the healing power of community.

Currently, Tim and Michael are both actively involved in the sponsorship program, giving back to other men the help and support they have received. They challenge men who insist on working 14-hour days and men who find justification in brutalizing their wives and children. Within this context of accountability, they provide role models for men struggling with issues of power and control, which occur for all men along a continuum.

Sharon and Mary similarly participate with other women in a range of community connections—from court-based work for women who lose children to father's rights groups, to helping women who need restraining orders to protect them from abusive husbands, to finding reliable babysitters for other women. For women, dealing with the issues of subordination and overresponsibility is a continuous struggle.

Together with other men and women, past clients of the cultural context model reach for new and humane solutions to family, work, and community life.

NOTE

1. "Gaslighting" is a term derived from the movie *Gaslight,* in which Charles Boyer tries to convince Ingrid Bergman that she is crazy when she notices things he is doing in their relationship and their home.

REFERENCES

Almeida, R. (1993). Unexamined assumptions and service delivery systems: Feminist theory and racial exclusions. *Journal of Feminist Family Therapy, 5*(1), 3–23.

Almeida, R. (Ed.). (1994). *Expansions of feminist family theory through diversity.* Binghamton, NY: Haworth Press.

Almeida, R., & Bograd, M. (1990). Sponsorship: Men holding men accountable for domestic violence. *Journal of Feminist Family Therapy, 2*(3–4), 234–256.

Almeida, R., Woods, R., & Messineo, T. (1998). The intersectionality of child development: Gender, race, and culture. In R. Almeida (Ed.), *Gender and race.* Binghamton, NY: Haworth Press.

Ainsworth, M. D. (1967). *Infancy in Uganda: Infant care and the growth of love.* Baltimore: Johns Hopkins University Press.

Bem, S. L.(1983). Gender schema theory and its implications for child development. *Signs, 8*(4), 598–616.

Broverman, I., Vogel, S., Broverman, D., Clarkson, F., & Rosenkrantz, P. (1972). Sex-role stereotypes: A current appraisal. *Journal of Social Issues, 28,* 58–78.

Dasen, P. (1977). *Piagetian psychology: Cross-cultural contributions.* New York: Gardner Press.

Erikson, E. H. (1950). *Childhood and society.* New York: Norton.

Erikson, E. H. (1959). *Identity and the life cycle: Selected papers* (Psychological Issues, Monograph No. 1). New York: International Universities Press.

Erikson, E. H. (1968). *Identity: Youth and crisis.* New York: Norton.

Freud, S. (1953). Three essays on the theory of sexuality. In J. Strachey (Ed. and Trans.), *The standard edition of the complete psychological works of Sigmund Freud* (Vol. 7). London: Hogarth Press. (Original work published 1905)

Fuentes, C. (1988). How I started to write. In R. Simonson & S. Walker (Eds.), *The Graywolf annual: Vol. 5. Multicultural literacy.* St. Paul, MN: Graywolf Press.

Gilligan, C. (1982). *In a different voice.* Cambridge, MA: Harvard University Press.

Gilligan, C., Ward, J. V., Taylor, J., & Bardige, B. (1988). *Mapping the moral domain.* Cambridge, MA: Harvard University Press.

Gunn-Allen, P. (1992). *The sacred hoop: Recovering the feminine in American Indian tradition.* Boston: Beacon Press.

Havighurst, R. (1976). The relative importance of social class and ethnicity. *Human Development, 19,* 56–64.

Kohlberg, L. (1969). Stage and sequence: The cognitive developmental approach to socialization. In D. Goslin (Ed.), *The handbook of socialization theory and research.* Chicago: Rand McNally.

Kohlberg, L. (1981). *Essays on moral development: Vol. 1. The philosophy of moral development: Moral stages and the idea of justice.* San Francisco: Harper & Row.

Maccoby, E. E. (1990). Gender and relationships: A developmental account. *American Psychologist, 45,* 513–520.

McGoldrick, M. (1989). In M. McGoldrick, C. Anderson, & F. Walsh (Eds.), *Women in families: A framework for family therapy.* New York: Norton.

Ogbu, J. U. (1988). Black children and poverty: A developmental perspective of cultural diversity and human development. *New Directions for Child Development, 42,* 11–28.

Tobin, J. J., Wu, D. Y. H., & Davidson, D. H. (1989). *Preschool in three cultures: Japan, China and the United States.* New Haven, CT: Yale University Press.

FILMS MENTIONED IN TEXT AND USED IN OUR WORK

Morning Voices (Available from Women Make Movies, Inc., 462 Broadway, New York, NY 10013)

The Color Purple (1985; director: Steven Spielberg)

Mississippi Masala (1992; director: Mira Nair)

Stand and Deliver (1987; director: Ramon Menendez)

Boyz N the Hood (1991; director: John Singleton)

The Great Santini (1979; director: Lewis John Carlino)

Straight Out of Brooklyn (1991; director: Matty Rich)
Jungle Fever (1991; director: Spike Lee)
Beauty and the Beast (1991; directors: Gary Trousdale, Kirk Wise)
Pretty Woman (1990; director: Garry Marshall)
The Little Mermaid (1989; directors: Jon Musker, Ron Clemente)
Steel Magnolias (1990; director: Herbert Ross)
The Joy Luck Club (1993; director: Wayne Wang)
Heaven and Earth (1993; director: Oliver Stone)
Corinna, Corinna (1994; director: Jessie Nelson)
20/20 episode on pornography (Available from ABC-TV, call 1-800-225-5222)
Gaslight (1944; director: George Cukor)
Voices of the Morning (1992; director: Meena Warji)

Note. Except for *Morning Voices* and the *20/20* episode, all films are major feature films; copies can be bought or rented at any video store.

Index

Religion (*continued*)
  differences, in intermarriage, 300–302
  Protestant, 242
  spirituality and, 72–74
Resentment, of sibling caretaker,
    286–287
Resilience
  acknowledgment of, 135, 355–356
  confidence and, 69–70
  encouragement and, 69–70
  growth and, 74–75
  healing and, 63
  humor and, 70–71
  individual traits and, 64–65
  initiative and, 68–69
  invention and, 68–69
  models/mentors for, 70
  perseverance and, 69
  positive outlook and, 67–68
  of refugee families, 355–356
  religious/spiritual beliefs and, 72–74
  view of adversity and, 66–67
Resilience-based approaches, need for, 62–
    63
Respect, cultural differences in, 408–409
Restorying
  of African American family, 188–190
  of past, 195
Re-visioning models. *See* Cultural context
    model; Fifth Province model
Rituals, of Nacirema, 153–157

S

Sacrificial losses, 395–399
Same-generation coalitions, 43–44
Savior, myth of, 291
Scapegoating
  family, 97
  prejudicial, 96
Search
  for biological aunt, 248–250
  for biological father, 245
Self-concept, cultural differences in, 406–
    408
Self-harming behaviors, intentional *vs.*
    nonintentional, 393–395
Self-hatred, 192
Self-identification, of homosexuals, 321–
    322
Self-narratives, cultural, deconstruction
    of, 31–32
Self-negation, 192
Self-reflexiveness, 136–137
Sensitization, 112

Separateness, triangles and, 38–39
Sexism
  associated advantaging, 151
  complexity of, 278
  learning, 106
  traditional universalist perspective and,
    13
Sexuality, homosexuals and, 324–326
Sexual orientation. *See also* Heterosexual
    relationships; Homosexuals
  differences, 100
  intermarriage and, 304–305
Sexual partners, male, parental irresponsi-
    bility of, 170
Shame, cultural differences in, 409
Slaves
  double binds and, 256, 259
  history, re-visioning of, 186–187
  identity of, 196
  learning to read and, 220
  roles of, 190
Social class
  becoming aware of, 226–228
  community aspects of, 52–53
  definition of, 50–51
  differences, postmigrational, 375–376
  economic aspects of, 51–52, 58–59
  hierarchies in, 5, 6–7
  individual attributes and, 54
  intermarriage and, 304
  patriarchy and, 53–54
  race and, 52–53
  resource access and, 52
  stratification in U.S. society, 104
  structure, 51
  therapeutic implications, 58–59
    importance of, 60–61
    two families example, 54–58
Social constructionist perspective, 133
Social disparities, 129
Social identities, multiple, 137–139
Socialization differences, by gender,
    271–272
Social problems, 106
Social projection process, 195–196
Social science
  reality constructions and, 404–405
  values and, 410–411
Social support, resilience and, 64
Social systems, redesigning, 152
Solution-focused therapies, 160
Soul, 73–74
Spirituality
  clinical implications, 84–88, 89
  cultural differences in, 409
  religion and, 72–74